Ploughshare of War

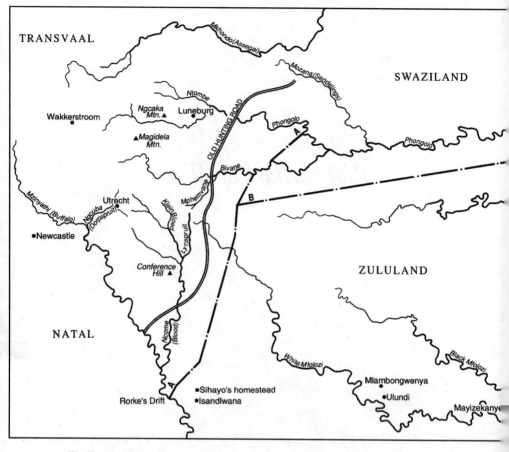

The Transvaal-Zululand disputed territory and environs. Line AA shows the 1861 boundary line, beaconed off in 1864, and line BB shows the encroachment by the 1875 proclamation.

Ploughshare of War

The Origins of the Anglo-Zulu War of 1879

Richard Cope

University of Natal Press
Pietermaritzburg
1999

© 1999 University of Natal Press
Private Bag X01
Scottsville 3209
South Africa

ISBN 0 86980 944 X

Cover design by Brett Armstrong

Typeset by the University of Natal Press
Printed by Kohler Carton and Print
Box 955, Pinetown 3600, South Africa

Contents

Abbreviations used in the References

A.S.N.A. .... Acting Secretary for Native Affairs, Natal
B.A. .... Border Agent
B.L. .... British Library, London, (Carnarvon Papers)
B.P.P. .... British Parliamentary Papers
Cape G.H. .... Government House records, Cape Archives, Cape Town
C.O. .... Colonial Office records, Public Record Office, London
C.O. 879 .... Colonial Office Confidential Print
C.O. 959 .... Colonial Office records, Public Record Office, London
(Frere Papers)
C.S.O. .... Colonial Secretary's Office records, Natal Archives,
Pietermaritzburg
G.H. .... Government House records, Natal Archives, Pietermaritzburg
G.R.O., PCC .... Gloucestershire Records Office, Gloucester
(St Aldwyn [Hicks Beach] Papers)
G.S. .... Government Secretary, Transvaal
H.C. Deb. .... House of Commons debates (Hansard)
H.L. Deb. .... House of Lords debates (Hansard)
K.C. .... Killie Campbell Africana Library, Durban
N.A.M. .... National Army Museum, London (Chelmsford Papers)
P.R.O. 30/6 .... Carnarvon Papers, Public Record Office, London
R.M. .... Resident Magistrate
S.N.A. .... Secretary for Native Affairs records, Natal Archives,
Pietermaritzburg
S.P. .... Theophilus Shepstone Papers, Natal Archives, Pietermaritzburg
S.P.G. .... United Society for the Propagation of the Gospel records,
London
S.P.G., W.P. .... Wigram Papers in the S.P.G. records
S.S. .... State Secretary records, Transvaal Archives, Pretoria
T.A. .... Administrator's records, Transvaal Archives, Pretoria
T.A., L.U. .... Landdrost of Utrecht records, Transvaal Archives, Pretoria
T.A., S.N. .... Secretary for Native Affairs records, Transvaal Archives,
Pretoria
U.W.L. .... University of the Witwatersrand Library, Johannesburg
Z.A.R. .... South African Republic (Transvaal)

Glossary

amakhafula .... (derogatory term for) Natal Africans

ibandla .... council of state

ibutho/amabutho .... age grades or regiments

ikhanda/amakhanda .... army barracks and royal homesteads ('military kraals')

inkosi/amakhosi .... chiefs, lords, kings

impi .... a military force

induna/izinduna .... officials in the service of the state

isigodlo .... king's private enclosure, women's quarters

isikhulu/izikhulu .... the great hereditary chiefs

izigqoza .... the party supporting Mbuyazi

khonza .... to give one's allegiance to

umkhosi .... the annual first fruits ceremony and military parade

umuzi/imizi .... homesteads

usuthu .... the party supporting Cetshwayo

Preface

The research for this book was carried on over a very long period. I first started working on Natal and Zulu history in 1962 when I began work at the University of Natal, under the supervision of the late Edgar Brookes, on an MA thesis on the relations between Shepstone and Cetshwayo. Professor Brookes encouraged me to approach the subject in terms of personalities and families: he told me that he had been approached many years earlier by a member of the Zulu royal family to stand as a Native Representative, that he had expressed a disinclination to stand against Denis Shepstone, but that he had been told that a Shepstone was not wanted. The question to be answered was thus seen as the origins of the hostility between the house of Senzangakhona and the house of Shepstone.

When I returned to the subject, some years after the completion of the MA thesis, there had been a great change in the approach to South African history. There had been a move away from purely political history; a greater awareness of, and curiosity about, the connections between the economy, social structure, politics and ideas of societies; and an interest in the dynamics of capitalist and pre-capitalist societies and in the changing relationships between the two in nineteenth-century South Africa. New ideas had been put forward about the role of the imperial factor in South African history, to the study of which I have also attempted to make some contribution in the form of articles in academic journals. In the light of these new ideas, a number of statements have been made about the genesis of the Anglo-Zulu war of 1879. I felt there was a need to test these statements against a detailed study of the evidence, and I felt that the research I had done for my MA thesis, and the considerable further research I have subsequently done, especially in British sources, put me in a good position to carry out this task. Hence I prepared a thesis which I submitted to the University of the Witwatersrand, and for which I was awarded the degree of PhD in 1995.

This book is a modified version of the thesis. A thesis is written for a captive readership of three. A book is intended for a much larger voluntary readership. In reworking the thesis I have therefore eliminated the academic longueurs necessary to satisfy examiners, and sought instead to arouse and retain the interest of the intelligent general reader. Judging by the number of books which continue to be published on the Anglo-Zulu war, the subject is one that retains the interest of the reading public. It is surprising therefore that there has never been a full-length study of how the war came about. There are numerous chapters and parts of chapters on the causes of the war, but this is the first book on the subject.

A study of the origins of the war casts light on more than the war itself. The Anglo-Zulu war of 1879, by any measure the biggest war fought between black and white in South Africa, occupies a crucial place in the history of South Africa, and an important place in the history of the relations between Europe and Africa. By the 1870s the whites in the interior of South Africa were losing ground to the blacks as the latter acquired the weapons which had enabled the former to establish their initial dominance. It was an exertion of British imperial power, of which the Anglo-Zulu war was the most conspicuous episode, which swung the balance of power against the blacks and cemented white supremacy in South Africa for more than a century. The war came on the eve of the partition of Africa by the European powers, and the forward British movement in the south, of which the war was a part, helped to precipitate the scramble. The springs of British imperial policy and practice in South Africa in the 1870s is a subject of absorbing interest and great importance.

In the course of research and writing I have become indebted to a great many people. Some of these debts date back a very long time, and any attempt to mention by name all the individuals who have helped me would produce a very long list as well as unjustifiable omissions. I will therefore express my gratitude in general terms. I am sincerely grateful to the numerous librarians and archivists in South Africa and in Britain who gave indispensable help in finding sources; to the historians whose work I have found stimulating and challenging; and the friends and colleagues who have given encouragement and help of all kinds. Among more recent debts, I must mention by name Noel Garson, the former head of the department of history at the University of the Witwatersrand, who supervised the thesis on which this book is based, and who was bravely prepared to take on a colleague whom he had every reason to believe to be set in his ways; Philip Stickler, chief cartographer in the department of geography at Wits, who converted my scrawled attempts at interpreting vague nineteenth-century descriptions and drawings into an elegant and useful map; Elaine Katz, who nobly volunteered to undertake the proofreading of the thesis; and my examiners, Noel Garson, John Benyon and Norman Etherington, for their helpful criticisms and comments. None of the above had any control over what finally went into the book, so I alone remain responsible for any factual errors or omissions and for what others may regard as errors of interpretation.

Richard Cope
History Department, University of the Witwatersrand

CHAPTER ONE

Introduction

The Significance of the Anglo-Zulu War

In 1879 Britain went to war with the most powerful African state in southern Africa. It was to prove the costliest in blood and treasure of any war the British had fought in the region. The official estimate of its cost to the British (and Indian) taxpayer was £4 922 140 18s 6d. This was nearly 90 percent of the total British military expenditure in South Africa in the second half of the 1870s, a period that included the last Cape eastern frontier war and the subjugation of the Pedi of the eastern Transvaal, as well as other engagements. The number of British subjects, officers and men, who were killed or died of wounds in South Africa between 1875 and the invasion of Zululand was officially estimated to be 179. The Anglo-Zulu war added another 1 386 to this toll.[1]

Few colonial wars had such an impact on Britain. The problem of paying for it caused something of a Cabinet crisis. The Chancellor of the Exchequer opposed borrowing the money and suggested instead a considerable increase in the duties on tea. Disraeli commented to Queen Victoria that it would be 'impossible to name a tax more unpopular'; his Cabinet colleague's suggestion, he told his sovereign, was motivated by the hope of winning 'an austere smile from Mr. Gladstone'.[2] For the Conservative party, with the economy depressed and an election approaching, the war could not have come at a worse time. The exhibition of British military incompetence at Isandlwana weakened Britain in its dealings with other powers[3] and together with other overseas disasters the war played a major part in losing the Conservatives the next election.[4]

The effect of the war on Zululand was obviously much greater. Probably about 7 000 Zulu died as a direct result of the war – even at Isandlwana the Zulu losses were not much less than those of the British – and the British crop-burning and cattle-looting wrought havoc on the Zulu economy. In time the Zulu could have recovered from this economic damage. The most lasting damage done by the war was political. Although Zululand was not annexed at the conclusion of the war, the monarchy was destroyed. The ensuing internecine conflict enabled Zululand's white neighbours to intervene, and the ultimate result was that the Zulu people lost most of their land as well as all of their independence.[5]

The Zulu were not alone in undergoing such a process of dispossession in this period. The 1870s also saw the final subjugation of the Xhosa, the Pedi and the peoples of East and West Griqualand, and the establishment of that untrammelled white supremacy which ended only recently. In the early 1870s white rule had been precarious over much of South Africa, and appeared to be becoming more so as Africans took advantage of the demand for labour at the diamond fields to gain the firearms which had defeated their fathers in the era of the Great Trek. By the early 1880s the picture was very different. Africans were defeated and disarmed, whites were enforcing their claims to land and taxes, and Africans were supplying cheap labour out of necessity, not in order to obtain guns. Hut-tax receipts in the Transvaal rose from £1 427 in 1876 to £33 690 in 1881, while between 1877 and 1883 the real cost of African labour on the Cape railways fell by half.[6] The overthrow of the Zulu kingdom played a major role in this transformation – both directly, and indirectly, as an example to others.[7]

This transformation was very largely the result of imperial intervention in South Africa. Africans were subjugated mainly by British troops under British officers, and taxes and labour were extracted by British administrators. This imperial intervention took the form of 'Carnarvon's Confederation Policy', that section of the history syllabus which generations of South African school pupils have toiled through with so little appreciation of its real significance. Carnarvon's confederation policy was a failure in the sense that it did not bring about a united federal dominion in Southern Africa, but is historically of great importance because the attempt to implement it produced a decisive shift in the balance of power between black and white, and led to the integration of blacks into the white economy on white terms.

It is generally agreed that the Anglo-Zulu war was a result of Carnarvon's confederation policy. The annexation of the Transvaal in 1877, carried out on the direct instructions of Lord Carnarvon, the Secretary of State for the Colonies, caused Britain to inherit the Boers' border dispute with the Zulu. It was this that put an end to the previously peaceful relations between British and Zulu and produced the crisis that led to war.

The confederation policy led to the war, and it also helped to produce a social and economic transformation in South Africa. Can one say that the war was fought deliberately in order to further such a transformation? It is questions such as this that form the subject of this book. There have been numerous books about the famous battles of the Anglo-Zulu war.[8] This is not another one. This book is concerned with the historical forces that led to the war. Let us see first what has already been written on the subject.

The Historiography of the War's Origins

In an important paper on the historiography of the origins of the war published in 1981,[9] the late Colin Webb identified three types of explanation. Since these types of explanation are roughly sequential, one might say that explanations of the causes of the Anglo-Zulu war have gone through three historiographical phases, though Webb's intervention itself has had a further effect.

The earliest type of explanation was (like most early explanations) essentially a repetition of the opinions and propaganda of the dominant and victorious participants in the events under discussion. It saw the fundamental cause of the Anglo-Zulu war as the incompatibility of barbarism and civilization: the savage, warlike Zulu kingdom was an anachronism in the late nineteenth century. 'What less could Sir Bartle Frere have demanded,' asked Theal in 1919, 'if the safety of Natal and the Transvaal was to be secured? . . . The question was simply whether civilisation or barbarism was to prevail in the country.'[10] Similarly, Cecil Headlam stated in 1936 that the question was 'whether the rule of law or the rule of the assegai was to prevail . . . If Africa was to be civilised, war with the Zulus at some time was, as Shepstone had declared, inevitable.'[11]

As Webb showed, later historians were distrustful of determinist explanations and of subjective phases such as 'barbarism' and 'civilization'. They also carried out more research and examined in more detail the series of events that led to the outbreak of war. It emerged from these researches that the 'barbaric' Zulu kingdom posed no threat to Natal, and that the tension between Zululand and the Transvaal was much more the result of Boer than of Zulu aggression. Shepstone's annexation of the Transvaal might have enabled Britain to resolve the border dispute between Zululand and the Transvaal by imposing a just settlement on the contending parties, a settlement which by satisfying the Zulu would have restored the peaceful relations that had always existed between the Zulu and the British. But Frere, egged on by Shepstone, chose instead to get up a war with the Zulu to nullify their legitimate land claims and thus reconcile the Transvaal Boers to the British flag. Frere also saw war as a means to eliminate Zulu military power and so reconcile the Cape to assuming a greater share of responsibility for the government of the interior. The ultimate purpose of reconciling and reassuring the Transvaal and the Cape was to achieve confederation, which Frere had been appointed to carry out and on which he had staked his reputation.

There was thus, on this view of the matter, nothing inevitable about the Anglo-Zulu war. It might almost be described as an accidental by-product of the policy of confederation. This raises the question of the purpose of the confederation policy. Was one of its purposes the elimination of such independent African polities as the Zulu kingdom, or were its purposes quite different?

The conventional view of the purposes of Carnarvon's confederation policy was that it was partly a product of the ambition of Lord Carnarvon to distinguish himself as the founder of another dominion, and partly intended to relieve Britain from the expense and responsibility of South Africa's troubled affairs. On this view, the overthrow of the Zulu kingdom did not flow directly from the confederation policy. Instead, the connection was indirect. The overthrow of the Zulu kingdom was a means to the achievement of confederation (by placating the Transvaal Boers and reassuring the Cape government) rather than one of the purposes of confederation.[12] Whatever the purpose of confederation might have been, on this view, the effects on the Zulu kingdom of the attempt to achieve it would have been the same; so the purpose of confederation might be considered ultimately as virtually irrelevant to the question of the origins of the Anglo-Zulu war. Thus the view which has more recently become established in certain circles,[13] that confederation was intended to ensure Britain's control over the naval bases on the southern tip of Africa and thereby secure the vital lifeline between Britain and its eastern empire, can have no effect on this view of the origins of the war. If the war was simply a by-product of the attempt to achieve confederation it makes no difference what the purpose of confederation was.

The third type of explanation identified by Colin Webb was marked by an impatience with what was seen as the superficiality of the purely political and personal type of explanation discussed above. It might be perfectly accurate as far as it goes to see the war as stemming from the attempt to implement the policy of confederation,[14] but if one understands this policy as intended simply to save money or maintain control over naval bases, and if one thus sees the Anglo-Zulu war as an incidental by-product of a policy carried out for quite different purposes, one is missing or ignoring the nature of the transition that came over South Africa in the 1870s and the deliberate intentions that helped to bring it about.

The seminal publication of this phase was the 1974 article by Atmore and Marks.[15] This was a wide-ranging survey of British imperial policy and practice in South Africa in the nineteenth century, and a critique of the prevalent political and personal interpretation of it. While feeling obliged to accept something of the established accounts of Carnarvon's personal and strategic predilections, Atmore and Marks argued for an essentially economic interpretation of confederation, pointing to Britain's changing position in the world, but more particularly to the changes and changing needs in South Africa following the discovery of diamonds, especially the growing demand for labour.

Other historians found this account of the 1870s more consistent with the results of their own researches, and they elaborated upon it. Norman Etherington stressed that the diamond fields were not the only part of South Africa to experience a 'labour shortage', and argued that Natal's dependence on migrant labour led its veteran Secretary for Native Affairs, Theophilus Shepstone, to seek British control over as much of its hinterland as possible. Etherington suggested that it was Shepstone's personal influence over Carnarvon which largely explained the latter's confederation policy: 'the perceptions of Shepstone and the expansive interests of Natal became, for a brief period, British imperial policy'.[16] Jeff Guy's view of confederation followed that of Atmore and Marks, and he boldly spelled out its implications for an African state whose King forbade his subjects to work for wages: 'in its most fundamental terms the Zulu kingdom was invaded to facilitate the advance of capitalist production in southern Africa'.[17]

In a sense, as Webb pointed out, the wheel had turned full cycle. Once again the explanation was seen to lie in an irreconcilable conflict of systems rather than in a not necessarily inevitable conjuncture of circumstances. One might argue that the first and third types of explanation make essentially the same point, the former being an ideological expression of the latter.

Webb remained dubious of both. He stated that arguments of the third type, if meant in any specific sense, had not been demonstrated with reference to the evidence, and he doubted that they ever could be. On the other hand, he argued, if meant in a more general sense, such formulations had no real explanatory power:

> Unquestionably, it is right to set historical events in context by taking cognizance of prevailing attitudes and assumptions. Thus, in the case under consideration, it is correct to point out that Carnarvon and Frere would have assumed without question that a federated South Africa would be supported by capitalist enterprise which would take advantage of the country's cheap and abundant black labour supply. That was part of the context of thought in which they operated. But to elaborate context to the position of prime cause of any event is to place explanation on a level of such generality that it ceases to be informative. Arguing that capitalism (in the form of the capitalist value system) caused the Anglo-Zulu war is as unedifying as arguing that feudalism (in the form of the feudal value system) caused the Norman conquest of England. Particular events cannot be explained by general conditions.[18]

Webb's argument has been influential, leading some subsequent writers to reject the Atmore-Marks-Etherington-Guy type of explanation.[19] Nevertheless, Webb is open to criticism. His chief concern seems to be to reject the notion that an abstraction caused the war and to insist that only people can bring about wars. But it may be doubted whether the shorthand expressions he quotes justify his summing up the type of explanation under discussion as 'capitalism caused the war'.[20] And his rejection of such a notion seems to have led him into something of an over-reaction. Webb appears to take it for granted that the motives for federation were purely political, and that capitalism was nothing more or less than the context within which the attempt was made to carry it out. But supporters of the view being criticised would argue that it was 'capitalist enterprise' that was intended to be supported by 'a federated South Africa' rather than the other way round, and that capitalist enterprise was still so undeveloped in South Africa in the 1870s that it can scarcely be described as the context within which the events of that decade occurred. The statement that South Africa possessed a 'cheap and abundant black labour supply' is especially surprising in view of the prevalent complaints of 'labour shortage' in the 1870s. It was certainly widely assumed that a country with a large black population ought to have an abundant labour supply – assumed, that is, that the proper position of black people was in the service of white employers. But in the 1870s this was still far from being the case, and it has been argued that part of the purpose of the confederation policy was to create an abundant supply of labour by shaking it loose from the pre-capitalist societies to which it was attached, and to regulate and rationalise its distribution.[21]

Perhaps eleventh-century European feudalism can be treated as a mere context in which particular things happened for particular reasons. No doubt the Franco-Prussian war can be explained without any reference to capitalist production since by 1870 it was so well established in both France and Prussia that it had become as much a general condition as the weather. But this was manifestly not the case in South Africa in the 1870s. Capitalist production was firmly established in Britain, but was struggling to be born in South Africa. The values of the British were capitalist, but those of the Zulu were most certainly not. The social and economic structures of Zulu and other African societies were incompatible with a capitalist economy predicated upon growth, innovation, capital accumulation and the employment of free labour. Self-sufficient households, households which produced all they consumed and consumed all they produced, did not constitute a market for manufactured goods, or supply commodities to the market; and since they were thus self-sufficient their members had no need to work for wages. But only capitalist production was capable of yielding the surplus necessary to support the civilization the British saw it as their duty and their mission to bring to the dark continent. One should not expect Englishmen in the 1870s to analyse their economic system in these terms, or in any terms. They simply took it for granted that the economy and culture in which they had grown up was superior to that of Africans and that the supersession of the one by the other was necessary, beneficial to all concerned, and inevitable.[22] Western Europe's conquest of the rest of the world, it has been argued,[23] was essentially different from such earlier movements as the Norman conquest of England. Except, to some extent, for the early Iberian conquests in America, it was not simply a case of one military class displacing another as the appropriators of wealth yielded up by a largely unchanging class of producers. The expansion of capitalist Europe revolutionized the non-capitalist societies with which it came into contact. The 'opening up of Africa' meant more than geographical exploration: it meant the opening up and transformation of African *society*. One is surely missing many of the dynamics of this period of history if one treats what was really a revolutionary force as nothing more than a 'context' or a 'general condition'.

The argument that Zululand was invaded to facilitate capitalist production is suspected by many as being dogmatic and teleological. Viewed in retrospect, the mineral discoveries, the confederation policy, the Anglo-Zulu war, and the other wars of the late 1870s, can be seen as having changed the racial balance of power and having begun the social and economic transformation of South African society. Critics suspect that those influenced by Marxist theory are too easily tempted to infer causes from results and confuse effects with intentions.

To claim that the discovery of diamonds did transform South Africa economically and advance the capitalist mode of production, and that this had political consequences, is an historical truism. It is, however, an over-long deductive step to move from this statement to an assertion that politicians were motivated in making political and military decisions by a desire to facilitate the advance of capitalist production. Unpacking the socio-economic perceptions of the Victorians is not always easy, partly because the British political and military elite did not reflect on or describe their actions in these terms. Guy's arguments are more of an *a posteriori* interpretation of events, than a reflection of contemporary conclusions.[24]

If it is possible to make any statement about 'contemporary conclusions' Victorians cannot have been entirely silent about their motives, and it should be possible, by a careful examination of the evidence, to find out whether the men who brought about the war did indeed envisage and intend a future of wage-labour for the Zulu people, and whether this was part of the reason why they acted as they did. This is what the chapters that follow attempt to do.

A further refinement of scepticism is possible. In her essay on Marxist economics, Joan Robinson quoted Voltaire to the effect that one could kill a flock of sheep by witchcraft provided one gave them plenty of arsenic at the same time.[25] Her point was that the empirical material accumulated by Marx was sufficient to demonstrate the exploitation of the working class, and that the labour theory of value, by which he sought to provide a scientific proof and measure of exploitation, was both spurious and unnecessary. Similarly, one might argue that the attempt to implement the policy of confederation in the circumstances then prevailing is a sufficient explanation of the Anglo-Zulu war, whatever the causes of the confederation policy might have been. Even if part of the purpose of the confederation policy was to incorporate the Zulu people into a capitalist economy, this does not really add anything to an explanation of why the war occurred. Whether confederation was wanted to save money, to safeguard naval bases, to facilitate capitalist production, or to do anything else, the Zulu kingdom would have been an obstacle to its achievement and so would have been removed. The attempt to implement the confederation policy thus does all the real explanatory work, while the talk of capitalist production is merely an accompanying incantation, performed only out of Marxist piety and not because it really does anything to further the explanation.

But would the Zulu kingdom have been invaded if the purpose of confederation had been something much more limited than the complete restructuring of South African society? How would an invasion for such purposes have been justified? Many years ago that perceptive historian C.W. de Kiewiet wrote: 'The manner in which the forces that bequeathed to modern South Africa its unique black proletariat were welcomed in the nineteenth century as forces of reform and civilization is one of the most amazing chapters in the country's social history.'[26] Describing something as 'amazing' comes close to describing it as inexplicable. But it is not impossible to understand why proletarianisation, an inescapable component of capitalist production, should have been regarded in nineteenth-century South African conditions as closely allied to civilization. In Britain the majority of the population were proletarians. Britain could not have achieved its economic progress without the free labour that only proletarianisation could provide, and could not have advanced in civilization without the surplus that only economic progress could yield. By de Kiewiet's time the social consequences of proletarianisation in South Africa were apparent, the Hammonds and others had written their classic and widely read threnodies on the process in Britain, and proletarianisation had come to be widely thought of as a bad thing rather than a good thing. *The Imperial Factor in South Africa* was essentially a defence of British imperial policy in South Africa, which de Kiewiet saw as humanitarian in intention and as a countervailing force to settler rapacity. He therefore found the nineteenth-century British attitude towards proletarianisation puzzling and anomalous.[27] He was too good a historian to glide silently over it as he might have been tempted to do. But this evidence needs to be incorporated into a coherent argument rather than remain an unexplained anomaly. From de Kiewiet's comment it appears that the Victorians were not as reticent about their socio-economic perceptions as has been alleged, and that there is evidence of a desire on their part to facilitate the advance of capitalist production. Perhaps this is why they acted as they did and why they felt justified in doing so. Whether this is so can only be settled by an examination of the available evidence, to which we must now turn.

Notes

1. BPP, Return of Casualties and Costs of South African and Afghan Wars 1875–1880, Vol. LVIII, no. 412 of 1881, pp. 2–3. These figures appear to be under-estimates. A footnote states that the figures for 'Natives (Colonial)' are 'as accurate as the imperfect Returns will admit'. Laband and Thompson estimate in their *Field Guide* that the total deaths on the British side in the battles of the Anglo-Zulu war were 1 583.
2. Cabinet Reports, Cab 41, 13/5, Secret, Disraeli to Victoria, 27 July 1879.
3. See ch. 10, p. 251.
4. Lovell, *Struggle for South Africa*, pp. 19 and 25; Beales, *Castlereagh to Gladstone*, pp. 228–9.
5. Laband, *Kingdom in Crisis*; Guy, *Destruction of the Zulu Kingdom*.
6. Delius, *The Land Belongs to Us*, pp. 245–6; Marks, 'Southern Africa', p. 397.
7. See ch.3, p. 49.
8. The best is Laband, *Kingdom in Crisis*.
9. Webb, 'Origins of the War'.
10. Theal, *History of South Africa*, Vol. X, p. 305. Sir Bartle Frere was the High Commissioner (1877–80) who sent the ultimatum to Cetshwayo, the Zulu King.
11. Headlam, 'Failure of Confederation', p. 475. Theophilus Shepstone was Secretary for Native Affairs in Natal for many years, and from 1877 Administrator of the Transvaal.
12. Brookes and Webb, *History of Natal*, ch. XIII; Thompson, 'Subjection of the African Chiefdoms', pp. 261–4. The introductory chapters of the numerous books on the Anglo-Zulu war generally follow this line of explanation.
13. Originating in Robinson and Gallagher, *Africa and the Victorians*, and elaborated in Goodfellow, *Great Britain and South African Confederation*.
14. Though Shula Marks seems to doubt even this: Marks, 'Southern Africa', p. 392. Shula Marks may be regarded as a co-founder of the new school of interpretation: see fn. 15.
15. Atmore and Marks, 'Imperial Factor'.
16. Etherington, 'Labour Supply', p. 239. I have argued that this is something of an ex-

aggeration in Cope, 'Local Imperatives' pp. 603–5. For Etherington's views see also his 'Frederic Elton', 'Anglo-Zulu Relations' and 'The "Shepstone System" '.

17. Guy, 'British Invasion', p. 8. It should be noted that this article appeared in a non-academic journal. In his *Destruction of the Zulu Kingdom* Guy is more cautious.
18. Webb, 'Origins of the War', p. 11.
19. Laband, *Kingdom in Crisis*, p. 5.
20. Webb, 'Origins of the War', p. 8 and notes 20 and 21.
21. Atmore and Marks, 'Imperial Factor', pp. 120–7; Etherington, 'Labour Supply'; Cope, 'De Kiewiet'.
22. Cope, 'De Kiewiet', esp. pp. 486–91.
23. Gellner, *Nations and Nationalism*, pp. 42–3.
24. Dominy, ' "Frere's War"?', p. 191.
25. Robinson, *Marxian Economics*, p. 22.
26. De Kiewiet, *Imperial Factor in South Africa*, p. 158.
27. I have discussed this question at greater length in Cope, 'De Kiewiet'.

CHAPTER TWO

The Zulu Kingdom and its Neighbours to 1873

Zulu, Boer and Briton to 1845

The Zulu kingdom was closely associated with whites from its beginning and whites were always a potential threat to it. The British appeared less of a threat than the Boers, and the Zulu Kings followed a policy of maintaining the best possible relations with the British colony of Natal as a counterweight to Transvaal Boer expansionism. This policy even led them to invite Natal to intervene in Zulu succession disputes. In the event this intervention facilitated the destruction of the Zulu kingdom when imperial policy took an expansionist turn.

The influence of the Zulu kingdom extended all over south-east Africa, but the core of the state established by Shaka lay between the Drakensberg and the sea, bounded in the north by the Swazi and the Tsonga, who were treated as tributaries by the Zulu Kings (the Tsonga more effectively than the Swazi), and in the south by the tributary peoples south of the Thukela river.[1]

In 1837 the Voortrekkers entered the region south of the Thukela and found it apparently almost empty of inhabitants. Their leader, Piet Retief, sought to negotiate a cession of land south of the river from Shaka's successor, Dingane. But Dingane feared the newcomers, and attempted to eliminate the danger by killing Retief and his immediate followers and attacking the main trekker encampment at Weenen. This pre-emptive strike failed. The trekkers received reinforcements and defeated the Zulu at the battle of Blood river. Dingane was defeated but not overthrown. A peace was patched up whereby the Thukela became the boundary between the Zulu kingdom and the trekker Republic of Natalia.

In 1839 Dingane's brother, Mpande, with thousands of his followers, defected to the trekkers. He succeeded in winning their confidence and support, and a joint invasion of Zululand resulted in the defeat and death of Dingane. Mpande was made Zulu King under trekker suzerainty. The trekkers, who had provided military support for Mpande but taken no part in the actual fighting, collected 30 000 cattle and claimed in addition a large sum in 'war expenses'. In lieu of this sum, the land between the Black Mfolozi and Thukela rivers was added to the Republic of Natalia.

The republic was short-lived. After much vacillation Britain annexed Natal, and in August 1843 the trekker *volksraad* tendered its submission to Commissioner Henry Cloete. A treaty concluded in October 1843 between Cloete and Mpande fixed the Thukela and Mzinyathi (Buffalo) rivers as the boundary between the British colony of Natal and the Zulu kingdom. There the boundary remained until 1897, when Zululand was incorporated into Natal.

Both countries were inhabited by Zulu-speaking people. It was the apparent emptiness of Natal that had attracted the Voortrekkers. But it was much less empty than it seemed. Many of the former inhabitants had probably taken refuge in inaccesible places from the disturbances of the early nineteenth century, and with the restoration of peace they re-emerged. Many of the Zulu who fled to Natal with Mpande never returned to Zululand, and they were later joined by their kinsmen and friends. Large numbers of such immigrants or refugees continued to enter Natal until 1854, when the Natal government required all such immigrants to enter the service of a colonist for three years at fixed wages. This appears to have stemmed the tide.[2] Nevertheless, by 1879 the black population of Natal was bigger than the population of Zululand.[3]

It was largely this black influx, and lack of confidence in the British ability to deal with it, that persuaded most of the trekkers to move to the Transvaal after 1843. The white population of Natal came to be predominantly British. But they were outnumbered by more than fifteen to one by Africans. To deal with this situation Theophilus Shepstone was appointed Diplomatic Agent to the Native Tribes in 1845. Like many 'native administrators', Shepstone was the son of a missionary, and grew up on mission stations in the eastern Cape, where he had learnt to speak the Xhosa language, which is very similar to Zulu. At the age of 18, during the frontier war of 1835, he entered the government service as an interpreter on the staff of the Governor, Sir Benjamin D'Urban. From 1839 to 1845 he was 'Diplomatic Agent' at Fort Peddie, in the 'Ceded Territory'.[4]

The Political Economy of Natal and its External Implications

The so-called 'Shepstone system' of indirect rule through chiefs, the recognition of customary law and the establishment of reserves, was very largely imposed on Shepstone by the Colonial Office as the cheapest means of maintaining control.[5] After the turmoil of the early nineteenth century many Africans were living in small groups without hereditary chiefs, and the establishment of a system of indirect rule required to a considerable extent that 'tribes' be constructed and chiefs appointed to rule them.

The degree of Shepstone's success in carrying out this task was measured by the internal peace which prevailed in nineteenth-century Natal, despite the smallness of the white population, the civil service and the garrison. This peace and the consequent avoidance of expense earned Shepstone the gratitude and respect of the Colonial Office. His opinions acquired great weight. During his 30 years as Diplomatic Agent and then Secretary for Native Affairs he dominated Natal in a way no relatively transitory Governor could do. His knowledge of and influence over Africans both in Natal and beyond its borders made him seem indispensable. The legend of 'Somtsewu', with his wonderful influence over the native mind, was born.

The documentary evidence shows that Shepstone did indeed acquire considerable influence over the minds of a number of Englishmen, in particular Sir Garnet Wolseley and Lord Carnarvon. It is likely that his dominating character and imposing demeanour had the same effect on the Africans with whom he came into direct contact. But Shepstone himself was under no illusions as to the fundamental reason for the quietness of Natal Africans at large. They were acquiescent because they retained their access to land. This fact dominated Shepstone's policies, both internal and external.

He consistently opposed the clamours of the colonists to break up the reserves (or 'locations' as they were called in Natal) and release the labour locked up within them. He was not unsympathetic to the labour needs of the colonists, but he knew that any sudden and forcible attempt to proletarianize Africans would be resisted and, in a country where Africans outnumbered colonists so overwhelmingly, this was something that could not be risked.

The reserves constituted less than a third of the land to which Africans had direct access. Some lived on unallocated crown land. Many more lived on the land of absentee landlords. Land had been granted on generous terms to the trekkers to encourage them to stay, but they left anyway, and most of this land came into the hands of speculators. The latter looked to European immigration to raise the price of land, but immigration was slow and in the meantime the only profitable use to which the land could be put was to let it out to Africans. A large proportion of the Africans in Natal thus had access to land but no security in the possession of it. This was what worried Shepstone about Natal's 'overwhelming and ever-increasing native population'.

> The occupation by natives of farms and crown lands unoccupied by whites as yet prevents much inconvenient pressure, but should any sudden and considerable accession of white population take place, a matter quite beyond the control of any government, it is impossible to foresee what solution will be found to so serious and dangerous a problem. A safety-valve in the shape of adjoining territory has always been looked to as the only source of relief.[6]

In the 1850s Shepstone sought this 'safety-valve' in the south. Much of the territory south of the Mzimkhulu river was sparsely inhabited, and Shepstone, supported by John Colenso, the Anglican Bishop of Natal, put forward various schemes for removing a proportion of Natal's Africans to this territory, including one in which he himself would move there and rule the people according to customary law, independently of the Natal government. But all these schemes foundered on the British government's reluctance to sanction such expansion and its possible expense, and the Cape's fear of such a move's possible repercussions on its eastern frontier.[7] In the late 1860s the possibility arose of acquiring Basutoland. Moshweshwe, hard-pressed by the Orange Free State, was prepared to come under Natal rule if this was the price of British protection. But the High Commissioner, Sir Philip Wodehouse, opposed this plan, and Basutoland came directly under the High Commissioner, later being added to the Cape.[8] The most promising direction in which a 'safety-valve' might be found remained Zululand. Its people spoke the same language as those of Natal. Many of the latter had indeed come from Zululand and might thus more easily be induced to go back.

Another advantage of controlling Zululand or part of it was that it would facilitate the passage of migrant labourers from the north. This was Shepstone's alternative to proletarianizing the Africans of Natal. It might seem paradoxical that Shepstone wished both to export Africans from Natal and simultaneously to import other Africans into Natal. But what Shepstone wished to export were self-sufficient households and small peasant producers who occupied land needed for prospective European immigrants, who competed as agriculturalists with whites and who supplied little or no labour. What he wanted to import was labour in its purest form – temporary migrants unencumbered by wives and children.

Agricultural competition from Africans and the shortage of labour resulted in the activities of the small white population of Natal becoming heavily concentrated in the commercial sphere. More than half the whites lived in the towns of Pietermaritzburg and Durban.[9] They could not live entirely by trading with each other or even with the agricultural producers of Natal. 'It was,' wrote Lieutenant-Governor Keate, 'the Overberg trade which is of such paramount importance to us.' 'Natal,' explained Lieutenant-Governor Maclean, 'is an entrepôt for a principal part of the trade of the interior.' The *Natal Mercury* stated in 1866 that the 'vast states of the interior . . . rank among the mainstays of our prosperity'.[10]

This prosperity was gravely threatened by the ambitions of the South African Republic (ZAR) in Zululand. These ambitions were not confined to the acquisition of land. The republic hoped to gain independent access to the sea and to acquire its own port. It would have been a disaster for white Natal if the colony had ceased to be the principal entrepôt for the interior. This explains the phenomenon which so struck Sir Bartle Frere, that white public opinion in Natal tended to be pro-Zulu and anti-Boer. In the land dispute between the Transvaal and Zululand, white Natal's interests were emphatically on the Zulu side. Transvaal expansion into Zululand would disrupt labour migration from the north, possibly send an influx of Zulu into the already 'overcrowded' Natal, certainly rule out any possibility of Zululand being used as a 'safety-valve' for Natal's 'surplus' black population, and destroy the Transvaal's dependence on the merchants of Natal.

White Natal's ideal solution to the problem would be to pre-empt the Transvaal by bringing Zululand under its own control. It was generally assumed by whites in Natal, both officials and colonists, that Zululand would eventually come under British rule or become part of the colony.[11] Shepstone certainly regarded this as a very desirable, indeed necessary, consummation. It was the dissension within Zululand in the 1850s that first lent urgency to the need for Natal to acquire a greater degree of influence over the Zulu kingdom, and at the same time seemed to provide Shepstone with the opportunity of doing so. It is to the politics of the Zulu kingdom that we must now turn.

The Politics of the Zulu Kingdom to 1856

There is much debate about what caused the Zulu kingdom to come into existence,[12] but there is no doubt that in the final stages it was Shaka's conquests or threats of conquest that imposed unity on what had formerly been the numerous independent chiefdoms of the northern Nguni region. Despite this imposition of unity most of these chiefdoms continued to exist, often under the same ruling lineages, recalcitrant rulers being replaced if necessary by more complaisant kinsmen. New chiefdoms were also formed, headed by Shaka's relatives and favourites. In all cases these local administrative positions became hereditary, if they were not so already, and constituted a potentially centrifugal, disintegrative force.

The main centralising agency in the Zulu kingdom was the *amabutho* ('regimental') system. Young men were enrolled in the *amabutho* (singular – *ibutho*) on the basis of age, not of locality, which were thus nationwide, not regional. Until they were permitted to marry (not usually much before the age of 40) they lived for most of the year in *amakhanda* ('military kraals'), which were technically royal residences, being presided over by a female relative of the King. They were thus removed from their fathers' homesteads and their local chiefs' jurisdictions and came under the direct control of the King. In this way military power and loyalties were transferred from the territorial chiefs to the King. The *amabutho* were more than regiments – they were also work parties. They built homesteads and cattle byres, tended cattle, cultivated crops and hunted. They did all this for the King, not for their fathers or local chiefs. The *amabutho* system was thus a means of transferring labour and hence wealth and power from the territorial chiefs to the King.

Memories still remained of the pre-Shakan days of independence and freedom from onerous duties to the state. The unity of the Zulu kingdom had been achieved by military conquest and was maintained by the regimental system. It was an artificial unity in the sense that it had no economic basis. Except that a greater surplus was appropriated by the newly-formed state, the economic system continued as before. The geography and ecology of Zululand was such as to provide all the types of soil and grazing necessary for this type of economy within quite small areas.[13] There was no economic necessity for political unity, nor any economic advantage to be gained from it. Economic forces were no barrier to separatist ambitions.

The political history of the Zulu kingdom centres around this conflict between centrifugal and centripetal forces. The power of pre-Shakan chiefs had been limited by the ease with which dissatisfied subjects could secede and attach themselves to another chief. Secession from the Shakan state was much more difficult. But it was made much easier by the establishment of a powerful alien state on its southern borders. Dingane's fate had been sealed when Mpande seceded to the trekkers. Mpande in his turn found his power eroded as a large proportion of his subjects re-established themselves in the British colony of Natal. The labour obligations imposed on such refugees by the Natal government in 1854 helped to check this process. Dissidence then became bottled up in Zululand. The balance between centrifugal and centripetal forces was sufficiently even – that is to say, separatist ambitions were sufficiently matched by the legitimacy of the monarchy – for dissidence to take the form of support for rival members of the royal family.[14]

Among the Nguni the normal rule of succession was that a chief was succeeded by the eldest son of his Great Wife. Neither Shaka nor Dingane ever married or acknowledged any sons. Dingane assassinated Shaka and Mpande defeated Dingane in battle. Precedent thus provided little clue as to who was Mpande's legitimate heir. Mpande had many sons, but never declared a Great Wife. Cetshwayo's mother was the only one of Mpande's wives who came of a chiefly family, and Cetshwayo was generally regarded as destined to succeed his father. It was said that Mpande had pointed him out as his heir to the trekkers in Natal in 1839 when Cetshwayo was still a child.[15]

By the mid-1850s Cetshwayo was approaching 30, and, like most heirs, was becoming impatient to obtain his inheritance. Like the eighteenth century Princes of Wales, he and his cause became a rallying point for dissidents of all kinds – not only territorial chiefs and their followers who hoped for greater autonomy under a young and untried King, but also younger men who, impatient with the military inactivity of the latter part of Mpande's reign, hoped for glory and booty under a more active young King.

By this time Mpande's eldest sons were established in separate *amakhanda* of their own. As Mpande grew old and sickly (though he did not die until 1872) so the attraction of the reversionary interest became stronger. For men who performed their annual period of service at the *amakhanda* of the King's sons, the separate princely residences became separate courts. Control of the *amabutho* seemed to be slipping out of the King's grasp. In these circumstances the best that Mpande could do was to keep the opposition divided. Of all the princes, Cetshwayo had the most support. Mpande therefore conferred marks of favour on Cetshwayo's chief rival, Mbuyazi, and urged his other sons to support him. In this way the Zulu kingdom became divided between two great factions, the *uSuthu* of Cetshwayo and the *iziGqoza* of Mbuyazi.

Shepstone and Cetshwayo, 1856 to 1861

The inevitable crisis came at the end of 1856. Mbuyazi attempted, through the Norwegian missionary Schreuder, to solicit the aid of the whites in Natal, as his father had done before him. Thus forewarned of the impending conflict,

Shepstone went to the border to mediate and prevent the conflict from spreading to Natal. When he arrived on 2 December he found that the battle had already taken place. Despite Mbuyazi receiving armed support from Natal hunters and traders, the battle of Ndondakusuka was a complete victory for Cetshwayo. Thousands of Mbuyazi's men were killed, and thousands more drowned in the swollen waters of the Thukela, including Mbuyazi himself. 'The effect of today's proceedings,' reported Shepstone, 'is to establish Cetshwayo as King of the Zulus. He will either pension his father or kill him, and that immediately.' 'I fear,' he wrote two days later, 'Cetywayo's success will make him a troublesome neighbour . . . Panda acquired his power in consequence and by the assistance of the white man, Cetywayo in spite of him; these opposite considerations will create corresponding sentiments.'[16]

Mpande was not so easily disposed of as Shepstone supposed he would be. For one conventionally represented as a 'weak king' he showed a surprising determination not to surrender to his victorious son. He still had political resources and he made the most of them. He retained considerable support within the Zulu kingdom, support which tended to increase as he demonstrated his staying power. He still had other sons and potential heirs. And he successfully propagated the belief that he had the support of his white neighbours, in particular the Natal government. In repeated messages he begged Natal to intervene on his behalf, either by sending Shepstone to investigate and settle affairs, or by armed intervention. His enemies, he said, were restrained only by the fear of incurring the displeasure of the Natal government. Its 'countenance was the only support he had . . . if it were withdrawn he would be put to death immediately'.[17]

Cetshwayo clearly believed that armed intervention by Natal was a distinct possibility. He attempted to ward it off by projecting a peaceful and conciliatory image of himself. He too urged Shepstone to come to Zululand so that he could explain his motives and conduct, which had been so misrepresented to the Natal government by the faction hostile to him. He meant no harm to his father, but merely wished to occupy his rightful place as *Induna* of Zululand, to which position, he claimed, his father had appointed him.[18] He made protestations of loyalty to Natal: he wished 'to shape all his actions in accordance with the wishes and advice of this Government'.[19]

In the four years after the battle of Ndondakusuka, the conflict between Mpande and Cetshwayo largely took the form of competition to gain the support of the Natal government. In their messages both emphasized their loyalty and obedience to the British. It seemed to Shepstone a favourable opportunity to extend greater control over Zululand. Since the conflict within the Zulu kingdom might provide the ZAR with a similar opportunity, it also made intervention more necessary. Another reason for intervention was that the continuing conflict there was sending waves of refugees into Natal and threatening to spill across the border. Shepstone was not convinced by Cetshwayo's protestations of loyalty to Natal. Mpande was not expected to live long. It seemed to be in Natal's best interests to ensure that the King had a more complaisant successor than Cetshwayo was likely to be once he gained full control of the kingdom.

It was widely believed in Zululand that Mbuyazi had survived and was living in Natal under the protection of the government. This was not in fact so; but what was true was that his mother, Monase, and another of her sons, Mkhungo, Mbuyazi's full brother, together with a half-brother, Sikhotha, were in Natal. Mkhungo was now the head of the *iziGqoza* faction. Shepstone had shown extraordinary eagerness to secure his person. Mkhungo had been held by a group of Boers in the Utrecht district while apparently on his way to Natal. Shepstone had insisted that the nearest Natal magistrate should obtain possession of him, even though this meant crossing the Natal border. Monase and her sons had been placed in the charge of Ngoza, one of Shepstone's most trusted chiefs, and the education of the princes had been entrusted to Shepstone's good friend, Bishop Colenso.[20]

It was widely believed, both in Natal and Zululand,[21] that Mkhungo was being groomed to succeed to the Zulu throne. This belief was probably correct. Shepstone appears to have left no record of such an intention, but Colenso was less discreet: he repeatedly described Mkhungo as Mpande's 'rightful heir'. Shepstone knew that the imperial government and the High Commissioner, Sir George Grey, in particular, were opposed to the Natal government becoming entangled in Zulu politics. The proposal that Bishop Colenso should resign his see and become Bishop of a new diocese of Zululand was in part a covert attempt to establish a Natal presence in Zululand in the interests of Colenso's protégé, Mkhungo.[22] Colenso told his Metropolitan that he felt 'a strong call within my heart for that work', but he added that 'the Providence of God, in bringing Panda's son, and intended heir, Umkhungo, under my charge, appears to have given me an external call, which I cannot neglect'. Shepstone himself even considered resigning his position and going with Colenso to Zululand, accompanied, it was hoped, by a '*vast body* of natives' from Natal. The scheme was a revival of their earlier scheme for the area south of the Mzimkhulu, so that, as Colenso said, 'that migration wd. then take place to the N.E. of this colony, which *was* to have gone to the S.W.'.[23]

Colenso's visit to Zululand in September and October 1859 forced a drastic modification of this visionary scheme. Colenso discovered that 'the whole strength of the Nation lies with Ketchwayo'. It would be 'absurd', he concluded, to support Mkhungo. But he still wished to establish a Zulu mission. His efforts, he said, would now be directed 'to try to bring the old King to acquiesce in the wish of the Nation'. With Cetshwayo made King with British support 'much may be done, under God, for the advancement of the whole Zulu people'.[24]

Nevertheless, Colenso was as reluctant to abandon his protégé as Shepstone was to abandon what he had supposed to be his trump card. In August 1860

Colenso was still hoping that Mkhungo might be restored 'by God's providence to a position of authority among his people'.[25] In September 1860 Sir George Grey visited Natal and, after conferring with Shepstone, produced a plan for the partition of Zululand between Cetshwayo, Mkhungo – and Shepstone! Shepstone was to have his 'safety-valve', in which the majority of Natal's black population was to be resettled and governed by him, while Cetshwayo and Mkhungo were to govern their portions of Zululand with the assistance of 'British officers', and thus effectively come under Natal's control.

Grey's uncharacteristic support for Shepstone's ambitions in Zululand was intended as the *quid pro quo* for Natal's acquiescence in his plans to extend the Cape's frontier to the Mzimkhulu, thus annexing territory which Faku, the Mpondo chief, had ceded to Natal. Lieutenant-Governor Scott of Natal refused to acquiesce in this, however, and was supported by the Secretary of State for the Colonies, whereupon Grey withdrew his support for Shepstone's plans.

By the time these diplomatic manoeuvrings had worked themselves out, the plan for partition had been overtaken by events in Zululand. News of the plan to partition Zululand leaked out to the newspapers,[26] and soon reached Cetshwayo's ears. He sent an alarmed message to Shepstone in January 1861, asking if it were true that he intended attempting to negotiate a cession of part of Zululand and seizing it by force of arms if negotiations failed. Shepstone denied contemplating the use of force but, still at that stage confident of Grey's support, confirmed his desire to negotiate the cession of part of Zululand 'to provide for the wants of the natives in the Colony'. This can have done little to reassure Cetshwayo. In March another shock followed. Cetshwayo learned of Mpande's plan to nominate a younger son, Mthonga, son of Nomantshali, as his heir. Cetshwayo contemplated fleeing to Natal, but in the event took sterner action. Nomantshali was put to death. Mthonga, with a brother and two *izinduna*, succeeded in escaping to the Boers of Utrecht. Cetshwayo followed with an armed force, but did not cross into the Utrecht district. He kept Shepstone informed of his movements and again requested his mediation.[27] But Shepstone learnt independently that Cetshwayo had succeeded in recovering Mthonga from the Boers.[28]

Cetshwayo's Nomination as Heir, 1861

It was probably this apparent evidence of collaboration between the Transvaal Boers and Cetshwayo, coming on top of the withdrawal of Grey's support for his more ambitious schemes, that persuaded Shepstone to abandon Mkhungo and throw the full weight of the Natal government behind Cetshwayo. He may also have heard that the ZAR, which had formerly supported Mpande, had decided to back Cetshwayo instead.[29] It would be disastrous for Natal if Cetshwayo became King with the support of the ZAR, in spite of the opposition of Natal. So, without the permission of the High Commissioner or the Secretary of State, Shepstone belatedly but hastily responded to Mpande's and Cetshwayo's four years of requests for mediation. His instructions from Lieutenant-Governor

Scott were to 'induce Panda to follow what is evidently the wish of his people, and to declare Cetywayo his heir'.[30]

Shepstone's reception in Zululand was unfriendly.[31] Mpande was much opposed to Cetshwayo's nomination as heir. He spoke fondly of his sons in exile, describing them as 'the seed which a wise man wishes kept until the sowing time arrives'. But since he believed that his position and even his life depended on the Natal government's support, and since Shepstone now demanded that he should name Cetshwayo his heir, he had no option but to comply. Cetshwayo received his nomination most ungraciously. He seems to have regarded Shepstone's belated patronage as Dr Johnson did Lord Chesterfield's: as the action of one who 'looks with unconcern on a man struggling for life in the water, and, when he has reached ground, encumbers him with help'.[32]

The nomination ceremony was something of a fiasco, and nearly a disaster. Cetshwayo at first refused to attend, and when he was eventually prevailed upon to do so he arrived with a bodyguard of 5 000 men. Shepstone noticed that each man had a single assegai, reversed to conceal the blade, in his small travelling shield. Heralds proclaimed Cetshwayo as heir and commander-in-chief of the army (and thus the real ruler of the country). They then turned to Shepstone and demanded, in the name of the Zulu nation, the return of Mkhungo and Sikhotha. Only their return would restore peace and quiet to the Zulu kingdom, they declared, for as long as they remained in the colony the constant rumours of the Natal government's intentions regarding them would cause apprehension and unsettledness. Shepstone agreed to convey this request to the Natal government, but gave no hope of compliance. A long and acrimonious argument then ensued. Tempers were inflamed by the action of Ngoza, Shepstone's *induna*, who without permission had entered the *isigodlo* (the women's quarters) of Mpande's residence. This in itself was a gross breach of etiquette, but it had political implications as well. Ngoza was the guardian of Monase, Mkhungo and Sikhotha, and he had entered the *isigodlo* to communicate with Monase's daughters. Cetshwayo and his supporters declared that it was this constant exchange of messages between the Natal and Zululand branches of the family that kept up a continual ferment about the Natal government's intentions and made it imperative that Mkhungo and Sikhotha should be returned. There were clamorous demands that Ngoza should answer for himself. Shepstone refused to allow him to do so and was insulted, and, according to one eye-witness,[33] spat at by Cetshwayo. Shepstone believed that if he had not firmly resisted the demand that Ngoza should answer for himself 'the meeting might have had a very serious termination'.

According to Shepstone, Cetshwayo apologized the next day for the intemperance of the meeting; but Shepstone was clearly not mollified. His description of Mpande's attitude towards the nomination of Cetshwayo was equally true of his own: he said he was 'induced by the force of circumstances alone to appoint Cetywayo his successor, he strongly deprecated the necessity, although he succumbed to it, and he fervently hopes that his appointment may prove a nullity'.

Shepstone returned to Natal in a dark mood. In his confidential report to Lieutenant-Governor Scott he described Cetshwayo as

> exceedingly intelligent and energetic . . . but peculiarly restless and impatient of restraint or contradiction. He was surrounded by men as Councillors, of a similar stamp, and I am inclined to the opinion that he will become sooner or later, a troublesome neighbour; he is at present the terror of the whole country, and surrounded as he constantly is, by a strong force of young restless men, there is no guarantee for moderation or prudence to be hoped for.

Mpande and the older men of Zululand, said Shepstone, were thoroughly loyal to the Natal government, 'but at present, all is overborne by the will and caprice of this young man'. It seemed to Shepstone that Cetshwayo was 'willing to carry on a sort of political dalliance, with either the Boers or Moshesh, or both; it flatters his vanity and is grateful to his ambition and that morbid feeling of animosity which he evidently feels towards the Native Tribes of Natal' (now the seat of the *iziGqoza* faction). Shepstone believed that Moshweshwe was planning to unite all the powerful African chiefs in a combination to resist and if possible destroy the white man, and that Cetshwayo was associated with this plan. Mpande, a shrewder judge than Shepstone, had scoffed at such stories: 'and do speculators suppose that Moshesh will ever venture for any political considera- tion to leave the rock that shelters him? He will do so when the rock rabbits feed on the plain.' But Shepstone considered that Mpande was either unaware of the extent of the negotiations being carried on, or else underrated them. In a final gloomy postscript to his confidential report Shepstone stated that he had heard that President Pretorius of the South African Republic was on a visit to Zululand to obtain the cession of a port in that country.[34]

In his other report of the same date, the one intended to be published, Shepstone stated that he had 'successfully accomplished the object of Your Excellency's instructions'.[35] It was of course true that he had, as instructed, induced Mpande to declare Cetshwayo his heir. But the real purpose of the visit had been to strengthen Natal's influence over Zululand by putting the latter's new ruler in its debt. Shepstone's belated expediency had failed to achieve this effect, and nowhere is the failure more eloquently exposed than in the pages of Shepstone's confidential report.

As it turned out, Shepstone need not have been so gloomy. If Cetshwayo had ever entered into an alliance, or even a dalliance, with the Boers, it was short- lived. Pretorius did not get his port. Cetshwayo denied the Boer claim that he had ceded land in return for Mthonga. The succession dispute within Zululand, which had made both Mpande and Cetshwayo reliant on Natal's favour, was for all practical purposes settled in 1861, but it was immediately replaced by a land dispute with the Transvaal. Natal had almost as great an interest in keeping the

Boers out of Zululand as had the Zulu themselves, and Cetshwayo came to rely on support from Natal in his resistance to the Transvaal's territorial claims. It remained essential for the ruler of Zululand to be on good terms with Shepstone, though now for a different reason. Right up to the Anglo-Zulu war of 1879 the Transvaal-Zulu border dispute remained the pivot around which the relations between the Zulu and their white neighbours turned, the question undergoing a dramatic change when Shepstone became the ruler of the Transvaal in 1877. It is to this dispute that we must now turn.

The Transvaal-Zulu Border Dispute: Origins and Merits

One may distinguish three distinct territories in dispute between the ZAR and the Zulu kingdom: the Utrecht district between the Mzinyathi (Buffalo) and the Ncome (Blood) rivers extended up to the Phongolo; the area between the Utrecht district, the Phongolo river, and in the east the line marked A-A on the map; and an ill-defined region north of the Phongolo.

This last region is not usually included within the 'disputed territory'; not only the ZAR but the British authorities in Natal took it as virtually axiomatic that the Zulu had never had any legitimate claim to land north of the Phongolo. But the Zulu certainly did claim land north of the Phongolo, and acted upon their claim, so we must consider what their claim rested upon, as well as the nature of the rival claims in this area.

The ZAR claimed land north of the Phongolo by virtue of cessions made by the Swazi King. A cession of 1855, which included a strip of land about 15 kilometres wide extending in an easterly direction towards the Lebombo mountains along the north bank of the Phongolo, was made partly in return for protection against the Zulu, but mainly in return for the Boers' promise to abandon the cause of a rival claimant to the Swazi throne. With the death of this claimant, and the failure of the Boers to pay all the cattle they had also promised, the Swazi King considered himself no longer bound by the cession and the Swazi resumed occupation of much of the land. In 1866, however, the regents for the King's minor successor ceded the land again, apparently in response to the growing Zulu threat.[36]

The Zulu claim to land north of the Phongolo rested upon the conquests of Shaka and the Zulu Kings' consequent overlordship of the rulers of the area, including the Swazi King himself, Sobhuza I having submitted to Shaka.[37] Even Shepstone stated on one occasion, at a time when he was particularly anxious to play down the claims of the ZAR over the Swazi, that 'the amaSwazi King and people have always been tributary to the Zulus'.[38] This claim was rejected by the Swazi as well as by the Boers and, as a rule, by the British. But the Swazi claim that the Phongolo was 'the ancient boundary that always separated our countries',[39] had the strength attributed to it by whites only in respect of the lower reaches of the river, near the Lebombo mountains. Further west, away from the centre of Swazi power, the claim became more dubious. The area north of this part of the Phongolo had been inhabited in pre-Shakan times by small independent chiefdoms which had submitted without resistance to Shaka, and since then the sovereignty of the Zulu Kings had been acknowledged at least intermittently in this area.[40] But the Swazi Kings also claimed these people as subjects and, in times of Zulu weakness, such as the period of conflict between Dingane and Mpande, and during the succession dispute of the 1850s, the Swazi Kings were able to secure from them an acknowledgement of their supremacy. The minor chiefs of this frontier zone were obliged in fact to *khonza* (submit) to either the Zulu or the Swazi King as circumstances dictated – sometimes they gave their allegiance to both simultaneously.[41] The Zulu claim to this territory was older, but the Swazi King exercised more effective control over it in 1855 when he ceded it to the Boers. Nevertheless, the Zulu never accepted that the Swazi had any right to cede this territory to the Boers,[42] and never accepted that the Phongolo was the boundary of Zululand.

They gave practical expression to their claims. From at least 1860 land north of the Phongolo was being colonized by Zulu from south of the river.[43] A ZAR border commission of 1866 found many homesteads belonging to Hamu, Masiphula, Mnyamana and other Zulu chiefs north of the river.[44] By the mid-1870s it is estimated that there were between 15 000 and 30 000 Zulu north of the Phongolo.[45]

The land south of the Phongolo making up the Utrecht district was almost unoccupied after the Hlubi and the Ngwe fled from Mpande to Natal in 1848, which might help explain why Mpande ceded it in that year for a mere 100 head of cattle to the men who made him King. The commission appointed by Lieutenant-Governor Bulwer of Natal in 1878 to investigate the border dispute expressed doubt as to the validity of this cession, but awarded the area to the Transvaal Province (as the ZAR had become following the British annexation of April 1877) on the grounds of established occupation and government and Zulu acquiescence in this.[46]

The disputed territory around which so much controversy centred, and which generated so much conflict, was the land between the Utrecht district and the line marked A-A on the map.[47] The alleged cession took place in March 1861, and resulted from the flight of Cetshwayo's rival Mthonga to the Utrecht district.[48] Mthonga and his attendants were detained by the members of a standing commission appointed in the ZAR the previous year to work for Cetshwayo's speedy accession to the Zulu throne and to obtain a cession of land. Cetshwayo followed Mthonga with an armed force, but did not cross into the Utrecht district. After a series of transactions, which it is difficult to reconstruct with any certainty owing to the dubious nature of the evidence, the fugitives were returned to Cetshwayo and the ZAR commission came away with a document bearing Cetshwayo's mark, ceding land to the line A-A. Cetshwayo acknowledged that he had signed a paper, but stated he had been given to understand that it contained the minutes of the discussions and a guarantee of the safety of the returned fugitives. Cetshwayo was not King and had no power to cede land. The documents suggest that the ZAR commission recognised Cetshwayo as King, or at least as heir. Nevertheless, another ZAR commission visited Mpande in August 1861 to obtain a ratification of Cetshwayo's cession. According to this commission, Mpande said that Cetshwayo had no right to cede land but signed a document ceding the same land himself. Mpande, however, always denied ratifying or making any cession.

This border dispute can be seen as the immediate cause of the war of 1879. By then the Transvaal was under British rule, so the war was fought between the Zulu and the British. As Administrator of the Transvaal, Shepstone supported the Transvaal case. He had become convinced that the Zulu were in the wrong, and that they knew they were in the wrong. The same applies to Sir Bartle Frere, the High Commissioner, whose ultimatum led to the war. But what seemed Zulu treachery and aggression would be something very different if the Zulu were in the right. To understand the genesis of the war of 1879, therefore, an attempt to reach some conclusion on the rights and wrongs of the border dispute is unavoidable.

It is difficult to think of a means by which the existence of an agreement between literate and illiterate parties could be proved or disproved by the production of documents. The Boers may have deceived the Zulu concerning the contents of the documents to which they affixed their marks. The documents presented to the commission appointed in 1878 to investigate the question may not have been those marked by the Zulu, but documents subsequently drawn up by the Boers with forged Zulu marks attached. Indeed, the document containing the alleged cession, initially supposed to be the original, turned out to be a 'copy', which was inexact at least to the extent that it contained the signature of a man who was not present on the occasion the original was drawn up.[49] Such documents, in fact, could be produced without the Zulu having signed anything. Conversely, of course, the Zulu could untruthfully but plausibly allege that such things had been done. Some of these difficulties could have been obviated had the Zulu been given copies of written agreements, but this was not done. The documents were drawn up, read out, interpreted, witnessed and preserved by an interested party. In these circumstances, the best one can do is to see if there are any particular reasons for distrusting the documents, and to consider the plausibility of what they contain.

The first dubious circumstance that should be noted is that Landdrost Smuts of Utrecht only informed Acting President Schoeman of the alleged cession seven weeks after it was supposed to have been made, in letters dated 20 May 1861.[50] What seems to have spurred Smuts to write was the news that a commission including Schoeman and M.W. Pretorius was approaching Utrecht.[51] But had the cession been genuine and unequivocal he would surely have reported the glad news without delay.

A document dated 16 March 1861 signed by Landdrost Smuts purports to give an account of the preliminary discussions between the ZAR border commission and Cetshwayo's representatives. In it the latter are represented as describing a recent meeting with Shepstone at which Cetshwayo refused to 'unite' with him as Mpande wished, saying 'Pretorius and the Boers made Umpanda king of Zululand; if Umpanda wishes to go over to the English, let him go, but we all join ourselves on the side of the Boers'. Cetshwayo, they said, offered reciprocal military assistance and 'would do as he was bid by the people there; if the people asked him for land he would give it'.[52]

But the only meeting between Shepstone and Cetshwayo in 1861 took place on 16 May, when Cetshwayo was recognised as heir.[53] This anomaly is not simply an error of dating. The meeting between the ZAR border commission and Cetshwayo's representatives unquestionably took place before Shepstone's meeting with Cetshwayo – the latter was in part a response to the former – and the ZAR commission and Cetshwayo's representatives cannot possibly have discussed something that had not yet taken place. On these grounds, and because all the persons present on the occasion of the receipt of this message from Cetshwayo denied to the 1878 commission that it had referred to Shepstone or declared that they could not remember any allusion to him, the commission dismissed this document as 'plainly a fabrication'.[54] The fact that fabrication was resorted to in the case of one document must cast doubt on the others, including the deed of cession (which was, as we have seen, a 'copy' containing at least one false signature), especially in view of the delay in reporting the alleged cession.

The documents with which the Transvaal supported its case before the 1878 commission represent only a selection of those available. The supposed cession of March 1861 was far from being the most favourable to the Transvaal. On the contrary, it was the most modest, and was presumably pushed because, this being so, it was the most plausible. There exists, for example, a document signed by five representatives of the ZAR, on the one hand, and Mpande, his chief councillor Masiphula and four other Zulu chiefs on the other, dated 30 March 1858, which declares Mpande's entire country, from the Thukela to the 'Comwoema', which flows through the Lebombo mountains to the sea, to be 'het Eigendom van die Goevernemend van de Suijd Afrecaansche Republiek'.[55] On a later occasion Mpande was somewhat less generous. On 16 December 1864 he allegedly ceded to the ZAR only the land to the south of the watershed north of the Mhlatuze river, although at the same time he acknowledged himself and his people to be subjects of the ZAR. The document containing this cession[56] is witnessed by Masiphula and another Zulu, and by three representatives of the ZAR.

No one could credit these 'cessions'. But in the case of the alleged agreement of March 1861 there was a good reason why Cetshwayo might have ceded some territory. Mthonga was a dangerous rival who threatened Cetshwayo's chances of becoming King. It would be worth Cetshwayo's while to cede a small part of the country, if by so doing he could secure his possession of the rest of it by recovering Mthonga and his brother from the Boers and gaining Boer support for his succession. The fact that the fugitives were returned appeared to Sir Bartle Frere a powerful argument in favour of the Transvaal case. If no land was ceded, why should the Boers have handed them over? 'Here,' wrote Frere, 'was a strong motive why Cetshwayo should make a cession, which at other times he would have refused; there appears no doubt that he did make some cession and got possession of the Princes of the Royal House.'[57] It is important to note, therefore, that the actual deed of cession contains no reference to the fugitive princes. When President Pretorius explained the land cession to the Lieutenant-Governor of Natal in 1865 he did not represent it as the *quid pro quo* for the two fugitives, but stated that the land had been obtained 'at a remuneration', presumably the 25 cows, bull, horse, bridle and saddle represented in the document as a present. Pretorius went on to explain:

> The reasons that gave rise to this agreement are simply that during the disturbances in the Zulu country between Panda and Cetywayo, the people of Cetywayo crossed the boundaries to follow up fugitive adherents of Panda, and thereby endangered the lives and property of the inhabitants of the Republic, and it was considered advisable to establish a boundary to prevent such incursions and inroads for the purpose of murder and bloodshed.[58]

Why then were the fugitives returned? Pretorius's letter provides a clue. The presence of the fugitives in Utrecht was a great temptation to Cetshwayo to send an armed force into the area to recapture them. Later in 1861 a rumour that Cetshwayo intended to seize Mkhungo had thrown the colony of Natal into a panic, had caused all available troops to be sent to the border, and had caused the Lieutenant-Governor to make urgent requests for reinforcements to the High Commissioner in the Cape, although the rumour later proved to be groundless.[59] It was the arrival of a strong armed force on the other side of the Ncome (Blood) river that prompted the Boers to open negotiations about the return of the fugitives. A border farmer, P.L. Uys, recollected that:

> a large Kafir Commando, of which the Captain Umzilikaza was headman, had at the same time come to the other side of the Blood River and threatened us that they had orders from Cetywayo to pursue Dingezi [one of Mthonga's attendants] and if we did not give up Dingezi and the two sons of Panda and the cattle, and the people, they would come amongst us and take them by force.[60]

The minutes of the meeting held on 1 April, at which it was decided to hand back the fugitives, confirm this view. The ZAR border commission informed the meeting that Cetshwayo was close by with a large force and had asked for the fugitives to be returned; upon this, 'considering that through the Kafirs having taken refuge with us our laws have already been transgressed, and that they endanger the safety of this State', it was resolved to hand them over. A further reason or justification for returning them mentioned in the minutes was that Cetshwayo and his captains had guaranteed their safety; but there is no mention of any cession of land.[61] No doubt the border commission tried to take advantage of the situation to extract a land cession from Cetshwayo; but the fact that they complied with the latter's demand for the return of the fugitives by no means proves that they were successful.

The failure of Landdrost Smuts to impart the glad news of the land cession would be intelligible if there were no glad news to impart. Seven weeks later the approach of Acting-President Schoeman and M.W. Pretorius might have led to the concoction of a land cession designed to show that the border commission appointed the previous year had not been idle.[62] Pretorius and the commission of which he was the head went on to visit Mpande on 19 June, taking with him a document for the King to sign stating that he approved, permitted and ratified the cession of land made by Cetshwayo. This document, bare of any signatures, is still in the archives in Pretoria. As the minutes of this commission record, Mpande stated that Cetshwayo had no right to cede land, that he had not ceded any, and that he, Mpande, would not cede any either. The members of the commission then visited Cetshwayo, who denied having ceded land.[63] Pretorius made a personal report to Schoeman concerning his visit to Cetshwayo, in which he stated that the people of Utrecht had misrepresented ('verbloemd') the transactions of March 1861, and that the Zulu had proved them to be liars to their face ('Overtuigd zijnde dat de kaffers de menschen in hun gesigt voor leugenaars hebben gemaakt . . .' etc).[64]

These events and the documents they generated were not brought to the attention of the 1878 commission of inquiry into the border dispute. Instead a document dated 5 August 1861 was produced. This bore the alleged mark of Mpande (though not those of any Zulu witnesses) and the signatures of three Utrecht farmers. It represents Mpande as stating that Cetshwayo had no right to cede land but that he would cede the same land himself.[65] In view of the fact that Mpande had refused less than two months earlier to ratify or make any cession to the son of the man who had made him King, it is difficult to take this document seriously.

The weight of all this evidence, in my opinion, makes it virtually impossible to believe that any cession of land was made by the Zulu in 1861, or to doubt that in this dispute the Zulu were in the right and the ZAR was in the wrong. It is possible that Mpande and Cetshwayo held out hopes of a land cession in order to gain the support of the Boers against each other during this period of internal conflict. Mpande appears to have considered himself under a particular obligation to the people of Andries Pretorius for their assistance in overthrowing Dingane and making him King. His expressions of loyalty to the Boers were no doubt construed as acknowledgements of their ultimate sovereignty. Just as the Zulu considered that Shaka's former dominance left them with rights to land and sovereignty across the Phongolo, so the Boers seem to have believed that their installation of Mpande gave them rights of a similar kind over Zululand.[66] Perhaps they regarded the documents with which they sought to prove their case in the same way as the monks of the Middle Ages are said to have regarded the charters they forged: as merely supplying formal proof for the benefit of inquisitive outsiders of what were undoubted rights sanctioned by history. There is certainly something medieval in the belief that the multiplication of deeds of cession would strengthen rather than weaken a claim. If their view of the matter was as I have suggested, it might explain what Frere found so difficult to accept: that 'so many men of fair repute in their own time among their own people conspired to perpetrate such a fraud'.[67] It was, as Gibbon would say, a 'pious fraud'.

History of the Dispute to 1873

In 1864 the ZAR beaconed off the line supposed to have been ceded in 1861. But, no doubt as a result of Zulu resistance, it made no immediate attempt to establish effective and permanent occupation down to this line. In fact, right up to 1879 a considerable part of the disputed territory remained occupied and ruled solely by Zulu. The highwater mark of Boer encroachment was reached in March 1876; after this the tide turned, and the Zulu took the offensive. The position in March 1876 was as follows:

- Land west of the Ncome (Blood) river was firmly in Boer control and was definitely part of the ZAR.[68]

- There were occupied Boer farms down to the Old Hunting Road (see the map), which seems to have been regarded in practice as the boundary of the Utrecht district and therefore of the ZAR. But there were also Zulu in this area who recognized only Zulu sovereignty and over whom the ZAR by a tacit agreement exercised no jurisdiction.[69]

- Boers used the land between the Old Hunting Road and the line supposed to have been ceded in 1861 (A-A on the map) for grazing purposes, but there was no permanent occupation of this area (although farms had been marked out and registered),[70] and the Landdrost of Utrecht exercised no jurisdiction in it.[71]

The gradual Boer encroachment provoked and was checked by Zulu protests, disturbances and war-scares in the border region. Several ZAR commissions visited Mpande in an attempt to effect a peaceful settlement, but the Zulu King refused to accept the 1861 line and refused to order the Zulu inhabitants of the disputed territory to leave. Indeed, it was observed that more Zulu were moving into it from other parts of Zululand. This Zulu settlement of the area may have been the result of population pressure in other parts of the country, but it seems likely that it was also intended to establish effective occupation, the better to resist Boer claims. Cetshwayo was reported in 1865 to have ordered the Zulu not to move out of the disputed territory on pain of death, to prevent the Boers from occupying it.

The Zulu authorities kept the Natal government informed of events on the border, and repeatedly requested its intervention. A message from Mpande and Cetshwayo described Pretorius's visit of June 1861. They stated that the Boers had been obliged to admit that their 'cession' was invalid. One might be inclined to doubt the accuracy of this statement, but Pretorius's letter to Schoeman of July 1861,[72] makes it plausible. Nevertheless, Mpande and Cetshwayo said that the Boers were persisting in demanding land, stating that they wanted a port and threatening to seize land by force. This attempt by the ZAR to obtain an independent outlet to the sea evidently caused the British some disquiet, for we find in June 1862 High Commissioner Wodehouse warning Pretorius, then on a visit to Cape Town, that St Lucia was British (by virtue of the 1843 treaty between Mpande and Cloete) and that Britain had objections to any further extension of the territory of the ZAR in the direction of Zululand. Wodehouse, however, accepted Pretorius's story that a cession had already been made.

The beaconing-off of the land claimed by the ZAR in 1864 led to another Zulu complaint to the Natal government and another inquiry by the High Commissioner to the ZAR. It was on this occasion that Pretorius explained that the land had been obtained at a remuneration and to prevent incursions.[73] The High Commissioner appears to have been convinced by this, and the Secretary of State agreed that there were no grounds for British interference.

It may have been this complaisant British attitude, together with disturbances on the border, that led Pretorius to make plans, in June 1865, to seize part of Zululand by force. He hoped to divide the Zulu by offering the throne to Hamu, Cetshwayo's brother, and to enlist the aid of the Swazi King in return for part of the territorial spoils. He hoped to annex all the land south of the Black Mfolozi. A force of 300 burghers was actually assembled in the Wakkerstroom district under Commandant-General Paul Kruger. But the weakness of the republic forced it to abandon this scheme. It was losing ground in the Soutpansberg, burghers were refusing to do military service, no help was forthcoming from the Swazi King, and the current war between Basutoland and the Orange Free State also had its dangers for the ZAR.

The Zulu took advantage of the ZAR's weakness. It was particularly during the period 1865 to 1868 that the formerly relatively sparsely inhabited disputed territory was settled by Zulu both south and north of the Phongolo. The Boers were unable to resist. The point was reached where the Landdrost of Wakkerstroom urged that Shepstone be asked to arbitrate.[74]

In 1869 a more determined attempt by the ZAR to achieve a more effective occupation of the disputed territory caused the Zulu both to resist the Boers and to request British arbitration. Cetshwayo also renewed an earlier request for the Natal authorities to take over the disputed territory, pointing out that there had never been any border dispute with Natal.[75] Shepstone had long sought a 'safety-valve' in adjoining territory[76] but what the Zulu hoped for from a British takeover of the area was the exclusion of Boers, not the inclusion of Natal's 'surplus' Africans.

Lieutenant-Governor Keate and President Pretorius eventually agreed that the former should arbitrate; but the attempt came to nothing. After Keate decided against the ZAR in the Diamond Fields border dispute in 1871, Pretorius resigned and the Volksraad resolved not to continue with the Zulu border arbitration. Keate left Natal in July 1872, and his successor seems to have known nothing about the proposed arbitration.[77] The Zulu were not told that arbitration had been abandoned, and Cetshwayo was still expecting it in November 1872, when he told the Natal government that he was taking no action in response to Boer acts of aggression because the matter was in the hands of the Natal government.

Shepstone told Cetshwayo in reply that the Lieutenant-Governor had recently written to the President of the ZAR on the subject, and urged, as he had done many times before, peace and forbearance. Lieutenant-Governor Musgrave had indeed written to President Burgers and told him of the wishes that the Zulu had repeatedly urged upon the Natal government concerning the border dispute, but he had made no suggestions regarding a solution. The letter was mainly concerned with Cetshwayo's brother Mthonga, whose flight to Utrecht in 1861 had been the first cause of the border dispute. Mthonga had escaped from Cetshwayo's custody in 1865, this time to Natal. He caused excitement in Zululand by secretly returning to visit Mpande and, having resisted the attempt of the Natal government to put him in the charge of a trusted *induna* remote from the Zulu border, he fled once more to the Transvaal. Musgrave's despatch informed Burgers of this, and pointed out that Mthonga's presence might embroil the ZAR with the Zulu.[78]

Perhaps Burgers felt that the presence of Mthonga might give him an advantage in negotiating directly with the Zulu authorities. Certainly he was opposed to any possible cession of the disputed territory to Natal.[79] He made an attempt to negotiate with the Zulu in January 1873, but found no one to meet him at the Zulu border on the appointed day. As he was returning, messengers overtook him with a gift of two oxen and the news that Mpande had died and that the Zulu nation was in mourning and therefore could transact no business. The messengers told the President that Cetshwayo would be glad to meet him in the winter.[80]

The further development of the border dispute was to wait until after Cetshwayo had been installed in the place of his deceased father.

The Zulu Succession: Zulu-Natal Negotiations, 1873

Mpande died in October 1872, but it was not until February 1873 that the Natal government was officially informed of his death. The Zulu messengers brought four oxen, which they said symbolized the head of the deceased King, and stated that they had been charged to make certain requests of the government. The first was that Shepstone might 'prepare himself to go to Zululand when the winter is near, and establish what is wanting among the Zulu people, for he knows all about it, and occupies the position of father to the King's children'. The messengers continued, even more obscurely:

> The Zulu nation wishes to be more one with the Government of Natal; it desires to be covered with the same mantle; it wishes Somtseu to go and establish this unity by the charge which he shall deliver when he arranges the family of the King, and that he shall breathe the spirit by which the Nation is to be governed.[81]

An explanation for this request is necessary, since it might be thought beneath the dignity of an independent kingdom for its new King to be installed by the agent of a foreign government. This was, indeed, the opinion of many of the most important men in Zululand.[82]

A statement by the Zulu messengers provides a clue. They stated that they were also commissioned to urge 'what has already been urged so frequently, that the Government of Natal be extended so as to intervene between the Zulus and the territory of the Transvaal Republic'.[83] Cetshwayo's invitation to Shepstone can be seen as part of his policy of maintaining the closest ties with Natal as a counterweight to the territorial encroachments of the ZAR. When Shepstone met Cetshwayo in Zululand, the first subject for discussion raised by the latter was the border dispute with the ZAR.

This, however, was not the only reason why Cetshwayo wanted his accession confirmed and supported by the Natal government. Although Cetshwayo had been publicly recognized as heir in 1861, there were still 'fears as to whether the succession would be disputed, and a civil war ensue'.[84] The loyalty of his brother Hamu was doubtful, and it was suspected that he had designs on the throne.[85] Cetshwayo had other brothers who would certainly have challenged his succession had they been able to get the necessary support from their protectors. Mthonga was in the Transvaal and Mkhungo was in Natal, and it was still widely believed that Mbuyazi, the leader of the *iziGqoza* faction, whose body had never been found after the battle of Ndondakusuka, was still alive and living either in Natal or in the Cape. In these circumstances it must have seemed prudent to Cetshwayo to invite the man who had presided over his nomination as heir to do the same for his installation as King.[86] This was a calculated risk – as Cetshwayo's encounter with Shepstone in 1861 had not been a happy one, and he still feared that Shepstone might take the opportunity to present a rival to the Zulu nation as their rightful King.

It was not only his position *vis-à-vis* potential rivals for the throne that Cetshwayo hoped Shepstone's presence would strengthen, but also his position as King *vis-à-vis* the territorial chiefs of Zululand.[87] There was a tendency for these chiefs to resume or acquire a greater degree of independence of the King. Neither Dingane nor Mpande had succeeded by simple indefeasible right; on the contrary, both had violently overthrown their predecessors, and to achieve this they had needed all the help they could get. The protracted conflict between Mpande and Cetshwayo had led to their both bidding for support not only from Natal and the ZAR, but from powerful chiefs in Zululand, who became more powerful as a result. There is evidence that Cetshwayo made deliberate attempts to arrest or reverse this tendency. Many observers commented on his attempt to revive the military system, which had evidently fallen into disarray during Mpande's troubled reign. This attempt was often attributed to a desire to emulate the conquests of Shaka, but in view of the centralising function of the *amabutho*, it is likely that part of Cetshwayo's motive was to strengthen the monarchy in relation to the territorial chiefs.

The 'coronation laws' proclaimed by Shepstone at Cetshwayo's installation should be seen in this context. Although they later came to be interpreted (from interested motives) as imposing restrictions on the King, their literal tendency was to strengthen the monarchy by restoring its monopoly of capital punishment. Shepstone stated that towards the latter part of Mpande's reign 'the nobles took upon themselves to exercise to a serious extent the power of putting to death those under them without previous reference to the King', which 'soon resulted in the diminution of the central authority'. The laws , which were drawn up in consultation with Cetshwayo, were, Shepstone reported after the installation, 'unpalatable to the nobles, but warmly supported by him [Cetshwayo]. He evidently felt that the heads of the people had become possessed of a power which it was his interest to curtail.'[88]

As one might expect, Shepstone was strongly in favour of acceding to the Zulu request that he should go to Zululand and install the new King. The proposal appealed to his vanity, and was calculated to enhance his prestige. In his writings on the subject he laid great stress on the high position he held in Zululand, claiming to have been accorded the rank of Shaka in 1861. This meant, he believed or asserted, that in Zulu eyes only he had the power to install the new King.[89] Acceding to the Zulu request would provide Shepstone with his long-sought 'safety-valve', if the ZAR could be persuaded to abandon a claim it was unable to enforce. This disputed territory was also one of the principal routes along which migrant labourers from the north travelled to Natal, so control of it would be desirable for this reason, too.[90]

But Shepstone's hopes and ambitions soared far above such relatively mundane considerations. He described the Zulu message requesting him to go to Zululand as 'the most important . . . one that has ever been addressed by the Zulu power to this Government'. He appeared to think that it introduced a fundamental change in the relations between Zululand and Natal, a change which would virtually bring Zululand under British rule. He stated that the heads of the Zulu people had assembled in two separate places, the older men at Nodwengu, the late King's residence, and the younger 60 miles (96 kms) away at Cetshwayo's residence. This division Shepstone attributed to apprehension on the part of the older men concerning their personal safety under the new regime, with its 'indications that Cetywayo intends to imitate Chaka in the severity of his rule'. The older section, Shepstone believed, was anxious for 'complete incorporation with this Government' and was willing to pay taxes. The 'thinking portion' of the younger section, he continued, was 'to some extent actuated by the same desire', and he went on to suggest in very vague language that the population at large also sought amelioration from harsh government and pressure of Boer encroachment in some closer association with Natal.

> Cetywayo may, and probably does feel, that some change is necessary to secure the Zulu position in the presence of surrounding events and, feeling the pressure of public opinion among his own people, is willing to occupy a position more subordinate to this Government than his father did and to submit himself to its guidance in his policy – domestic as well as foreign.

Shepstone believed that the 'compromise measure' which the Zulu would agree on was to cede to Natal not merely the disputed territory but a section of Zululand clear of ZAR claims; and that a British commissioner resident within this ceded territory would also exercise advisory powers in the remaining part of Zululand that remained nominally independent. This would represent a 'compromise' between the 'incorporation' desired by some and the continued independence desired by others. Shepstone stated that he had regarded previous acknowledgements of the supremacy of the Natal government as being 'more complimentary than real'. But the driving to Pietermaritzburg of four oxen, representing the King's head, was a public and therefore much more serious and substantial acknowledgement of 'vassalage on one side and supremacy on the other'. The Zulu invitation, Shepstone considered, afforded the Natal government 'an opportunity of acquiring a good deal of additional influence and real power not only over the Zulus but over all other Native powers of South East Africa, for the power to control the Zulus includes that of controlling all the rest'.[91]

The statement of the Zulu messengers that the Zulu nation wished 'to be more one with the Government of Natal' and 'covered with the same mantle',[92] was presumably the basis of these soaring hopes. Shepstone's more specific expectations seem to have been based on wishful thinking rather than on any definite information. There was no reason why the Zulu should want to have any of their land other than the disputed territory under the control of Natal, and no reason why they should want the disputed territory filled up with resettled Africans from Natal. Shepstone's belief that the Zulu or any section of them wanted to come under British rule was equally implausible. All these hopes, as we shall see, were doomed to disappointment.

The Installation of Cetshwayo

Shepstone eventually set off on 30 July 1873 at the head of a large expedition which included a military escort of colonial Volunteers and Natal Africans.

On both sides there were fears of treachery. Cetshwayo suspected that Shepstone was bringing a rival claimant to the throne, while Shepstone and his entourage suspected that Cetshwayo might be planning a pre-emptive attack on the expedition. Shepstone's force of Volunteers was by no means only for the purpose of display. They were armed and took precautions against a surprise attack.[93] The size of Shepstone's expeditionary force in its turn aroused Cetshwayo's apprehensions. Viewing the approach of the expedition through a telescope, Cetshwayo was heard to say that there were too many waggons for peace.[94] Shepstone attempted to reassure Cetshwayo by sending a message to him:

> I shall not condescend to contradict the foolish rumours that I am bringing a rival heir to the Zulu authority, I leave those to be corrected by the Zulu messengers who travel with me. I come in good faith to carry out the wish of the Zulu people, and must be looked upon as fully intending to keep my word.

Cetshwayo in his turn attempted to reassure Shepstone by sending him a message stating that he was well aware that killing him would do nothing to vanquish the English, and that even Shaka had recognized the English as his superiors.[95]

Shepstone's plan had been to meet Cetshwayo at his residence near the Norwegian mission station of Eshowe, 'take possession' of him there, and then present him to the assembled Zulu nation as their King. When the expedition reached Eshowe, however, they found that Cetshwayo and his followers had withdrawn further into the interior. The expedition pressed on towards the Isiklebhe residence, where the coronation ceremony was to take place. On 15 August, before they reached it, Shepstone received a message stating that Cetshwayo and his party had joined Mpande's chief counsellor, Masiphula, and the headmen of the Zulu nation, and that the great men had in their impatience found themselves trespassing and had saluted Cetshwayo with the royal salute. At the same time Shepstone received a note from Cetshwayo's white chief, John Dunn, stating that a portion of the coronation ceremony had been completed and had gone off quietly.

This was disconcerting news for Shepstone. The theory on which his intervention in Zulu affairs was based was that only he, as holder of the rank of Shaka, as representative of the British government, and as chief witness to the nomination of Cetshwayo as heir in 1861, had the authority to install the new Zulu King. He knew that many influential Zulu, led by Masiphula, regarded it as derogatory to call in the assistance of foreigners to install a Zulu King, and he feared that Masiphula had persuaded the Zulu to install Cetshwayo themselves, declining Shepstone's services except as secondary and inessential. He therefore sent a message requesting an explanation of the nature of the ceremony that had occurred, stating that if he did not have the complete and sole authority to install Cetshwayo as King, he would have no alternative but to return to Natal immediately.

There can be little doubt that the ceremony conducted by Masiphula was, in Zulu eyes, the real ceremony which made Cetshwayo King. It appears to have been attended by virtually the entire Zulu army, that is the manhood of the nation, while only 5 000 Zulu were present at Shepstone's ceremony (possibly as a result of food shortage).[96] Cetshwayo stated after the Anglo-Zulu war that he had been 'proclaimed King by Masiphula, the late King's prime minister, and all the chiefs'. Whites whose view of the matter was derived from Zulu sources represented the earlier ceremony as the real one. John Dunn stated that Cetshwayo 'had been proclaimed King by Masiphula before the arrival of Mr Shepstone, and now this had merely been confirmed by him'. The missionary Robert Robertson's wife wrote that Cetshwayo 'was virtually crowned a fortnight before Mr Shepstone appeared', many of the great men being 'jealous of British sanction being supposed to be necessary to the ceremony'. J.Y. Gibson, whose pioneering history of the Zulu was based largely on Zulu sources, treats Masiphula's ceremony as the essential coronation and Shepstone's as a mere repetition.[97]

Before a reply to Shepstone's message could be received, a further message came from the Zulu, stating that Masiphula had died. 'A lucky thing for us as he would have caused us trouble,' commented Henrique Shepstone, a sentiment no doubt shared by his father. It appears to have been a sentiment shared by Cetshwayo, too: according to a member of his *isigodlo*, Cetshwayo had Masiphula poisoned, fearing that this relic of the old reign might prove a threat to the new.[98]

The reply to Shepstone's message came on 18 August. It assured him that only he, as representing Shaka, could install Cetshwayo and that no one had attempted to contest that. Masiphula had only told the young people escorting Cetshwayo that he and the other elders were 'willing to accept this child of Panda, and to give him the Royal Salute, when we are authorized to do so by him whose arrival we expect'. The royal salute had not been used by authority.[99] Shepstone may not have believed this, but he had at least succeeded in eliciting a formal statement from Cetshwayo that confirmed and acknowledged his view of the theory behind his intervention in Zulu affairs. This, together with the death of his rival king-maker, was sufficient to enable him to avoid the humiliation of returning unsuccessfully to Natal. There were further long-distance negotiations, necessitated by continued mutual suspicion, but Shepstone and Cetshwayo eventually met at the Mlambongwenya *ikhanda* or 'military kraal' on 28 August, 12 years after their first stormy encounter.

Cetshwayo had with him the men who had participated in the major events connected with the border dispute, and a long discussion ensued on this subject. Shepstone found that the Zulu considered all Boer occupation of land below the Drakensberg an encroachment on their territory, and regarded the whole of the district of Utrecht and part of that of Wakkerstroom as rightfully part of Zululand. He expressed surprise at hearing the ZAR title to the districts of Utrecht and Wakkerstroom called in question, but the Zulu insisted that the

Boers had never been given the right to occupy these areas permanently. Individual Boers had been allowed to graze cattle in these areas, but only on condition that they came under Zulu law as Zulu subjects, as long as they remained on Zulu soil. There had been no transfer of sovereignty. No documents purporting to cede territory to the Transvaal had ever been knowingly signed by any Zulu in authority. The Boers were behaving in an extremely aggressive fashion. Acts of aggression were of daily occurrence, and in some of these Zulu had been killed. Shepstone laid stress in his report on the vehemence, anger and bitterness with which Cetshwayo and his people spoke on the subject: their evident feelings, he said, could scarcely be described in language too strong. Cetshwayo said that unless the government of Natal stepped in a very serious catastrophe must soon occur, as the Zulu would rather die than submit to having their rights trampled underfoot. He wished the British to take over and occupy the territory in question; the Zulu had never had a border dispute with the British whereas they were never without one with the Boers, and every year brought a new encroachment.

Shepstone stated in reply that the British government could not accept land burdened with such questions as was the land that the Zulu wished it to occupy. He promised to tell the Lieutenant-Governor of Natal of their wish, but could hold out no hope of its being granted. He advised the Zulu that the government of the ZAR doubtless assumed that the land in question was its by a valid cession, and that it did not necessarily know what was done by its subjects on distant frontiers, and he advised them to make a full representation of the whole matter to the government of the republic.[100]

Shepstone had earlier hoped that the Zulu might be prepared to cede to Natal land clear of ZAR claims as a means of stopping further Boer encroachments. After these discussions it was apparent that the Zulu were prepared to cede nothing on their side of the line claimed by the ZAR (but a great deal on the other side of it, including much land that Shepstone had assumed to be undisputed ZAR territory), and that it was the title to the land rather than the use of it that they were offering to Natal.

On the following day there was a five-hour discussion on other matters. On the question of relations between Natal and Zululand,

> Cetywayo wished for an offensive and defensive arrangement, said his army was ours, and that his quarrels ought to be ours also. I told him that, when we wanted the services of his army, we should consider it to be ours and send for it, but that we must form our own judgement as to his quarrels.

Shepstone had built extravagant hopes upon the Zulu statement that they wished 'to be more one with the Government of Natal' and 'covered with the same mantle', but he found that they did not seek any degree of incorporation into Natal. All that was agreed was that the relations between Natal and Zululand should be 'continued on the same footing on which they had been heretofore under Panda's reign', Cetshwayo adding 'only let them be more intimate and more cordial'.[101]

The laws that Shepstone was to proclaim at the installation were decided upon at this meeting: the 'indiscriminate shedding of blood' should cease; no Zulu should be executed without trial and without the right of appeal to the King; and for minor crimes a fine should be substituted for death.[102] The message inviting Shepstone to Zululand had asked him to 'breathe the spirit by which the Nation is to be governed'.[103] Shepstone took this to mean that he would have to deliver a 'charge to the new King' stating publicly the principles upon which he was supposed to base his foreign and domestic policy.[104] Such a 'charge' would have imposed duties and restrictions on the King himself, but the tendency of the laws agreed upon at this meeting was to restrict the power of the chiefs and thus enhance the power of the King.

On the question of missionaries Shepstone commented, 'it is clear that Zululand is at present not a field favourable to missionary operations, as it is unlawful for a Zulu to be a Christian'.[105] A Christian Zulu, maintained Cetshwayo, was a Zulu spoiled. The missionaries had done no actual wrong, but the tendency of their teaching was mischievous. Cetshwayo wanted them to go or to confine themselves to secular education. Shepstone argued that the missionaries had entered Zululand with the avowed object of teaching the people new beliefs and habits; they had not disguised this and they had been admitted by Cetshwayo or his father, so the Zulu rulers could not find fault when the teaching started to take effect. The Natal government believed in the objects of the missionaries and respected them, and its convictions ought to be treated with some deference by those whom it had befriended. But the only agreement that could be reached was that no missionary already in the country should be expelled without the assent of the Natal government. Shepstone did not consider it wise even to attempt to reach any agreement on the subject of converts.

Migrant labourers passing through Zululand sometimes robbed Zulu of food on their way to Natal and were sometimes robbed of money on the way back. Employers in Natal were prepared to provide rest-houses with supplies of food, but a white man was considered necessary to supervise this arrangement. Shepstone gathered that Cetshwayo feared that such an arrangement might lead ultimately to the occupation of his country by whites. Eventually it was agreed that John Dunn, already resident in the country as a subordinate chief under Cetshwayo, should take charge of the coastal route, the one most used. The inland route was also discussed, but since this ran through the disputed territory, Cetshwayo was disinclined to do anything that might complicate this issue.

This concluded the discussions of the day. Shepstone's estimation of Cetshwayo is of interest, and is in striking contrast to the jaundiced view he took of him in 1861:

Cetywayo is a man of considerable ability, much force of character, and has a dignified manner; in all conversations with him he was remarkably frank and straightforward, and he ranks in every respect far above any Native Chief I have ever had to do with. I do not think that his disposition is very warlike; even if it is, his obesity will impose prudence; but he is naturally proud of the military traditions of his family, especially the policy and deeds of his uncle and predecessor, Chaka, to which he made frequent reference. His sagacity enables him, however, to see clearly the bearing of the new circumstances by which he is surrounded, and the necessity for so adjusting his policy as to suit them.[106]

The installation ceremony took place on 1 September and passed off without untoward incident. The 'coronation laws' were first proclaimed. Then Cetshwayo retired from view and donned a scarlet mantle and a scarlet and gold head-dress provided by Shepstone. Re-emerging, he was formally presented to the people as their new King. After further proceedings, Shepstone and his entourage departed on 3 September, reaching Pietermaritzburg on 19 September.

Cetshwayo's Installation: Reactions and Results

Shepstone's official report on the installation leaves one with the impression that it was an important, dignified and successful event. Not everyone agreed. Many regarded the 'tin-pot coronation' as something of a farce.[107] The unimpressive nature of the ceremony, the small numbers attending it and the 'tinsel crown' were much commented on in the Natal newspapers.[108] *The Natal Witness*, the leading advocate of responsible government and champion of colonial as opposed to imperial interests, produced a scathing attack on the entire expedition, stating that the ceremony had been unimpressive, the real coronation had been that conducted by Masiphula, the new laws had been broken immediately and the arrangement for the passage of labourers would be ineffective, the only benefit being the campaigning experience gained by the Volunteers.[109] There were more favourable comments. *The Natal Mercury*, the representative of coastal sugar interests, welcomed the arrangement concerning the passage of labourers through Zululand, and even the *Witness* was later compelled to admit that the arrangement was working.[110] The expedition produced a widespread impression that the Zulu kingdom was no longer a formidable military power, an impression apparently based on the small number of soldiers at the installation, their apparently poor discipline and the shortage of food on the occasion.[111]

The reaction of Shepstone's superiors in the Colonial Office to the expedition was at first distinctly negative. The Earl of Carnarvon, who, with the Conservative election victory of 1874 had become Secretary of State for the Colonies, minuted: 'I greatly doubt the wisdom of the expedition' since it 'pledges us to a protectorate or something very like it' and so was likely to embroil Britain with the ZAR.

> It must always be remembered that the very qualities & merits & past successes of Mr. Shepstone in native affairs tend to blind him to the danger of these future complications and make him set a horribly undue value on what he describes as British prestige.[112]

Carnarvon's official reply to the despatch enclosing Shepstone's report on the expedition was sent only after he had seen Shepstone personally. The contrast between this despatch and the above-quoted minute illustrates the influence Shepstone gained over Carnarvon. Carnarvon stated that although he was still not altogether convinced that it had been wise to undertake the mission, on account of the risk involved, he placed 'much confidence in his [Shepstone's] belief that it was very important not to lose this opportunity of causing his influence to be asserted and recognised, as well as that its results are likely to be of value'.[113]

For both Cetshwayo and Shepstone the results of the expedition proved disappointing. Cetshwayo became King to the exclusion of his rival claimants, but his other objectives were not achieved. If, as I have argued, the 'coronation laws' were designed to strengthen the King's power relative to that of the territorial chiefs by giving him an appellate jurisdiction in their areas, it is clear that they did not have this effect. There is much evidence that Cetshwayo never succeeded in making the right to inflict capital punishment a royal monopoly and that the chiefs retained the power to execute without reference to the King.

In fact the only real limitation on the chiefs' power over their own subjects lay in the King's control over the *amabutho*, which Cetshwayo maintained despite some strain and conflict. In the sphere of central government Cetshwayo had to rule in conjunction with the *izikhulu*, the great chiefs who made up his *ibandla* or council of state. Again there is evidence of conflict. Cetshwayo's wishes were sometimes frustrated by the *izikhulu* but, equally, he was sometimes able to overrule their objections.[114] Cetshwayo was a constitutional rather than an absolute monarch. R.C.A. Samuelson, who was the son of a missionary brought up in pre-war Zululand, described the great chiefs as 'the real rulers of Zululand'.[115] This is probably an exaggeration. Cetshwayo was not a cipher, even though his attempt to curb the power of his chiefs by means of Shepstone's coronation laws was unsuccessful.

Cetshwayo's hope of gaining Shepstone's and Natal's active assistance in Zululand's border dispute with the ZAR was also disappointed. Indeed, if he really hoped to recover all the land up to the Drakensberg,[116] which would include territory long since settled by Boers and incorporated into the ZAR, such a hope can only be regarded as completely unrealistic. In any case Shepstone had his own aims and ambitions in this area. If British rule had been extended to the disputed territory, however defined, it would have been filled with 'surplus' Africans from Natal and would therefore not have been available for Zulu settlement and as a field for Zulu royal patronage.

Shepstone succeeded in negotiating a satisfactory agreement concerning the passage of migrant labourers along the coastal route through Zululand, but otherwise the high hopes with which he had entered Zululand were not fulfilled. As we have seen, the flattering remarks made by the Zulu about their desire for greater unity with the Natal government, which led Shepstone to expect a virtual surrender of sovereignty, turned out to be, as he had characterized such utterances earlier, 'more complimentary than real'. And the only land the Zulu were willing to cede to Natal was land which it was not in their power to give, being territory claimed by the ZAR, most of it under its effective occupation and rule. If Natal were to obtain a 'safety-valve', an opening to the north, which Shepstone considered a necessity, it would be able to do so only by the exercise of imperial force, physical or moral, against either the ZAR or Zululand, or both. Imperial policy was about to take a turn which would bring this consummation within the bounds of practical politics.

Cetshwayo appears to have believed in a special relationship between the Zulu and the British, as represented by the Natal government, and he acknowledged the superior power of the British Empire. 'But you must know', he told a British official in 1877, 'that from the first the Zulu nation grew up alone like a tree, separate and distinct from all the others, and has never been subject to any other nation.'[117] Nevertheless, the fact that Shepstone installed Cetshwayo and proclaimed the fundamental laws of the kingdom made it appear, or made it possible to make it appear, that Zululand was henceforth in some sense subject to Britain. It could be, and was, used to justify further intervention. In particular, the new laws proclaimed at the coronation were used to justify the invasion of 1879. In his ultimatum to the Zulu King, the High Commissioner, Sir Bartle Frere, stated:

> These laws for the well-being of the Zulu people were the conditions required by the British Government in return for the countenance and support given by it to the new Zulu King by the presence of its representative, and by his taking part in the King's coronation; and once spoken as they were, they cannot be broken without compromising the dignity, the good faith and the honour of the British Government.[118]

As we have seen, these laws were probably intended to limit the powers of the chiefs. But they came to be regarded as promises made by the King, promises which it was alleged he had broken by ruling in a sanguinary and lawless fashion.[119] It should be noted that neither Lieutenant-Governor Pine nor Shepstone expected the new laws to have an immediate or sweeping effect. Pine wrote that they would probably not be strictly observed, but that they would be a 'beacon to guide future generations into the path of higher civilization'. Shepstone stated that

> it cannot be expected that the amelioration described will immediately take effect. To have got such principles admitted and declared to be what a Zulu may plead when oppressed, was but sowing the seed which will still take many years to grow and mature.[120]

The more important point is Frere's assertion that Cetshwayo's assent to these laws was the condition required by the British government for Shepstone's presence at the coronation, and that his alleged disregard of them therefore compromised that government's dignity, good faith and honour. This is simply not true. The British government proper, the imperial government, did not know about the expedition until after the event. All that the Natal government required was that the occasion would not be marred by bloodshed, and this condition was kept. The initiative for the new laws did not come from the British side. Shepstone stated that it was only after entering Zululand that he found that the Zulu regarded him as 'clothed with the power of fundamental legislation', that this 'was a responsibility [he] had not contemplated' but from which he felt he 'could not withdraw'.[121]

One could also argue that it was Masiphula who had really installed Cetshwayo as King, and that Shepstone's ceremony had been nothing more than a recognition of his installation; and that since Cetshwayo therefore did not owe his crown to Shepstone or the British government, any breach of any undertaking made on the occasion of Shepstone's visit could not affect his legitimacy or right to rule. The fact remains that by inviting Shepstone to Zululand and by apparently recognizing Shepstone's sole authority to install the new King,[122] Cetshwayo had given hostages to fortune and facilitated future British intervention in the Zulu kingdom.

Notes

1. Wright and Hamilton, 'Traditions and Transformations', pp. 71–3.
2. Mael, 'Political Integration', pp. 116–17 and 146–8.
3. Colenbrander, 'Warriors, Women, Land and Livestock', p. 3; *Blue Book of the Colony of Natal*, 1879, pp. V4–V5.
4. Gordon, *Shepstone,* provides details of Shepstone's early career.
5. Etherington, 'Origins of "Indirect Rule" '. See also Etherington, 'The "Shepstone System" '. The most detailed account of the Shepstone system is Welsh, *Roots of Segregation.* On the political economy of Natal see Slater, 'Land, Labour and Capitalism'; Bundy, *Rise and Fall,* ch. 6; Slater, 'Changing Pattern of Economic Relationships'; and Harries, 'Plantations, Passes and Proletarians'.
6. SNA I/6/3, private memo by Shepstone, 28 February 1874.
7. Gordon, *Shepstone,* ch. 17.
8. Uys, *Era of Shepstone,* pp. 47–51.
9. De Kiewiet, *British Colonial Policy,* p. 204; Brookes and Webb, *History of Natal,* p. 158.
10. De Kiewiet, *British Colonial Policy,* pp. 206 and 258.
11. Uys, *Era of Shepstone,* p. 131.
12. Recent summaries are Wright and Hamilton, 'Traditions and Transformations'; and Peires, 'Paradigm Deleted'.
13. Sansom, 'Traditional Economic Systems' and 'Traditional Rulers and their Realms'; Guy, 'Ecological Factors'; Hall, *Settlement Patterns,* chs 8 and 9.
14. I have relied extensively on Mael, 'Political Integration', for this account of the internal conflict in the Zulu kingdom.
15. Webb and Wright, *Stuart Archive,* Vol. 2, pp. 165 and 215–16; Fuze, *Black People,* p. 98.
16. KC, Uncat Ms 26515, folder of typed transcripts entitled 'Cetshwayo and Zululand Affairs', nos 3 and 4, Shepstone to Scott, 2 and 4 December 1856.
17. SNA I/6/2, no. 34, message from Mpande, 18 February 1859. See also other messages from Mpande in this period in SNA I/7/3.

18. SNA I/7/4, p. 4, message from Cetshwayo, 9 June 1859.
19. SNA I/7/4, p. 34, message from Cetshwayo, 7 February 1860. See other messages from Cetshwayo in this period in SNA I/7/3 and I/7/4.
20. Kennedy, 'Fatal Diplomacy', pp. 144–5.
21. Nourse, 'Zulu Invasion Scare', pp. 35–6; SNA I/8/7, p. 385, Shepstone to Scott, 22 June 1861.
22. Kennedy, 'Fatal Diplomacy', pp. 145–6 and 175.
23. UWL, Selected Records of the Archbishop of Cape Town, Ba 3, Colenso to Gray, 8 June 1859.
24. Kennedy, 'Fatal Diplomacy', p. 182.
25. UWL, Selected Records of the Archbishop of Cape Town, Ba 3, Colenso to Gray, August 1860 [no day specified].
26. Kennedy, 'Fatal Diplomacy', pp. 184–7.
27. SNA I/6/3, memo by Shepstone on events since January, 30 March 1861; ibid, message from Cetshwayo, 11 March 1861.
28. Kennedy, 'Fatal Diplomacy', p. 190.
29. McGill, 'History of the Transvaal', pp. 257–8.
30. SNA I/6/3, no. 246, Scott to Shepstone, 15 April 1861.
31. Information on the 1861 nomination of Cetshwayo as heir comes from: (1) SNA I/8/7, pp. 382–394, Shepstone to Scott, 22 June 1861, and Confid, Shepstone to Scott, 22 June 1861; (2) a manuscript in Shepstone's handwriting dated 'May', evidently written at the time as a sort of diary, formerly in SP 22 – I have not been able to locate it since the Shepstone Papers were re-arranged; (3) 'John Dunn's Notes' in Moodie, *Battles and Adventures*, Vol. II, pp. 458–9; (4) KC, James Stuart Papers, File 9, no. 13, KCM 23401, 'story of Xubu ka Luduzo' (son of one of Shepstone's messengers – both were eyewitnesses) recorded 26 May 1912; (5) testimony of Gxubu ka Luduzo (the same man as the preceding though his name is spelt differently) recorded 27 January 1912 (a shorter and less detailed account) in Webb and Wright, *Stuart Archive*, Vol. 1, pp. 158–9; (6) a letter written by an unspecified person in Natal to the *Mission Field*, quoted in Mackenzie, *Mission Life*, pp. 150–3; (7) Bishop Schreuder's narrative, quoted in Etherington, 'Anglo-Zulu Relations', pp. 19–20.
32. Boswell, *Life of Johnson*, Vol.I, p. 156; see Webb and Wright, *Stuart Archive*, Vol. 2, p. 166; and UWL, Selected Records of the Archbishop of Cape Town, Ba 3, Colenso to Grey, 29 June 1861.
33. Xubu (or Gxubu) ka Luduzo – see fn 31.
34. SNA I/8/7, p. 395, Confid, Shepstone to Scott, 22 June 1861.
35. Ibid, p. 385, Shepstone to Scott, 22 June 1861.
36. Bonner, *Kings*, pp. 74–6, 110–13.
37. BPP, C1961, p. 27, Dunn to Bulwer, 20 April 1876.
38. BPP, C1748, p. 56, minute by Shepstone, 3 June 1876.
39. BPP, C2220, p. 393, statement of messengers from the Amaswazi Tribe, 31 May 1869.
40. Colenso, *Commentary*, second pagination series, p. 129. Colenso obtained his information about the region north of the Phongolo from members of the house of Masobhuza, Langalibalele's chief wife, who was a sister of Mswati, the Swazi King, and who settled at Bishopstowe after the exile of her husband. Colenso also pointed out that the Ngwe, under their chief, Phutini, Langalibalele's uncle, lived both north and south of the Phongolo before 1848, when, with Langalibalele's Hlubi, they fled from their overlord Mpande to Natal (ibid, p. 117). See also Natal Archives, Colenso Papers, Vol. 2, p. 258, Colenso to Bulwer, 26 and 28 March 1879.
41. Bonner, *Kings*, pp. 45, 49 and n. 19, 92–3.
42. Van Rooyen, 'Verhouding', pp. 68–9.
43. Bonner, *Kings*, pp. 76 and 132–3; Webb and Wright, *Stuart Archive*, Vol. 4, p. 315.

44. BPP, C2220, p. 375, border commission report, 20 June 1878.
45. Colenso, *Commentary*, second pagination series, p. 117; Bonner, *Kings*, p. 133.
46. BPP, C2220, pp. 371 and 381, border commission report, 20 June 1878.
47. McGill, 'History of the Transvaal', chs. IX, XVII and XVIII, is the most thorough and detailed account of the question. I have checked Dr McGill's most important references in the Transvaal Archives. The question is also discussed in less detail in Stander, 'Verhouding', chs VI, VII and VIII. This work is written from a strongly and uncritically Afrikaner nationalist standpoint, and its usefulness is limited by the author's tendency to treat all sources, contemporary documents, later recollections and secondary sources, both scholarly and popular, as having the same evidential status. The report of the border commission set up in 1878 to investigate the question is in Appendix II of BPP, C2220.
48. See p. 18.
49. BPP, C2220, p. 379, border commission report, 20 June 1878.
50. SS 40, sup 1/61 and 2/61, Smuts to Schoeman, 20 May 1861.
51. McGill, 'History of the Transvaal', p. 268.
52. Ibid, p. 261.
53. See p. 19.
54. BPP, C2220, p. 378, border commission report, 20 June 1878; McGill, 'History of the Transvaal', p. 261n.
55. SS 19, R1981A/58, Treaty, 30 March 1858; the full text is quoted in McGill, 'History of the Transvaal', p. 428.
56. SS 62, R1181A/64, treaty with Mpande, 16 December 1864; the full text is in McGill, 'History of the Transvaal', pp. 428–9.
57. BPP, C2222, p. 43, memo by Frere, n.d. [November 1878].
58. BPP, C1961, p. 22, Pretorius to Maclean, 23 March 1865.
59. Nourse, 'Zulu Invasion Scare'.
60. BPP, C2242, p. 76, 'A Remembrance between Us and the Zulu Tribes, how Matters Went on', by P.L. Uys, 1 December 1877.
61. CO 879/13, African no. 150, p. 98, minutes of meeting at Waaihoek, 1 April, 1861.
62. See p. 23.
63. SS 38, R4489/61, Proes to Schoeman, 26 June 1861, encl 1, treaty; encl 2, minutes; encl 4, report of visit to Cetshwayo.
64. SS 38, R4489/61, Pretorius to Schoeman, 14 July 1861; see McGill, 'History of the Transvaal', pp. 268–72 for this commission's visit to Zululand.
65. An English translation is in BPP, C2242, p. 64,
66. This comes out strongly in Stander, 'Verhouding'; and the author seems to be of the same opinion.
67. BPP, C2222, p. 27, minute by Frere [1 August 1878]. The date appears in the original in the Natal Archives though not in the Blue Book.
68. BPP, C2220, p. 381, border commission report, 20 June 1878.
69. TA, SN 6, Minutes, p. 163, evidence of G.M. Rudolph (Landdrost of Utrecht) before 1878 border commission.
70. BPP, C2242, p. 57, appendix 3, no. 1, Shepstone to Carnarvon, 1 December 1877.
71. TA, SN 6, Minutes, p. 163, evidence of Rudolph before 1878 border commission.
72. Quoted on p. 26.
73. See p. 25.
74. McGill, 'History of the Transvaal', pp. 279–300.
75. SNA I/7/6, p. 87, message from Mpande, Cetshwayo and the Zulu People, 5 June 1869. The earlier requests for British arbitration were in SNA I/7/4, p. 238, message from Mpande, 24 April 1865, and SNA I/7/4, p. 235, message from Cetshwayo, 25 April 1865.

76. See pp. 12–13.
77. BPP, C1961, pp. 1–5, minute on the history of the disputed territory, by Shepstone, 25 June 1876; Stander, 'Verhouding', p. 374; GH 1325, no. 91, Musgrave to Bishop Wilkinson, 21 December 1872.
78. SNA I/7/6, p. 179, Dunn to Musgrave, 9 November 1872, and p. 181, Shepstone to Dunn, 20 November 1872; GH 1325, no. 86, Musgrave to Burgers, 30 October 1872.
79. Appelgryn, *Burgers*, p. 70.
80. *The Natal Mercury*, 13 February 1873, letter from Utrecht correspondent, 30 January 1873.
81. BPP, C1137, p. 22, statement of Zulu messengers, 26 February 1873.
82. BPP, C1137, p. 9, Shepstone's report on the installation of Cetshwayo, n.d. Except where otherwise specified, information on Cetshwayo's installation in this and the following sections of this chapter comes from this source, which will normally be cited only in the case of direct quotations.
83. BPP, C1137, p. 22, statement of Zulu messengers, 26 February 1873.
84. *The Net*, 1874, p. 101, quoting the missionary Robert Robertson, 22 January 1874.
85. *The Net*, 1873, p. 25, and 1874, p. 24; BPP, C1137, p. 17, Shepstone's report.
86. BPP, C1137, p. 26, memo by Shepstone, 11 June 1873; Fuze, *Black People*, p. 100.
87. I argue this in detail in Cope, 'Political Power'.
88. BPP, C1137, pp. 6 and 19, Shepstone's report.
89. BPP, C1137, pp. 11 and 26, Shepstone's report, n.d., and memo, 11 June 1873.
90. SNA I/6/3, private memo by Shepstone, 18 February 1874; BPP, C1137, p. 20, Shepstone's report.
91. SNA I/7/6, pp. 191–7, memo by Shepstone, 3 March 1873, on message from Zulu nation, 26 February 1873.
92. See p. 30.
93. KC, Uncat Ms 13665, 'The Crowning of Cetshwayo', by A. Blamey (a member of the expedition); *The Natal Witness*, 3 October 1873, letter from 'Volunteer of 13 years standing', 24 September 1873.
94. KC, GC Cato Papers, File 2, no. 14, Ms 16006, Cato to William Shepstone, 20 August 1873. Cato obtained this information from Bishop Schreuder.
95. BPP, C1137, pp. 8 and 12, Shepstone's report.
96. *The Natal Colonist*, 5 September 1873, editorial; ibid, 23 September 1873, 'Monthly Summary'; *The Times of Natal*, 30 August 1873, 'Zulu expedition' (by Charles Barter).
97. Webb and Wright, *Zulu King Speaks*, p. 18; Moodie, *Battles and Adventures*, Vol. II, p. 477; *The Net*, 1874, p. 24; Gibson, *Story of the Zulus*, pp. 124–30.
98. Natal Archives, HC Shepstone Papers, Vol. 2, diary, 16 August 1873; Dlamini, *Paulina Dlamini*, pp. 60–2.
99. BPP, C1137, p. 11, Shepstone's report.
100. Shepstone kept his report of this discussion separate from his general report: SNA I/7/10, minute on Zulu-Transvaal relations, described from a Zulu point of view, by Shepstone, 20 February 1874.
101. BPP, C1137, pp. 14 and 18, Shepstone's report.
102. Ibid, pp. 15–16.
103. BPP, C1137, p. 22, message from Zulu, 26 February 1873.
104. BPP, C1137, p. 26, memo by Shepstone, 11 June 1873.
105. BPP, C1137, p. 19, Shepstone's report.
106. Ibid, p. 21.
107. Etherington, 'Anglo-Zulu Relations', p. 33, quoting John Akerman, a Natal politician, and Robert Robertson, the missionary.
108. *The Natal Colonist*, 9 September 1873, editorial; *The Natal Witness*, 23 September 1873, 'Monthly Summary, the Coronation of Cetywayo'; *The Natal Mercury*, 9 September

1873, editorial; *The Times of Natal*, 10 September 1873, 'Zulu Expedition'.

109. *The Natal Witness*, 23 September 1873, 'Monthly Summary, the Coronation of Cetywayo'.

110. *The Natal Mercury*, 9 September 1873, editorial; *The Natal Witness*, 2 June 1874, 'Monthly Summary, the Coast', 15 December 1874, 'Amatonga Labourers', 15 January 1875, 'Amatonga Labourers'.

111. *The Natal Mercury*, 9 September 1873, editorial, and 16 September 1873, 'The Coronation of Cetywayo' by Thomas Baines; *The Times of Natal*, 10 September 1873, 'Zulu Expedition', and 17 September 1873, editorial; *The Natal Colonist*, 23 September 1873, 'Monthly Summary, the Zulu Coronation Expedition'.

112. CO 179/114, minute by Carnarvon, 20 June 1874, on Natal 5791, Pine to Kimberley, 13 April 1874.

113. BPP, C1137, p. 27, no. 2, Carnarvon to Pine, 7 November 1874.

114. Cope, 'Political Power', pp. 11–31.

115. Samuelson, *Long, Long Ago*, p. 27.

116. See p. 34.

117. GH 1397, report on Zululand, by F.B. Fynney, 13 July 1877.

118. BPP, C2222, p. 206, message no. 2 to Cetshwayo, 11 December 1878.

119. Whether this allegation was true or not is considered in Cope, 'Characters of Blood?'

120. BPP, C1137, p. 3, no. 1, Pine to Kimberley, 13 April 1874; ibid, p. 16, Shepstone's report.

121. Ibid, p. 18.

122. See p. 34.

CHAPTER THREE

Black and White Diplomacy in South-East Africa 1873 to 1877

This chapter examines the relations between Natal, the South African Republic (ZAR), the Zulu kingdom, the Swazi kingdom and the Pedi paramountcy in the mid-1870s. The focus is on the dangers to continued Zulu independence from local circumstances and ambitions. But it will become apparent that these local forces were increasingly influenced and then overtaken by imperial forces.

Langalibalele, Shepstone and Carnarvon, 1873 to 1875

On his return from Zululand, Shepstone had to deal with the question of the Hlubi. These were people who had fled from the Zulu King Mpande in 1848. They had been granted land in the foothills of the Drakensberg to protect the colony from San raiders. Young Hlubi, like other Africans in Natal, went to work at the diamond fields of Griqualand West and, like other Africans in Natal, many of them failed to register the firearms they brought back with them, especially when they discovered that they were liable to be confiscated. Their chief, Langalibalele, was on bad terms with the local magistrate, who tried to compel him to enforce the gun-registration law. When the chief failed to do so, Shepstone summoned him to Pietermaritzburg. Langalibalele's brother had lost his life when he had obeyed a similar summons by Mpande, and Langalibalele's grasp of the difference between civilized and uncivilized governments was weakened by the fact, well-known among Africans in Natal, that another Natal chief, Matshana kaModisa, had been fired upon when he had obeyed a summons by Shepstone's brother. Consequently Langalibalele made a number of excuses for not going to Pietermaritzburg. In October 1873 an armed force was sent to arrest him, and he and most of his people fled to Basutoland. Some of them were intercepted by a government force at the top of the Bushman's river pass. The commander was under orders not to fire the first shot so his attempts to persuade them to return to Natal were unsuccessful. Finding themselves being surrounded, the government troops retired, and while doing so five of them, three colonists and two Africans, were shot in the back. This event produced great fear and anger among the colonists. The Hlubi remaining in Natal, together with their neighbours, the Ngwe, who had done nothing more than harbour some of the fleeing Hlubi's cattle, were driven off their land. Between 150 and 200 Hlubi were killed, their cattle seized and prisoners were compelled to enter into contracts with white employers. When Langalibalele was captured he was accorded a travesty of a trial by a special tribunal under what was deemed to be 'native law' and sent to Robben island.[1]

These events aroused the attention of the formidable Bishop Colenso. Alarmed at the effects of his investigations and disclosures, Lieutenant-Governor Pine sent Theophilus Shepstone to England to explain things to the Secretary of State for the Colonies. Colenso, once Shepstone's great friend and supporter, now his bitter enemy, followed a month later.[2]

Carnarvon had no reason to be favourably disposed towards Shepstone and at first seemed reluctant to meet him.[3] But his attitude towards him was transformed by their first meeting. On the day they met, 12 September 1874, Carnarvon entered in his diary:

> He is very able and I think as straightforward as able. He said all that he properly could in vindication of Pine & the Natal Govt. but he also answered all my questions truthfully. I talked to him for an hour and a half and had a very interesting as well as a valuable conversation with him.

The following day he wrote: 'Again a long, a valuable & a very interesting conversation with Shepstone. He impresses me very much.' By the time Shepstone left England Carnarvon had hinted at a knighthood and an increase in salary.[4] Shepstone was to have a considerable influence on Carnarvon in the future. One historian goes so far as to say that 'the perceptions of Shepstone and the expansive interests of Natal became, for a brief period, British imperial policy'.[5] This is an exaggeration. Carnarvon was thinking along the lines of confederation well before he met Shepstone[6] and his ideas on 'native policy' differed considerably from Shepstone's, as we shall see in a moment.[7] Nevertheless it is true that Carnarvon came to rely heavily on Shepstone's knowledge and advice in pursuing his policy in South Africa.

He remained convinced, however, that the Natal government had acted incorrectly and unjustly in the Langalibalele affair, a view confirmed by his meetings with Colenso.[8] This was reconciled with his new-found admiration of Shepstone by putting all the blame on 'that poor old dotard of a Governor', as Mrs Colenso called him: Pine was recalled despite his protests that he had acted throughout on the advice of Shepstone.[9]

Carnarvon believed that it was not enough simply to rectify the injustices of this particular case: what was needed was a thorough reform of native administration so as to prevent a repetition of such events. In this he was influenced by his friend, the historian James Anthony Froude, whom he asked to visit South Africa. Froude was a disciple of Thomas Carlyle, and what he emphasized was not the oppressiveness but the weakness of the Natal government:

> I cannot but regard the state of feeling here as exceedingly serious. The colonists find themselves a small minority surrounded by multitudes of daring natives who will not

work for them or work very irregularly and who swarm over the frontier in increasing numbers owing to the ease and license which they enjoy under British rule.[10]

The imperial government, he said, had made a mistake in maintaining tribal organization and the authority of chiefs, and in conferring arbitrary power on the Lieutenant-Governor in his capacity of 'Supreme Chief'. The tribes were growing in wealth and power and chiefs were becoming more independent and insubordinate. The colonists feared insurrection, and were tempted to exaggerate any evidence of disaffection to create an opportunity for the draconian powers of the Supreme Chief to be used. The result was a lack of normal control punctuated with such lamentable episodes as the brutal suppression of Langalibalele's Hlubi. In place of the existing mixture of weakness and ferocity, Froude advocated the dissolution of tribal authority, the scrapping of representative government, the imposition of direct imperial control, the establishment of a police force and the enforcement of vagrancy laws and contracts for service.[11]

Carnarvon's despatch conveying his decision on the subject expressed views very similar to those of Froude. He stated that the existing system 'depended too much upon the maintenance of friendly relations, and too little upon a firm enforcement upon the Kafirs of the obligations of individual citizenship'.[12] He pointed out that the tribal system, the recognition of native law, and the maintenance of the authority of hereditary chiefs, originally intended only as temporary expedients until Africans were fit for the duties of civilized life, had not been phased out as intended but had become more firmly entrenched. This perpetuation of tribalism and native law meant the perpetuation of barbarism, while the power of tribal chiefs militated against the spread of Christianity. What was needed, in Carnarvon's view, was the replacement of the tribal system by individual citizenship, of chiefs by white magistrates, of native law by the common law of the colony and of communal land tenure by individual proprietorship.[13]

This meant dismantling the 'Shepstone system'. Shepstone did not express disagreement with these proposals. Indeed, he pointed out that they were very similar to the proposals he had made 30 years earlier: in the 1840s he had advocated a policy of civilization and amalgamation of the races in one body politic, but it had been vetoed on grounds of expense, and he had since then been obliged to make bricks without straw and rule the Africans of Natal as best and as cheaply as he could.[14] There was considerable truth in this; but it was also true that Shepstone had become converted to what circumstances had made his life's work, and that he had come to regard the authority of chiefs (appointed rather than hereditary), tribal structures, collective responsibility and native law as essential for control in the peculiar circumstances of Natal.[15] The result was that the great reform of 'native policy' intended by the Colonial Office for Natal amounted in practice to little more than the provision of legal warrant for doing what Shepstone had always considered circumstances required him to do, and what he had therefore always done.[16] To those who complained that the 'new native policy' as implemented by Shepstone was indistinguishable from the old, the Colonial Office response was that such critics overlooked 'the peculiar condition of the natives of Natal, the extraordinary influence wh. Mr. Shepstone possesses over them, & the weakness of our military force there, all wh. reasons make it advisable that the introduction of reforms should be entrusted to Mr. S.'[17] Shepstone succeeded in convincing the Colonial Office of 'the necessity of extreme and constant caution' in making any changes, and that they could not 'be hurried on without great risk to the Colony'.[18] Sir Garnet Wolseley, the distinguished soldier whom Carnarvon sent to Natal to implement the changes he wanted, wrote privately to him:

> No matter what may be the change considered necessary here in Native affairs, or no matter how trifling may be the service or the duty I wish to see carried out where Kaffirs are concerned, I am always met by Mr. Shepstone, my adviser upon such matters, upon whom your Lordship told me to rely, with the objection that we are too weak to run the risk of the excitement that any such attempt on my part to carry out existing laws would occasion.[19]

As a result of Shepstone's great reluctance to dismantle the system he had built up over his years of maintaining control with minimal resources, it became firmly established in the official mind that Natal was in a very dangerous condition. Sir Garnet Wolseley and his 'brilliant staff' were sent out not only to dazzle the colonists into surrendering some of their constitutional powers, but also because it was believed that their military abilities might be needed. Wolseley asked for a fast despatch boat so that he could summon all available troops from the Cape and Mauritius without delay if necessary.[20] Despite the apparent note of scepticism and exasperation in Wolseley's comment on Shepstone quoted above, he agreed with him on the weakness of the British hold on power in Natal. He believed that more direct control over the African population was necessary to retain Natal as a British colony, and that big changes could not be safely carried out in existing circumstances.[21] Carnarvon stated in a letter to the Secretary of State for War in October 1875 that he agreed with Wolseley's 'statement that Natal – & generally speaking S. Africa – is the most dangerous point at present in the whole Colonial Empire'.[22]

Shepstone, Wolseley and the Zulu Kingdom, 1875

The Zulu kingdom was part of this danger. In discussing the hazards of trying to introduce reforms without a strengthened military force, Wolseley wrote:

> Amongst the elements of danger existing here the fact of our having on our North-Eastern frontier a powerful native kingdom in which every man is a trained soldier must not be forgotten. The Zulu army, well-organized after their own fashion, numbers between 30,000 and 40,000 warriors, well-armed. I am informed that the result of the unfortunate skirmish [with Langalibalele's Hlubi] in the Bushman's River Pass is much

talked of amongst them, and regarded by them as a proof that the Kafirs, when armed with guns, are more than a match for the white men of Natal.[23]

Carnarvon made a much-quoted reference in Parliament to 'a force of 30,000 armed Natives resting like thunder clouds upon the frontier of the Colony'.[24] Wolseley stated that his military preparations were intended primarily for the 'contingency of a war with the Zulus', though he added that such a contingency was improbable.[25] Cetshwayo showed a distinct interest in the Langalibalele affair, making numerous requests that the chief be given up to him 'ostensibly to act as his rain-doctor', Pine stated, implying that the real reason was something more sinister.[26] Cetshwayo's explicit desire to go to war with the Swazi and his mustering of his army in May 1875 apparently for that purpose (events that will be discussed below) were reminders of the dangers inherent in the existence of large independent African kingdoms.[27]

The belief that the existence of an independent African kingdom on the borders of the colony made the Africans of Natal less amenable to control may well have been correct. Robert Robertson, the Zululand missionary, stated that it was a common opinion among Natal Africans that 'if the Zulu power were ended, the white men would be able to do what they liked with them, make Coolies of them, etc.'. This perception was shared, from his own point of view, by a future Prime Minister of Natal who remarked in January 1878 that 'the kaffirs will never be thoroughly quiet till the Zulu chief is deposed'. After the Anglo-Zulu war a Natal magistrate commented on the 'marked difference' in the conduct of blacks, 'the late war having had a salutary effect on their behaviour towards the whites'. Another British official commented in June 1879, after a visit to Natal, that he was 'much struck with the improved demeanour of our natives', a change which he attributed to the recent display of British power.[28]

Carnarvon's proposals for change in Natal made Shepstone's long search for a 'safety-valve', in the form of adjacent territory to which dissatisfied Africans could remove, all the more urgent. Even before Carnarvon put forward his proposals, Shepstone had expressed the opinion that 'with such an outlet all reasonable legislation would be safe, without it every measure must be specially considered with reference to its popularity or otherwise among our natives'.[29] When Shepstone was in Zululand for the installation of Cetshwayo, the latter had urged that the disputed territory be taken over by the British. Shepstone had pointed out the difficulties in the way of such a step, and had promised no more than to inform the Lieutenant-Governor of Natal of the Zulu request,[30] but he was anxious to seize whatever opportunity this request might provide. He went to Britain not only to explain the actions of the Natal government in the Langalibalele affair, but also, as Pine told Carnarvon,

to explain to your Lordship, more fully than could be done in written communications, the grounds which render it necessary that an outlet should be afforded to the overwhelming kafir population of this Colony by the acquisition of some territory intervening between the occupied country of Cetywayo, the King of the Zulus, and the Transvaal Republic.[31]

In Britain Shepstone argued that negotiations should be opened with the ZAR to induce it to abandon any claim it believed itself to possess to the territory. Citizens of the republic with claims to farms in the territory should be compensated. The territory, once acquired, should not be an integral part of Natal and subject to its laws – in other words, the Natal colonists should be allowed no power over it. But it should be ruled through the Natal Department of Native Affairs, since, Shepstone claimed, Africans would more readily move to a territory under a familiar government.

> Of course much difficulty could be removed from the native mind if I could go with them; how far this may be feasible when the time comes I cannot say, but it may be possible for me to afford occasionally personal supervision; and I shall be glad to contribute as far as I may be able towards the abatement of a danger which no-one sees more clearly than I do.

Shepstone also advocated the purchase of a strip of Zulu territory 20 miles wide along the Natal border from the disputed territory to the sea:

> This portion of Zululand is but sparsely inhabited by the Zulus, and I have reason to believe that Cetshwayo's policy is to withdraw himself and his people more towards Delagoa Bay, so that, to him, the value of this land will be less than it has hitherto been.

What reason he had to believe this he did not say; and in view of the Zulu attitude to land which emerged during his discussions with Cetshwayo on the question of the disputed territory the previous year,[32] it is difficult to see how he could have believed that Cetshwayo or his advisers would have been prepared to relinquish any rights over any territory beyond the land in dispute with the ZAR. It seems that he was expecting some eventuality to change Zulu attitudes; for he stated that he did not think that the chance to make such a purchase was likely to present itself very soon but that the Natal government should have the discretion to make the purchase when the opportunity presented itself without the delay of a reference to Britain, which might cause the opportunity to be lost. He thought that £15 000 would be a sufficient sum both for buying out Boer claims in the disputed territory and for acquiring the further strip of Zulu territory, and that it would be possible to repay this sum from revenues derived from the newly acquired territory. The further strip of Zulu territory would be a valuable addition to Natal.

> That ultimately this will also be occupied by Europeans cannot be doubted; but if the land can be acquired and put to the purpose I have suggested, the present tension in Natal will be relieved, and time be gained to admit of the introduction of a larger proportion of White colonists.

The relief obtained by the acquisition of the disputed territory would on the other hand not be merely temporary, 'because the outlet lying to the North, the abatement admits of permanent extension towards a climate unsuited to Europeans, but not so to natives'. Shepstone here seemed to be envisaging a Natalian empire under the Native Affairs Department extending indefinitely in the direction of the tropics.[33]

The problem with this expansionist dream was that the ZAR had no intention of relinquishing its claims to the disputed territory. One of Wolseley's staff, Colonel George Pomeroy Colley, went on a tour of the Transvaal in June and July 1875, and one of the things Wolseley asked him to investigate was the possibility of this territory being ceded to Natal. He evidently hoped that the prospect of peace following the setting up of a British buffer between the Transvaal and Zululand would cause the Boers to favour such a proposal.[34] Colley found that this was not the case. The territory in question provided valuable winter grazing for the Boers and they had no desire to withdraw from it. In any case, a British occupation of what they and the ZAR regarded as the disputed territory, the land between the Mzinyathi and the Phongolo, would not greatly lessen the chance of conflict, since the Zulu also claimed and occupied land north of the Phongolo.[35] Acting President Joubert (President Burgers was overseas raising funds for a railway to Delagoa Bay) simply would not admit to Colley that any border dispute existed, blandly informing him that there had been no representations on the subject from the Zulu, and that when Keate had proposed arbitration a ZAR commission had visited Mpande who had denied any cause of complaint. Colley found that the disputed territory, together with an additional slice of Zululand, had only recently been formally incorporated by proclamation within the borders of the ZAR.[36] War with the Zulu was looked on in the Transvaal as inevitable sooner or later, and the frontier farmers seemed disposed to hasten it rather than delay it. Colley gained the impression that such a war would be generally supported in the Transvaal, and would be brought on immediately were it not for fear of British intervention. Colley reported that the ZAR would welcome a British annexation of Zululand (presumably on the assumption that the Delagoa Bay railway project would be successful and give the ZAR access to a port free of British control) but that it resented the existing semi-protectorate, which gave the Boers no security and at the same time tied their hands in dealing with the Zulu. Colley did not even raise the question of a cession of the territory with the republic's government. Clearly there was no possibility of such a cession being made, and he did not want to arouse suspicion or hostility on the eve of Lord Carnarvon's confederation conference (to be discussed in the next chapter), which it was hoped that the ZAR would attend.[37]

Wolseley's reaction to the news of the proclamation incorporating the disputed territory within the Transvaal was that the opportunity for Natal to acquire this territory had irrevocably passed and that 'all hope of being able to locate our super-abundant Kafir population thereon is for ever put an end to'.[38] Even before Colley returned from the Transvaal, Wolseley's and Shepstone's ambitious gaze had shifted from the disputed territory and gone beyond even the 20-mile wide strip of Zululand that Shepstone had advocated buying. They now aimed at bringing all Zululand under British rule.

There were a number of reasons why they considered the annexation of Zululand desirable, necessary indeed. It would solve Natal's 'native problem'. Zululand would be an admirable 'safety-valve': 'with such a territory in our possession and kept as a Kaffir province under the superintendence of white magistrates, we should get rid of our surplus native population here', Wolseley told Carnarvon. The ending of Zulu independence, as we have seen,[39] would facilitate the introduction of the 'new native policy' in Natal by reducing the independent mentality of Natal's Africans. Shepstone extended this principle to South Africa at large. By 1875 he was already elevating Cetshwayo to the position formerly held by Moshweshwe:[40] that of the leader of a black conspiracy against the whites of South Africa.

> Again there seems to be growing in the minds of all the native powers outside Natal a spirit of restlessness at the encroachment of white people, all are getting firearms and all think themselves so much the stronger for their possession. That such a feeling should arise is natural and that the struggle must come on a large or small scale is inevitable.

It was, he said, 'the Zulu power' that was a 'growing source of unquiet, because its prestige and influence with all other natives are so great'.

There were also imperial reasons for annexing Zululand. The republics looked to access to a non-British coastline as the source from which their real independence was to come, wrote Shepstone, 'so that the possession by England of the East Coast from Natal to the Zambezi appears to be the only certain preventive to the growing up of two antagonistic interests in South Africa'. Wolseley also argued that the annexation of Zululand was necessary to achieve the confederation Carnarvon desired, by preventing the ZAR from gaining independent access to the sea.

Humanitarianism was also enlisted in the campaign against Zulu independence. By freeing the Zulu people from the bloody despotism of Cetshwayo, claimed Wolseley, the annexation of Zululand would be a blessing to humanity.

This last consideration was also a reason why an annexation might be relatively easily effected. Since Cetshwayo's rule was murderous and he was hated by his subjects, a thousand British soldiers crossing the Thukela and announcing British rule, Shepstone persuaded Wolseley, would be sufficient to win over the Zulu people. If Cetshwayo were deposed the whole country would voluntarily accept British rule. Shepstone told Wolseley that if Cetshwayo were assassinated Britain might be formally invited to take over the country: the great men would rather be annexed to Natal than ruled by another Zulu King.[41]

With the benefit of hindsight it is easy to see how absurd it was to say that the Zulu wanted British rule. Did Wolseley and Shepstone really believe it? Beneath

Wolseley's surface brusquerie and braggadocio a much less self-assured character emerges from a careful reading of his diaries. He was easily influenced by those whom he could find no reason for dismissing as fools or scoundrels – and Shepstone was then at the height of his reputation as an astute and immensely knowledgeable African diplomat. Shepstone himself had a great capacity for wishful thinking. We have seen in chapter two what extravagant expectations the Zulu request that he should attend Cetshwayo's installation aroused in him.[42] We saw too how these expectations were disappointed.[43] But he was very ready to entertain them again. There were many unsuccessful missionaries in Zululand who were eager to assure him that the Zulu would welcome the British as liberators. Shepstone was quite uncritical of the information or misinformation he was fed if it accorded with his desires or prejudices. It seems likely that Wolseley and Shepstone did believe what they said. Indeed, had they been able to foresee that more than a thousand British troops would be wiped out in a single battle shortly after crossing the Thukela and that the Zulu people would rally behind their King in the defence of their country's independence, it is scarcely possible to believe that they would have offered Carnarvon the advice that they did.

It was in private letters that Wolseley and Shepstone urged Carnarvon to annex Zululand, but the step was also publicly urged in the Natal press, evidently as a result of events in Zululand. During May 1875 the Zulu army was mustered. The apparent intention was to attack the Swazi, but there were rumours, 'industriously circulated', that Cetshwayo intended to invade Natal. These rumours evidently caused some alarm in the colony.[44] *The Natal Mercury*, which had earlier commented on Cetshwayo's acquisition of large numbers of firearms and on his restoration of 'the discipline and system of his uncle Chaka', referred to this mustering, and commented:

> It is hoped in many quarters that before our eminent Administrator leaves South Africa something will have been done to establish more definitely the northern boundaries of British rule in South Africa . . . The immediate abutment of powerfully organized nations of armed and independent kafirs upon British territory has obvious perils and inconveniences, and must be a considerable bar to peaceful purpose and to perfect security. Sir Garnet Wolseley's able administrative power and experience will probably be directed upon the solution of this difficulty.

The *Mercury* believed that Cetshwayo's intentions towards the British were pacific, but Natal was trying to build a railway and needed to raise loans, and warlike demonstrations in a neighbouring savage kingdom were not encouraging to investors:

> If the British Government desire to exercise in their African dominions the beneficent function to which it aspires as an imperial dispenser of peace, civilization and security, it is surely called upon to remove from its borders a condition of things so fraught with disquietude and menace.[45]

At the same time there appeared in the press, especially in *The Natal Mercury* and *The Natal Colonist,* a wave of reports of cruelties and atrocities in Zululand. Cetshwayo, it was said, was putting his subjects to death in a wholesale manner and on the most frivolous pretexts. The point was made that this was a breach of the 'coronation laws', and in the *Colonist* the conclusion that this would justify British intervention was explicitly drawn.[46] On the other hand the papers that published these reports expressed reservations and doubts concerning their veracity, and also published letters by travellers and residents in Zululand denying their truth. The point was made by some correspondents that the executions that occurred were mostly the work of chiefs rather than of the King himself. John Dunn wrote to *The Natal Colonist* stating that there existed not the slightest foundation for the account of atrocities in Zululand contained in a letter signed 'J.L.H.', which it had printed.[47] Cetshwayo himself sent a message to Bishop Colenso, assuring him that the rumours of wholesale killing were untrue, and that only eight people had been executed since the coronation, all for very good reasons. John Dunn, in a letter to Colenso, put the figure at not more than 12.[48]

There can be no doubt that Cetshwayo and his chiefs did not observe the coronation laws in the sense that they sometimes executed people without the 'open trial and the public examination of witnesses for and against' that the laws required. Where guilt was flagrant, or regarded as such, a trial was considered purposeless and unnecessary. People were also killed for witchcraft after procedures very different from the sort of trial that the coronation laws required. But the evidence does not support the accusations of wholesale slaughter made against Cetshwayo at this time and later in his reign.[49] This wave of atrocity stories in 1875 looks very much like a systematic campaign of denigration. The fact that these stories were useful to and were used by Shepstone and Wolseley in their attempt to persuade the British government to take over Zululand suggests that they were the inspirers of the campaign. This was a conclusion drawn at the time. The secretary of the Aborigines Protection Society, writing to the London *Times,* and evidently representing Bishop Colenso's views, stated that 'the reports are supposed to have been circulated for a political purpose'.[50] *The Natal Witness,* which advocated responsible government and saw itself as the defender of colonial as opposed to imperial interests, considered that the rumours of Zulu atrocities and aggressive intentions were part of an official attempt 'to impose upon our credulity, to excite our fears, and to make our passions the instruments of a dangerous and ruinous aggression', aimed at adding Zululand as a 'new satrapy' to the 'Native Affairs' *imperium in imperio*. Like the *Mercury,* the *Witness* was concerned about railway loans – but drew rather different practical conclusions:

> for, now that we have come into the region of railway loans, and are parties to an application for favourable notice in the money market, we really cannot afford to allow false reports of war, insurrection, bloodshed, and massacre, to circulate with impunity, at the risk of an extra two per cent.[51]

What at first sight makes it seem plausible that these rumours of atrocities in Zululand were inspired from Government House is the fact that Wolseley had taken a great deal of trouble to get newspaper support for his constitutional changes, and had succeeded in persuading, as he said, all but *The Natal Witness* into 'something like reason'.[52] But whether this support necessarily extended to all Wolseley's aims and ambitions is a different matter. It is surely significant that *The Times of Natal,* which had been not merely persuaded but actually bribed to act as the government mouthpiece,[53] was singularly free of Zulu atrocity stories. The increasing scepticism of the newspapers towards these stories suggests that they were being used as the vehicles of a campaign rather than that they were parties to it. If the stories were officially inspired, the connection between the government and the newspapers was probably indirect. The circuit probably ran through certain missionaries in Zululand.

As we have seen,[54] conversion to Christianity was actively discouraged in the Zulu kingdom. Mpande and Cetshwayo had admitted missionaries for purely expedient and secular reasons, and by the 1870s these reasons had largely disappeared. The succession dispute between Mpande's sons had been settled and was no longer a reason for attempting to gain Natal's support by appearing to favour missionaries. European artefacts were now easily obtainable from traders, and firearms (which the missionaries refused to supply) from John Dunn, who was entirely dependent on his patron Cetshwayo, shared his interests and was thus a more reliable scribe and diplomatic agent than the missionaries. The Zulu acquisition of firearms strengthened them against the ZAR and may have made them feel less dependent on the missionaries' British patrons and protectors. In these circumstances, the life of a Zululand missionary was one of extreme frustration, and it is not surprising that the missionaries should have seen the replacement of a heathen by a Christian government as their only hope, and that they should have done all they could to facilitate a British takeover of the country.[55]

What they could do was spread stories of misgovernment and cruelty in the Zulu kingdom. The possibility of British intervention spurred them on to make such reports: there is a distinct temporal correlation between the two, especially in the case of Shepstone's principal contact among the missionaries, the Anglican, Robert Robertson of Kwamagwaza.[56] In later years there is no doubt that many of the reports of Zulu atrocities came from his pen,[57] and there is no doubt that in 1875 Robertson was in communication with Shepstone and knew of his plans to acquire at least part of Zululand. This is shown by letters from Robertson to Shepstone (which were sent on to Carnarvon), assuring him that he agreed with every word Shepstone had written (and that he had burnt the letter he had received from him) and encouraging him in his plans, at the same time urging a British protectorate up to Delagoa Bay. There was, he said, 'a great deal of bloodshed' in Zululand and 'a very great deal of discontent and disaffection towards the present King'.[58]

Carnarvon was in principle in favour of the annexation of Zululand. Indeed, the logic of his confederation policy required it, as we shall see in the following chapter. But there was always, in practice, some reason for delay. A constant reason was the power and organization of the Zulu kingdom. Carnarvon wrote to a cabinet colleague in September 1875 that he would 'probably be obliged to annex Zululand' but added that it would be 'a tough nut to crack'. He was also, he said, under pressure to annex Malaya and 'beset on all sides with applications to take New Guinea'.[59] Too many annexations all at once were sure to arouse opposition among members of parliament and the public. As far as South Africa was concerned, he was at this time trying to persuade the colonies and republics of the merits of confederation. His attempt to organize a conference in Cape Town on the subject proved abortive. In 1876 he held a poorly attended conference in London, which achieved nothing. Meanwhile, relations between the ZAR and its black neighbours deteriorated sharply. The increasingly impatient Carnarvon believed he saw in this an opportunity to achieve by a *coup de main* what he had been unable to achieve by persuasion. When Shepstone returned from the London conference in late 1876 it was to annex not Zululand but the Transvaal. It is to the relations between the ZAR and the black population of the Transvaal and its environs that we must now turn.

Boer, Swazi and Zulu to 1875

As we have seen,[60] Froude ascribed the labour shortage and the insecurity in Natal to the 'ease and license' Africans enjoyed under British rule. He gained the impression while in Natal (no doubt from the colonists) that things were very different in the republics:

> The Dutch in the Free States manage their relations with the natives successfully. They have severe laws but no harrying of tribes or arbitrary violence. They have few coloured men among them. Those that they have are fed and clothed and made to work and though not slaves, to be bought and sold, they are not allowed to be idle or leave their farms. In consequence they have no trouble there.[61]

When he reached the Transvaal Froude discovered in fact that things there were just as bad as they were in Natal, if not worse. He wrote to Carnarvon:

> You ought to be here to see how absurdly the policy of the Transvaal has been misrepresented. The Kafirs are as idle as they please. Here as in Natal the women are the slaves of the men and you have a vast and increasing colonial population growing up in idleness and in all the vices which idleness breeds . . . You perhaps do not realise the enormous disproportion of numbers between the Blacks and the Whites. If the Whites were drilled and organized they might laugh at the notion of danger – but they are defenceless both here and in Natal. They have no armed force on which they can rely.[62]

In the Transvaal as in Natal untrammelled white supremacy and the reduction of the blacks to wage labour were still things of the future. In both territories the practical liberties that blacks enjoyed were the result not of liberal principles but of black power. The spectacular victories won by the Voortrekkers over Mzilikazi's Ndebele and Dingane's Zulu give the impression that the whites who settled in the interior of South Africa established their complete domination over the blacks from the start. This impression is misleading. The power of a concentrated military expedition with superior mobility and a monopoly of firearms was dissipated when the Voortrekkers dispersed to the farms they had staked out in the Transvaal. Political unity was not attained for many years. Even when a central government was established, it was singularly weak. It had great difficulty in extracting taxation from its citizens and subjects, white and black. Consequently the administrative machine was rudimentary and a regular army non-existent. Burghers were as reluctant to turn out on commando as they were to pay taxes, so the force at the disposal of the Pretoria government was minimal. Only in the central, southern and south-western districts of the Transvaal, which had been partly depopulated during the wars among the blacks in the period before the entry of whites from the Cape, and over which the Voortrekkers established their dominance while still organized as a military expedition, was Boer control reasonably secure. In the northern and eastern districts powerful chiefdoms remained unsubdued. Although the Pretoria government claimed them as its subjects, it exercised no control over them, and Boer occupation of land and access to labour supplies in these areas rested on diplomacy rather than on *force majeure*. Even in the 'white heartland' Boer domination was limited as long as Africans had the alternative of withdrawing to areas outside Boer control.

The principal prop of the Boers in the eastern Transvaal was their alliance with the Swazi. The basis of this alliance was their common hostility towards the Pedi in the north and the Zulu in the south. The Swazi also supplied the Boers with labour in the form of *inboekselings* or 'apprentices' captured in their wars with other African peoples.[63] These people, deracinated and acculturated, constituted the nearest thing to a stable and permanent labour force that the Boers possessed.

The constitutional relations between the ZAR and the Swazi kingdom were as confused and disputed as those between the ZAR and other African kingdoms and chiefdoms. A proclamation of 29 April 1868 purported to annex Swaziland to the Transvaal, but the Swazi refused to accept that they were subjects of the ZAR,[64] and the latter made no attempt to tax them or exercise any form of practical sovereignty over them. Cetshwayo also claimed that the Swazi were his subjects and had 'always been Zulu subjects ever since Chaka's time',[65] but this claim too the Swazi repudiated. As we have seen,[66] the Zulu claimed land north of the Phongolo which was also claimed by the Swazi and the ZAR, and from at least 1860 the Zulu were colonizing this land.

Throughout his reign Cetshwayo wished to launch an attack upon the Swazi, a wish which was thwarted by the consistent opposition of the ZAR and Natal governments, as well as of his own *izikhulu*. He nevertheless persisted in this ambition. There were various possible motives for it. It may have been to facilitate Zulu expansion across the Phongolo. It may have been to replenish his cattle stocks, which were much reduced by lung-sickness. As we shall see below, there is some evidence that Cetshwayo's motive was to assert his rights as suzerain over the Swazi, and possibly to install his own candidate as their King. But the reason Cetshwayo gave most often was simply that he wished to 'wash his spears':

> It is the custom of our country when a new King is placed over the nation, to wash their spears, and it has been done in the case of all former Kings of Zululand. I am no King, but sit in a heap. I cannot be a King until I have washed my assegais.[67]

Besides its ritual importance, washing his spears would have materially enhanced his power as King. Many observers gained the impression that the obstruction and opposition of the old guard of *izikhulu* led Cetshwayo to rely upon the support of the younger regiments[68] so that they became 'his most important political prop'.[69] Cetshwayo stated after the war that 'the young men in Zululand were getting very restless and quarrelsome, being anxious to get a chance of "washing" their spears', that they 'proposed a raid into Swaziland solely for this purpose' and that he was 'pressed by them' to comply.[70] It was reported in 1875 that the disbandment of a force called up for this purpose led to expressions of anger and accusations of cowardice being directed at the King by the young regiments.[71] Cetshwayo had washed his own spears in Swazi blood, having played a prominent role in the Zulu attack on Swaziland in 1852, the year after his own regiment, the Tulwana, had been enrolled.[72] It is very likely that he would have dearly loved to have complied with his young supporters' wishes and repeated the exploits of his youth.

The immediate cause of Cetshwayo's first attempt to organize an attack on Swaziland arose from a palace revolution in that country. King Mswati had been succeeded in 1865 by a minor, Ludvonga. The country was ruled by a council of regency, of which the most prominent member was Ndwandwe, the new young King's uncle. By the 1870s Ludvonga was becoming impatient to assume active control of the country, a move known to be resented and resisted by Ndwandwe. To prolong his regency he was apparently even prepared to allow the country to come under a greater degree of Zulu influence. It was said that he had sent to Cetshwayo to ask for one of his sisters in marriage, promising that her eldest son should become King, while he acted as regent in the meantime. When Ludvongo suddenly and inexplicably died in March 1874, Ndwandwe was believed to have poisoned him, and he and a large number of his followers were put to death.[73]

It was this event that Cetshwayo considered a reason, or opportunity, for intervention. In April he began talking of retaliation for the killing that had occurred in Swaziland.[74] In October 1874 he informed the Natal government that he intended going to war with the Swazi unless it could be shown that he would not be right by so doing. Cetshwayo's justification for war was that the killing of Ndwandwe and a large number of his people had been done without apprising the Zulu nation of it. 'Cetywayo and the Zulu nation feel that just cause has been given them, by such an act of disrespect, to punish the Amaswazi.'[75]

This suggests that the purpose of Cetshwayo's proposed attack was to enforce his rights as suzerain. But he may also have had ambitions to put his own candidate on the throne. Ndwandwe, whose death Cetshwayo wished to avenge, had been prepared to accept a greater degree of Zulu influence. He was now dead. The new King, Mbandzeni, was in the following year to acknowledge himself a subject of the ZAR, something no previous Swazi King had done. Meanwhile, Cetshwayo harboured a rival claimant to the Swazi throne. This was Mbelini, a son of Mswati who had been excluded from the succession in 1865, despite what he said were his father's wishes. He went into exile shortly after his father's death, and after spending a short time with the Lydenburg Boers, found a refuge in Zululand. In the month following the deaths of Ludvonga and Ndwandwe he made attacks on the Swazi border, which were assumed to be in pursuance of his kingly aspirations. It was also naturally assumed that Cetshwayo was behind these attacks, and that his real object in wishing to invade Swaziland was to install his client Mbelini as King.[76] Cetshwayo disclaimed responsibility for Mbelini's attacks, not altogether implausibly, since Mbelini certainly acted independently of his patron on occasion. The truth probably is that Cetshwayo used Mbelini as a convenient cat's-paw whose actions might be taken advantage of if possible or repudiated if necessary.[77] Just as Shepstone would have put Mkhungo on the Zulu throne had circumstances been propitious, so Cetshwayo, in all probability, would have taken the opportunity to install Mbelini as Swazi King after Ludvonga's death, had the opportunity occurred.

Whatever his motives for wishing to invade Swaziland, he did not treat the Natal government's refusal of permission as final. In March 1875 he informed the ZAR government of his intention to punish the Swazi for the deaths of Mswati, Ludvonga and Ndwandwe, and asked for permission to do so. This was of course refused.[78] According to Acting President Joubert, Cetshwayo then announced that he intended attacking in any case.[79] In May he showed that he meant what he said by mustering his army.[80] The ZAR responded by assembling over 300 men under Gert Rudolph, the Landdrost of Utrecht. The government also supplied him with artillery. This was one the biggest forces that the ZAR had assembled in years. Before it set out for Swaziland the news came that the Zulu army had once again dispersed. Nevertheless it was decided to take advantage of the scare to demonstrate to the Swazi that the ZAR was in earnest in its promises of protection, and to extract from them a recognition of ZAR sovereignty over Swaziland. Having succeeded in the always difficult task of raising a commando, the ZAR authorities did not want to waste the opportunity of using it. The members of the commando, who were not told where they were going or why, were undisciplined and mutinous; but Rudolph managed to get them to the

Swazi Great Place, where he followed Shepstone's example by 'installing' or recognizing Mbandzeni as King. He also concluded a treaty in terms of which the Swazi accepted the status of subjects of the ZAR while retaining possession of their land. The original intention had been that the commando on its return journey should beat the bounds between Zululand and the Transvaal, but the increasingly mutinous temper of the members of the commando, as well as a fear of collision with the Zulu, caused this project to be abandoned, and after leaving Swaziland the commando dispersed.[81]

Zulu, Swazi, Boer and Briton, 1875 to 1876

Cetshwayo's project to attack the Swazi evidently caused violent altercations between himself and his advisers. The Norwegian missionary Bishop Schreuder told Wolseley that 'the King was very angry with his Captains refusing to go to war without our permission'.[82] The Landdrost of Wakkerstroom reported a rumour that two military commanders had been executed for opposing Cetshwayo's plans.[83] Rudolph mentioned that a man named 'Umkokwaan' (perhaps one of the above) had been executed for his opposition to the proposed Swazi raid: in the following year he reported that Cetshwayo had declared that he intended going to war with the Swazi regardless of his chiefs' opposition, and that anyone who attempted to hinder him would share 'Umkokwaan's' fate.[84] Mkhokhwana was a regimental *induna* and was executed ostensibly for witchcraft.[85] Cetshwayo himself reported the execution of 'Umkokwana' to the Natal government (without, however, specifying his offence): he was clearly an important man.[86] The Zulu opponents of the projected attack on Swaziland were able to point to the opposition of both the ZAR and Natal to the scheme. With regard to Natal, they were not entirely correct. Pine had opposed the project in October 1874 when Cetshwayo had asked permission, but by 1875 his successor had imperial as well as local considerations in mind and these caused him to take a rather different view. When Shepstone told him Cetshwayo intended fighting the Swazi, Wolseley wrote in his diary:

> I wish his attention could be diverted to the Transvaal; he hates the Dutch who have always cheated and dealt unfairly with him; a war between those two parties would be very useful to us. It would reduce the King's power immensely perhaps break it up altogether and it would prevent the Transvaal from obtaining money to make the Delagoa Bay Rl. Rd. and make it more keenly anxious to give us the strip of disputed territory lying between them & the Zulu kingdom, a piece of land that we want very badly as a home for all discontented Kaffirs. I have only to give the King the slightest hint, and he would pitch into the Transvaal there and then. I wish I could do so without compromising the Govt. at home. When his messengers arrive I will see what can be done. It is a glorious opportunity for England, for we ought to try and force the Transvaal into our arms.[87]

But the opportunity did not occur. Cetshwayo clearly had no inkling of Wolseley's attitude towards the Transvaal. Having perhaps heard rumours of

Wolseley's wish to annex Zululand – he would almost certainly have heard that Natal newspapers were advocating such a step – he believed that the Transvaal commando to Swaziland had mustered at the instigation of the Natal government. When his messengers arrived in Pietermaritzburg, it was not to request permission to attack the Swazi but to assure the Natal government that in accordance with its wishes he had no intention of doing so. He had lately assembled his army, as was customary for a new King, the messengers explained, but he intended harming no one.

The messengers stated that

> Cetywayo has been informed that the Boers, the Amaswazi and the Amatonga are arming against him and that they have received the sanction of the Government of Natal for their so doing . . . Cetywayo says who has turned me out of my own house, I belong to the British Government and when I became King of the Zulus it was the British Government that made me so.

Cetshwayo was told in reply that the Natal government had sent no communications to the Boers, the Swazi or the Tsonga of the kind suggested by Cetshwayo, and that the Transvaal commando was the sort of response one might expect to the assembling of the Zulu army, but that the ZAR had told Natal nothing about it.[88] If this reassuring reply (not to mention any informal hints and suggestions that might have accompanied it) was designed to revive Cetshwayo's interest in military adventures, it did not succeed: the proposed Swazi campaign was abandoned, for the time being.

The sending of the commando under Rudolph to Swaziland had been occasioned by the threat of a Zulu invasion, but the opportunity was taken to reduce the Swazi themselves to a greater degree of subordination. In somewhat similar fashion, the duty of protecting the Swazi was used by the ZAR as an excuse for claiming more Zulu territory. On 25 May 1875 a proclamation was issued, signed by Acting President Joubert, which laid down as the boundary between the Transvaal and Zululand the line 'ceded' in 1861, together with an extra slice (bounded by the line B-B on the map) running along the southern bank of the Phongolo to the Lebombo mountains, the purpose of which was said to be to act as an additional buffer between the Zulu and the Swazi. No attempt was made to claim that the Zulu had ceded this territory. The proclamation made no mention of the 1861 'cession', and the line it laid down was clearly not intended to be final: it was stated twice in the document that the line was made 'with reservation of all further claims and rights of the said Republic after'.[89]

Such paper claims were of no value unless they could be enforced, and any attempt at enforcement was certain to encounter resistance from the Zulu. President Burgers was anxious to preserve peace, which he considered essential for the progress and development of the Transvaal; but Burgers had gone to Europe in February 1875 to raise funds for the construction of a railway to Delagoa Bay, and he did not return until April 1876. In his absence Acting

President Joubert pursued an aggressive policy towards the Zulu, influenced, it seems, by Rudolph, the Landdrost of Utrecht.

Rudolph had until 1873 been a British official in Natal, and was to co-operate loyally with Shepstone after the British annexation of the Transvaal in 1877, but in the intervening period he actively pursued the ZAR's interests in Zululand in opposition to those of Natal and Britain. At first he urged Joubert to inform Cetshwayo that unless those Zulu living on the Transvaal side of the newly proclaimed boundary were moved within two months they would be treated as subjects of the ZAR. If Cetshwayo refused to accept this, which Rudolph considered likely, then war should be declared. Rudolph later decided that war should be avoided if possible, a decision perhaps influenced by the mutinous character of the commando he took to Swaziland. He pointed out the danger of British ambitions in Zululand, especially with regard to the disputed territory. War between the ZAR and the Zulu kingdom was likely to lead to British intervention and the annexation of the disputed territory to the exclusion of both Boer and Zulu. At the same time British expansionist ambitions made it a matter of urgency that the ZAR's claims to land between the Mzinyathi and the Phongolo rivers should be established. Since British expansionism was a threat to the Zulu as well, Rudolph believed that by bringing this to the attention of Cetshwayo he might be able to persuade him to acquiesce in the ZAR's claims without war. He intended, he told Joubert, to make it clear to Cetshwayo that 'Jan Bull' wished to annex the entire coast up to the Portuguese line, and that if the Zulu King sought help from the British it would be at the cost of his kingship.[90]

The official message sent to Cetshwayo on 23 August 1875 contains no warning of British ambitions, but it is likely that something of the sort was transmitted verbally, as Cetshwayo's reply contains a statement that the British were his friends and that he had always been badly treated by the Boers. The fact that Cetshwayo did not report this message to the Natal government, as one would expect him to have done, suggests that Rudolph might have succeeded in instilling some doubts in his mind about the friendliness of the British.[91] The ZAR's official message, a copy of which was sent to Natal, demanded the extradition of certain criminals and an assurance that there would be no further hostile movements against the Swazi. It also required Cetshwayo to make his subjects acquainted with the boundary proclamation and to prohibit them from living beyond the boundaries thus laid down. It concluded by urging him 'earnestly to weigh these matters . . . if you . . . wish that peace and friendship shall be maintained between you and us'.

Shepstone's comment on this message was that it had 'the look of an ultimatum'; but he did not consider that the ZAR was 'in a position to proceed to extremities'.[92] Cetshwayo's response to this 'ultimatum' was to refuse to comply with any of its demands[93] and to summon his army.[94] Joubert reported this to the Natal government and added that Cetshwayo had also made an inroad on the boundary and caused 'defenceless Kafirs' to be killed. His letter made it clear that he intended, in Shepstone's phrase, to resort to extremities. He stated that Cetshwayo's 'vague and impudent' reply to the message of 23 August made it necessary to send him another message 'requiring a positive answer'; and he continued:

> However much the Government may wish to keep peace with Cetywayo, it is obvious that an end must be put once for all to such atrocities, and the Government will be under the necessity of adopting strong measures, unless a very marked change should occur. It is therefore the wish of this Government to enquire in what position Cetywayo stands to Her Majesty's Government, in order that, in the event of any further complications with Cetywayo, the amicable relations existing between Her Majesty's Government and that of the Republic may not, by ignorance in that respect, be disturbed.[95]

In effect, the ZAR was asking if the Natal government had any objection to its declaring war on the Zulu. On the same date Joubert sent another message to Cetshwayo, repeating the requirement that Zulu subjects should vacate the disputed territory. Cetshwayo reported this message to the Natal government, and made it clear that he was determined not to yield to the ZAR demands. He said the matter was urgent as the ZAR government had already ordered the Zulu occupying the land it now claimed to desist from cultivating the soil. As Cetshwayo had no intention of submitting to this dictation, great mischief would happen unless the Natal government intervened. The Zulu messengers stated:

> Cetywayo desired us to urge upon the Government of Natal to interfere to save the destruction of perhaps both Countries, Zululand and the Transvaal; he requests us to state that he cannot and will not submit to be turned out of his own house, it may be that he will be vanquished, but as he is not the aggressor, death will not be so hard to meet.

In an evident attempt to encourage Natal to intervene, Cetshwayo stated that his installation by Shepstone was the cause of jealousy on the part of the Boers, who considered that their support and installation of Mpande entitled them to the loyalty of the Zulu. It was Shaka, however, who had determined that the Zulu should be subject to the British government, and 'the accidental interruption of Panda's falling into the hands of the Boers is not considered sufficient by the Zulu people to set aside the policy of Chaka which the Zulu nation had adopted'.[96]

The new Lieutenant-Governor, Sir Henry Bulwer, who had succeeded Sir Garnet Wolseley at the end of August 1875, was thus confronted within three months of assuming office with the possibility of war between two of Natal's neighbouring states. He of course referred the matter to Shepstone. Shepstone reported that no treaty or formal protectorate existed between the Zulu and the British government, but that the Zulu recognized the superior standing of the British government. Shepstone claimed further that Cetshwayo had given him to understand that his installation by a representative of the British government

'had altered the relations of the Zulu people towards that Government to such
an extent as to introduce the relationship of parent and child, and that this
involved care of the child and fighting for him if necessary'. This comparison, he
said, he had not entirely repudiated, but he had reserved for the British government the right to act at its own discretion, according to circumstances.

It is instructive to compare this report with Shepstone's report on Cetshwayo's
installation written about 18 months earlier. The earlier report shows that
Cetshwayo did ask for a mutual 'offensive and defensive arrangement', and that
Shepstone, while not rejecting his offer of military assistance, had told him that
'we must form our own judgement as to his quarrels'. But there is nothing in the
earlier report to suggest that Cetshwayo asked for British assistance as a child to
a parent, or to suggest that the installation had introduced a new relationship
between Natal and Zululand. On the contrary, Cetshwayo is quoted as stating
that the relations between them should continue as they had been in Mpande's
time, and Shepstone's discussion of the subject is devoted entirely to the princi
ples which he said had enabled Natal 'to maintain peaceful and even cordial
relations during twenty-seven years of close contact with the Zulus'. Shepstone's
later report was no doubt designed to encourage Bulwer to exaggerate the
subordination of Zululand to Natal to discourage the ZAR from attacking it; but
it also shows that Shepstone was still trying to impose on the installation of
Cetshwayo a meaning that he had hoped it would have but which the event had
not borne out.[97]

Bulwer's reply to Joubert, based on a draft by Shepstone, was designed to
discourage the ZAR from going to war despite the absence of any formal British
protectorate over the Zulu. It pointed out that the Zulu were Natal's immediate
neighbours, separated only by a stream of water, and that their intercourse,
which had always been 'frequent and intimate', was 'regulated by a sort of tacit
understanding which has grown out of our relative positions', and had 'been
effectual in maintaining peace and goodwill between this Government and the
Zulus'.

> Although therefore no technical diplomatic relations exist between us, the position
> between the two countries is such that any hostile collision between the South African
> Republic and the Zulus would most seriously affect the interests of this Colony, and Her
> Majesty's Government could not fail to look with the greatest anxiety upon an event that
> would produce grave embarrassment and difficulty in this part of Her Majesty's
> possessions.[98]

When Bulwer reported all these events to the Secretary of State, he commented that 'the differences and causes of difference are not new, but of late the
Government of the Transvaal appears to have set its mind upon bringing them
to a conclusion, and to be taking measures that can scarcely fail to produce a
collision'.[99]

Nevertheless, the ZAR did not go to war with the Zulu. Bulwer's letter to Joubert probably had some effect. Bulwer also enclosed Cetshwayo's message to him in his letter, and from this Joubert could see that Cetshwayo was determined to resist. The ZAR was in no position, financial or military, to wage war with the Zulu in opposition to the wishes of the British government. Cetshwayo's reply to Joubert's second message was much more polite than his reply to his first, so this helped the ZAR government to save face. Nevertheless, the Zulu King still made it clear that it was out of the question that he would move his people from the land that the ZAR claimed.[100]

For the next few months an uneasy peace prevailed on the frontier. When conflict erupted again it was the result not of the ZAR's trying to drive the Zulu out of the disputed territory, but (as we shall see in a moment) of its trying to treat them as its subjects.

The Natal government's warning to the ZAR against expansion at the expense of the Zulu was followed a little later by a similar warning from the imperial government. But Carnarvon's despatch of 25 January 1875 contained an important qualification. It warned that the extension by the Transvaal either of territory or of influence, whether by way of a protectorate over the Swazi, or the assertion of territorial claims against the Zulu, made without the previous concurrence of Her Majesty's Government, could not be recognized by it. In particular, the appropriation of Zulu territory was not acceptable since it could only lead to war, which would have a dangerous and disturbing effect on the black population of Natal and endanger European lives and property nòt only in Natal but throughout South Africa. Then came the qualification. All that had been stated applied only so long as South Africa continued to be 'split up into several provinces having no common bond of union between them'.

> Should a Confederation of all or most of the Provinces of South Africa be accomplished, as I hope may be the case at no distant day, the extension of territory under the jurisdiction of any particular Province would cease to be a very serious danger, and the point of view from which Her Majesty's Government is now constrained to regard the question would obviously become changed.[101]

As originally drafted by Sir Robert Herbert, Lord Carnarvon's cousin and the Permanent Under-Secretary at the Colonial Office, the despatch had run:

> If it should hereafter be the desire of the Republic to unite with the British Colonies in a confederation, H.M. Government will be ready to take a liberal view of the limits to which the territory, jurisdiction or influence of each Colony or State shall extend.

Sir Garnet Wolseley, by this time back in Britain, to whom the draft was referred for his comments, objected that this passage was 'capable of being construed by the Boers as somewhat in the light of a bribe and might therefore convey to them the idea of weakness on our part'. His own draft, which was substantially accepted, had, he explained, the merit that the Boers would be sharp enough to read between the lines . . . whilst if hereafter the despatch has to be published, the bribe would be well smothered up in the expression of our dread of a Native war – a feeling that is always deemed in England to be sufficient excuse for any line of policy that has that object in view.

The confederation policy required that not only the Transvaal but Zululand come under the British flag. The annexation of Zululand would be a means of containing the Transvaal. Wolseley continued:

> It is generally felt in S.A. that Zululand must sooner or later in the natural course of events be ruled by us: the Natives themselves I believe entertain this feeling. [It is not difficult to guess who instilled this convenient belief in Wolseley.] Come what may, we must not permit any S.A.[n] State or foreign power to occupy it. If we allowed the Transvaal to occupy the 'Disputed Territory' it would only be the first step towards further encroachments on their part, and ere many years elapsed, we should find them with a frontier on the seaboard.

The process of encroachment, said Wolseley, would lead to war and anarchy 'destructive to all trade and agriculture', and to an influx of Zulu into Natal where blacks were already too numerous. He evidently believed it would be possible to annex Zululand without conflict with the Zulu:

> I venture to suggest that perhaps it might be possible in the present aspect of affairs to induce Cetywayo formally to ask us to take him and his people under our protection. I have no doubt that Mr. Shepstone could devise some good plan for having this proposal made to the King, and if, as would appear from the late reports from his country, he is really expecting to be attacked by the Boers and is determined to fight them for the 'Disputed Territory' he might feel it to be in his true interests to have the aegis of our protection thrown over him as the Transvaal has done for the Amaswazi.[102]

How the interests of both the Transvaal and Zululand in the matter of the disputed territory were to be satisfied, Wolseley did not explain. This contradiction in imperial policy manifested itself in an acute form after the British annexation of the Transvaal in 1877 and led inexorably to the war of 1879.

The Colonial Office did not succeed in bribing the ZAR into confederation nor in deterring it from attempting to make good its claim to the disputed territory. The ZAR's renewed attempt in March 1876 had explosive results. The first news Shepstone received of the impending storm was in a letter from John Dunn dated 13 March:

> I am requested by Cetywayo to state that he has received information from his people living in the North Border of the Zulu Country that a party of Dutch with a lot of Kaffirs have been distributing a lot of notes, as enclosed, amongst his subjects, and seizing 25 head of cattle and beating and otherwise illtreating his subjects and have threatened to return in six days with an armed force.[103]

The enclosed note revealed that this curious occurrence was a Boer tax collection. The ZAR was now attempting to make good its claim to the disputed territory not by expelling the subjects of the Zulu King but by treating them as subjects of the republic. The Zulu of the disputed territory refused to pay the tax, stating that they were subjects of Cetshwayo. 'What is Cetywayo but a Kaffir and a dog', the tax-collectors are said to have retorted, and they seized cattle in default of payment.[104]

All this was reported to Cetshwayo, who instructed his subjects in the disputed territory to resist, by physical force if need be, any seizure of cattle at the next attempted collection, which they had been told would be on 10 March. He also sent an armed force of several thousand men to back up his subjects' resistance. By 9 a.m. on the morning of 10 March there were 500 Zulu near Potter's store, where the 'Old Hunting Road' crossed the Mphemvane river. According to Potter they were 'all armed to the teeth in full war costume . . . they were dancing and yelling, defying the F. Cornet to come, and I believe if he had showed his face he would have been certainly killed'.[105] Only after receiving assurances that no attempt would be made to collect the tax did this Zulu force begin to disperse. Zulu forces also assembled at other places in the disputed territory to provide armed resistance to any attempt at taxation and, despite Cetshwayo's instructions that they were to act solely on the defensive, and despite the Zulu commanders' attempts to enforce this order, a certain amount of damage was done to Boer property.

This disturbance caused great alarm among the frontier farmers, who retreated into laager. The Landdrost of Utrecht, Gert Rudolph, visited the disturbed areas the following day and, finding that first reports had been very much exaggerated and that the Zulu force had retired, tried to persuade the Boers to leave the laagers and return to their homes, promising that the tax would remain in abeyance until he heard from Pretoria. But though the frontier was outwardly calm, nothing had been resolved, and the situation was still tense. Few Boers heeded Rudolph's recommendation to return to their farms. The prevalent feeling seemed to be that things could not simply be allowed to drift on as they had done for so many years, and that the time had come to decide once and for all whether the disputed territory belonged to the Zulu or the Boers.

Cetshwayo sent a message to Rudolph complaining of the levying of tax on his subjects and explaining that he had sent the armed forces into the disputed territory to prevent its collection. Rudolph replied that he had stopped the collection of the tax and asked Cetshwayo to make any complaints to him in future rather than send in 'commandoes' to rob homesteads. He also desired the Zulu King to order his people on the border to be quiet. But this was easier said than done. The ease with which they had driven the Boers off their farms emboldened the Zulu, and their speech and acts of robbery and destruction seemed to indicate a wish to provoke a war. Cetshwayo himself appeared peaceably inclined, and claimed to be unable to control the turbulent spirits of his young warriors; but he cannot have failed to be impressed at the contrast between the effects of one short sharp military demonstration, on the one hand, and the years of patient appealing to the government of Natal, on the other. Now it was the turn of the Boers to submit without resistance to insult and injury. Rudolph realized that any retaliation by the Boers would mean war, so, to reduce the chances of a conflict, he reversed his earlier policy, and advised or ordered the frontier farmers, some of whom had returned to the farms, to go into laager.

From this time on the disputed territory remained in an almost permanently disturbed condition. Sporadic attempts were made to reoccupy farms, but at the time of the British annexation of the Transvaal in April 1877 many if not most of the owners of farms in the more exposed areas were still in laager or had trekked out of the district altogether.

Boer, Pedi and Zulu to 1876

Meanwhile, in another part of the Transvaal eastern frontier zone, occurrences of a strikingly similar nature were taking place. In March 1876 Sekhukhune, the Paramount of the Pedi, sent an armed force to uphold his claims to territory in which citizens of the ZAR had settled. As on the Zululand frontier, this caused panic among the whites and drove them into laager.[106]

The heartland of the Pedi polity lay between the Olifants and Steelpoort rivers, but the limits of Sekhukhune's authority were indefinite and fluctuating, as his influence over other groups ebbed and flowed according to circumstances. He made formal claims to land as far south as the Komati river, which would have included the entire Lydenburg district within his domain. The ZAR on the other hand claimed that the whole of Sekhukhune's country was an integral part of the republic and that the Pedi were its subjects, a claim which Sekhukhune rejected and which the ZAR was unable to enforce. In practice the Steelpoort river marked the boundary of undisturbed Pedi control, while to the south-east of it lay a frontier zone of interspersed settlement and indeterminate authority.

By the late 1860s Boer power in the Transvaal had reached a low ebb. In 1867 it collapsed altogether in the Soutpansberg region of the northern Transvaal. Even in the white heartland of central, southern and south-western Transvaal the effective authority of the central government seemed to be dwindling. In 1868 a tax on blacks, which it was estimated would bring in the modest sum of £1 500, in fact brought in the extremely modest sum of £3 5s 9d.

In the 1870s there was an attempt to revive the effectiveness of the central government. In 1872 the burghers of the ZAR followed the earlier example of their fellows in the Orange Free State and elected an educated man from the Cape, Thomas François Burgers, as President in place of the frontiersmen who had formerly held that position. A more energetic attempt was made to collect taxes and extract labour from the black population. The Boers needed more labour as the discovery of minerals in the interior had created markets for agricultural produce. But the diggings also exacerbated the shortage of labour by diverting it from the farms. The result was coercive legislation in the 1870s which, though largely ineffective in producing more labour, did have the effect of increasing the white pressure upon blacks in those areas of the Transvaal that were under Boer control.

The response of many such blacks was to withdraw from the white heartland of the Transvaal to those parts of it which were under the effective control of black rulers. Blacks inhabiting frontier zones of dual or indeterminate authority were able to make such a change of allegiance without changing their residence. So increasing white pressure on blacks paradoxically led to an extension of black authority in the borderlands and hence increasing black pressure on whites. It was the conflict thus engendered that led to war between the ZAR and the Pedi in 1876.

It was around Sekhukhune's brother, Dinkwanyane, that the conflict in the Lydenburg district centred. Missionaries of the Berlin Missionary Society had been permitted to work among the Pedi in 1861. They met with some success, but they also aroused popular hostility. When Dinkwanyane was converted, taking the Christian name of Johannes, Sekhukhune saw the Christians in his realm under the leadership of his brother as a possible threat to his paramountcy. He therefore expelled the missionaries in 1866. Johannes Dinkwanyane and his followers accompanied the missionaries to their new station at Botsabelo, near Middelburg, in republican territory. But they became dissatisfied with the auto-cratic regime of Alexander Merensky, the missionary in charge of Botsabelo, particularly since he insisted upon their fulfilling all the demands made on them by the ZAR, demands which other blacks even in the white heartland of the Transvaal were able very largely to evade.

On the other hand Dinkwanyane did not wish to return to the Pedi heartland since this would mean abandoning Christianity, to which he was genuinely devoted. The solution was to move, in 1874, to a semi-independent position in the frontier zone between the Pedi heartland and the ZAR. Here Johannes Dinkwanyane and his people were sufficiently independent of Sekhukhune to practise their religion without interference, but at the same time able to refuse Boer demands for tax and labour on the grounds that they were the subjects not of the ZAR but of Sekhukhune.

Sekhukhune welcomed the accession of strength and expansion of territorial influence that the return of his brother to his allegiance represented. At the same time he wished to avoid open conflict with the ZAR. Although he undoubtedly wished to expand his territory at the expense of that of the ZAR, his ambitions were probably not the prime motor of the Pedi expansion that took place in this period. To a great extent he was pulled in the wake of his brother. But to the Boers and to the British gold-diggers (and to most subsequent historians) it seemed that he was determined to drive the whites out of the Lydenburg district, and that he was using Dinkwanyane as a stalking-horse in pursuit of this aim.

The Landdrost of Lydenburg and Acting President Joubert became increasingly convinced that war with the Pedi would be necessary. The crisis came in March 1876. A farmer named Jancowitz attempted to establish himself on a farm which the Landdrost of Lydenburg had obtained for him in the immediate environs of Johannes Dinkwanyane's village. Dinkwanyane saw this as a deliberate provocation, which perhaps it was. His people prevented Jancowitz and an assistant-veldkornet from erecting beacons, and overturned a wagon on which Jancowitz had loaded timber that he had collected on the land he claimed to be his. The Landdrost threatened Dinkwanyane with attack, attempted to raise a commando, and appealed to Pretoria for help. Sekhukhune's response to this threat to his brother was to send an armed force to his support. This invasion of republican territory (as whites saw it) caused panic in the Lydenburg district. The Boers moved into laager, and the predominantly British gold-diggers appealed for British intervention.

Sekhukhune soon withdrew the force he had sent, and he and Dinkwanyane made conciliatory overtures; but the Boers were convinced that this was merely a cunning move to ensure that any overt act of war would appear to the British (whose possible intervention was a factor in the minds of both Boer and Pedi) to be the initiative of the Boers. Although an outward calm descended upon the Lydenburg district, the Boers did not believe that it was safe to resume the occupation of their farms.

This was the situation that confronted President Burgers on his return from Europe in April 1876. In two parts of the eastern Transvaal frontier zone whites had been driven from their farms by military demonstrations of powerful black rulers. What made the situation seem even more ominous was the belief that Cetshwayo and Sekhukhune were acting in collusion. Contemporary newspapers show that it was widely believed that Cetshwayo and Sekhukhune were allies. The belief was not of recent origins, nor was it confined to newspaper editors and correspondents. In 1871 the Swazi regents expressed fears of a combined Zulu-Pedi attack on their country.[107] President Burgers said that the expedition sent to Swaziland in 1875 was the result of the ZAR government hearing that Cetshwayo was preparing to attack the Swazi 'in conjunction with Secucune'. Shepstone commented on this statement that 'these two acting in concert against the Amaswazi may mean doing the same against the Republic when opportunity offers'.[108]

It is not at all certain that there really was an alliance between Cetshwayo and Sekhukhune. The fact that both rulers made armed demonstrations at about the same time is suggestive. The basis for an alliance existed: the Swazi and the ZAR had long been allies, and both the Pedi and the Zulu had a history of conflict with both of them. Cetshwayo and Sekhukhune were certainly in communication with each other. But all black rulers in South Africa were in communication with each other, as well as with white governments, and there is no special significance in the fact that this was true of the Zulu and Pedi rulers as well. The armed demonstrations they both made in March 1876 have the appearance of collusion, but their subsequent dealings with the Transvaal show no sign of their acting in concert with each other.[109] And the events of March 1876 in the Zulu and the Pedi borderlands respectively are independently explicable without recourse to the hypothesis of collusion. The most we can say is that events on Sekhukhune's frontier may at times have had an influence on Cetshwayo, and vice versa, but it is clear that both were more influenced by things nearer home.

The Boer-Pedi War, 1876

Even though their respective actions are independently explicable, the belief in an alliance between Cetshwayo and Sekhukhune is of great importance, as it influenced perceptions of and responses to their actions. Since the war between the ZAR and the Pedi led to Shepstone's annexation of the Transvaal, Shepstone's perceptions and responses are particularly important. He was a firm believer in a Zulu-Pedi alliance, and interpreted the events of March 1876 entirely in such terms. He stated that it was probable that Cetshwayo had sent messengers to Sekhukhune and other Transvaal chiefs describing the situation in the disputed territory

> in pursuance of an arrangement which is believed on very good grounds to have been in existence for some time past between Cetywayo and those Chiefs, namely, that if ever active hostilities should commence between the Zulus and the Government of the Republic, the powerful Tribes to the North and East of the Transvaal should make use of the opportunity by operating against the rear of the Boers and so paralyse their effort against the Zulus. This is probably the cause of the attitude assumed by Sikukuni and Johannes as described in communications from the Transvaal, and the time that elapsed between the disturbance in the disputed territory and the show of Sikukuni's hostility in the Transvaal seems to correspond with the time the Zulu messengers would take to reach those Chiefs.[110]

Shepstone saw Sekhukhune's inaction no less than his actions as entirely determined by events not on his own frontier but on Cetshwayo's. In June 1876 Shepstone wrote:

> As far as Sikukuni is concerned, the hostile attitude he had shown appears to have been abandoned and this is evidently because later information from the Zulus told him that the actual rupture between the Republic and Cetywayo on the question of the disputed territory, which was so imminent in the preceding March, had contrary to his expectations not taken place.

But if the ZAR went to war with Sekhukhune, Shepstone continued,

> the danger is that Cetywayo may feel bound to assist a tributary chief suffering in the Zulu cause, and whose destruction he will consider as seriously weakening the position he evidently so much relies on should actual warfare ever break out between him and the Government of the Republic.[111]

When President Burgers returned to the Transvaal from Europe in April 1876 his inclination was to attempt to maintain peace, which he considered necessary for the credit-worthiness, economic development and modernization of the ZAR. But the Volksraad was determined upon war with the Pedi, a decision in which Burgers reluctantly acquiesced. Sekhukhune posed a greater threat to the Transvaal than Cetshwayo. De Kiewiet stated that Sekhukhune's land 'lay across the line of the projected railway' to Delagoa Bay. As Goodfellow pointed out, it was in fact well to the north of it.[112] Even in his most expansive moments Sekhukhune claimed land only to the Komati river, while the projected railway was intended to run to the south of it.[113] Nevertheless the railway is possibly of some relevance to the decision to go to war, since some of the land Burgers had mortgaged to raise the loan to build the railway was in territory occupied by the Pedi.[114] But much more important than this was the threat that Sekhukhune appeared to pose to the Lydenburg district in general. 'Unless we now shut up Secoecoene,' wrote Burgers, 'we may as well drop the whole district of Lydenburg and more.'[115] Lydenburg was no newly occupied frontier territory like the land in dispute with the Zulu; with the exception of the Potchefstroom district, it was the oldest and most long-established district of the ZAR. The Soutpansberg district had recently been abandoned; it would be intolerable for the ZAR were Lydenburg to go the same way.

War with Sekhukhune required peaceful overtures towards Cetshwayo; and the ease with which their supposed alliance was split must have seemed surprising. Burgers sent Rudolph to Cetshwayo with a letter to his 'Good Friend' regretting the border disturbances during his absence in Europe and suggesting a meeting of plenipotentiaries in a few months to settle the border dispute.[116] Cetshwayo was quite agreeable to such a meeting, but wished for an Englishman (meaning, it was assumed, Shepstone) to be present as well. He also asked for permission to attack the Swazi, and suggested that were he to receive such permission the border dispute could be more easily settled.

Both the presence of Shepstone at the proposed meeting and the proposed attack on the Swazi were unacceptable to the ZAR, but it was possible to agree that peace should be maintained on the border and that there should be no warlike demonstrations pending the proposed meeting to settle the border question. Rudolph told Cetshwayo that the ZAR intended to attack Sekhukhune, but Cetshwayo said that his relationship with Sekhukhune was nothing more than one of friendship: he obtained certain skins and feathers from him as well as the services of doctors. He volunteered the information that Pedi doctors had recently arrived to treat redwater disease in his cattle; this confirmed information Rudolph had received from other sources concerning the movements of certain Pedi, and constituted a reassuring explanation for them. It had been decided to station 300 burghers on the border to reassure the Swazi that they could aid the republic against Sekhukhune without a Zulu attack in the rear. Rudolph told Cetshwayo that this would be done, and the latter thanked him for his candour.

Rudolph was confident that Cetshwayo would not aid the Pedi or attack the Swazi.[117]

Stationing the force on the frontier proved difficult. Only half the burghers commandeered for this purpose turned up, and many of them refused to take orders from the commandant appointed to lead them. Equal reluctance to turn out on commando was manifested in other parts of the republic. It was with great difficulty that a force of about 2 000 burghers was eventually mustered to take the field against the Pedi.[118] The Swazi were also hesitant, but were eventually prevailed upon to send a force of about 2 000 men.[119] At the head of this unenthusiastic army was the incongruous figure of President Burgers, a clergyman by profession, who in default of anyone else, was reluctantly obliged to lead the forces in person.

By the time the war began Shepstone was at the seat of imperial power, having gone to England to attend Carnarvon's confederation conference as the official representative of Natal. Carnarvon intended that this should be a conference of all the colonies and republics in South Africa, including the ZAR, and Shepstone and Bulwer hoped that it would provide an opportunity for settling the Transvaal-Zululand border dispute. The matter was becoming urgent, as the situation was becoming more dangerous. It was evident that Cetshwayo's patience was wearing thin, that his hopes of intervention by Natal were dwindling, and that he would not for much longer heed the Natal government's counsels of peace and forbearance. As Shepstone commented at the time of Cetshwayo's forcible resistance to the attempted tax-collection, 'messages from the Zulu King are becoming more frequent and urgent, and the replies he receives seem to him both temporizing and evasive'.[120]

Shepstone told Cetshwayo at the time of the attempted tax collection that he hoped to be able to settle the dispute at the conference to be held in London later that year, and he also said that if the Zulu King wished to make any further statement on the subject it would be conveyed to the Secretary of State.[121] Cetshwayo and his advisers accordingly met and composed a lengthy statement of their case which John Dunn wrote down and sent to Shepstone.

The statement was not confined to the question of the disputed territory. It began with a history of the Zulu nation's relationships with the British and the Boers designed to show that the Zulu had been allies of the former since Shaka's time. When Mpande had formed an alliance with the Boers against Dingane he had intended to ally with the British, but at that date the distinction between the two had not been clear to the Zulu. The statement pointed out that Dingane had been defeated by Mpande's soldiers without the assistance of the Boers, and 'it was a mere form saying he was made King by the Dutch, for which the Zulu Nation had to pay heavily in cattle and children'. The hostility of the Boers towards the Zulu was attributed to the latter's alliance with the British.

Turning to the land dispute itself, the statement admitted that the Zulu had permitted a party of Boers to settle between the Mzinyathi and Ncome (Buffalo and Blood) rivers in return for a present of 100 cattle, but they rejected any further claim to land. The Boers had tried to persuade Cetshwayo to cede them land when they returned his brothers (in 1861) but he had refused to do so. An account of the later disputes and negotiations followed, together with details of aggressive acts on the part of the Boers. The statement ended by urging the intervention of Natal as the only way in which the dispute could be settled without recourse to war.[122]

Shepstone drew up a full report on the history of the dispute, which together with the appended documents ran to 30 pages when printed in the Blue Books. Forwarding this to the Secretary of State for the Colonies, Bulwer stressed the forbearance that the Zulu had always shown, and their reliance on the good offices of Natal to settle the dispute; he also pointed out that this had achieved nothing. The attempt by the ZAR to give practical expression to its claims by levying a tax in the disputed territory had created a situation that threatened to produce war. It was therefore 'due not less to the good faith than to the interests of this Government that some endeavour should be made without delay to bring about a final settlement of this question'.[123]

Bulwer told Cetshwayo that the statement written down by Dunn, together with other papers relative to the question, had been sent to England to be 'submitted to the consideration of the Councillors of the great Queen'. Shepstone, he told him, had also gone to England.[124] It is very likely that Cetshwayo and his advisers gained the impression that Shepstone had gone to England specifically to settle their dispute with the Transvaal. This may explain their reaction to the steps taken by Shepstone on his return. Since the ZAR was not represented at the conference, he returned empty-handed as far as the Zulu were concerned. When next they had dealings with him over the disputed territory he was no longer a friendly intermediary but the ruler of the very country with which they were in dispute.

It was the failure of the ZAR's expedition against Sekhukhune that brought Shepstone hurrying back to South Africa and enabled him to annex the Transvaal. Yet the war with the Pedi was by no means the complete fiasco it was represented as being.[125] An important stronghold, Mathebe's mountain, declared by Burgers to be the 'Kaffir Gibraltar', was captured on 4 and 5 July. This victory led many minor chiefs to surrender. On 13 July Johannes Dinkwanyane's stronghold was stormed by the Swazi contingent, and Johannes was killed. The Boer force that was supposed to have assisted in this attack did nothing, with the result that the Swazi refused to take any further part in the war. They returned home and the stronghold was reoccupied by the Pedi. Nevertheless, by the end of the month the Boer forces were approaching Sekhukhune's mountain, the Lydenburg district was no longer under threat from the Pedi, and much of the Pedi heartland was in Boer hands. An attempt was made to storm Sekhukhune's mountain on 2 August. The lower reaches were gained, but the Boers refused to advance in the face of the fire from the Pedi guns. On the following day they again refused to make a frontal attack, suggesting instead a form of siege warfare aimed at starving the Pedi into submission. President Burgers had no alternative but to comply with this suggestion, whereupon most of the commando disbanded and returned to their homes.

Various explanations have been offered for this refusal of the Boers to fight. Distrust and dislike of their heretical President and his new-fangled schemes was probably an *ex post facto* rationalisation.[126] The contemporary English language press confidently ascribed the Boer behaviour to simple cowardice. In the sense that they were not prepared to die for their country, it might be argued that this was correct. 'Cowardice' is natural: to flee from danger is instinctive. For men to be prepared to sacrifice their lives for an abstraction such as 'the nation' or 'the fatherland' requires a long process of conditioning which the Boers of the Transvaal had not yet undergone. Their loyalties were to their farms, their families and their local communities (or factions within them). Their country meant little to them at this stage of their history. To risk their lives for other men's farms seemed little more than folly.[127]

The guerrilla warfare resorted to after the failure to storm Sekhukhune's stronghold was effective in the long run. The republican forces, reinforced by a contingent of volunteers from the diamond fields, destroyed the enemy's crops and so harassed the Pedi that Sekhukhune was eventually (early in the following year) forced to sue for peace. The ZAR was also in urgent need of peace. The war had exhausted it financially; and a greater threat than Sekhukhune was looming. By the time peace with the Pedi was signed Theophilus Shepstone was in Pretoria, with the British flag in his baggage.

Notes

1. Guest, *Langalibalele*; Wright and Manson, *Hlubi Chiefdom,* chs 5 and 6.
2. For Colenso and Langalibalele, see Guy, *Heretic*, chs 13–15.
3. CO 179/114, minutes by Norris, 20 July, and Herbert, 21 and 23 July, on Natal 8271, Pine to Carnarvon, 12 June 1874; CO 179/115, minute by Herbert, 26 August, on Natal 9861, Confid, Pine to Carnarvon, 20 July 1874.
4. BL Add Mss 60906, Carnarvon's diary for 1874, entries for 12 and 13 September, and 2 December.
5. Etherington, 'Labour Supply', p. 239.
6. See ch. 4, p. 89.
7. See also ch. 4, p. 90, and Cope, 'Local Imperatives', pp. 603–5.
8. BL Add Mss 60906, Carnarvon's diary for 1874, entries for 5 and 31 October 1874.
9. Rees, *Colenso Letters,* p. 315; BPP, C1121, p. 94, no. 28, Carnarvon to Pine, 3 December 1874; BPP, C1187, p. 10, no. 11, Pine to Carnarvon, 19 January 1875.
10. BL Add Mss 60798, no. 51, Froude to Carnarvon, 4 October [1874].
11. Ibid, nos 51, 53 and 56, Froude to Carnarvon, 4, 11 and 20 October [1874].
12. BPP, C1121, p. 91, no. 26, Carnarvon to Pine, 3 December 1874.
13. Ibid, pp. 92–4, no. 27, Carnarvon to Pine, 3 December 1874.
14. CO 879/8, Natal no. 80, p. 7, memo by Shepstone, 14 June 1875.

15. CO 879/7, Natal no. 66, memo on native affairs, n.d. [by Shepstone] printed 28 November 1874.
16. CO 879/7, Natal no. 65, memo by Shepstone, 28 November 1874; GH 64, no. 28, Carnarvon to Wolseley, 15 March 1875, encl the bill on native administration which Shepstone played a major part in drawing up.
17. CO 179/122, minute by Malcolm, 26 February 1876, on Natal 2289, Chesson to Carnarvon, 25 Febuary 1876.
18. CO 879/9, African no. 83A, p. 223, Colonial Office to Aborigines Protection Society, 6 December 1875.
19. PRO 30/6/38, no. 25, Wolseley to Carnarvon, 12 June 1875.
20. Ibid, no. 1, Wolseley to Carnarvon, 16 February 1875, and memo., n.d.; PRO 30/6/5, p. 62, Carnarvon to Ward Hunt, 18 February 1875. See also ibid, p. 65, Ward Hunt to Carnarvon, 25 February 1875 for other naval and military precautions.
21. CO 879/8, Natal no. 80, pp. 1–6, Wolseley to Carnarvon, 14 June 1875; PRO 30/6/38, no. 15, Wolseley to Carnarvon, 12 June, 1875. See Cope, 'De Kiewiet', pp. 498–500 for more detail on Wolseley's views.
22. PRO 30/6/12, p. 97, Carnarvon to Hardy, 26 October 1875.
23. CO 879/8, Natal no. 80, p. 4, Wolseley to Carnarvon, 14 June 1875.
24. HL Deb, Vol. CCXXV, col 1896, 23 July 1875.
25. PRO 30/6/38, no. 2 [? unnumbered but between nos 1 and 3], memo, on the evidence of handwriting and content by Wolseley, n.d.; ibid, no. 4, Wolseley to Carnarvon, 27 February 1875.
26. GH 1218, p. 429, no. 81, Pine to Kimberley, 13 April 1874; In ibid, p. 519, no. 173, Pine to Carnarvon, 23 September 1874, Pine stated that Cetshwayo had sent six embassies, the last of 80 men, 'demanding' Langalibalele.
27. Ibid, p. 535, no. 189, Pine to Carnarvon, 23 October 1874; *The Natal Mercury*, 8 May 1875, editorial; *The Natal Witness*, 11 May 1875, 'Zululand'.
28. GH 1053, p. 117, Robertson to Bulwer, 24 May 1878; Child, *Charles Smythe*, p. 80 (Charles Smythe was Prime Minister of Natal, 1907-8); Natal Blue Book for 1879, p. JJ18; CO 959/1, Clarke to Frere, 6 June 1879.
29. SNA I/6/3, private memo by Shepstone, 28 February 1874.
30. See ch. 2, p. 35.
31. GH 1218, p. 489, Confid, Pine to Carnarvon, 20 July 1874.
32. See ch. 2, pp. 34–5.
33. GH 64, Confid, Shepstone to Herbert, 30 November 1874, encl in no. 60, Carnarvon to Wolseley, 30 April 1875.
34. GH 1300, p. 41, Confid, Wolseley to Carnarvon, 14 June 1875.
35. See ch. 2, pp. 21–2.
36. See p. 61.
37. CO 879/9, African no. 83A, pp. 97–107, no. 75, report on the Transvaal by G. Pomeroy Colley, 10 August 1875.
38. GH 1219, p. 146, no. 172, Wolseley to Carnarvon, 14 August 1875.
39. See p. 49.
40. See ch. 2, p. 20.
41. PRO 30/6/38, no. 30, Wolseley to Carnarvon, 8 July 1875; PRO 30/6/47, Shepstone to Carnarvon, 26 August 1875; PRO 30/6/49, p. 159, memo of conversation with Wolseley, by Carnarvon, 7–8 October 1875.
42. See p. 31–2.
43. See p. 35–6.
44. *The Natal Colonist*, 15 June 1875, editorial.
45. *The Natal Mercury*, 2 March 1875, editorial; 29 June 1875, editorial; 8 May 1875, editorial; 1 June 1875, 'The Month'.

46. *The Natal Mercury*, 15 April, editorial; 1 May, 'The Month'; 25 May, editorial; 15 June, letter from 'Rusticus' 5 June; 6 July, 'The Month'; 5 October, 'The Month'. *The Natal Witness*, 18 June, 'Short Notes'; 13 July, letter from 'a traveller' 26 June. *The Natal Colonist*, 15 June, editorial; 25 June, letter from J.L.H. 21 June; 29 June, editor's reply. All dates 1875.

47. Letter from Dunn, 3 July 1875, in *The Natal Colonist*, 9 July 1875.

48. *The Natal Witness*, 5 October 1875, report of letter from F.W. Chesson to *The Times*, London.

49. Cope, 'Characters of Blood?'

50. Chesson to *The Times*, 12 August 1875, quoted in *The Natal Mercury*, 5 October 1875.

51. *The Natal Witness*, 12 October 1875, editorial.

52. De Kiewiet, *Imperial Factor in South Africa*, p. 43.

53. Hove Central Library, Wolseley Papers, NAT 1, Minute Book Natal, 1875, no. 49, 29 August 1875.

54. See ch. 2, p. 36.

55. On missionaries in Zululand in this period see Etherington, *Preachers*, pp. 74–86; Etherington, 'Anglo-Zulu Relations', pp. 13–52; Hernaes, 'Zulu Kingdom', pp. 102–86. For an attempt to set Zulu missions in a broader 19th century South African context, see Cope, 'Christian Missions'.

56. Cope, 'Characters of Blood', pp. 7–10.

57. See ch. 6, pp. 144-5. See also SPG, WP, no. 204, Robertson to McCrorie, 6 February 1878.

58. PRO 30/6/38, nos 32 and 33, Robertson to Shepstone, 18 and 25 June 1875.

59. PRO 30/6/10, no. 20, Carnarvon to Salisbury, 3 September 1875.

60. See, pp. 46–7.

61. BL Add Mss 60798, no. 51, Froude to Carnarvon, 4 October [1874].

62. BL Add Mss 60798, no. 62, Froude to Carnarvon, Pretoria, 10 November, and addition to letter, 12 November [1874]

63. Bonner, *Kings*, pp. 80–4.

64. Ibid, pp. 118–21.

65. SNA I/7/6, p. 237, message from Cetshwayo, 11 November 1875.

66. See ch. 2, pp. 21–2.

67. BPP, C1961, p. 46, report on Zululand by F.B. Fynney, 4 July 1877.

68. SP 19, Gallwey to Shepstone, 3 May 1877; SNA I/1/29, confid minute, R.M. Umsinga, to ASNA, 24 December 1877; CSO 1925, Special BA, Umvoti, to Colonial Secretary, 12 January 1879.

69. Colenbrander, 'Zulu Political Economy', p. 92.

70. Webb and Wright, *Zulu King Speaks*, p. 25.

71. Letter from Zululand correspondent, 1 July 1875, in *The Natal Mercury*, 27 July 1875.

72. Bonner, *Kings*, pp. 62–3 and 130.

73. Bonner, *Kings*, pp. 123–5. See also letter from D. Straker, 8 April 1874, in *De Volksstem*, 2 May 1874, quoted in *The Natal Mercury*, 19 May 1874.

74. Bonner, *Kings*, p. 129.

75. SNA I/6/2, no. 60, Dunn to Shepstone, 4 October 1874; ibid, no. 59, message from Cetshwayo, 19 October 1874.

76. Bonner, *Kings*, pp. 120 and 129–30.

77. Ibid, p. 134. This was the view taken by Bulwer: GH 1220, p. 24, no. 14, Bulwer to Carnarvon, 12 January 1877.

78. Rudolph to SS, 17 March 1875, quoted in Monteith, 'Cetshwayo and Sekhukhune', p. 58.

79. CO 879/9, African no. 83a, p. 99, no. 75, report on the Transvaal, by G. Pomeroy Colley, 10 August 1875.

80. *The Natal Mercury*, 8 May 1875, editorial; *The Natal Witness*, 11 May 1875, 'Zululand'; Monteith, 'Cetshwayo and Sekhukhune', p. 58.

81. Bonner, *Kings*, pp. 134–7; *De Volksstem's* correspondent, 13 June 1875, quoted in *The Natal Mercury*, 13 July 1875; letter from a member of the commando, 3 July 1875, in *The Natal Mercury*, 3 August 1875.

82. Preston, *Diaries 1875*, p. 195, entry for 11 June.

83. Monteith, 'Cetshwayo and Sekhukhune', p. 59.

84. SS 213, R2187, Rudolph to SS, 24 August 1876.

85. Webb and Wright, *Stuart Archive*, Vol. 4, pp. 320 and 352; Cope, 'Political Power', p. 24.

86. GH 1396, no. 14, message from Cetshwayo, 7 June 1875.

87. Preston, *Diaries 1875*, p. 175, entry for 4 May.

88. SNA I/7/6, p. 229, message from Cetshwayo, 7 June 1875; ibid, p. 231, message to Cetshwayo, 14 June 1875.

89. Van Rooyen, 'Verhouding', Vol. I, pp. 79–90. A translation of the proclamation is printed in BPP, C1961, p. 19.

90. Monteith, 'Cetshwayo and Sekhukhune', pp. 61–3.

91. Ibid, p. 64. Bulwer commented on this omission in GH 1219, p. 180, no. 214, Bulwer to Carnarvon, 26 October 1875.

92. GH 854, message to Cetshwayo, August 1875, encl in State Secretary, ZAR, to Colonial Secretary, Natal, 15 September 1875, and memo on ibid by Shepstone, 13 October 1875.

93. Monteith, 'Cetshwayo and Sekhukhune', p. 64.

94. GH 1219, p. 179, no. 214, Bulwer to Carnarvon, 26 October 1875.

95. GH 856, no. 1961, Joubert to Bulwer, 13 October 1875.

96. Message to Cetshwayo, 13 October 1875, cited Monteith, 'Cetshwayo and Sekhukhune', p. 66; SNA I/7/6, p. 237, message from Cetshwayo, 11 November 1875.

97. SNA I/7/7, p. 157, report on the nature of the relations between HM Government and the Zulus, by Shepstone, 30 October 1875; BPP, C1137, p. 18, Shepstone's report on the installation of Cetshwayo, n.d.

98. GH 1325, no. 247, Bulwer to Joubert, 15 November 1875.

99. GH 1219, p. 195, no. 221, Bulwer to Carnarvon, 26 November 1875.

100. Monteith, 'Cetshwayo and Sekhukhune', p. 67, quoting Rudolph to SS, 10 December 1875.

101. GH 68, Carnarvon to Barkly, 25 January 1876, encl in no. 186, Carnarvon to Bulwer, 31 January 1876. High Commissioner Barkly was instructed to forward the despatch to the government of the ZAR

102. CO 179/118, minutes by Herbert, 7 December 1875, and Wolseley, 21 January 1876, on Natal 13203, Bulwer to Carnarvon, 26 October 1875.

103. SNA I/6/3, Dunn to Shepstone, 13 March 1876.

104. SNA I/7/6, p. 246, message from Cetshwayo, 25 March 1876.

105. SNA I/7/7, p. 197, extract from Charles Potter to his father, George Potter, 12 March 1876. Besides this letter, information on the attempted tax-gathering and its results comes principally from SNA I/1/27, no. 66, George Potter to Shepstone, 18 April 1876; reports from Rudolph in SS 205, 206 and 207; a letter from a correspondent on the Zulu border, 14 March 1876 in *The Natal Witness*, 24 March 1876; a letter from its Utrecht correspondent, 22 March 1876, in *The Natal Mercury*, 4 April 1876; and from ibid, 12 and 17 April 1876, in ibid, 25 April 1876.

106. Except where otherwise stated, this account of Pedi-ZAR relations is based on Delius, *The Land Belongs to Us*.

107. Bonner, *Kings*, pp. 120 and note 106.

108. GH 66, minute by Shepstone, 20 October 1875, on Burgers to Colonial Office, 4 August 1875, encl in no. 116, Carnarvon to Bulwer, 18 August 1875.

109. See Monteith, 'Cetshwayo and Sekhukhune', esp pp. 170–6; and Cope 'Origins', pp. 100–1.
110. SNA I/7/7, p. 239, minute on the condition of Zululand and the Transvaal government, by Shepstone, 28 April 1876.
111. Ibid, p. 257, minute on ZAR-Sekhukhune affairs, by Shepstone, 5 June 1876.
112. De Kiewiet, *Imperial Factor in South Africa*, p. 100; Goodfellow, *Great Britain and South African Confederation*, p. 113 and n.
113. Monteith, 'Cetshwayo and Sekhukhune', p. 99.
114. De Kiewiet, *Imperial Factor in South Africa*, p. 100; Monteith, 'Cetshwayo and Sekhukhune', p. 100; letter from Middelburg correspondent, 16 June 1876, in *The Natal Witness*, 7 July 1876; Public Record Office, London, Foreign Office records, FO 63/1039, Pol Ser no. 8, Confid, Elton to Derby, 25 September 1876.
115. Delius, *The Land Belongs to Us*, p. 204.
116. Burgers to Cetshwayo, 26 April 1876, quoted in Dunn, *John Dunn*, p. 132.
117. SS 209, R1270/76, Rudolph to SS, 27 May 1876; SS 210, R1534/76, Rudolph to SS, 15 June 1876; letter from Utrecht correspondent, 4 June 1876, in *The Natal Mercury*, 13 June 1876; 'Cetywayo's reply' (apparently from *De Volksstem*) in *The Natal Mercury*, 15 June 1876; letter from Pilgim's Rest correspondent, 12 June 1876, in *The Natal Witness*, 23 June 1876.
118. Van Rooyen, 'Verhouding', pp. 55 and 251–2.
119. Bonner, *Kings*, pp. 141–2.
120. SNA I/7/7, p. 101, minute on affairs in the disputed territory, by Shepstone, 30 March 1876.
121. SNA I/1/28, Confid Shepstone to Dunn, 3 April 1876.
122. BPP, C1961, pp. 26–8, Dunn to Shepstone, 20 April 1876.
123. Ibid, p. 1, no. 1, Bulwer to Carnarvon, 29 June 1876.
124. SNA I/7/13, p. 9, message to Cetshwayo, 25 July 1876.
125. On the war see Van Rooyen, 'Verhouding', pp. 254–74.
126. Van Rooyen, 'Verhouding', p. 264.
127. Ibid, pp. 263–4; Delius, *The Land Belongs to Us*, p. 206.

CHAPTER FOUR

Carnarvon and Confederation

The Purposes of Confederation

Britain occupied the Cape, temporarily in 1795 and permanently in 1806, for its strategic position on the sea route between the British Isles and British India. Cape Town and Simonstown were all the British really wanted, and on a number of occasions Secretaries of State expressed regret that they could not retain only the peninsula and abandon the rest of the colony. Despite these views, British territory in South Africa continued to expand. Boer land-hunger and aspirations to independence, the destabilization of frontiers, missionary agitation and the desire of British settlers for a more propitious framework for economic enterprise were some of the pressures driving the British frontier forward. It is significant that before 1877 all annexations were the work of the 'man on the spot', the Governor or High Commissioner, who was subject to these pressures. Expansion was merely acquiesced in by a reluctant imperial government – except in the cases of Queen Adelaide Province and (after an interval) the Orange River Sovereignty, when it was repudiated and reversed. This is what makes the annexation of the Transvaal in 1877 such an important departure, for it was carried out on the direct instructions of the Secretary of State for the Colonies.

For many years the Colonial Office adhered to the policy of the Conventions in terms of which the Orange River Sovereignty was retroceded and authority over the Transvaal was disclaimed. When Sir George Grey advocated a South African confederation including the Orange Free State for the sake of frontier stability and free trade, he was censured and recalled. In the late 1860s and early 1870s, however, the Colonial Office became more receptive to proposals for confederation. The policy of confederation pursued by Carnarvon from 1874 might be seen as nothing more than a continuation of the policy of the previous Liberal administration. But this would be a mistake. Carnarvon's confederation policy represents not continuity but a sharp break with the past.[1]

The policy of the Liberal administration of 1868 to 1874 was essentially anti-imperial. Britain's industrial supremacy and commitment to free trade made the costs of empire seem greater than its benefits. The Liberals were inclined to hasten what they saw as the inevitable independence of the colonies of settlement. They encouraged them to become self-governing and militarily self-sufficient so that the expensive imperial garrisons could be withdrawn. It was to facilitate such a withdrawal that the Liberal government wished to see the South African colonies and republics combined into a stronger self-sufficient whole.

These were not Carnarvon's motives. He wished to reverse the Liberal policy of withdrawing redcoats from self-governing dominions[2] and, although the War Office still favoured the reduction of the imperial garrison in South Africa, the Colonial Office under Carnarvon was strongly opposed to any such move.[3] Treasury parsimony was something that Carnarvon and his Colonial Office staff always had to take into account, but they saw it as an obstacle to be surmounted, not a goal to be attained. When the news came of Shepstone's annexation of the Transvaal, Robert Herbert, the Permanent Under-Secretary at the Colonial Office, wrote to his cousin Carnarvon: 'ask Sir S.N. [Stafford Northcote, the Chancellor of the Exchequer] for a quarter of a million immediately after you have read him the telegram!'[4] The view has been expressed that the annexation of the Transvaal 'was intended to be a step towards withdrawal from responsibility for the internal affairs of South Africa',[5] which in itself has a somewhat paradoxical ring to it. But in fact Carnarvon and his associates envisaged the northern frontier of the new confederation as extending beyond the Transvaal to the Zambezi and the Portuguese lines on the east and west coasts,[6] which makes it surely impossible to believe that this was simply a continuation of the Liberals' cost-cutting exercise.

Another line of argument in the historical literature is that the strategic importance of the Cape required confederation. Robinson and Gallagher wrote that 'supremacy in southern Africa seemed indispensable to British statesmen of the Eighteen seventies and eighties for much the same reason as it had to Pitt', and that the

> control of the naval base at Simon's Bay and the south African shores . . . required the exclusion of other European Powers and control of the potentially hostile republics inland. These were chief among the arguments which moved Carnarvon and his colleagues to confederate south Africa.

This line was followed by Goodfellow, the author of the standard work on Carnarvon's confederation policy. He wrote that confederation was designed 'to erect from the chaos of the subcontinent a strong, self-governing, and above all loyal Dominion behind the essential bastion at Simon's Bay'. Goodfellow was well aware of the expansive nature of Carnarvon's designs – it was he, indeed, who first drew attention to them – but he attempted to accommodate them within his explanation by saying that 'the southernmost sixth of the African continent would have to be firmly British before the Secretary of State could rest from anxiety about Simon's Bay'.[7]

There is no doubt about the continuing strategic importance of the Cape, even after the opening of the Suez Canal in 1869. There is also no doubt about Carnarvon's concern with the naval defence of the empire. He expressed anxiety about the poor state of Simonstown's defences. Some historians feel that there must have been some connection between these concerns and his confederation policy. But the suggested connection proves, upon closer examination, to be both implausible and unsupported by evidence, while there is some evidence which tells directly against the hypothesis.[8] Goodfellow was obliged to admit that there was no particular threat to the Cape sea route in the 1870s to which confederation might be seen as a response.[9] Did the southernmost sixth of the African continent really have to be British to ensure British control of Simonstown? Was not the Cape Colony sufficient? And surely the dominion behind Simonstown would become less rather than more loyal by incorporating within its electorate the burghers of the ex-republics? This danger was pointed out to Carnarvon by Froude, for whom Simonstown and Table Bay were the only imperial interests in South Africa. Carnarvon did not disagree with Froude about this danger, but he pressed on with his plans nonetheless.[10] The only member of the British Parliament who alluded to the naval importance of the Cape when debating South African confederation, a former Lieutenant-Governor of Bengal, used it as an argument *against* confederation on the very reasonable grounds that 'it was not likely that in the case of this confederation being brought about, it would be English either in nationality or in sentiment'.[11] In the absence of any evidence that Carnarvon's motives were those attributed to him by Robinson and Gallagher and by Goodfellow, it is more plausible to argue that confederation was desired despite, rather than because of, the strategic importance of the Cape.

A reason for confederation Carnarvon often gave was the need for a 'uniform native policy'. This was arbitrarily dismissed by Goodfellow as a 'smokescreen' to conceal his 'true intentions', but de Kiewiet took it more seriously, interpreting it in liberal and humanitarian terms. Carnarvon, he believed, was hoping 'to find some more ample place for the native population', and trying to 'win for the natives a higher and better place in the future of the land they lived in'. The failure of confederation, he wrote, was a 'failure of high motives and worthy ends' – a 'failure to do anything to stem the torrent that was rushing the native population into political helplessness and economic hopelessness'.[12]

The evidence for this view consists of statements by Carnarvon and provisions of the South Africa Act of 1877, which might more accurately be interpreted as evidence for the need to mollify British public opinion or allay stirrings of conscience. The evidence against de Kiewiet's view is much stronger.[13] A confederation with its northern border on the Zambezi implied an end to the remaining independent southern African kingdoms and chiefdoms, and Africans were to get little in return. It is a remarkable fact that the constitution drawn up by white South Africans in 1909 was more liberal as regards the franchise than the constitution drafted by the Colonial Office under Carnarvon, since the latter failed to provide any representation for Africans in the federal legislature.[14] The draft bill provided that the existing franchise was to be retained in the provincial legislatures, although some senior members of the Colonial Office favoured limiting the non-white franchise in the Cape by means of an educational test or even explicitly on grounds of race.[15] The draft bill provoked a protest from the Aborigines Protection Society.[16] More remarkably, the Cape government itself protested at the retrograde native policy they believed the imperial government, under the influence of Froude, intended to foist upon them.[17] If Carnarvon was really seeking a higher and better place for Africans, it is strange that he should have relied on the advice of Froude, a man who regretted the abolition of slavery, admired the republics' native policy and urged the introduction of some form of forced labour in South Africa. Froude did not conceal his opinions from Carnarvon, who valued his advice.[18]

To a considerable degree, in fact, the Colonial Office intended to achieve uniformity in native policy by adopting elements of republican policy. It was believed in the Colonial Office that republican policy had been much ameliorated and that further amelioration was possible. On the other hand the opinion was expressed that 'the Cape may perhaps go too far in an opposite direction'.[19] A confidential memorandum drawn up in the Colonial Office for the information of the cabinet expressed the hope that the Boers would 'relieve the Kafirs from their legal disabilities in respect of property and personal rights', in return for the benefits such as cheap railway loans that would follow from 'British connection and support'. But it continued:

> on the other hand, there are points in the Boer policy towards the natives which are not unworthy of our attentive consideration . . . The Dutch make the Kafirs work; they do not allow them to squat and multiply in savage sloth. Undoubtedly a Kafir should be compelled, as the Dutch compel him, to work.[20]

Some idea of what sort of 'uniform native policy' Carnarvon had in mind is gained from his request to Froude to suggest 'a common system of treatment which shall be clear of the reproach of a system of servitude, and yet shall put that moral screw on the native which is desirable for the safety and interest of all parties'.[21]

It is difficult to see in all this an attempt 'to stem the torrent that was rushing the native population into political helplessness and economic hopelessness'. If anything, it seems to indicate a fear that the 'torrent' was drying up. de Kiewiet, like his mentor W.M. Macmillan, was a defender of the imperial factor as a counterweight to settler rapacity. Such a view came naturally to Macmillan, writing of an age when the imperial government intervened to emancipate the slaves, protect the Khoisan from exploitation and reverse the annexation of Xhosa territory.[22] It becomes much more artificial when applied to the 1870s. The springs of philanthropy were flowing much less strongly by this time. The slaves had long since been emancipated throughout the British empire and the subsequent decline of the West Indian plantation economy produced some disillusionment with the results of emancipation. Partly as a result there was a noticeable hardening of racial attitudes. Besides slavery, a great stimulus to philanthropy in the early nineteenth century had been the decline in indigenous populations in the Americas, Australasia and elsewhere, in the face of European colonisation. It was sometimes assumed, feared, or hoped that the Bantu-speaking people of South Africa would follow the example of the Khoisan and diminish in the face of the European advance, and that South Africa would become literally a 'white man's country'. By the 1870s it was clearly apparent and widely commented on that this had not happened and was not going to happen.[23] The Colonial Office in the 1870s was much more impressed with the precariousness than with the oppressiveness of white rule in South Africa. This was the lesson Carnarvon learned from the Langalibalele affair in Natal. Froude was not his only adviser who was explicitly anti-philanthropic. Wolseley described the policy that had led to the Langalibalele affair in Natal as 'dictated by high philanthropic sentiments'. A Colonial Office memorandum stated that British policy had 'sacrificed our safety and our commerce to uninformed theory and sentiment'.[24]

In more recent explanations of confederation, in contrast to the Robinson and Gallagher thesis of continuity, the emphasis has been on discontinuity. In place of an argument for consistent imperial policy for unchanging strategic reasons, recent writers on the subject have emphasized the changes brought about by the mineral discoveries.[25] This reflects a sense of discontinuity felt by contemporaries – surely a point in favour of this view. Bishop Colenso predicted that the discovery of diamonds would cause South Africa to be 'revolutionized'.[26] By 1876 the general manager of the Standard Bank could comment that there was 'a general spirit of enterprise abroad, which some ten years ago would hardly have been considered possible of such a country'.[27] South Africa was no longer the economic backwater it had been. Diamonds, moreover, had been discovered in the most remote and backward part of the country. This, as a Colonial Office memorandum of 1875 noted, was likely to produce political as well as economic effects, political problems as well as economic benefits. Referring to the Sand River and Bloemfontein Conventions, it stated:

> It was not then supposed that any political importance would attach to the small and isolated communities thus contemptuously abandoned in the interior, and it was predicted that for years to come European colonization would find an ample field for its energy in cultivating to their highest capacity the terraced shores of the Southern Ocean. Since that time mineral wealth of unprecedented and, indeed, untold extent has been discovered in the interior, dissipating those anticipations, and showing that the most active field of industry and the centre of political importance are no longer to be sought in the southern country.[28]

Recent writers have given plausible reasons why the new conditions required political unity. It is less clear why it was Carnarvon who pressed ahead so decisively with confederation, and persisted in it despite apathy and even opposition in South Africa. The subject needs to be looked at not only from the South African end. The British context within which Carnarvon operated requires examination. The 1870s were also a period of change in Britain, not only in the material sphere but also in the sphere of ideas: it was a period of anxious doubts and questionings about Britain's place in the world. It is when South Africa's problems are viewed within this mental framework that Carnarvon's aims become clearer.[29]

Britain in the 1870s

Events in Europe in the late 1860s gave rise to a growing feeling in Britain that the country was not playing the role it should as a great power. The balance of power in Europe was changing, as Prussia defeated Denmark, Austria and finally France itself, and the German empire was formed. Britain had exercised no influence during this 'German Revolution', as Disraeli called it:[30] peace, retrenchment, reform, and what might nowadays be called appeasement were the watchwords of the Liberal administration. When Russia reneged on its treaty obligations, Gladstone was content with a face-saving manoeuvre.[31] Britain's isolation and passivity was noted on the Continent and produced in Britain itself a flood of criticism of the government's 'Pharisaical neutrality', its 'pulpit good advice', its 'peace at any price principles', and 'the doctrine of non-intervention, as interpreted by Manchester', or, in short, in the vogue word of the day, the 'effacement' of England.[32] Carnarvon expressed his disquiet thus:

> In continental phraseology, we are 'effaced' from the roll of great powers, and it is not only known that we have no means of fighting, but it is thought we will not fight. Nor can we complain of it as unreasonable if foreigners inquire whether those who showed such unmistakable reluctance to support Savoy and Denmark, and Luxembourg and Turkey, would be very eager to compromise themselves on behalf of Switzerland, or Holland, or Belgium.

Such a national policy, Carnarvon believed, was not only dishonourable, but dangerous.

> Heavily weighted in the race of commercial competition; consuming with improvidence the resources on which much of commerce depends; loved by none, envied by many; with enormous wealth to tempt, and with little power to defend; undermined by a pauperism which is growing up by the side of and in deadly contrast to our riches; with power passing from the class which had been used to rule and to face political dangers, and which had brought the nation with honour unsullied through former struggles, into the hands of the lower classes, uneducated, untrained to the use of political rights, and swayed by demagogues, we talk as if Providence had ordained that our Government should always borrow at 3 per cent, and trade must come to us, because we live in a foggy little island set in a boisterous sea.[33]

As this statement suggests, underlying the disquiet at the diplomatic 'effacement' of Britain was the knowledge that the era of Britain's undisputed supremacy in the economic sphere was drawing to a close. Britain's aloofness, pacifism, complacency – and its loss of interest in colonies – were all based on the commanding lead in industry and commerce it had enjoyed in the mid-nineteenth century. As other countries industrialized and as their commitment to free trade lessened so this lead was eroded and doubts and anxieties grew. Froude in 1870 attributed the prevalent indifference towards the empire to the apparently endless prosperity that Britain was then enjoying, but asked 'whether our confidence is justified; whether the late rate of increase in our trade is really likely to continue'.[34] Others warned that outlets in the colonies might be needed if Britain's pre-eminence in manufacture passed away.[35]

Italy and Germany were both unified by 1870. The United States had fought a great war to preserve its unity (and had subsequently retained most of its high wartime tariffs) and was expanding rapidly westwards. Russia was expanding eastwards and southwards. In these circumstances the Gladstonian belief that England's strength lay in England and not in her empire appeared increasingly implausible, and Gladstone's supposed policy of dismembering the empire came to seem an act of consummate folly. That dismemberment was his policy appeared to be confirmed by the Colonial Secretary Lord Granville's recall of British garrisons from the self-governing colonies at a time when they could ill afford to lose them, by the peremptory and even hostile tone of Granville's despatches, and by his and Gladstone's evasive replies to the charge that they wished to get rid of the colonies.[36]

The protest against this policy or supposed policy of dismemberment (and the supposition was not as mistaken as it has sometimes been represented)[37] began among the colonists themselves. A series of noisy protest meetings attended by colonists, ex-colonists and Englishmen with colonial connections was held in London in late 1869 and 1870 and aroused much comment in the press. The attention of the public was focused on the empire to an extent unprecedented in recent years. The protest was taken up in Parliament, a campaign in which Carnarvon took a prominent part. The belief or hope was stimulated that the empire was not destined for certain disintegration but that it might be given more institutional coherence and become an additional source of strength to Great Britain.[38] Carnarvon attacked the folly of attempting 'to abandon these sources of possible – and if possible then of incalculable – strength, and to allow this country to subside into the position of a second Holland'.[39] He asked: 'Heavily pressed as we are in the race of international competition, are our fortunes so well assured that we can afford to throw away the affection, the loyalty and the warm feeling of the colonists as if they were merely so much idle lumber?'[40] Much of the protest came from the Liberals,[41] but Disraeli adroitly captured the rising imperialist sentiment for the Conservative party. The imperial programme adopted by the Conservatives was not intended to be one of wholesale annexation; rather, it was a policy of attempting to bind the self-governing colonies of settlement closer to the mother country. Consolidation, not expansion, was its watchword. Self-government should have been granted, said Disraeli, 'as part of a great policy of Imperial consolidation'. His proposals in this connection were vague, but they included 'an Imperial tariff', securities for the continued access to the unappropriated land of the colonies by emigrants from England, reciprocal defence arrangements and 'the institution of some representative council in the Metropolis'.[42]

Schemes for imperial federation proliferated in the 1870s.[43] Carnarvon had little faith in such blueprints, but as a practical statesman he believed that opportunities should be taken as they arose to work towards the goal 'which may yet in the fullness of time be realised, of a great English-speaking community united together in a peaceful confederation, too powerful to be molested by any nation, and too powerful and too generous, I hope, to molest any weaker State'.[44] When in 1877 he introduced his South African Confederation bill into Parliament he stated: 'It is possible that Confederation is only one stage in the political journey of the Empire and that it may even lead in the course of time to a still closer union.' He also said there had been a 'remarkable tendency' towards 'aggregation' in recent years, citing the examples of Italy, Germany and the United States of America.[45]

When the Conservatives won the election of 1874 Carnarvon became Secretary of State for the Colonies. He was an ambitious man and hoped to make his mark. He had been Secretary of State for the Colonies for eight months during 1866 and 1867 and had thus presided over the later stages of the confederation of the Canadian colonies. Ambition to repeat this success probably helps to explain why he was inclined to see the solution of South Africa's problems in confederation.

The first year of the new Conservative administration was marked by British advance in West Africa, Malaya and the South Pacific. But this cannot be seen as the implementation of a new policy of imperialism. The groundwork for these advances had been prepared by the previous Liberal administration in response to local problems; the extension of British influence stopped short of formal sovereignty in West Africa and Malaya; and Carnarvon plainly disliked the necessity of annexing Fiji.[46] The Conservatives' imperial policy was not one of territorial aggrandizement but of consolidating the existing empire of white settlement. Elsewhere, like the Liberals, they wished, ostensibly at least, for nothing more than a 'fair field and no favour' for British trade. Perhaps it might be more accurate to say that they wished to preserve the advantages of the informal hegemony that Britain possessed through her old-established trade links and her influence with indigenous rulers. This 'imperialism of free trade', as Gallagher and Robinson called it, had the advantage of avoiding trouble and expense. It had the disadvantage of being insufficient to prevent the intrusion of other European powers. Britain had come to regard its virtual commercial monopoly in sub-saharan Africa[47] as its right. But as other countries industrialized, and as the deepening depression of the 1870s caused competition to intensify, so this virtual monopoly appeared to be coming under threat. The ancient claims of the Portuguese had long been a source of irritation. The claims of the Boer republics to be independent civilized states and to be recognized as such by European powers, were a potential threat to Britain's paramountcy in southern Africa. The original purpose of a self-governing confederation, as I will argue in the next section, was to solve immediate South African problems. It was also intended to make a contribution towards imperial consolidation, and, one might add, to make Carnarvon's reputation as an imperial statesman. But it came to be seen as a means of preventing Britain from being excluded from African territory without the necessity of bringing it under direct British rule.[48]

South African Problems

Two major South African problems confronted Carnarvon when he became responsible for the colonies: the diamond fields dispute and the Langalibalele affair.

The location of South Africa's diamond deposits in the arid region north of the Cape Colony seemed calculated to multiply the effects of their discovery and spread them over the widest area. Agriculturally uninviting and sparsely populated, this was a region of indefinite boundaries. The discovery of diamonds caused them to become disputed boundaries. The sparse population resulted in labour being drawn from all over southern Africa, from Natal and the eastern Transvaal, and even from as far afield as Zimbabwe and Mozambique. The aridity of the region to which thousands of fortune-seekers flocked stimulated agricultural production over a wider area than would otherwise have been the case. The distance of the diamond fields from the nearest port stimulated the transport industry, and the aridity of much of the intervening terrain, with its shortage of grass for the increasing number of trek-oxen, encouraged the building of railways. All these activities increased the demand for labour, which, in a country where most people still retained access to land, led initially to high wages, but led later to forceful measures to shake loose the labour needed.

Had the geology of South Africa permitted the discovery of diamonds near, say, Port Elizabeth, the effects of their discovery would have been far fewer. The diamond-mining industry would have constituted something of an economic enclave, connected with the international economy, but largely insulated from the rest of South Africa, the political disunity of which would have been irrelevant. The discovery of diamonds would not have caused any border disputes, railways would not have been necessary, a larger proportion of necessities including even food could have been imported, the demand for labour would consequently have been less, and this fact, together with the existence of a relatively dense and already partially proletarianized population in the region, would have made labour supply much less of a problem.

It was the diamond fields dispute that first led Carnarvon to suggest confederation. The High Commissioner, Sir Henry Barkly, had annexed the diamond fields in 1871 at the urging of interested eastern Cape merchants and politicians and over the protests of the Orange Free State. Molteno's western-dominated ministry then refused to take it over, thus leaving it in Britain's hands as the separate colony of Griqualand West. This was a source of great irritation to the Colonial Office, which had given Barkly permission to annex the territory only on condition that it was incorporated into the Cape. The change of government in Britain made no difference to the attitude of the Colonial Office because, as we have seen,[49] it was no part of Conservative policy to bring further territory under direct British rule. To make matters worse, Barkly and Richard Southey, the Lieutenant-Governor of Griqualand West, with the support of petitions from the merchants of Kimberley and Hopetown and the Port Elizabeth Chamber of Commerce, went on to urge the British annexation too of 'Batlapinia', the territory to the north of Griqualand West, to prevent the ZAR from expanding across the Keate award line and disrupting Griqualand West's trade and labour supply routes.[50] Sir Robert Herbert, the Permanent Under-Secretary at the Colonial Office, described this as an 'even less inviting annexational prospect' than the annexation of Fiji. It was this situation that led Carnarvon to ask 'whether some form of federation might not solve many of the existing difficulties'.[51] He told Barkly that he recognized that 'the annexation of the Batlapin district . . . might be a solution of some awkward and pressing questions . . . but I cannot undertake further annexations with Fiji and the G[old] coast on my hands . . .' He preferred to achieve his ends, he said, by a 'conciliatory and friendly policy as regards the Dutch states' and mentioned the possibility of forming a 'closer connection' with the Transvaal.[52] The same applied to the border dispute with the Orange Free State. Herbert wrote that confederation would be the means 'of putting Griqualand West back into the Orange state, without surrendering the territory from under the British flag'.[53] Carnarvon wrote to Froude, whom he sent to represent Britain at the confederation conference in Cape Town, that if President Brand of the Orange Free State

> comes into Confederation, there need not be any great difficulty, as far as I can see, in making over such parts of Griqua-Land to the Orange Free States [sic] as may be desirable. If it is all a part of the English Empire, it will not signify whether one province or another has the disputed territory; so, too, as regards the Transvaal; if they will confederate they may have a great deal of the Batlapin and Baralong territory.

Carnarvon made it clear that territorial concessions could be made only in return for confederation. The Transvaal, he wrote

> cannot be allowed to annex Zulu-land, as they seem half inclined to do. This would make them independent of us, and we must not throw away a single card in this game. Nothing must be given up by us except for a clear equivalent. But both with Brand and with the Transvaal, a friendly adjustment of boundaries may be quite possible if they come into Conference.[54]

The Cape Town conference never took place, so what Wolseley candidly described as a 'bribe' of Zulu territory had to be made in writing, suitably 'smothered up' in more respectable expressions.[55]

These statements make it clear that one of the purposes of confederation was to settle border disputes by abolishing borders or by rendering them merely provincial. A related purpose was to bring territory under the British flag without

Britain herself having to assume the trouble and expense of ruling it. It was not often stated explicitly that confederation meant the end of independent African states, probably because it was felt to be self-evident, but these statements clearly imply that African territory was regarded as available for the British government to dispose of as it saw fit.

One reason why it was considered desirable that territory should come under the British flag was the need to prevent the flow of labour from being obstructed. This applied not only to the northern route through the territory of the BaThlaping ('Batlapinia'); it applied to the republics as well. The burghers of the republics resented the diversion of labour from their farms to the diamond fields by the attraction of higher wages and the opportunity to buy guns. They took to intercepting Africans crossing republican territory in order to press them into service or seize their weapons. This led Africans to travel in large armed bands. It was this state of affairs that caused the Liberal Under-Secretary for the Colonies to reverse his earlier opinion on the wisdom of the Bloemfontein Convention of 1854: 'every day shows in a stronger light the mistake that was made in abandoning the Orange River territory'.[56] Confederation would end this anarchy and enable the supply of labour to be regulated in a calm and rational manner by the new central government.

Natal was also dependent on migrant labour, which was also liable to be obstructed, in this case by Zulu and Portuguese as well as by Boers. For this reason, among others, Shepstone desired the British control over the interior that confederation would bring. But whether Carnarvon favoured confederation as a means of facilitating migrant labour to Natal, as Etherington has argued, is much more doubtful.[57] As we have seen,[58] there were fundamental differences between Shepstone's and Carnarvon's views on the subject of native administration in Natal. Shepstone wanted to avoid undue pressure on Africans, to secure a 'safety-valve' beyond the borders of the colony for those squeezed off the land, and to facilitate migrant labour from across the borders as a means of mitigating the labour shortage. Carnarvon's response to the Langalibalele affair was to push for direct rule and firmer control of the black population. Even after Shepstone's personal explanations, Carnarvon remained dubious about his proposals for a 'safety-valve',[59] and he was quite explicitly opposed to Natal remaining reliant on migrant labour from the north: 'with good wages & treatment the Natal colonists ought not to need foreign labour'.[60] Migrant labour might be unavoidable in the sparsely populated Griqualand West but it seemed unnecessary in the relatively densely populated Natal.

The labour shortage in Natal, however, was not simply the result of low wages and poor treatment: it was the result of a lack of control. This is what Froude and Wolseley impressed upon Carnarvon. The insecurity of white rule in Natal, the labour shortage and economic stagnation were all closely interlinked. And what was true of Natal was also true to some degree of all the territories beyond the borders of the Cape.

Far from dying out in the face of a stronger race and a higher civilization,[61] the black population of Natal was growing. This growth was sometimes reconciled with the expectation of its decline by postulating, in Carnarvon's words, 'an inexhaustible swarm of warlike Native Tribes, pouring down from the North'.[62] A Colonial Office memorandum similarly stated that beyond the outposts of colonization there were 'hundreds of millions of inhabitants, who, ever since we have record of them, have always been pushing southwards, impelled by causes and objects which are but imperfectly understood'. This memorandum was drawn up by Edward Fairfield to explain the Colonial Office's South African policy to the cabinet. It continued:

> It is this continuous pressure southwards which imparts the most formidable aspect to native affairs in South Africa. In other quarters of the globe where colonists and natives have met as rival occupiers of the soil, the latter were limited in numbers, and when they dwindled before the destructive agencies of civilization, their places were not supplied, and the native question in time settled itself by the disappearance of the natives; but in South Africa the native question will not so be disposed of. The number of natives with whom we have to deal is increasing and practically unlimited . . . The native danger lies chiefly on the side of Natal and the South African Republic . . . The recent affair of Langalibalele brought out with formidable distinctness the precarious position of civilization and British rule in Natal . . . The disagreements of the South African Republic with its native neighbours, chiefly the Zulus, are numerous and bitter . . . It was, then, primarily, with a view to lay the foundation of a sound system of self-protection against native danger, and to shift the burden of that protection on the right shoulders, that Lord Carnarvon moved in the question of Confederation.

Fairfield also stated that 'the most immediately urgent reason for a general union is the formidable character of the native question, and the importance of a uniform, wise and strong policy in dealing with it'.[63]

The idea that Africans were migrating southwards seems to have been derived from white Natal ideology. Colonists liked to believe that Natal had been virtually empty when the first whites arrived and that the existing black population consisted of refugees from the Zulu kingdom, who had no ancestral right to the land they occupied but who did have an obligation to work for their protectors. These ideas are reflected in the statements of Froude and Wolseley. Froude wrote of blacks who 'swarm over the frontier in increasing numbers' and who 'will not work' for the colonists.[64] Wolseley stated that the black population of Natal had grown by 350 per cent, chiefly as a result of 'the large influx of Kafirs from all the neighbouring States, especially from Zululand'. For such an immigrant 'Natal is a sort of earthly paradise, where he can live in slothful ease, almost entirely unsubjected to any claim upon his labour'. If the present mild policy was persisted in, warned Wolseley, 'the whole province will become fully occupied by natives, who, learning of their own strength, will not long brook a European rule over them'. The past generation regarded the British as protectors, but 'to the young men of today we appear in the light of alien rulers, who tax them for occupying districts and farms which they have learned to regard as their own'.

Meanwhile, said Wolseley, the white population had remained stationary, and its military power had declined, since so many men had left for the diamond and gold fields that the proportion of men to women had decreased considerably, and those that were left were no longer expert shots owing to the disappearance of game. 'On the part of the whites there is an ever growing sense of insecurity; they hesitate to invest largely in a colony which threatens soon to pass altogether into the hands of the black man.' Many talked of emigrating. With this despatch Wolseley sent a private letter in which he said the despatch 'in no way overstated my feeling as to the insecurity of our tenure of power here'.[65]

Carnarvon shared Wolseley's views on the insecurity of white rule in Natal and the consequent economic stagnation. He told the House of Lords:

> There has not in my opinion been that control over Native affairs which is required by the public interest. The result is that there has been a stagnation, so to speak, of many of the industrial interests of the Colony. There has been – as I think Sir Garnet Wolseley pointed out to the Legislature – that want of internal security which leads in the long run, to a want also of external confidence – which hinders emigration and which prevents the real development of the Colony.[66]

Reform was 'essential to the prosperity of the colony in its development'; without it 'you would end by having a black colony, which means decay of its resources, the absence of prosperity, and general falling away of its means of subsistence'.[67]

Confederation would strengthen white rule. Speaking of South Africa in general on another occasion he stated that confederation

> would certainly create strength, diminish the risk which is inseparable from the existence of these great native tribes, preserve the European communities from sudden panics, and tend at least to tranquillize the native mind, because the natives would see in times of disturbances that there was little chance of their being able to combine for mischief. And thus the ultimate result would be to raise and improve and consolidate with the European communities the native races.

Firmer control over the native population was necessary simply in the interests of tranquillity; but it seems clear from the statements by Carnarvon, Wolseley and Froude quoted above that it was also regarded as necessary for economic development.

The diamond-diggers of Griqualand West were notorious for obtaining labour by supplying Africans with guns. This was, said Carnarvon, 'a dangerous form of wages'.[68] But what other means could be found to obtain sufficient supplies of labour?

Froude was quite explicitly in favour of coercion. A loyal and prosperous confederation was only possible, he wrote to Carnarvon from South Africa, if

Britain would 'permit a *system of forced labour* to be established here'. He added that he believed that 'the Natives would in the long run be happier under such a policy and certainly would have a better chance of becoming useful industrious men'.[69] When Froude visited the Transvaal in 1874 he found, contrary to his original expectations, that the Africans were just as 'idle' and out of control as in Natal. In a statement rich in unintended historical irony he told the British Secretary of State for the Colonies that unless 'you can make up your mind to introduce some system of *apprenticeship* by which the future generation of natives can be educated in industrious habits . . . the Transvaal . . . will prove a perilous acquisition'.[70] We have already quoted[71] the Colonial Office memorandum of January 1876 stating that 'a Kafir should be compelled, as the Dutch compel him, to work'. But Carnarvon knew that the most they could hope for was a 'moral screw', which would be `clear of the reproach of a system of servitude'.

If bribing Africans with the weapons of war and forcing them into a system of servitude were both excluded, what else was there? Proletarianization was another possibility. Schemes were put forward calculated to make it more difficult for African tenants to retain their direct access to land. Under Wolseley's direction one of his aides, Major (later General Sir William) Butler, drew up a scheme for the compulsory lease or sale of absentee-owned land to white immigrants. Wolseley recommended that Africans squatting on crown land be charged a rent.[72] Carnarvon wanted communal land tenure in Natal to be replaced by individual tenure, a change likely to yield a certain proportion of landless people.[73] He told Wolseley's successor that he wished to see some scheme 'under which the proprietors of land unoccupied, or occupied only by Kafirs, may be required to grant leases on reasonable terms to European settlers'.[74] The African occupants of such land, who though often called 'squatters' were in fact legal rent-paying tenants, would presumably have to work for the new leaseholders.

Besides creating an adequate labour force, confederation would promote economic growth in other ways. Economic growth was quite clearly one of its chief purposes. A Colonial Office memorandum pointed to the disadvantages of disunity: 'European immigration and capital flow slowly into countries under small and isolated Governments, whose financial solvency is questionable, and where there is no adequate security for property or confidence in prudent legislation.'[75] Carnarvon emphasised South Africa's great resources and their undeveloped state in existing conditions. He said he wanted greater unity in order 'to see the development of those great resources which South Africa possesses'.[76] His hope was that South Africa would be enabled 'to combine her resources, and to develop the prosperity which the gifts of Nature and her geographical position enable her to command, but to which, while divided into separate factions, she cannot attain'.[77] Confederation would mean that

many public works which are now neither undertaken nor dreamt of would become possible. That which is not the business of any one individual member of the family politic is the business of none; and considering her great resources . . . it must be owned that in this part of the race of civilisation South Africa is somewhat . . . in arrear.[78]

Confederation was intended to be South Africa's great leap forward. Sir William Butler recalled: 'How eager we were at our writings, our proposals, our plans for colonisation, for native government, better land division and tenures, extensions of railways and telegraphs, and half a dozen other matters – so hopeful about it all.'[79]

Economic development might be expected to be of benefit to all in the long run, but it is clear that in this case it was to be achieved by bringing pressure to bear on Africans to do what they would prefer not to do: to work for white employers rather than only for themselves. As we have seen,[80] the implications of confederation were inimical to African independence. So an independent African kingdom whose King forbade his subjects to work for white employers was surely quite incompatible with the proposed new order.

The Cape Town Conference, 1875

Since confederation was clearly intended to benefit the whites of South Africa, one might expect them to have eagerly embraced it. It is understandable that the burghers of the republics should have valued their independence more than the prospect of economic progress of which they might not be the chief beneficiaries. But even in Natal the Lieutenant-Governor described the 'preponderating feeling' towards confederation as one of 'apathy and indifference',[81] and the attempt to implement it foundered chiefly on the opposition of the Cape government. Carnarvon's policy won support from certain interest groups in South Africa, particularly in Natal and in the eastern Cape, but what they were really supporting was the British expansion that they saw it as representing, expansion which was calculated to benefit their trading, prospecting, investing and speculating activities in the interior. As Sir Henry Barkly said of the eastern Cape members of the legislature who urged the annexation of Griqualand West, they wished to 'employ British bayonets to make their fortunes'.[82] But while Carnarvon's South African supporters wished to use Britain's power and wealth to further their interests, Carnarvon wished to use South African revenues and capacity for effective administration as a means of developing southern Africa and keeping it open to British trade and enterprise, without Britain itself having to bear all the necessary responsibility and expense. Both Carnarvon and his supporters wished to use each other. Though superficially the same, their aims were fundamentally contradictory and incompatible. Since the Cape Colony was the wealthiest state with the largest white population, the contradiction found expression in conflict between Carnarvon and the Cape government.

Lord Carnarvon's first attempt to implement his confederation scheme was to call a conference of South African states and colonies to be held in Cape Town. In a despatch dated 4 May 1875[83] to the High Commissioner, Sir Henry Barkly, he pointed to the disadvantages of disunity: the border and territorial disputes, the absence of a common policy in respect of such things as the trade in arms and ammunition, and above all the lack of white unity in the face of the native population. This, he wrote, contained 'the germs of a great danger', and also resulted in the diversion of resources to control and defence which ought to be used in furthering the material progress of the country. In the first draft of this despatch confederation had been a specific item on the conference agenda and had been described as 'over-shadowing them all'.[84] In the final version it was given the more modest status of something that might arise in the course of discussion, in which case, Carnarvon said, the imperial government would provide the most 'cordial assistance' towards its achievement.

To Carnarvon the advantages of confederation were so obvious that he could not believe that they would not be apparent to all. The republics might have been expected to cherish their independence, and the acrimonious and still unresolved territorial disputes arising out of the Keate award and the annexation of the diamond fields might have been expected to have instilled in them a heightened aversion to the British flag. But far from seeing these disputes as an obstacle to confederation, Carnarvon saw them as a means by which it might be brought about: the republics were to be lured into confederation by generous border settlements, which would not endanger British interests once the whole country was under the British flag.[85]

Carnarvon did not anticipate the opposition his proposal immediately encountered, nor the quarter from which it came. J.A. Froude, whom he had appointed as the imperial government's representative, was shocked to discover when he arrived at Cape Town on 19 June 1875 that the Cape government, supported by its Parliament, refused to have anything to do with Carnarvon's proposed conference. Prime Minister J.C. Molteno and his colleagues were not opposed in principle to confederation, but they saw no urgent necessity for it, and envisaged its coming about by the gradual absorption of the outlying colonies and republics into the Cape. They suspected Carnarvon's scheme of being an attempt to foist the responsibility and expense of defending the rest of the country on to the shoulders of the Cape. They were jealous of the responsible government they had attained in 1872 and felt that Carnarvon was ignoring it by initiating the proposal for a conference without consulting them first, by deciding the number of delegates the Cape should have, and by naming the persons who should represent it. Above all, they saw the designation of the Prime Minister as the representative of only half the colony, while the leader of the separatist movement in the eastern Cape was designated as representative of the other half, as a gross and mischievous interference in a most delicate aspect of the colony's internal affairs.[86]

The situation confronting Froude on his arrival aroused all his considerable combative instincts. He assumed the role of leader of the opposition to the Molteno ministry, and in a series of speeches in the country (so he told Carnarvon) he made 'the valleys ring with cheers for Lord Carnarvon', 'set Port Elizabeth on fire', and set Grahamstown 'off like a rocket'.[87] He succeeded in arousing public opinion sufficiently to oblige Molteno to recall Parliament. But then Carnarvon, assuming (on Froude's advice) that victory was certain and that the Molteno ministry was doomed, announced the removal of the proposed conference from Cape Town to London. This ensured Molteno's survival by enabling him to withdraw his motion condemning Froude's unconstitutional agitation. And Molteno also succeeded in persuading Parliament to vote down an opposition motion to send delegates to the London conference.[88]

The failure of Carnarvon's attempt to hold a conference in South Africa might have discouraged a less determined or more realistic politician. But Carnarvon was encouraged by Froude, in whom he had the most extraordinary faith, to believe that, despite everything, confederation was on the brink of achievement. Froude in his more sober moments had grave doubts about even the desirability of confederation, which he felt would weaken Britain's hold over the Cape naval bases. But the Cape's opposition turned him into a violent and uncritical partisan of Carnarvon's scheme. He assured the latter that conciliation of the republics would cause them to 'agree to anything that you wish', and that once the obstruction of the 'paltry, mean, worthless knot of Cape Town politicians' was overcome, 'the different States will run together into one like so many drops of quicksilver'.[89]

This advice was utterly unrealistic and misleading. But Carnarvon was completely taken in. 'I consider that I am most fortunate,' he wrote, 'in having such a man as Froude to deal with so difficult a question, very acute in his perception of men and events.'[90] So valuable did he consider Froude's vapourings that he had them printed and bound for easy reference.[91] He also sent some of them to Disraeli. Disraeli returned them without comment, but a little later offered Carnarvon the Viceroyalty of India (technically a demotion) and when he turned that down, the Admiralty (a real promotion). But Carnarvon felt his work in the Colonial Office was too important to relinquish when South African confederation was about to be achieved.[92] Disraeli's reference, only a few months later, to 'Froude's agitation' as one of the 'blunders' of 'little Carnarvon'[93] suggests that when he read Froude's excited outpourings, and Carnarvon's uncritical reception of them, his fine political antennae sensed impending disaster, which he tried to avoid by getting Carnarvon out of the Colonial Office.

Carnarvon was led to believe that it was only through unlucky accidents that he had narrowly missed success in South Africa. A conference in London under his personal supervision would, he believed, have much more chance of success than a conference in Cape Town where everything lay 'at the mercy of intrigue and accident'.[94] He was optimistic that he would be able to win over the Cape Prime Minister and the republican Presidents.

Britain and the Republics, 1874 to 1876

President Brand of the Orange Free State attended the London conference, but there was no representative from the ZAR. Why this was so is a question to which there is no easy answer. Burgers' explanation was that he was not invited, an explanation accepted by his most recent biographer.[95] But behind the absence of a formal invitation lies the long and confused story of Burgers' ambiguous relationship with Britain. Since its ultimate outcome was the annexation of the Transvaal, a crucial step towards the Anglo-Zulu war, this relationship must be briefly explored.

Burgers' ideal was a united South Africa, and there is evidence that what he wanted was a united South Africa under its own flag, independent of Britain.[96] Yet Englishmen who had dealings with him – Froude in 1874, Carnarvon in 1875, Shepstone in 1877 – persistently gained the impression that he sought, or at least was prepared to accept, a union within the British empire.[97] When Froude visited the Transvaal in 1874, Burgers told him of his dream of a united South Africa. Froude tried to find out whether he contemplated an independent united state.

> To my surprise he said he deprecated most earnestly the separation of the Colonies from Great Britain. These were not the days of such states. If Great Britain abandoned South Africa it might fall into the hands of some other Power which would be less tender of Colonial liberties – and I soon found he was thinking of Germany.

Burgers also favoured, so he told Froude, the introduction of British capital and immigrants to the Transvaal to develop its abundant resources.[98]

A few days later Burgers made a public speech in favour of confederation which was evidently capable of being interpreted in the same way. But afterwards the State Secretary, N.J.R. Swart, an Anglophile Hollander, took Froude aside and told him that he was being purposely misled, that Burgers was working for an independent South Africa and that he 'never contemplated for a moment the return of the two Republics under the British flag'. Froude thereupon demanded to know of Burgers whether he advocated a confederation under the British crown or an independent confederation. The president, Froude reported, hesitated and seemed embarrassed. At length he said that he did look forward to a time when South Africa might be independent, and strong enough to sustain its independence; but, with a sigh, he admitted that that time had not yet come and that it might not even be near. He would therefore accept confederation in the only form in which it was attainable. 'He assured me solemnly,' wrote Froude, 'that whenever the question of Confederation came on in a practical form, the word "independence" should never be heard from him.'[99]

Nevertheless, he sought to promote the economic development of the Transvaal (and his remarks to Froude suggest he saw economic strength as necessary to political independence), and he also sought friendly relations with Continental powers. It was to achieve both these ends that he travelled to Europe in April 1875 to negotiate the construction of a railway to the Portuguese possession of Delagoa Bay.

A railway between the ZAR and Delagoa Bay was recognized by all concerned as disastrous to British interests and ambitions in South Africa. Delagoa Bay was potentially the most convenient port for both republics – only the tsetse fly and the absence of a railway prevented it from being so in reality. The Colonial Office learned in April 1876 that the Portuguese foreign minister, in recommending a commercial treaty with the Orange Free State to the Cortes, had told it that 'there is every reason to think that, at a not distant period, the whole of its maritime import and export trade will be carried on through the port in question'.[100] The same would of course be true of the ZAR. This would greatly damage mercantile and government revenue in the Cape and especially in Natal. It would make the ZAR and OFS economically independent of the British colonies, put an end to any hope of confederation and cause the republics and the land beyond to move permanently out of Britain's sphere of influence.[101] Such a railway could not, however, be objected to on any legitimate ground. Representatives of British interests were therefore very ready to attribute nefarious designs to President Burgers.

Barkly, the High Commissioner, an old enemy of Burgers, reported to Carnarvon that the railway scheme was just a blind, pointing out that the line had not even been surveyed. Burgers' real purpose, he asserted (on the flimsiest evidence), was to assist Germany to acquire Delagoa Bay and to put the Transvaal under German protection. The 'intervention of Germany in the affairs of South Africa', he stated, 'would create endless political and commercial complications' and put an end to all hope of confederation.[102] 'I fancy Mr. Froude thought he had converted him to federation under the British flag,' wrote Barkly, who disliked Froude almost as much as he disliked Burgers. He went on to report that on his way through the Cape to board the ship to Europe Burgers had preached what the newspapers called rebellion, described English as a foreign language, and told schoolboys in Uitenhage that amongst them might be found the future Washington of South Africa.

I mention these things not to set Your Lordship against the man, but to put Her Majesty's Government on their guard, as he is a very chameleon in his moods and may to carry his objects pass himself off as a loyal subject of the Queen.[103]

Carnarvon (who trusted Froude and distrusted Barkly) went out of his way to treat Burgers with assiduous courtesy. He showed him his despatch of 4 May 1875 calling a South African conference before it was published. Burgers said that he 'approved of every word', and promised him every assistance.[104] This despatch[105] alluded to confederation only as something that might arise during the proposed conference. There can be no doubt that for Carnarvon confederation was the real purpose of the despatch; but Burgers (naturally enough) took it at its face value. He clearly appreciated Carnarvon's conciliatory approach (so different from the acrimonious dealings he had had with Barkly) and promised him the ZAR would be represented at the conference. He meant this. He wrote to Acting President Joubert that advantage should be taken of the conference to settle border and other disputes. But he also told Joubert that although Carnarvon hinted at confederation in his despatch he did not press for it and that he had 'told him that at the moment we will not think of it'.[106] Carnarvon's impression, however, was that Burgers wished 'to support the policy of a conference & ultimately a Confederation'.[107] These statements are perhaps compatible if 'at the moment' and 'ultimately' are left undefined, but there is no doubt that Carnarvon and Burgers put the emphasis in very different places.

Carnarvon believed that Burgers would leave England with friendlier feelings towards it than those with which he arrived. This was quite possibly correct. The British Minister in Lisbon told Carnarvon that Burgers was enthusiastic in praise of him and his policy.[108] Carnarvon expressed the hope that Burgers would be disposed to see that the true interests of his country lay not in German alliances but in a better and closer relationship with England. Nevertheless, he asked the Foreign Office to investigate Barkly's allegations about Burgers' intrigues with Germany. The British ambassador in Berlin reported that Burgers had indeed written to Bismarck, enclosing a gold medal, which the latter had accepted ('as a votive offering', according to Froude) but that if Burgers were to offer the Transvaal to the protection of Germany it would be refused. The German government, the ambassador was assured, had no desire to acquire Delagoa Bay, the Transvaal or any other colonial territory.[109]

The Colonial Office kept an anxious eye on Burgers' railway proceedings. Burgers failed to raise a loan in London, and had difficulty doing so in Amsterdam, from where he wrote to Joubert of the endless difficulties placed in his path by malicious intrigues from Britain, possibly meaning the Colonial Office.[110] Nevertheless, having eventually succeeded in raising a loan in the Netherlands, he assured the Colonial Office that he would do his utmost to ensure the ZAR was represented at the proposed conference, although he could not promise to be present in person, being about to return to South Africa.[111] When he passed through Cape Town in March 1876 Barkly understood him to say that he would propose to the Volksraad that a representative should be sent. But when he opened the Volksraad he made no reference to the question and Froude received a letter from him to say that in the existing position of affairs he did not think it in the interests of the ZAR to be represented at the conference.[112] In these circumstances it is not surprising that no formal invitation was issued to him.

The reasons for Burgers' change of attitude on reaching the Transvaal can only be surmised. Probably he felt that having (as he supposed) successfully arranged for the construction of an independent outlet to the sea there was no further need to collaborate with Carnarvon and his schemes. This feeling would have been reinforced by the hostility of Transvaal Boer opinion to the idea of confederation, and by the decision to go to war with Sekhukhune, a step that Burgers knew Carnarvon opposed.

Although Burgers continued to express appreciation of Carnarvon's 'kind and liberal policy',[113] Carnarvon henceforth regarded him as untrustworthy and hostile. His changed attitude to the conference, his allegedly anti-English speech in Graaff-Reinet on his way back to the Transvaal, and his declaration of war on the Pedi, all led to Herbert's portentous conclusion that since Burgers was no longer in a 'reasonable frame of mind . . . we shall probably be obliged to despair of any *suaviter in modo* with him'.[114]

Members of the Colonial Office expressed scepticism about the viability of Burgers' railway scheme; nevertheless, the clause in the treaty with Portugal by which the ZAR undertook to 'induce' Africans to work on the construction of the railway was noted as a possible means of intervening to thwart the scheme on ostensibly humanitarian grounds.[115] Even if this scheme failed it was clear that the aspiration to independence would persist as long as Delagoa Bay remained in foreign hands. Pomeroy Colley, after visiting the Transvaal and Delagoa Bay stressed 'the extreme importance – I might almost say necessity – of our acquiring this port, if ever the Colonies and States of South Africa are to be united into one great dominion, and their resources developed'.[116] Carnarvon needed little prompting. He tried to induce the Portuguese to sell the Bay to Britain; indeed the records of the Colonial Office for 1875 and 1876 are full of plans for acquiring the whole of the east coast in order to seal out foreign powers and seal in the Transvaal.[117] But the most Carnarvon was able to achieve was an agreement with the Portuguese that the party to whom the French President Macmahon awarded the disputed southern shores of Delagoa Bay, which had been submitted to his arbitration, should not sell it to any third party without giving first refusal to the other party to the dispute.[118] But Portugal, in whose favour Macmahon decided in July 1875, had no intention of selling any territory to anyone.

The fears of the Colonial Office went beyond the apprehension that the republics might become economically independent of British territory through a railway to a Portuguese port. There were fears that the republics themselves were bent on extending their territory to the sea. In October 1875 Carnarvon told Lord Derby, the Foreign Secretary, that 'the Dutch states – particularly the Trans Vaal – are seeking to enlarge their bounds & to get down if possible to the sea coast & *under existing circumstances* this would be extremely inconvenient'. Shortly afterwards Carnarvon heard from the British Minister in Lisbon that one of Burgers' aides had told the American Minister that the ZAR possessed between 80 and 100 miles of coastline around the mouth of the Limpopo – though when the British Minister questioned him he denied it.[119] The conclusion of a commercial treaty between the Orange Free State and Portugal containing a clause referring to the *ships* of the former produced a nervous reaction. The stipulations of this treaty were the same as those of the treaty concluded with the ZAR three months earlier, and the presence of the clause in both was probably nothing more than the result of some draftsman's addiction to routine; but in the anxious state of the Colonial Office it was seen as portending the acquisition by the republics of a seaboard on the east or west coasts. Walvis Bay was considered a distinct possibility. The Palgrave expedition to Damaraland was greeted with satisfaction because 'as long as he is in the country it will scarcely be possible for the Dutch Republics to act'.[120]

The Colonial Office wanted British sovereignty to be declared over all the coastline not actually in the possession of another power, but the Foreign Office opposed claims without occupation. Herbert commented that this should not be allowed to 'lose us the territory now slipping from us. Perhaps a man of war cruising on the coast might be occupation enough'. Carnarvon added that the ship might visit landing places as 'evidence of interest and supervision'.[121] But these were desperate, indeed absurd, suggestions. The rather more rational hope was that the London conference, which President Brand at least was expected to attend, might achieve something.

Brand arrived in London on 6 May 1876 to discuss the diamond fields dispute. Carnarvon described him in his diary as 'incurably obstinate, narrow and dull'.[122] He refused to undertake to confederate, or to promise to abstain from foreign alliances without British concurrence, or to do anything else in return for concessions in the diamond fields dispute. He simply wanted what was his by right, and would concede nothing in return, beyond an agreement to participate in the conference. To secure this at least, Carnarvon eventually accepted Brand's case and agreed to a border adjustment and monetary compensation. But when the conference opened, Brand stated that his Volksraad's instructions would not allow him to participate if there were 'any mention of Confederation'.[123]

The only concession the Cape government made to Carnarvon was to offer to assist in settling the diamond fields dispute. The ever-hopeful Carnarvon seized on this as a cause for optimism. He said it was an 'undertaking . . . of very great consequence', which would give him a 'great advantage',[124] and probably lead to the Cape agreeing to be represented at the London conference.[125] But when Molteno arrived in Britain at the end of July 1876 and found the diamond fields dispute already settled, he stated that he was not empowered by his Parliament to do anything else, and refused to attend the conference.[126]

Despite the absence of representatives from the Cape and the ZAR, an attempt was made to hold a conference. Carnarvon, with his deputy Sir Garnet Wolseley, presided. Sir Theophilus Shepstone, newly knighted for the occasion, together with two unofficial delegates, represented Natal. Brand was there to represent the OFS. He had earlier stipulated that he could not confer with any representatives of Griqualand West, which he regarded as part of the OFS; the settlement of the dispute had removed this difficulty, but there was no time for a representative to be summoned from South Africa, so the ubiquitous Froude, who had been sent to South Africa to represent Great Britain, was now deemed to represent Griqualand West, a territory in which he had spent about a week. Carnarvon raised the great question of confederation in his opening address on 3 August 1876, but thereafter the participants confined themselves to desultory discussions on the 'native question', on which some resolutions of a very general nature were passed. After the first of the seven sessions Carnarvon attended for only half an hour a day, except for the second and seventh sessions, which he did not attend at all. After the second session verbatim records of the proceedings ceased to be kept. On 15 August the conference 'adjourned', never to reassemble.[127]

The conference had achieved nothing, confederation was as far off as ever, and the republics were slipping from Britain's grasp. 'The Transvaal . . . *must* be ours,' wrote Carnarvon in late 1876.[128] It was too rich a prize to lose. It was an essential part of the envisaged great South African dominion with its northern boundary on the Zambezi. But it was much more than just a means of access to the far interior: by the 1870s it was a commonplace that the Transvaal, undeveloped though it was, was potentially the richest part of South Africa.

'The Transvaal,' Froude told Carnarvon in 1875, 'is one of the richest countries in the whole world in its natural resources.' According to a report in *The Morning Advertiser* of 19 February 1876, a cutting of which is in Carnarvon's papers, 'the land of promise, the seat of future wealth and greatness in the southern part of this continent is undoubtedly the Transvaal'. 'There can be no question that the resources of the Transvaal are greater and more varied than are those of any of the other states of South Africa,' wrote Francis Oats, FGS, the Provincial Engineer of Griqualand West, in a report of his tour of the country printed by the Colonial Office in November 1876.[129] The fertility of the soil, the well-watered nature of the country, and its healthy climate and hence suitability for white settlement were frequently remarked upon. But it was more particularly its mineral wealth that caused it to be 'regarded by many who have seen it as the richest country in the world',[130] or as 'one of the finest and richest countries in the world'.[131] The discovery of the vast Witwatersrand gold fields in 1886 has tended to obscure in retrospect the fact that even before this date the Transvaal had the reputation of being, in the recurring phrase, 'very rich in minerals'.[132] Gold, diamonds, silver, iron, coal, tin, nickel, lead, cobalt, plumbago and copper were said to be found in workable grades and quantities. Francis Oats, the geologist quoted above, was (ironically enough) sceptical of the reports of vast deposits of precious metals in the Transvaal, but he found other minerals in 'great abundance'. The iron ore of the Steelpoort valley he said was not only 'most abundant' but of 'the greatest possible excellence of quality'; and he expressed the belief that 'the whole of the sandstone formation of the "Hooghte Veldt" is a coal formation'.[133] This immense coalfield, another visitor to the Transvaal believed, was 'destined to play a most important part in the history of the world's industry'.[134]

Not everyone agreed. Charles Warren (later General Sir Charles Warren) visited the Transvaal shortly after it was annexed, and commented 'I have not seen the great richness of this country so much talked of'. He said he 'thought that the account of its wealth had been exaggerated . . . A great influx of British might stir up the country, but otherwise I cannot understand how it is to develop suddenly in the manner so often forecast.'[135] As time went on growing numbers of people came to share these views, but Warren's remarks make it clear that in 1877 the prevailing opinion was the opposite of his own.

The need to justify Britain's annexation of the Transvaal in 1877 called forth statements to the effect that it was a treasure chest sat on by people who could not or would not release its potential riches but that henceforth things would be very different. It was 'owing to the unenterprising character of its inhabitants and their predilection for pastoral occupations', wrote Herbert in June 1877, that 'the resources of the country have remained undeveloped, except to a very small extent'.[136] The enemies of 'improvements – railways, telegraphs and everything – which might introduce British influence into the Transvaal' could not be allowed to 'obstruct the path of colonisation, as it advances towards the equator'.[137] What was needed was good government, peace and law and order. 'Capital is sure to follow in the steps of law and order, neither of which they have hitherto had there,' wrote a Natal settler in 1877. The Parliamentary Under-Secretary for the Colonies assured the House of Commons shortly after the annexation that good government would 're-assure capitalists and encourage European immigration'. Shepstone gave the assurance that firm control over the natives would give a 'great impetus' to 'the development of the immense resources of this country by the release of . . . a large body of labourers . . . from the thraldom . . . of inter-tribal wars'.[138]

These statements represent British views on the condition of the Transvaal shortly after the annexation, or after the decision to annex had been taken. The most commonly expressed fear for the future in the pre-annexation period was not that the Transvaal would remain undeveloped but that it would be developed under foreign auspices and become economically independent of the British empire. President Burgers was no enemy of progress. He certainly wished to develop the immense resources of the Transvaal – but not as part of the advance of British colonization to the equator. On the contrary he was trying to develop the country with the aid of foreign capitalists and governments with a view to keeping the Transvaal permanently out of the British sphere of influence. He therefore had to be stopped.

Britain, the ZAR and the Pedi, 1876

Carnarvon's two attempts at achieving confederation by conciliation and discussion had failed. He now intervened more forcibly. The ZAR's war with Sekhukhune's Pedi provided the opportunity for intervention. On hearing of Burgers' intention to make war on the Pedi, whom the British government did not accept were subjects of the ZAR, Carnarvon caused Burgers to be informed that this 'engagement of the Republic in foreign military operations' was a source of great danger to the British communities in South Africa, and potentially productive of a 'general native war'. Such actions, and any attempt to extend the frontiers of the Republic, Carnarvon warned, would be regarded as a breach of the Sand River Convention, the charter of the ZAR's independence. The nature of Carnarvon's preoccupations at this time is shown by his statement that 'designs and objects, such as the annexation of territory on or near the East or West Coasts, have been attributed to the Transvaal Republic'.[139] Although in this public despatch Carnarvon stated that he could not believe such allegations, a private letter of the same date shows quite clearly that he did believe them. Writing to Bulwer on the same subject he said that 'under no circumstances can we permit any further undefined annexations of territory towards the sea coast. The Dutch policy is clear enough in this respect and we cannot allow it.' Another fear was expressed in this private letter. He continued: 'Nor is it sound policy to allow the Dutch under present circ[umstance]s so to cripple the Zulus & the g[rea]t native tribes as to secure an ascendancy for themselves in S. Africa.'[140]

Already the Zulu were seen as potential unwitting allies in the task of establishing the hegemony of Briton over Boer. It is ironic that in the event it was the forward policy of Carnarvon himself which, by destroying Pedi and Zulu power and forging a sense of Afrikaner unity, established the conditions for just such a 'Dutch ascendancy' as he feared.

At first, then, Carnarvon feared that the Boers would be victorious, and saw hope only in the possibility that this might provide a justification or opportunity for revoking the Sand River Convention. Edward Fairfield of the Colonial Office, in a memorandum on the subject of relations between the ZAR and the Zulu written at the request of Carnarvon's private secretary, then raised the possibility that a Boer defeat at the hands of Sekhukhune's Zulu allies 'would open the way to our intervention in the affairs of the Country as a peace making power alone capable of defending the interests of civilization'. This would give Britain 'paramount influence' in South Africa; 'and we would more easily deal with the separatist tendencies of Mr. Brand if we surrounded him on all sides'. Shepstone arrived in London on 31 July 1876. As we have seen,[141] Shepstone was convinced that an attack on the Pedi might very well result in a Zulu invasion of the Transvaal. A despatch from Bulwer, written shortly after Shepstone left Natal, warned of this possibility. Shepstone no doubt emphasised this point in his personal discussions with Carnarvon and the officials of the Colonial Office. Barkly, in despatches written in July, described the situation of the ZAR as 'alarming', and stated that 'nothing but a rapid and brilliant series of victories can avert terrible disasters'. By August Carnarvon was envisaging the possibility of a Boer defeat: 'His own people, as well as the English settlers in the Transvaal, may perhaps find out that confederation under the English flag wd. have great practical advantage.'[142]

Carnarvon's interests and desires, together with the nature of the advice and opinion he received, had thus put him in a very receptive frame of mind when on 14 September a telegram from Barkly was received:

> Army of President totally routed deserters pouring into pretoria Sickakuni pursuing in force meeting at Landrosts office Leydenburg agreed to ask British government to take over Transvaal Volksraad summoned fourth September am I to accept the proposed cession?[143]

Herbert sent the telegram by messenger to Carnarvon, who was in the country, stating that it 'will show you that our anticipations as to President Burger's failure & the consequent desire of the Transvaal to come under British rule are being fulfilled very rapidly'. Herbert did not 'think it a case for acting in a hurry, especially as we shall have to wait some time for the resolution of the Transvaal Volksraad & that will very probably be adverse to annexation in the first instance'. But Carnarvon would not hear of such doubts and delays.[144] The opportunity now presented had to be grasped without hesitation. Bold and immediate action alone could prevent a great South African war and enable Britain to acquire the Transvaal 'at a stroke'; after this the Orange Free State would not be able to retain its independence for long, and confederation would be achieved.[145]

Barkly was instructed, in reply to his telegram, to allow no opportunity to be lost to acquire the Transvaal, but to accept as few conditions as possible.[146] Shepstone suggested that negotiations would have a better chance of success if conducted by Bulwer rather than Barkly, whose earlier dealings with the ZAR had been of a most acrimonious nature.[147] He also thought that he himself should return to South Africa, and suggested that Wolseley should go with him.[148] Wolseley urged that Shepstone should be sent out to bring the Transvaal under British rule.[149]

Carnarvon thereupon decided that Shepstone should return immediately as Special Commissioner to conduct the negotiations, 'with a secret despatch empowering him to take over the Transvaal Govt. & Country and to become the first English Governor if circumstances on his arrival render this in any way possible'. Carnarvon told Shepstone on 21 September, to the latter's 'consternation', that he had to leave the following day.[150] Just nine days after the receipt of Barkly's telegram, Shepstone was on the high seas.

Shepstone's negotiations proved to be protracted, and news from South Africa, still unconnected by telegraph, took a long time to come. Meanwhile, a further development on the Continent caused Carnarvon disquiet and must have convinced him that he had been right to send Shepstone to the Transvaal. This development was the inaugural conference of King Leopold's International Association. Sir Bartle Frere, whom Carnarvon had appointed to succeed Barkly as High Commissioner, attended it and returned full of enthusiasm. Carnarvon's suspicions illustrate the nature of his preoccupations.

I have little doubt that his real hope is to get a footing in S. Africa for some Belgian colony . . . and a colony in or near S. Africa would be full of objections. We find it hard enough to absorb the two Dutch Republics even under present circumstances: and it would be very unwise to encourage the creation of any new State near us. We are the paramount and we ought, if only as a matter of political convenience to be the sole Power in that part of the world.

Frere assured Carnarvon that the purpose of the Association was not to found colonies, that it would not operate south of the Zambezi, and that the King hoped Britain would play the leading part in its activities. Carnarvon still felt that its proceedings should be watched with a careful eye.

I should not like any one to come too near to us either in the south towards the Transvaal, which *must* be ours: or on the north too near to Egypt and the country which belongs to Egypt. In fact when I speak of geographical limits I am not expressing my real opinion. We cannot admit rivals in the east or even the central parts of Africa: and I do not see why, looking to the experience which we have now of English life within the tropics, the Zambezi should be considered to be without the range of our colonisation. To a considerable extent, if not entirely we must be prepared to apply a sort of Munro [*sic*] doctrine to much of Africa.

W.R. Malcolm, the legal adviser to the Colonial Office, discussed the matter with an international lawyer, Sir Henry Thring, and the latter's advice caused Carnarvon to oppose the Association unreservedly. Malcolm reported that England would 'suffer the intrusion of a Society over whose actions she has no control & whose power for evil is immense'. Foreign countries might 'direct its operations so as to annoy this country' or 'take a sinister interest in it to the detriment of English power'. Thring himself commented that there was 'something in the background besides philanthropy and I cannot imagine a more cunningly devised scheme for faltering England in enterprize'.[151]

It was the mutual fear of exclusion by other European powers that played the major role in the Scramble for Africa. The Scramble is usually dated from the 1880s, when the chain-reaction began in earnest. But 'the colonial rivalry of the mid-1880s was to a considerable extent to grow out of the economic anxieties of the previous decade'.[152] Carnarvon's anxieties about Britain's position in the world and his fear of exclusion from Africa are palpable. His activities in southern Africa and other parts of Africa in turn aroused similar suspicion and concern on the Continent.[153] The change in the balance of power between black and white that took place in South Africa in the 1870s could be seen in purely local terms as a continuation of the history of conquest that began in 1652; but the initiative taken by the imperial power suggests that it should rather be seen as an early stage of that late nineteenth-century process which led in a few years to the whole of Africa coming under European rule.

Notes

1. For a judicious account of the debate on the question of the break in imperial policy generally in the late nineteenth century, see Kennedy, 'Continuity and Discontinuity'. For some of the contributions to the debate see Cope, 'Local Imperatives', n. 44.
2. BL Add Mss 60763, Carnarvon to Disraeli, 30 November and 10 December 1875.
3. See the correspondence in CO 879/12, African no. 144; and the minutes on CO 48/ 477, Cape 7422 and Cape 14135, War Office to Colonial Office, 30 June and 29 December 1875, and on CO 48/480, Cape 4145 and Cape 9817, War Office to Colonial Office, 6 April and 14 August 1876.
4. BL Add Mss 60793, Herbert to Carnarvon, 19 May 1877. In the event only £100 000 was extracted.
5. Thompson, 'Great Britain and the Afrikaner Republics', p. 289.
6. CO 179/122, minute by Carnarvon, 17 March 1876, on Natal 2622, printed copy of memo of Portuguese possessions on east coast of Africa; ibid, minute by Malcolm, 5 April 1876, on Natal 3995, Foreign Office to Colonial Office, 3 April 1876; PRO 30/ 6/4, no. 67, Carnarvon to Frere, 12 December 1876.
7. Robinson and Gallagher, *Africa and the Victorians*, pp. 59–60; Goodfellow, *Great Britain and South African Confederation*, pp. 70, 117 and 72.
8. I have examined this hypothesis in detail in Cope, 'Strategic and Socio-economic Explanations'.
9. Goodfellow, *Great Britain and South African Confederation*, p. 83.
10. BL Add Mss 60798, no. 104, Froude to Carnarvon, 27 September [1876]; ibid, no. 106, Carnarvon to Froude, 16 October 1876; ibid, no. 110, Froude to Carnarvon, 24 October [1876]; ibid, no. 111, Froude to Carvarvon, 21 November [1876].
11. HC Deb, Vol. CCXXXV, col 1755, Campbell, 24 July 1877.
12. Goodfellow, *Great Britain and South African Confederation*, p. 210; De Kiewiet, *Imperial Factor in South Africa*, pp. 5, 7 and 135.
13. For a fuller discussion of this question see Cope, 'De Kiewiet'.
14. Goodfellow, *Great Britain and South African Confederation*, p. 121.
15. CO 107/3, minute by Malcolm, 21 July 1876, on GW 8679, Brand to Carnarvon, 19 July 1876; Goodfellow, *Great Britain and South African Confederation*, pp. 43 and 105.
16. Goodfellow, *Great Britain and South African Confederation*, pp. 139–40.
17. BPP, C1631, p. 13, ministerial minute, 14 March 1876, encl in no. 10, Barkly to Carnarvon, 16 March 1876; Lewsen, *Correspondence of Merriman*, pp. 16–25; Trapido, ' "Friends of the Natives" ', pp. 253–4.
18. BL Add Mss 60799A, Froude's letters to Carnarvon in 1874, especially those of 5 July and 4, 11 and 20 October; PRO 30/6/2, no. 7, Carnarvon to Ponsonby, 11 August 1875.
19. CO 107/3, minute by Malcolm, 21 July 1876, on GW 8679, Brand to Carnarvon, 19 July 1876.
20. CO 879/9, African no. 84, p. 8, memo on South African affairs by E[dward] F[airfield], January 1876. Fairfield added that the African's work ought to be of profit to himself as well as to his white masters.
21. PRO 30/6/84, p. 36, no. 18, Carnarvon to Froude, 2 September 1875.
22. Saunders, *De Kiewiet*; Macmillan, *Cape Colour Question*; Macmillan, *Bantu, Boer and Briton*.
23. Cope, 'De Kiewiet', pp. 496–7.
24. PRO 30/6/38, no. 25, Wolseley to Carnarvon, 12 June 1875; CO 879/9, African no. 84, confid memo on South African affairs, by E[dward] F[airfield], January 1876, p. 8.
25. Atmore and Marks, 'Imperial Factor', pp. 120–7; Etherington, 'Labour Supply'.
26. Guy, *Heretic*, p. 193.
27. Standard Bank Archives, GMO 3/1/6, p. 200.

28. CO 879/9, African no. 86, 'The Native Question in South Africa' by E[dward] F[airfield], 9 December 1875; see also CO 107/5, Lanyon to Frere, 27 February 1878, enclosed in GW 4075, Frere to Carnarvon, 5 March 1878, for an expression of similar views.

29. I have attempted to consider both the imperial and the South African sides of the question in Cope, 'Local Imperatives'.

30. Kennedy, *Anglo-German Antagonism*, pp. 24–7; Monypenny and Buckle, *Life of Disraeli*, Vol. V, pp. 126–38.

31. Bourne, *Foreign Policy of Victorian England*, pp. 124–5.

32. Cairnes, 'Our Defences', p. 167; Harrison, 'Effacement', p. 165; According to Ludlow, 'Reconstitution', p. 499, the phrase 'effacement of England' originated in the German *Moniteur* of Versailles during the occupation.

33. Carnarvon, 'Army Administration', pp. 539–40. Much of this phraseology is taken over from G.T. Chesney's imaginary account of Britain's defeat and occupation by Germany, *The Battle of Dorking*, published in 1871, of which this article was in part a review.

34. Froude, *Short Studies*, Vol. II, pp. 194–5, a reprint of an article first published in *Fraser's Magazine* in 1870.

35. Hynes, *Economics of Empire*, p. 15. On the effects of Britain's changing diplomatic and economic position on attitudes to empire see n. 1. More recent summaries include Chamberlain, *'Pax Britannica'?*, chs 8 and 9; and Cain and Hopkins, *British Imperialism*, Vol. I, pp. 204–7.

36. Eldridge, *England's Mission*, ch. 3.

37. See Benians, Butler and Carrington, *Cambridge History of the British Empire*, Vol. III, pp. 22–4; Kimberley, 'Journal of Events', p. 29.

38. Eldridge, *England's Mission*, chs 4 and 5.

39. Bodelson, *Mid-Victorian Imperialism*, p. 113.

40. Eldridge, *England's Mission*, p. 63.

41. See eg the Liberal Parliamentary Under-Secretary for the Colonies, Edward Knatchbull-Hugessen's anonymous article 'South Africa and her Diamond Fields'.

42. Monypenny and Buckle, *Life of Disraeli*, Vol. V, p. 195.

43. Bodelson, *Mid-Victorian Imperialism*, pp. 130–45.

44. Carnarvon, 'Imperial Administration', p. 760.

45. HL Deb, Vol. CCXXXIII, cols 1657–8, 23 April 1877.

46. McIntyre, *Imperial Factor*, BL Add Mss 60906, Carnarvon's diary for 1874, entry for 15 April 1874 (on Fiji).

47. Munro, *Africa and the International Economy*, p. 67.

48. This argument is developed in more detail in Cope, 'Local Imperatives'.

49. See p. 87.

50. CO 48/468, Cape 3836, Barkly to Kimberley, 4 March 1874, encl Southey to Barkly, 18 February 1874; ibid, Cape 3837, Barkly to Kimberley, 4 March 1874, encl petitions.

51. BL Add Mss 60791, Herbert to Carnarvon, 10 April 1874; PRO 30/6/32, no. 6, Carnarvon to Barkly, 27 May 1874.

52. Ibid, no. 13, Carnarvon to Barkly, 22 August 1874.

53. CO 48/477, minute by Herbert, 18 August 1875, on Cape 8825, Foreign Office to Colonial Office, 31 July 1875.

54. PRO 30/6/84, p. 37, no. 18, Carnarvon to Froude, 2 September 1875. One must assume that Carnarvon meant to write 'Confederation': his earlier remarks surely make it clear that merely participating in the conference would not be enough.

55. See ch. 3, pp. 65–6.

56. Etherington, 'Labour Supply', p. 245.

57. Etherington, 'Labour Supply'; see my comments in Cope, 'Local Imperatives', pp. 603–4.

58. See ch. 3, p. 47.
59. CO 179/116, minute by Carnarvon, 18 September 1874, on Natal 10652, Lucas to Herbert, 9 August 1874; ibid, minute by Carnarvon, 5 December 1874, on Natal 13808, Confid, Shepstone to Herbert, 30 November 1874.
60. CO 179/115, minute by Carnarvon, 12 December 1874, on Natal 13802, Pine to Carnarvon, 22 October 1874.
61. See pp. 83–4.
62. HL Deb, Vol. CCXLIV, col 1655, 14 March 1879. See also ibid, Vol. CCXXXIII, col 1660; Vol. CCXLIV, col 1937; Vol. CCXLV, col 121; Vol. CCXLVIII, col 1889.
63. CO 879/9, African no. 84, confid memo on South African affairs, by E[dward] F[airfield], January 1876, pp. 5–6.
64. BL Add Mss 60798, no. 51, Froude to Carnarvon, 4 October [1874].
65. CO 879/8, Natal no. 80, pp. 2–4, Wolseley to Carnarvon, 14 June 1875; PRO 30/6/38, no. 25, Wolseley to Carnarvon, 12 June 1875. For the sense of insecurity felt by Natal colonists, see Etherington, 'Natal's Black Rape Scare', especially pp. 50–3.
66. HL Deb, Vol. CCXXV, col 1896, 23 July 1875.
67. CO 179/122, Carnarvon's reply, 21 March 1876, to Natal 2836, Natal Land and Colonisation Company to Carnarvon, 9 March 1876, in cutting from *The Standard*, 22 March 1876.
68. CO 879/10, African no. 102, p. 3, conference on South African affairs, 3–15 August 1876.
69. BL Add Mss 60798, no. 53, Froude to Carnarvon, 11 October [1874]. Emphasis in original.
70. Ibid, no. 65, Froude to Carnarvon, 19 November [1874]. Emphasis in original.
71. See, p. 83.
72. CO 879/8, Natal no. 80, p. 3, Wolseley to Carnarvon, 14 June 1875.
73. BPP, C1121, p. 94, Carnarvon to Pine, 3 December 1874.
74. BPP, C1401–1, p. 85, Carnarvon to Bulwer, 20 October 1875.
75. CO 879/9, African no. 84, p. 5, memo on South African affairs, by E[dward] F[airfield], January 1876.
76. HL Deb, Vol. CCXXIII, col 693, 12 April 1875.
77. Carnarvon, *Speeches*, p. 315, a speech made on 6 March 1878.
78. HL Deb, Vol. CCCXXXIII, col 1651, 23 April 1877.
79. Butler, *Sir William Butler*, p. 184.
80. See pp. 89–90.
81. Le Cordeur, 'Relations', p. 233.
82. PRO 30/6/32, no. 17, Barkly to Carnarvon, 23 September 1874. Etherington, 'Labour Supply' has much information on Natal's expansionist urges in the 1870s; Le Cordeur, 'Relations' has similar information for both the Cape and Natal in the 1870s and earlier; see also Cope, 'Local Imperatives'.
83. BPP, C1244, 'Proposal for a Conference of Delegates from the Colonies and States of South Africa'.
84. Goodfellow, *Great Britain and South African Confederation*, p. 63.
85. PRO 30/6/84, pp. 36–7, Carnarvon to Froude, 2 September 1875.
86. De Kiewiet, *Imperial Factor in South Africa*, pp. 60–5 and 73–5; Goodfellow, *Great Britain and South African Confederation*, pp. 73–4.
87. PRO 30/6/84, Froude to Carnarvon, 25 July 1875, p. 31; Goodfellow, *Great Britain and South African Confederation*, p. 83.
88. Goodfellow, *Great Britain and South African Confederation*, pp. 74–98; Lewsen, 'First Crisis', pp. 228–31; Lewsen, *John X. Merriman*, pp. 52–4.
89. PRO 30/6/84, pp. 81, 26 and 57, Froude to Carnarvon, 24 October, 8 July and 19 September 1875.

90. PRO 30/6/2, no. 7, Carnarvon to Ponsonby, 11 August 1875.

91. Only three copies were printed, one each for Froude, Herbert and Carnarvon – BL Add Mss 60798, no. 78, Carnarvon to Froude, 18 January 1876. Carnarvon's copy is in the Carnarvon Papers in the Public Record Office, PRO 30/6/84.

92. BL Add Mss 60763: Carnarvon to Disraeli, 2 September 1875; Secret, Disraeli to Carnarvon, 5 November 1875; Carnarvon, 'Mem: of argts for and against my accepting the Govnship Genl. of India' (5–9 Nov. 1875); Carnarvon to Disraeli, 9 November 1875; Carnarvon, 'Mem: as to Admy.', n.d. Also BL Add Mss 60907, Carnarvon's diary, 1875, entries for 5, 6, 7, 16 and 18 November.

93. Disraeli to Lady Bradford, 26 April 1876, in Monypenny and Buckle, *Life of Disraeli*, Vol. II, p. 815.

94. PRO 30/6/84, pp. 51 and 91, Carnarvon to Froude, 12 October 1875 and 15 November 1875.

95. BPP, C1748, p. 142, Burgers to Barkly, 15 September 1876; Appelgryn, *Burgers*, p. 162.

96. Appelgryn, *Burgers*, p. 48.

97. Shepstone in 1877 represented Burgers as collaborating with him in bringing the Transvaal under British rule, a view which Uys accepted: Uys, *Era of Shepstone*. But Appelgryn, *Burgers*, cogently argues that the evidence can be differently interpreted.

98. BL Add Mss 60798, no. 62, Froude to Carnarvon, 10 November [1874].

99. BL Add Mss 60798, no. 65, Froude to Carnarvon, 19 November [1874].

100. CO 48/480, Corvo to Cortes, 22 March 1876, encl in Cape 4711, Foreign Office to Colonial Office, 20 April 1876.

101. PRO 30/6/38, nos 22, 25 and 36, Wolseley to Carvarvon, 29 May, 12 June, 16 August 1875.

102. CO 537/124a, ff. 38 and 54, Secret, Barkly to Carnarvon, 5 April 1875 (quotation) and 15 April 1875.

103. PRO 30/6/32, nos 42 and 43, Barkly to Carnarvon, 5 and 10 (quotation) April 1875.

104. BL Add Mss 60907, Carnarvon's diary for 1875, entries for 8 and 11 May.

105. See pp. 94–5.

106. Engelbrecht, *Burgers*, pp. 126–8.

107. PRO 30/6/2, vol. 2, no. 92, Carnarvon to Ponsonby, 7 January 1876.

108. PRO 30/6/38, no. 18, Carnarvon to Wolseley, 13 May 1875; BL Add Mss 60797–2, Lytton to Carnarvon, 11 December 1875.

109. CO 537/124a, f. 59, draft, Colonial Office to Foreign Office, 15 May 1875 (based on a minute by Carnarvon, 13 May 1875).; CO 537/124a, f. 77, Confid, Russell to Derby, 1 June 1875, encl in Confid, Foreign Office to Colonial Office, 10 June 1875; BL Add Mss 60798, no. 28, Froude to Carnarvon, 20 May [1874].

110. Appelgryn, *Burgers*, p. 90; Uys, *Era of Shepstone*, p. 155; Engelbrecht, *Burgers*, pp. 119 and 132.

111. CO 107/3, f. 225, Burgers to Herbert, 1 February 1876.

112. PRO 30/6/32, no. 103, Barkly to Carnarvon, 26 May 1876; Engelbrecht, *Burgers*, p. 136.

113. PRO 30/6/23, no. 26, Burgers to Carnarvon, 8 May 1876.

114. CO 48/478, minute by Herbert, 12 July 1876, on Cape 8162, Barkly to Carnarvon, 13 June 1876.

115. CO 179/122, minutes by Malcolm, 21 February 1876, and Herbert, 22 March 1876, on Natal 1917, Foreign Office to Colonial Office, 18 February 1876.

116. CO 879/9, African no. 83a, p. 102, report on Transvaal by G. Pomeroy Colley, 10 August 1875.

117. See especially CO 179/119 and CO 179/122.

118. BPP, C1361, p. 246, correspondence concerning Delagoa Bay.

119. PRO 30/6/8, p. 81, Carnarvon to Derby, 27 October 1875; BL Add Mss 60797–2, Lytton to Carnarvon, 11 December 1875.

120. CO 48/480, minutes by Malcolm, 22 April 1876, and Carnarvon, 23 April 1876, on Cape 4711, Foreign Office to Colonial Office, 20 April 1876; CO 48/478, minute by Malcolm, 5 May 1876 (quotation), on Cape 5355, Barkly to Carnarvon, 4 April 1876.
121. CO 48/480, minutes by Herbert and Carnarvon, 23 April 1876, on Cape 4711, Foreign Office to Colonial Office, 20 April 1876, and draft, amended by Carnarvon, Colonial Office to Foreign Office, 29 April 1876.
122. BL Add Mss 60908, Carnarvon's diary, 1876, entry for 30 May.
123. Goodfellow, *Great Britain and South African Confederation*, pp. 97–101.
124. PRO 30/6/2, no. 75, Carnarvon to Victoria, 21 December 1875.
125. CO 879/9, African no. 84, memo on South African affairs, by E[dward] F[airfield], January 1876, p. 11, presumably reflecting Carnarvon's views.
126. Goodfellow, *Great Britain and South African Confederation*, pp. 101–4.
127. Ibid, pp. 104–6; CO 48/484, Cape 1222, 'Conference on Sth. African Affairs'; CO 879/10, African no. 102, is the printed version, which, however, omits the verbatim record of the second day's proceedings.
128. PRO 30/6/4, no. 67, Carnarvon to Frere, 12 December 1876.
129. BL Add Mss 60798, no. 15, Froude to Carnarvon, 17 March [1875]; BL 60937, cutting from *Morning Advertiser*, 19 February 1876; CO 879/10, African no. 112, p. 9, 'Notes of information on the resources of South Africa in general, and of the state of the Transvaal republic in particular', by F. Oats, 12 November 1876.
130. BL 60937, cutting from *Morning Advertiser*, 19 February 1876.
131. Child, *Portrait*, p. 88.
132. This particular phrase occurs in BPP, C1814, p. 5, no. 3, Herbert to Treasury, 8 June 1877; Jeppe, *Transvaal Book Almanac*, p. 32; Moodie, 'Population' p.607 (lecture of 3 May 1878, comment by chairman, Sir Arthur Cunynghame); Durnford, *Soldier's Life and Work*, p. 160. References in other terms to the mineral wealth of the Transvaal are too numerous to itemise.
133. CO 879/10, African no. 112, p. 6.
134. Atcherley, *Trip to Boerland*, p. 220.
135. Warren, *On the Veldt*, pp. 175 and 199. This book was published well after the discovery of gold on the Witwatersrand, but consists mostly of unmodified extracts from his much earlier journals and letters (see pp. v and 3 of the book).
136. BPP, C1814, p. 5, no. 3, Herbert to Treasury, 8 June 1877.
137. BL Add Mss 60937, *The Standard*, cutting, 15 March 1877 (in Carnarvon's papers).
138. Child, *Portrait*, p. 88; HC Deb, Vol. CCXXXV, col 979, Lowther, 9 July 1877; BPP, C1961, p. 71, no. 27, Shepstone to Carnarvon, 11 August 1877.
139. BPP, C1748, pp. 46–7, no. 31, Carnarvon to Barkly, 12 July 1876.
140. PRO 30/6/38, no. 77, Carnarvon to Bulwer, 12 July 1876.
141. See ch. 3, pp. 70–1.
142. CO 107/1, f. 90, memo on question of Transvaal encroachment, by Fairfield, 10 July 1876; GH 1219, p. 396, no. 117, Bulwer to Carnarvon, 12 June 1876; Kennedy, 'Fatal Diplomacy', pp. 287–8; CO 879/10, African no. 104, pp. 2–3, Barkly to Carnarvon, 14 and 21 July 1876; PRO 30/6/38, no. 78, Carnarvon to Bulwer, 5 August 1876.
143. CO 48/479, Cape no. 11178. The telegram came from Madeira, which was as far as the telegraph cable extended; it had perforce travelled by ship from Cape Town. The last seven words were in cypher.
144. BL Add Mss 60793, Herbert to Carnarvon, 14 and 15 September [1876], the latter in response to a telegram from Carnarvon.
145. PRO 30/6/3, no. 28, Carnarvon to Victoria, 15 September 1876; Carnarvon to Disraeli, 15 September 1876, in Uys, *Era of Shepstone*, p. 174; PRO 30/6/38 no. 43, Copy, Carnarvon to Wolseley, 17 Sept 1876; BL Add Mss 60796, Carnarvon to Hardy, 17 September 1876.

146. GH 597, Tele, Carnarvon to Barkly, received 25 August 1876, encl in Private and Confidential, Barkly to Bulwer, 14 October 1876.
147. BL Add Mss 60796, Meade to Carnarvon, 17 September 1876.
148. BL Add Mss 60793, Herbert to Carnarvon, 18 September 1876.
149. PRO 30/6/38, no. 44, Wolseley to Carnarvon, 20 September 1876. This is the same day that Carnarvon took the decision to send Shepstone (see next footnote) which makes it look as though Wolseley's letter was probably too late to have influenced him. But Wolseley says that he had earlier scribbled a note to Herbert saying the same thing, which Carnarvon said he received on 20 September 1876 (BL 60769, Carnarvon to Hardy, 20 September 1876). Carnarvon told Wolseley that his letters were 'most valuable to me and I have fully acted on them' (Hove Central Library, Wolseley Papers, WA, no. 1, Carnarvon to Wolseley, 24 September 1876).
150. PRO 30/6/11, no. 79, Carnarvon to Disraeli, 20 September 1876; SP 5, Shepstone's diary for 1876, entry for 21 September.
151. PRO 30/6/4, no. 64, Carnarvon to Frere, 8 December 1876; no. 67, Carnarvon to Frere, 12 December 1876; no. 70, memo by Malcolm, 16 December 1876; no. 71, Thring to Carnarvon, 30 December 1876.
152. Kennedy, *Anglo-German Antagonism*, p. 51.
153. Sanderson, 'European Partition', p. 23.

Sir Theophilus Shepstone, Diplomatic Agent to the Native Tribes
of Natal, 1845–1856, and Secretary for Native Affairs, 1856–1876;
Administrator of the Transvaal Province, 1877–1879.

Cetshwayo kaMpande,
Zulu King, 1872–1879.

Lord Carnarvon,
Secretary of State for the
Colonies, 1874–1878.

Sir Henry Bulwer, Lieutenant-Governor of Natal, 1875–1880.

Sir Garnet Wolseley, Administrator of Natal, April–September 1875;
High Commissioner for South-East Africa, June 1879–April 1880.

Paramount Chief Sekhukhune of the Pedi, 1861–1879.

Thomas François Burgers, President of the ZAR, 1872–1877.

John Dunn and his *iziduna*, a photograph taken after the
British annexation of Zululand.

Sir Theophilus Shepstone as Special Commissioner and his staff, on his way to
annex the Transvaal. Rear: Lieut. Phillips, M. Osborne, Col. Brookes, Capt. Jarvis.
Seated: W. Morcom, J. Henderson, Sir Theophilus Shepstone, Dr Lyle, Fred
Fynnie. Reclining: Rider Haggard.

John William Colenso, Bishop of Natal, 1853–1883.

Sir Bartle Frere, High Commissioner, 1877–1880.

Lord Chelmsford, Commander-in-Chief, 1877–1879.

CHAPTER FIVE

The Annexation of the Transvaal

Shepstone and the ZAR, October to December 1876

Shepstone's instructions were to bring the Transvaal under British rule, with the consent of its government if possible, and without it if not. This last part of his instructions was never so baldly stated; but there can be no doubt that Shepstone understood that Carnarvon wished him to annex the Transvaal if at all possible even without the consent of its government.[1]

With no telegraphic link Carnarvon was too remote to control South African events; but with the eager collaboration of Barkly, to whose policy of enmity with the ZAR he was now reverting, as Froude pointed out,[2] he did all that he could to weaken the republic and make it less able to resist annexation.

Carnarvon instructed Barkly and Bulwer to issue proclamations warning British subjects not to volunteer for military service in the Transvaal. The Law Officers reported that Britain had no grounds in international law for protesting at the ZAR's calling up of British subjects resident in the Transvaal for commando service but, discovering that, by agreement, Dutch, Belgian and Portuguese citizens were exempt from commando service, Carnarvon instructed Barkly to demand that British subjects be similarly exempted. He ordered Barkly not to provide the ZAR with any assistance except in return for confederation.[3] He empowered Shepstone to warn Brand that any attempt to assist the ZAR would jeopardize the payment of his compensation for the diamond fields.[4] A proposal from the Foreign Office to put pressure on Portugal to stop arms imports through Delagoa Bay was described by Herbert, with Carnarvon's concurrence, as 'inapplicable to the condition of affairs at this moment, as we can hardly provide President Burgers with arms & prevent poor Secocoeni from defending himself'.[5] Britain did not have the legal power to prohibit arms imports by the ZAR government, but Barkly, with Carnarvon's approval, did his best to delay them.[6] A newspaper report on the intended use of explosive bullets by the ZAR was investigated as a possible propaganda weapon against it.[7] Barkly sent numerous newspaper clippings and other reports of Boer atrocities, past and present, to Britain, where they were published in the Blue Books. 'We shall have a great deal of indignation against the Boers from wh. not even Mr Froude can save them as soon as these reports become more widely known', remarked an official of the Colonial Office.[8]

Only the man on the spot, the Special Commissioner, could consummate the policy of annexing the Transvaal. But when Shepstone arrived at Cape Town on

21 October 1876 he found the situation to be very different from what Barkly's telegram had led him to expect. Sekhukhune had not 'pursued in force'; the temporary panic in the Lydenburg district had subsided; the Landdrost of Lydenburg (an Englishman named Cooper) who had called the meeting requesting British intervention, had been dismissed;[9] and the Pedi were being successfully contained and harassed by a band of volunteers drawn mostly from the diamond fields. The war with Sekhukhune was clearly insufficient to induce the ZAR to request or accept British intervention.

Disappointed by Sekhukhune, Shepstone saw a gleam of hope in another direction. He learned for the first time of the perilous financial condition of the ZAR. It appeared that President Burgers's attempts to modernize the republic had succeeded only in ruining it.

Of the £300 000 loan floated in Amsterdam, less than a third had been subscribed, much of it at a discount, so that although a debt of £93 833 had been incurred only £80 745 had been realized. By the beginning of 1877, £8 660 of this amount been consumed in interest charges, banker's commission and other expenses connected with the raising of the loan. Almost all the remaining £72 085 had been spent on rail and rolling stock, so that a further loan had to be raised in South Africa at exorbitant rates of interest to pay for the transport of this material to Delagoa Bay. There it lay and rusted, for there was no more money to build the line, which had not even been surveyed. It was eventually sold for £15 000.

Burgers had earlier borrowed £60 000 from the Cape Commercial Bank in order to redeem the republic's depreciated paper currency. The war with the Pedi and local expenses connected with the proposed railway had necessitated further loans, some at very high rates of interest, so that the total debt of the republic stood at well over £250 000. Its credit was exhausted and no further loans could be raised at any rate of interest, so extraordinary taxation was resorted to. The war tax was resented by burghers in the frontier regions who received no protection in return for it, as well as by burghers in other regions who had no need of protection.

The railway tax was resented by all since there was no railway and no likelihood of one being built. Both these taxes were consequently very poorly paid. All available revenue was swallowed up by the attempts to pay the interest charges on the loans, so there was no money to carry on the administration. Official salaries were in arrears, and the postal service to Kimberley continued only because it was paid for by the government of Griqualand West. Burgers had earlier alienated the conservative elements in the Transvaal through his liberal religious views, and especially by his attempts to establish a secular system of education. As the facts of the financial morass he had plunged the country into became known (and the truth about the railway loan was extracted from him only with great difficulty), Burgers also lost the support of the 'progressive' elements who had formerly been his supporters.[10] 'So it appears,' concluded Shepstone, 'that what Sekukuni has forborne doing towards swamping the State is being fully made up for by the rash and inconsiderate measures of the State Government itself.'[11]

The bankruptcy of the state, the collapse of credit, the war, and the disruption of labour supplies, brought mining and trade within the republic to a virtual standstill and contributed to a trade depression elsewhere in South Africa, especially in Natal.[12] This helped to produce the demands expressed in the colonies and even in Britain for British intervention.[13] But in the Transvaal the agitation for British intervention was confined to mining and mercantile interests, representing a minority of the white population that was almost entirely British. The Boers, who were (or who could if necessary become) largely self-sufficient, were not as severely affected by purely economic and financial factors. For this reason Shepstone began to pin his hopes on another possible source of pressure – the Zulu.[14]

The assumption in the Colonial Office had been that the danger presented by Africans would terrify the Transvaal into confederation. Indeed, there was some concern at first that the pressure from this quarter might be greater than necessary or desirable. Carnarvon expressed fears of 'a great Kaffir War', and a 'great S. African War wh. would be an extremely serious affair'. Herbert expressed the 'hope that the Kafirs will not have pressed their advantage to a destructive length, & that Sir T. Shepstone may be in time to direct the storm'. Great danger was seen in the possibility that Cetshwayo and his big, disciplined army might intervene: 'any rash move on his part would be a very serious matter', wrote Carnarvon to General Ponsonby, the Queen's private secretary; 'I am very glad I did not lose a mail in despatching Shepstone to the scene of action – for if any man can guide these wild men it is he.' What was needed was sufficient pressure to topple Boer hegemony, but not so much as to threaten British hegemony as well. Ponsonby, after many letters from Carnarvon, caught the point nicely: 'The crisis is rather an anxious one as if the Kaffirs exterminate the Boers I suppose they might turn on us.'[15]

The situation that Shepstone found on his return to South Africa was very different from what had been hoped and feared in Britain, and needed different handling. Not only was Sekhukhune successfully contained by the forces of the ZAR, but his supposed ally Cetshwayo had made no attempt to come to his rescue. The latter's responses to events in the Transvaal must now be examined.

Cetshwayo, Rudolph and Bulwer, June to November 1876

As we have seen,[16] Burgers made peaceful overtures to Cetshwayo on his return from Europe and Cetshwayo responded in kind. He agreed to a meeting to settle the border dispute, though his wish for an Englishman (meaning, it was presumed, Shepstone) to be present was no more acceptable to the ZAR than his request for permission to attack the Swazi. Cetshwayo also agreed that peace should be maintained on the border pending a settlement. He responded to the news that the ZAR intended going to war with his supposed ally Sekhukhune by saying that the latter was no more than a friend.

Friendly communications and reassuring reports continued through June, July and early August. The Swazi entry into the war against Sekhukhune did not produce the feared reaction. Gert Rudolph, the Landdrost of Utrecht, heard that Sekhukhune had asked Cetshwayo for help, but that the latter had refused it. Cetshwayo made it clear that he still wished to 'punish' the Swazi, but it also seemed clear that he would not do so without the consent of the President.[17] One may surmise that his advisers, the *izikhulu* of Zululand, insisted upon this condition. They had no interest in military expeditions calculated to boost the monarchy, many of them had marriage connections with the Swazi, they feared that war with the Swazi would lead to war with the whites, and they consistently opposed Cetshwayo's Swaziland ambitions.[18]

More disturbing for Rudolph was the behaviour of the Zulu on the border. Despite Cetshwayo's undertaking to order them not to give offence, they were clearly determined not to allow the Boers who had gone into laager at the time of the attempted tax collection in March 1876[19] to resume the occupation of their farms. Boer cattle were driven off these farms, other cattle were stolen, abandoned farm houses were broken into and robbed, some were burnt down, and the bearing and speech of the Zulu were reported to be insolent and threatening. All this produced feelings of fear and despair among the frontier Boers.[20]

These disturbed conditions in Utrecht were reported to Sir Henry Bulwer, the Lieutenant-Governor of Natal, by the Magistrate of the adjacent Natal division of Newcastle. Bulwer, consistent with his belief in the existence of an alliance between Cetshwayo and Sekhukhune, believed that these events might be the result of the war between the ZAR and Sekhukhune. He accordingly sent a message to Cetshwayo alluding to the war in the Transvaal, urging him to maintain his usual moderation and forbearance, and expressing the hope that nothing would be done to hinder a peaceful solution of the disputed territory question. Cetshwayo assumed that this message was the result of Rudolph's having written to Bulwer, and he asked Rudolph why he had done so when he, Cetshwayo, had promised him that he would not intervene in the war with Sekhukhune. Rudolph denied having sent any such letter.[21]

It was on 2 August 1876 that the ZAR commando failed against Sekhukhune and disintegrated. News of this would probably have reached Zululand before the messengers from Natal left Cetshwayo (they returned to Pietermaritzburg on 28 August). This manifestation of Boer weakness may have caused Cetshwayo to decide that he could safely risk an expedition against the Swazi even without the ZAR's permission. At any rate he took advantage of the presence of Natal messengers to ask permission of the Natal government to 'wash his spears'. He did not say whom he intended attacking, but the messengers gained the impression that it was the Swazi.[22] Rudolph reported on 10 August that he had heard that Cetshwayo was calling up his people to attack the Swazi. The Landdrost of

Wakkerstroom heard similar reports a little later, and also got a message from the Swazi King saying that he had heard them too. On 22 August Rudolph received a message from the Swazi King stating that his people on the border had heard that Cetshwayo was busy preparing a force to invade Swaziland, probably at the place of Mshelekwana, one of his chiefs, who lived on the Lebombo mountains. Rudolph was inclined to believe that this was true since he had recently received reports from his African police that Cetshwayo was collecting his army in order to send it to Mshelekwana, that he was determined to carry out his plan despite the opposition of his counsellors, and that in reply to the latter's protests that such an expedition would bring the Zulu into conflict with the Boers, Cetshwayo had said 'let them stop my army if they can'. According to Rudolph it was an old ambition of Cetshwayo's to obtain possession of the caves of Mshelekwana since his own country lacked such natural fortifications. Perhaps the failure of the Transvaal Boers to take Sekhukhune's mountain fortress had rekindled these ambitions. Whatever the reason for it, Cetshwayo's evident intention to go ahead with his plan to attack Swaziland in defiance of his counsellors and the ZAR was extremely worrying for Rudolph, for the ZAR would have to make some attempt to protect the Swazi if it were to retain their alliance in the future, and this would mean war with the Zulu.[23]

But like so many previous scares, the Swazi expedition never came off. Bulwer, in reply to Cetshwayo's request, politely but firmly deprecated any thought of washing his spears. Cetshwayo accepted this veto:

> The English nation is a just and peace loving one, and I look upon the English people as my fathers. I shall not do anything outside of their Government. I cannot understand though how I am a King, as from the time the Zulus became a nation it has been the custom – or law – to wash spears after the death of a King and I have not washed mine.[24]

After the audience, Cetshwayo's counsellors, led by Mnyamana, the Chief Counsellor, privately told the Natal messengers to thank their government for disapproving of the idea of washing spears, 'stating that it was only the King and young men that desired it, but that they (the Headmen) wished for peace'.[25]

An event of this time that may have distracted Cetshwayo's attention from the Swazi was the 'marriage of the *inGcugce*'.[26] In 1876 Cetshwayo, for the first time in his reign, gave permission for two of his regiments to marry. They were expected to find wives from among the *inGcugce*, an age-set much younger than themselves. But some of these girls had entered into relationships with younger men from whom they were extremely reluctant to part. Many of these couples now fled to Natal or the Transvaal. In other cases their relatives connived at their evasion of the law by representing the girls as members of younger age-sets or else as the wives of their lovers' elder brothers. Cetshwayo received numerous complaints from disappointed suitors, and sent out armed parties to investigate and punish. The result was widely reported to be a wholesale massacre of young women and their relatives. The number of people killed, however, was nothing like the hundreds reported and was possibly not more than 10, fines being imposed in most cases.[27] Bulwer responded to the reports reaching Natal by sending a message stating that he hoped 'to hear from Cetywayo that these reports are incorrect, believing as he does that Cetywayo remembers and is guided by the words spoken and the counsel given to him and the Zulu Nation by the Representative of this Government at his (Cetywayo's) installation as King'.[28]

The marriage of the *inGcugce* had significant political overtones. The King's control over marriage was one of his most important prerogatives. It was essential to his control of the army and of the social and economic life of the country as a whole. It was imperative for him to retain this prerogative if the kingdom were not to dissolve into virtually independent chiefdoms under the untrammelled control of the great territorial chiefs. If the marriage law were broken, said Cetshwayo, he 'would be a shadow instead a king'.[29] It is therefore quite likely that what Gert Rudolph heard was true: that the King was extremely angry with his chiefs and accused them of disloyalty for not taking care that the marriage law was observed in their various districts. It was not in their interests as territorial chiefs that the marriage law should be strictly observed, but rather the reverse.[30]

Thus Bulwer's message of 3 October was on a very sensitive subject and came at a very sensitive time. The *izikhulu* had frustrated Cetshwayo's kingly ambition to send a military expedition to Swaziland, and it was the intervention of the Natal government that had assisted them to do so. They had also been negligent in upholding the prerogative of the King in their districts; and now the Natal government seemed to be encouraging them in this too. It was doing so, moreover, in the name of the 'coronation laws' which in Cetshwayo's eyes had been intended to limit the power of the chiefs and strengthen those of the King.[31] When the messengers arrived, Mnyamana, the Chief Counsellor, was not at Ulundi.[32] Contrary to custom, Cetshwayo saw the Natal messengers without any of his counsellors being present. In the messengers' report of what he said, his concern with both internal law and order and external military affairs is clearly apparent (perhaps more mixed up together in the report than in reality):

> Did I ever tell Mr. Shepstone I would not kill? Did he tell the white people I had made such an agreement, because if he did he has deceived them. I do kill, but I do not consider that I have done anything yet in the way of killing. Why do the white people start at nothing? I have not yet begun. I have yet to kill, it is the custom of our nation, and I shall not depart from it. Why does the Governor of Natal speak to me about my laws? Do I come to Natal and dictate to him about his laws? I shall not agree to any laws or rules from Natal and by so doing throw the large kraal which I govern into the water. My people will not listen unless they are killed, and while wishing to be friends with the English, I do not agree to give my people over to be governed by laws sent to me by them. Have I not asked the English to allow me to wash my spears, since the death of my father Umpande and they have kept playing with me all this time, treating me like a child?
>
> Go back and tell the English that I shall now act on my own account and if they wish me to agree to their laws I will leave and become a wanderer but before I go it will be seen,

I shall not go without having acted. I am not Mr. Shepstone who went back and deceived the white men, saying I had agreed to his laws.

Go back and tell the white men this, and let them hear it well, the Governor of Natal and I are equal, he is Governor of Natal, and I am Governor here.[33]

This 'formidable message', as it became known, came as a considerable shock to Bulwer. He interpreted it, not in the Zulu context which had produced it, but in the light of his own preoccupations as an agent of the imperial government. In this he was probably influenced by Shepstone, who arrived in Natal the day after the message was received. For Bulwer and Shepstone the central issue of the time was not the maintenance of monarchical authority in Zululand, but the Boers' failure against Sekhukhune. 'The deadly hatred that the Zulus bear for the Boers is now mixed with an undisguised contempt for them,' Bulwer told Carnarvon. Cetshwayo's revived ambition to wash his spears would probably lead to an attack on Swaziland or even the Transvaal itself, he continued. Only a desire to avoid offending the British government had kept him quiet hitherto. 'In the present message Cetywayo throws off any concealment of his intention to "wash his spears", and repudiates the moral influence which this Government has exercised with him.' Cetshwayo, Bulwer wrote privately,

finds his relations with this Govt. which have hitherto been his support & strength, to be now an irksome restraint. Hence his message. He wants to shake off the burden of the moral influence which this Govt. has exercised with him, and to be free to follow his own desires wh. are bent on mischief.[34]

It must be noted that, even on the information available to Bulwer, these comments are scarcely accurate. Even after the news of the Boers' failure against Sekhukhune must have reached him Cetshwayo had dutifully said that he regarded the English as his fathers and would not act against their wishes.[35] This suggests that the 'formidable message' was not simply the result of the events in the Transvaal. Even in the 'formidable message' itself he stated that he wished to be friends with the English and, although he complained of not being permitted to wash his spears, he did not declare that he would go ahead without this permission; what he repudiated was specifically the Natal Lieutenant-Governor's interference in the internal administration of his country.

A little earlier Bulwer received from East Griqualand, which had recently come under Cape administration and in which disturbances had broken out, reports of communications between Zulu, Basotho and Mpondo. He also received reports of rumours among the Basotho that Cetshwayo had proposed a combination between the Zulu, the Basotho and other African peoples against the whites generally.[36] He had earlier been inclined to suspend judgement on these reports; after the receipt of Cetshwayo's 'formidable message' (and, one should probably add, after the arrival of Shepstone), he became convinced that Cetshwayo had 'not only been preparing for war, but that he has been sounding the way with the view to a combination of the different races against the White man'.[37] The belief that Cetshwayo was the senior partner in an alliance between himself and Sekhukhune was beginning to develop into the belief that Cetshwayo was the evil genius of a country-wide black conspiracy to drive the white man into the sea. This hypothesis was later to be repudiated by Bulwer; but it was taken up by Shepstone, and especially by Frere, and swollen to monstrous proportions as an all-purpose explanation and justification.

Shepstone and Cetshwayo, November to December 1876

What was for Bulwer a cause for concern was for Shepstone a source of hope. Carnarvon had stressed the importance of annexing the Transvaal with the consent of its government and people, if at all possible, and Bulwer was strongly of the same opinion. But the Boers would not consent to British rule except under great pressure. The pressure produced by the financial condition of the ZAR was too slow and indirect. The pressure produced by Sekhukhune was too slight since he was fighting purely on the defensive. Hence the importance of the Zulu. Shepstone hoped that the Zulu King would go ahead with his attack on the Swazi, as this would 'also involve Cetywayo with the Transvaal, & tend to bring matters to a more speedy issue'. Cetshwayo's 'formidable message' to Bulwer was described by Shepstone as 'a very fortunate one, because it relieves us of an unpleasant responsibility on his behalf'.[38] The responsibility was presumably that of attempting to restrain the Zulu King from acts of war; his defiance of Natal showed, or could be used to show, that any further attempts at restraint would be useless.

Bulwer heard that Burgers had sent Rudolph to see Cetshwayo once again in connection with the border dispute; it seemed to him that war or peace between the Zulu and the Transvaal depended on the outcome of this meeting.[39]

Rudolph had been given plenary powers by Burgers to settle the border dispute, including the power to agree to a line more favourable to the Zulu than that claimed by the ZAR. He arrived at Ulundi on 23 October 1876. It was evident that the Boer failure against the Pedi had had its effects. Cetshwayo asked pointed questions about the commando the ZAR had sent against Sekhukhune, and boasted of the power of the Zulu army. Despite this implicit comparison he still considered it necessary to obtain the President's consent to an attack on the Swazi, which Rudolph told him was impossible. On the subject of the boundary Rudolph and Cetshwayo never came within sight of any agreement. Rudolph said that he was prepared and empowered to accept less than the ZAR's full claim, but Cetshwayo and his counsellors denied having made any cession at any time and declared that all the land to the Drakensberg belonged to the Zulu.[40]

Rudolph's mission was thus a complete failure. Despite Cetshwayo's claim that the districts of Utrecht and part of Wakkerstroom were Zulu territory, Rudolph did not believe that he would attack the ZAR; but he thought it likely that he would send a 'commando' against the Swazi in December,[41] when the annual *umkhosi* (which was in part a military review) was due to take place; and this, as he told Cetshwayo, would be tantamount to an act of war against the ZAR.

Having heard that Shepstone was back in South Africa, Rudolph wrote to him about his interview with the Zulu King. 'Without flattery,' he wrote, 'I feel much safer now that you are back in Africa.'[42] He would have felt much less safe had he known that Shepstone had not the slightest intention of trying to restrain Cetshwayo.

Shepstone wished to find out more about Cetshwayo's intentions. He could not communicate directly with him without making some allusion to his 'formidable message', and he could not do that without expressing disapproval, and he feared that this might have a restraining effect on Cetshwayo. So he asked John Dunn to pay Natal a visit after having seen Cetshwayo, hoping in this way to ascertain the state of things.

But he evidently wished to do more than obtain information. He feared that even if he said nothing to Cetshwayo his mere presence in the Transvaal might have a restraining effect upon him. He explained to Wolseley:

> But if I go to the Transvaal without ascertaining previously the real state of the Zulu mind & taking the precautions that may be necessary, Cetywayo may suppose that I have gone to form a coalition with the Boers against him, become amiable to the Boers & so remove a very wholesome pressure.

He did not say what these 'precautions' were. He had asked Dunn to inform Cetshwayo of his arrival 'as a matter of news'.[43] Perhaps the news was to include the information that he was not going to the assistance of the Boers.

Although Shepstone waited until 27 December, he never saw Dunn. For some reason Dunn did not visit Natal. Shepstone had to make do with Nunn, a white trader who held a similar position under Hamu as Dunn did under the King. From Nunn he received the unwelcome news that an attack upon the Swazi was unlikely.[44] Shortly before Shepstone left Pietermaritzburg he heard indirectly from Dunn. He saw a letter from Dunn to a friend in Natal dated 15 December, in which Dunn wrote:

> I've had a long talk with Cetywayo, & he has come to the conclusion that as affairs have gone on so long without the intervention of the English Govt. although requested to do so several times, he will allow matters to take their course, especially as he has heard about the move said about to be taken by the English Govt. in the Transvaal; Cetywayo is however determined to hold the boundary against the Dutch.[45]

The meaning of this is not very clear. It might mean that he would make no attempt to prevent the border dispute from drifting into war. But it suggests that he had no intention of taking any active steps. Shepstone had to search for crumbs of comfort. The annual *umkhosi* was being held earlier than usual. This was probably the result of food shortage (the effect of drought) but Shepstone hoped that it might have some sinister significance, and that the ceremony might culminate in an attack on Swaziland.[46]

Shepstone found another crumb of comfort in the activities of Gert Rudolph. The latter believed that a faction in Wakkerstroom was planning to do a separate deal with Cetshwayo and obtain the disputed territory for themselves in return for 1 000 cattle. In order to knock this idea on the head (and, according to Shepstone, to induce the voters to support the re-election of Burgers) Rudolph held several meetings at which he stressed the Zulu danger and the necessity for unity in the face of it. Shepstone had hoped to gain information which would have enabled him to speak with authority on the dangers of Cetshwayo's intentions; now he found Rudolph was doing just that: 'my object is therefore so far attained'.[47]

Shepstone in the Transvaal and the Zulu on the Frontier, January to April 1877

Shepstone wrote to Burgers on 20 December 1876, nearly seven weeks after he had arrived in Natal, and told him he was coming to the Transvaal to institute a 'special inquiry into the origin, nature and circumstances' of the Transvaal disturbances, with a view to securing 'the adjustment of existing disputes and difficulties, a settlement of the questions out of which they have arisen, and the adoption of such measures as may appear best calculated to prevent their occurrence in the future'.[48] A week later, without waiting for a reply, he left Pietermaritzburg with his staff and an escort of 25 mounted policemen, entering the Transvaal on 4 January 1877. En route he met Gert Rudolph, who had come across to Newcastle on New Year's Day to see him. The meeting was cut short by the arrival of a messenger from Utrecht demanding Rudolph's immediate return as 'Cetshwayo's boys' were out and had attacked an African homestead under Transvaal protection in the disputed territory.[49] Shepstone's reaction to this is not recorded, but one may suspect that he saw it as an omen of success for his mission.

This attack, it turned out, had taken place, not in what the ZAR considered to be the disputed territory, but on land well to the north of the Phongolo river, in the Wakkerstroom district, on a farm belonging to Assistant Veldkornet Kohrs, between the Ntombe and Mkhondo (Assegai) rivers. Four 'kraals' or African homesteads were 'eaten up', 30 people were killed and a large quantity of livestock was taken. The attack was the work of Prince Mbelini, the Swazi exile, who lived in the vicinity. According to Cetshwayo's later testimony, the attack arose out of a quarrel between Mbelini and his uncle 'Umshiani'. The latter had formerly lived under Mbelini, but had subsequently left him, taking a large number of cattle and 'joined the Boers'. Mbelini claimed that one of his people had tried to assassinate him; hence the attack on his homesteads.

This explanation of the occurrence suggests that it was not intended as an act of hostility towards the Boers. No attack was made on Kohrs' farmhouse;

indeed, Kohrs went to see Mbelini the following morning to demand an explanation; and when Mbelini was told that some of the livestock taken from the 'eaten-up' homesteads belonged in fact to Kohrs he readily returned them.

The attack on homesteads on the Kohrs' farm took place on the night of 31 December 1876. A few days later Mbelini attacked a homestead on Meyer's mission station at the German settlement of Luneburg, at the junction of the Ntombe and Phongolo rivers, killed an African woman, and reportedly made threats against the whites.

The local Zulu assured Rudolph that Mbelini was acting entirely on his own initiative and that Cetshwayo had nothing to do with these attacks. Rudolph did not believe them. He believed that Mbelini was a tool in Cetshwayo's hands, and that Cetshwayo was seeking a *casus belli* and hoping the Boers would provide him with one by attacking his subject, Mbelini.[50] Shepstone took a similar view. Cetshwayo, he wrote, seemed 'determined to pick a quarrel'.

> I believe that Cetywayo still respects, & to some extent fears, the Govt. of Natal & that his object in permitting the raids and murders of natives committed by Umbelini on farms occupied by white subjects of the Transvaal is to provoke retaliation & so furnish himself with a justification to meet any remonstrance from the Lt-Gov of Natal.[51]

Proof of Cetshwayo's unfriendly intentions seemed to be provided by a message he sent to Rudolph, received on 10 January 1877, consisting of a list of complaints about the frontier Boers and a recommended solution for the problem. The complaints concerned the harbouring of Zulu fugitives and cattle, and the solution was that Rudolph should order all Boers living among his people to depart. Although the Utrecht district west of the Blood river was claimed as part of Zululand, Cetshwayo exempted the people living there from this order as he said they gave him no trouble.[52]

This demand, which Rudolph made public, coming on top of Mbelini's attacks and Cetshwayo's assumed complicity in them, caused alarm and dismay on the border. The government of the ZAR was appealed to but was unable to provide any assistance. Many Boers abandoned their farms and went into laager or trekked further inland.[53] The Utrecht correspondent of *The Natal Mercury* wrote:

> In this district and Wakkerstroom public opinion is daily becoming more in favour of federation, those who were the most anti-English two months since, are today in favour of it. The pressure put on by Cetshwayo is driving many to their wits end . . . The prospects of federation look blooming this side of the Vaal river. There is a large majority in favour of any government that will ensure peace and security to life and property.[54]

The fact that the pressure exerted by Cetshwayo was conducive to the success of Shepstone's mission raises the suspicion that it was the result of the communications he had had with John Dunn before leaving Natal. This suspicion is heightened by the fact that Cetshwayo's messengers to Rudolph brought a letter written by Dunn confirming the eviction notice, and by the fact that Dunn also wrote at Cetshwayo's instance to Shepstone informing him of the notice.[55] But these facts are far from conclusive. All Cetshwayo's letters were written by Dunn; there was nothing unusual in Cetshwayo keeping Shepstone informed of the state of the border dispute; and there is nothing in either of these two letters to suggest that the eviction had been made at Shepstone's suggestion. In the letter to Shepstone Cetshwayo stated that the Boer farmers living among his subjects had been the cause of constant disturbances by their ill-treatment of the Zulu, and that this was likely to endanger the peace between Zululand and the Transvaal, which it was his wish to maintain.

Cetshwayo's eviction order caused some farmers to leave; but he made no attempt to compel those who did not leave to do so. Rudolph did not believe that there was any danger of Cetshwayo making an attack on the Utrecht district. He believed that his aim was to frighten the Boers by the insolence ('brutaliteit') of the local Zulu and induce them to leave by these indirect means. The danger Rudolph feared was that one of the Boers might shoot at the Zulu out of fear or anger, and thus spark off a general massacre.

On 22 January 1877 Rudolph received Cetshwayo's reply to the message that he had sent to him informing him of the the the actions of Mbelini. Cetshwayo thanked Rudolph for the information, and said that he knew little about Mbelini's doings because he lived so far away, that he was a villainous dog like all Swazi, and that Rudolph should deal with him as he saw fit. He assured Rudolph that if he attacked Mbelini with an armed force he would not be hindered by the Zulu of the area, who would do nothing to help Mbelini. In later messages Cetshwayo said that Mbelini was not his subject and that he was an evil-doer subject to no one; and he positively urged Rudolph to attack him and root him out, assuring him that the Zulu would not interfere.[56]

These reassuring messages from the Zulu King, together with the news of a peace treaty with Sekhukhune, apparently restored some confidence among the frontier farmers. The Utrecht correspondent of *The Natal Mercury*, himself firmly in favour of British rule, reported:

> Burgers and Independence for ever is now the cry of those who a month ago were willing to accept unconditionally, annexation, and are today as braggart and bounceable as ever, and fancy themselves capable of conquering single-handed all the native tribes in South Africa.[57]

Rudolph did not share this confidence (if it really existed). He hesitated to act against Mbelini because he feared, despite Cetshwayo's assurances, that it would provoke the local Zulu. He also feared that Cetshwayo's messages might themselves be a trick to entice him into striking the first blow. The decision was taken out of his hands by Assistant Veldkornet Kohrs, who gathered a force and attacked Mbelini on 24 February. The attack was unsuccessful; but the local Zulu made no attempt to hinder Kohrs' commando nor to help Mbelini; and this emboldened Rudolph to make a second attack. Action was especially necessary, he felt, as Kohrs' unsuccessful attack was bound to provoke Mbelini into retaliating. He then discovered that Mbelini had left his stronghold between the Mkhondo (Assegai) and Ntombe rivers and retreated to another stronghold near the Dumbe mountain, on the Zulu side of the line that the Transvaal had claimed since 1861. Rudolph therefore abandoned his plan to attack him since it would constitute an invasion of Zululand. The Landdrost of Wakkerstroom was neither so scrupulous nor so prudent and took a force against Mbelini at his new abode. But he discovered that Mbelini had again retreated further into Zululand, so after burning the deserted homestead the Wakkerstroom commando returned home. This incursion into Zululand caused some alarm among the border farmers, as they feared it would excite the wrath of the Zulu King. It produced no apparent reaction, however, and the alarm soon subsided.[58]

The Transvaal-Zululand border situation was one of inherent conflict. Two populations lived interspersed and held allegiance to two different governments. Since Boer and Zulu recognized no common law the most petty dispute had to be settled by diplomatic rather than by judicial means: a cow straying into a mealie-field could cause an international crisis. Each government and population claimed exclusive ownership of the same land. Cetshwayo and the local Zulu tried to induce the Boers to leave and to induce those Africans who had submitted to the hegemony of the ZAR to give their allegiance instead to the Zulu King. The ZAR and the local Boers tried to induce the Zulu to leave or to remain as subjects of the ZAR and servants of the Boers. The ZAR was in no position to exert its claims by force. The great fear of Gert Rudolph, the republican officer with overall responsibility for frontier affairs, was that hasty action might spark an explosion, and he was tireless in urging patience and forbearance on the Boers. Cetshwayo was determined to resist further encroachment, and he wished to regain territory which had been lost in the past; but it is clear that he wished to do so by measures which fell short of force, and that he had no wish for a war with the Transvaal. The resulting situation was one of continual tension interspersed with occasional alarms. It seems that during the alarms a substantial number of Boers were prepared to welcome the prospect of British rule. But this was only in the Utrecht and Wakkerstroom districts. Elsewhere in the Transvaal the Zulu frontier situation seems to have had little effect on the Boers, who at this stage in their history had little sense of national unity.

Shepstone thus had no easy task in attempting to magnify the Zulu danger to proportions sufficient to terrify the Boers of the Transvaal into accepting British rule. He was all the more dependent on the Zulu since the Pedi had been so thoughtless as to conclude peace with the republican government while Shepstone was actually in Pretoria negotiating its downfall. Shepstone was able to show that Sekhukhune had not agreed to become a subject of the ZAR as its plenipotentiaries had claimed,[59] but that was small compensation for the role he had originally envisaged himself playing – commanding Sekhukhune in the Queen's name to spare the Transvaal while sheltering the terrified Boers under the folds of the British flag. Nothing of that sort was possible now.

Shepstone suspected that the relative inaction of the Zulu was the result of his own presence in Pretoria: 'they appear to be quietly awaiting the result of my mission', he wrote to Barkly.[60] He feared that Rudolph might, by 'artfully alluding to my presence', suggest to Cetshwayo 'that the British Govt. has in some way sanctioned & is a party to the demand in the matter of Umbelini'. He therefore asked Bulwer to tell the Zulu King to believe no messages that connected him or the British government with the politics of the Transvaal unless they came directly from him, Shepstone, or from Bulwer, and that Rudolph represented only the Boer government.[61] There is no evidence that Rudolph did use Shepstone's presence in Pretoria in the way that he feared, or that it had any influence on Cetshwayo's refusal to protect Mbelini from the consequences of his atrocious act.

Shepstone's dealings with the tottering republican regime can be dealt with here only in the most schematic way.[62] Shepstone revealed his true purpose only gradually. As we have seen,[63] he initially told Burgers in the vaguest terms that his purpose in coming to Pretoria was to inquire into the war in the Transvaal, to adjust existing disputes and to secure the adoption of measures calculated to prevent such occurrences in the future. On the road to Pretoria he emphasized the need for 'some change', a sentiment which was well received, not only by English shopkeepers but by Boers. Considering the state of the country and the unpopularity of President Burgers this is not surprising, but Shepstone chose to interpret it as a desire for British rule. In Pretoria he told Burgers and his Executive Council that he had come to negotiate a federation of the Transvaal with the other states and colonies of South Africa. Only after some time did he reveal that he was authorized to bring the Transvaal under British rule, and that he would be obliged to do so if it proved unable to pull itself together. Finally he declared that no internal reforms could save the republic and that he must declare the Transvaal British territory, which he did on 12 April 1877.

There was no resistance. Shepstone had with him only 25 mounted police, but there were British troops poised on the border, and beyond them lay the whole might of the British empire of which Shepstone was the immediate representative. The republic on the other hand was in a weak and vulnerable condition and its citizens were deeply divided. The predominantly English commercial and mining population, as well as some of the Boers in the frontier regions, welcomed British rule as the only way to safeguard life and property. It is difficult to believe Shepstone's claims that a majority of the Boers welcomed British rule. But they were demoralized by the manifest failure of the republic and had no alternative focus of loyalty. Burgers was discredited, and his opponent in the forthcoming presidential election, Paul Kruger, was an untutored frontiersman and seemed to many entirely inadequate to guide the republic through its complex difficulties. All attempts to find a third candidate had failed. Shepstone himself had been seriously suggested as a candidate in the previous presidential election. Now he had become the ruler of the Transvaal, under somewhat unusual circumstances it is true, and under the British flag. But he undertook that the Transvaal would remain a separate government with its own laws and legislature and that Dutch would remain an official language along with English. And the British connection was not without its advantages, in the form of financial, military and administrative assistance. Burgers issued a protest against the annexation, and the Executive Council appointed two of its members as a deputation to the British government to seek its reversal, but Burgers' last act as President was to order his burghers to refrain from any violent act that might jeopardize the success of the deputation's mission – and thus a patriotic reason or excuse was furnished for what might otherwise have seemed unpatriotic inaction.

Shepstone's Use of the Zulu Threat

All Shepstone's attempts to gain the consent of the government or the legislature of the ZAR to the annexation of the country ended in failure. Both these attempts and their failure led him to lay a heavy stress on the danger facing the Transvaal from its black inhabitants and neighbours, and especially from its most powerful black neighbours, the Zulu. He first invoked the black peril in an attempt to frighten the republican authorities into consenting to British rule, and when that failed he invoked it as a means of justifying his having annexed the Transvaal without their consent. The effect of the annexation of the Transvaal was therefore to promote the image of the Zulu as a fierce and aggressive menace to white people.

Shepstone's dealings with the ZAR authorities were mainly verbal, and there is not much direct evidence of what he said to them. An exception is provided by his formal meeting with the Executive Council on 1 March, when minutes were kept. In reply to Shepstone's insistence on the inherent weakness of the republic, Kruger said that a strong police force could be formed which would be adequate for most purposes, and that the burghers would have to be called out only to deal with a powerful people such as that of Cetshwayo. This gave Shepstone his cue:

> Look at the real facts. Cetshwayo actually exercises power on land belonging to this state. He is hostile to the people here and says that they killed Dingaan. The British Government holds him back from attacking you. Are you in a position to overcome him?[64]

These words contain an implicit threat. 'The British Government' in this context really meant Shepstone himself. If he intended to continue to hold Cetshwayo back, his question would become superfluous. Shepstone was later remembered as having made the threat much more explicit. According to a version of this conversation given by the Boer 'Volkskomitee' to Sir Bartle Frere in April 1879, Shepstone, after stating that Cetshwayo ruled part of the country continued:

> We have restrained him and he will not do anything as long as I am here, but does the State possess the power to resist that man if I remove my hand from him?[65]

Such a master of the art of vagueness as Shepstone is unlikely to have been so explicit, but it is likely that he wished to introduce into the minds of his hearers the idea that he might cease to restrain Cetshwayo, and the Volkskomitee's statement suggests that he succeeded.[66]

The main point of his remarks was that the ZAR was only in appearance an independent state, but was not so in reality since it depended for its very existence upon the exertions of a more powerful neighbour; and that the continuance of this anomalous state of affairs was a threat to the whites of South Africa. This became the major theme of Shepstone's writings, public and private, in the weeks leading up to the annexation.

Bulwer's reaction to the news of the conclusion of peace between Sekhukhune and the ZAR was to comment that it was this question which had really produced Shepstone's mission, and that its settlement 'removes one of the difficulties which turned men's minds in the Transvaal to the necessity of a stronger Government'. Perhaps the greatest difficulty, Bulwer had continued, was the Zulu question; and they too had 'subsided for the present'.[67] Shepstone's response was to say that even if Sekhukhune had accepted the status of a subject of the ZAR this meant little since the ZAR had little control over its black subjects.

> They decline to pay taxes, make war upon each other, deny the authority of the State Govt. & allow Boers to occupy the farms to wh. they have received titles from the Govt. of the Republic on condition only that they pay annual tribute to the native chiefs claiming jurisdiction. If the imbecility of the Govt. is such as to be obliged to bear with these things from its own subjects in what condition is it to face its foreign relations? How can it inspire respect abroad? What effect has it already produced upon the powerful Amaswazi, & the still more powerful Zulus? And what may it not, *must* it not yet produce? All these considerations show sure signs of fatal weakness & this weakness is inherent in the circumstances of the country & in its form of Govt.; nothing within the compass of its own means can redeem it. I conclude therefore that it would be unkind to the people of this country both white and black & that it wd. be destructive of the security of H.M. Possessions in S. Africa to allow this seeming but unreal independence longer to tempt the ambitions and cupidity of the native Chiefs and Tribes within & without the boundaries of the Republic. If it had not been for the good offices of the Govt. of Natal this country would have been overrun long ago, & for these people to talk of their independence and freedom is simply to talk of enjoyments which they don't possess.[68]

On 22 February the Volksraad rejected Carnarvon's Permissive Confederation Bill. Shepstone's hopes of annexing the Transvaal with the consent of its government dwindled to virtually nothing. It seemed certain, he wrote to Barkly on the following day, that troops would be needed to overawe the ignorant and fanatical portion of the population:

> even if anything like universal opposition were shown, it wd. be impossible for H.M. Govt. to allow this State to drift into the anarchy that is inevitable if it retains its nominal independence, & to become an easy prey to its half million so called native subjects, to say nothing of the powerful tribes by which the Transvaal is surrounded. I am satisfied that if I were now to abandon my mission, & leave the country as it is, that in six months it wd. be overrun & annihilated as a state, & that we should soon have a war of races in S. Africa.[69]

Sir Arthur Cunyngehame, the general commanding in South Africa, was alarmed at the prospect of troops being used to conquer the Transvaal. Shepstone explained:

> My reason for desiring to have a considerable force at first is because I fear that if the fanatical portion of the Boers were tempted by the exhibition of a small force to fire a shot at it, nothing could prevent the Zulus & Amaswazi from falling upon the white people in the Republic & committing horrible ravages before they could be stopped. They would assume that they were bound to defend H.M. Govt. & as their inclination would strongly suit their sense of duty they would not wait to ask if their assistance were wanted or not. Of the Boers themselves I have no fear, they may possibly a few of them discharge their consciences by discharging their firearms, but it will most probably be at a safe distance to both parties. The great danger will be as you will see, that which I have described concerning the Zulus.[70]

Sekhukhune could no longer be represented as a threat to the ZAR; but Shepstone ingeniously found a way of making a virtue of this necessity. He had not, he said, been in the Transvaal for more than a few days before finding that the war with the Pedi was 'but an insignificant item' among the many dangers which beset the republic. The Pedi were 'unwarlike, and of no account in Zulu estimation'. Nevertheless this 'little episode' was enough to bring about the bankruptcy and collapse of the state.

> The Sikukuni storm, small though it was, had been enough to show that the Transvaal bark was unseaworthy and to make it unmanageable, and the discovery that such a serious effect had been produced by so small a cause had sent the thrilling intelligence through all the immense masses of natives between the Zambesi on the north and the Cape Colony on the South that the relative positions of the white and the black man had been seriously changed; and had prompted the thought that the supremacy of barbarism was no longer hopeless provided only that the effort be well planned and simultaneously executed.

As Shepstone explained it, the Boers had been able to establish themselves in the Transvaal because its native inhabitants, being of the Basotho race, were unwarlike and docile compared to the Zulu, and initially regarded the Boers as 'protectors against their dreaded enemies of the Zulu race'. Closer contact soon estranged them, however, and these 800 000 to 1 000 000 blacks who formed a dark fringe around the sparse white population became more hostile. Tribe after tribe successfully resisted the authority of the Boer government, and whole districts were abandoned by Boers except for those few who were permitted to remain as tributaries of African chiefs. Nevertheless, the Transvaal blacks, being unwarlike, made 'no attempt to follow up their victories; and this ebb of white power occurring piecemeal in a series of local incidents, the overall tendency was not clearly perceived. 'It was only when the whole available strength of the country was called up against Sikukuni and so signally failed, that the prestige of the state vanished from the minds of the natives.'

Beyond the dark fringe of relatively unwarlike Basotho tribes within the nominal borders of the ZAR, Shepstone continued, lay the more powerful, better organized and more aggressive tribes of Zulu race. To the north were the people of Lobengula, who still cherished hostile memories of former encounters with the Boers. To the east lay the extensive territory from Delagoa Bay to the Zambezi under the chief Mzila. To the south-east, the Swazi were looked on as subjects of the ZAR, but they repudiated this and since the war with Sekhukhune they had become impatient of restraint. 'Their experience of the prowess of their white allies on that occasion has destroyed their respect, and made them both defiant and aggressive.' To the south was the head of the Zulu race.

> Cetywayo is the most formidable as he is the most hostile to this state, of all the surrounding native powers. He can, it is believed, send 30,000 soldiers into the field; his men are under the strictest discipline, embodied in regiments in every way well organized; most are provided with firearms a large proportion of which are of a superior description.

Cetshwayo's 'hatred of the Boers is notorious', while his 'regiments are continually clamouring to be allowed to emulate their predecessors who overran and conquered for Cetywayo's uncle Chaka the whole of the territory now forming the Transvaal Republic'. Cetshwayo had long been anxious to wash his spears. Formerly the Swazi had been the intended victims,

> but since the result of their encounter with Sekukuni, the Boers have been promoted to the preference, because it is believed that they could be more easily dealt with than the Amaswazi, while the glory of washing his weapons in white blood would be greater.

In the case of both the Zulu and the Swazi, 'the Government of Natal has been the only obstacle to attacks on the Republic being made by those tribes, which, judged by the light afforded by the Sikukuni war, would, if made, most assuredly have annihilated the state'. The ZAR had thus for long been unable to maintain its independence by its own strength, and given the recent large-scale acquisition of firearms by Africans it was improbable that it would ever be able to do so. Cetshwayo was 'watching the progress of events' and would commit no aggressive act as long as Shepstone remained in the country; 'but if I am obliged to leave without accomplishing my mission he will at once claim the right of independent action'.[71]

There are elements in Shepstone's analysis which are not entirely devoid of truth. The situation of the whites who settled in the heart of Africa was inherently precarious. They had been able to establish themselves in the Transvaal partly because wars preceding the Great Trek had disrupted its African polities but mainly because of their monopoly of horses and firearms. Nevertheless, the peripheral areas of white settlement remained 'open frontiers',[72] frontier zones in which the Boers were unable to dominate the Africans and had to deal with them as equals or even as superiors. To an extent the Boers became incorporated into the existing African system of political and diplomatic relationships.[73] In the 1860s they lost power in the northern Transvaal, and it was not inconceivable that as they lost their monopoly of the most effective weapon of war this process of decline might have gone further, leading either to withdrawal to the more secure base of the Cape Colony or to growing accommodation with and incorporation into African polities. The extent to which such a process could go is shown by the history of the Portuguese *prazeiros* of the Zambezi valley, who during the course of the seventeenth and eighteenth centuries became transformed from Portuguese settlers virtually into African chiefs.[74] It was never likely that such a process would go so far in the Transvaal in the nineteenth century. The nineteenth century was not the seventeenth century. In an age of rapidly expanding industrial capitalism in Europe, it is almost inconceivable that European settlers would have been thus marooned in Africa, left to find their own salvation, and forced either to retreat or to adapt to the African environment and circumstances as best they could and become transformed in the process. The *prazeiro* regime itself was replaced by direct Portuguese rule in the Zambezi valley later in the nineteenth century. In the Transvaal it was Shepstone's annexation which arrested and reversed the tendencies towards the sort of regime that existed in the Zambezi valley.[75]

Such tendencies did then exist. There were in a broad and general sense elements of truth in Shepstone's representation of the situation of the whites in the Transvaal. But his contention that the ZAR faced imminent invasion and annihilation at the hands of its African neighbours was certainly untrue. There is evidence that Lobengula was worried by the possibility that Boers might attempt to settle in his country and that he intended resisting any such attempt,[76] but there is no evidence of any intention on his part to invade the Transvaal. The remote figure of Mzila was even less of a threat. The Swazi were far too afraid of the Zulu to contemplate any aggression toward the Boers. Moreover, while it is true that the Swazi contingent withdrew from the war against the Pedi in disgust at the Boers' failure to participate in the assault on Johannes Dinkwanyane's stronghold, the 'prestige' of the Boers does not seem to have diminished in Swazi eyes to the extent represented by Shepstone. Well after this Swazi withdrawal and after the Boers' failure against Sekhukhune, as we have seen,[77] the Swazi King was still anxiously seeking the aid of the ZAR against a threatening Zulu attack on his country. I have found no evidence which in any way supports Shepstone's statement that Cetshwayo had decided to wash his spears in 'white blood' instead of in that of the Swazi. It is probably true that Cetshwayo was deterred by fear of offending the British government from taking more active steps to drive the Boers out of the disputed territory. But there is no evidence that he entertained any thought of 'overrunning' the Transvaal or claiming any more of it than the Utrecht district and part of the Wakkerstroom district. Moreover it is very doubtful that the Zulu would have been successful had they had any such ambition. The war with the Pedi was misleading. What the Boers had failed to do was to dislodge Sekhukhune from a formidable natural fortress, a position which it later took the British two years to capture (and then only with massive assistance from the Swazi). From this failure of the Boers against Sekhukhune nothing can be inferred about what they might have been able to do had the Zulu invaded the open country of the Transvaal, and had such a real threat forced united action upon them. The firearms the Zulu had acquired were mostly of an inferior description, and they had not (as the Anglo-Zulu war of 1879 was to show)[78] become at all skilled in their use or able to adapt their warfare to their possession. It is quite possible that a Zulu attack on a Boer laager would have suffered much the same fate as Dingane's army at Blood river, and mounted Boer marksmen might have wrought havoc upon the Zulu foot-soldiers.

Did Shepstone really believe what he wrote in his public proclamations and despatches? One might expect his private letters to tell a different story. But they do not. There is no inconsistency between his private and public writings. Having been entrusted with the task of annexing the Transvaal, and being determined to succeed, it was necessary for Shepstone to persuade not only the public but his superiors and colleagues, and himself too, that the black danger, and expecially the Zulu danger, to the Transvaal was such that he had no alternative but to bring it under British rule.

Shepstone was generally successful in this campaign of persuasion. It became the prevalent belief in Britain and among many in South Africa that only Shepstone's annexation had saved the Transvaal from the Zulu. The annexation of the Transvaal therefore helped to foster the belief that the Zulu were a menace, and thus helped to facilitate the invasion of Zululand less than two years later.

The Zulu had done little to warrant such a belief. At the end of March, however, only a fortnight before Shepstone proclaimed the Transvaal British, there was a scare on the Transvaal-Zulu frontier. It was reported that the Zulu army was assembling and that an attack on the Transvaal was intended. Many Boers crossed over into Natal, or drove their cattle across and went into laager themselves in the Utrecht district, while others trekked further inland.[79]

The report that the Zulu army was mustering was not mere idle rumour. The Zulu army was indeed called up and, according to the missionary Robert Robertson, who was at Cetshwayo's residence at the time, the summons was issued on 24 March. All fighting men, it was reported, were ordered to join their regiments except those living near the Transvaal frontier, and three regiments were sent to the vicinity of this frontier. This military muster, however, had not been ordered with any aggressive intentions. It was ordered in response to a report that the Boers were invading Zululand, possibly with the intention of making another attempt to seize Mbelini. As soon as Cetshwayo realised that this report was false, he disbanded his army, except for some men whom he retained to begin work on a new *ikhanda* in the dense bush near the junction of the White and Black Mfolozi, a project planned the previous December.[80]

Bulwer informed Shepstone of the Zulu military muster.[81] The news reached Shepstone literally on the eve of the annexation, on 11 April 1877. He immediately sent to C. Boast, the Acting Resident Magistrate at Newcastle, asking him to send a messenger to Cetshwayo to tell him that news had reached him of some hostile intention on the part of the Zulu King towards the people of the Transvaal, and that if this were so all such intentions were to be given up and any force assembled for aggressive purposes was to be disbanded as the country was about to be placed under the sovereignty of the Queen.[82] In due course Shepstone received a reply to this message, conveyed to Newcastle by Kabana, Boast's messenger to Cetshwayo, and by letter from Boast to Pretoria. Cetshwayo is thus reported to have said:

> I thank my Father Somtseu for his message. I am glad that he has sent it because the Dutch have tired me out, and I intended soon to fight with them once, only once and to drive them over the Vaal. Kabana, you see my 'Impis' (armies) are gathered. It was to fight the Dutch I called them together. Now I will send them back to their homes.

'I attach considerable importance to Cetywayo's answer,' Shepstone told Carnarvon,

> because it shows clearly the pinnacle of peril which the Republic, and South Africa generally, had reached at the moment when the annexation took place; it also fully justifies the description of the dangerous condition of the country which my Proclamation and address to the people of the 12th April set forth.[83]

It is very doubtful that it does justify Shepstone's lurid descriptions of the impending annihilation of the ZAR. In the first place, the statement 'my "Impis" (armies) are gathered. It was to fight the Dutch I called them together' may have been true, but it was misleading. Some or possibly all of the men gathered at the royal residence at the time Kabana arrived there had *originally* been called together to 'fight the Dutch', but according to all other accounts they were retained for the very different purpose of building once it had been established that the reports

of a Boer invasion were false. Second, this message seems to be a somewhat free
rendering of what Cetshwayo actually said. In a report to the Natal government
Boast represented Kabana as reporting Cetshwayo thus:

> You see Kabana my armies ('Impi') are collected. I called them together to fight the
> Dutch if they again complained to me of the acts of Umbelini . . . or sought him from
> me. They will now return to their homes.[84]

In this version of Cetshwayo's statement, fighting the Dutch is contingent upon
their taking some action first. If 'sought him from me' is taken to mean sought by
physical force, that is, by making another armed incursion into Zululand in
pursuit of Mbelini, this version of Cetshwayo's words would accord better with
other accounts of the reasons for the military muster, and confirm its essentially
defensive purpose. Boast nevertheless offered the opinion to Bulwer that had
Shepstone's message not reached Cetshwayo when it did a Zulu invasion of the
Transvaal would have taken place in a few days. Bulwer, in sending this report to
Carnarvon, commented that he did not think there were sufficient grounds for
Boast's opinion: that the cause of the Zulu muster had been an apprehension
that an attack would be made by the Boers in pursuit of Mbelini; that had such a
pursuit taken place there would have been a collision between the Boers and the
Zulu; but that there was no reason to suppose that Cetshwayo intended fighting
the Boers unless compelled to do so in self-defence.

Carnarvon's comments on Bulwer's despatch are illuminating. He ordered
that it should not be published in the Blue Books.

> It is not I think desirable to raise any doubt as to Sir T. Shepstone's judgement amongst
> people who know less of him than we do. If indeed it were a question as between his
> view & that of Sir H. Bulwer on the motives of a Native Chief acting as Cetawayo has
> done I should be disposed to accept Sir T.'s opinion.[85]

This was more than an expression of confidence in Shepstone's knowledge of
Africans. Bulwer's remarks were subversive of the whole elaborate justification
Shepstone had developed for the British seizure of the Transvaal. Imperial policy
required Cetshwayo and his people to be ferocious and aggressive, burning to lay
waste the Transvaal and wash their spears in white blood. Shepstone had built up
this image of the Zulu in order to cover up his failure to secure the Boers'
consent to the annexation of their country. This image was now a necessity and
had to be sustained. A balanced and evidence-based judgement which under-
mined this image had to be suppressed.

Notes

1. SP 15, Carnarvon to Shepstone, 4 October 1876; BL Add Mss 60798, no. 106, Carnarvon to Froude, 16 October 1876.
2. BL Add Mss 60798, no. 104, Froude to Carnarvon, 27 September 1876.
3. BPP, C1748, p. 47, nos 32 and 33, Carnarvon to Barkly and Bulwer, 12 July 1876; CO 48/480, Cape 8317, Law Officers to Colonial Office, 12 July, and minutes; GH 597, Barkly to Bulwer, 12 October 1876, encl Barkly to Burgers, 4 October 1876; SP 65, Secret, Carnarvon to Barkly, 22 September 1876, copy in Shepstone's handwriting.
4. Appelgryn, *Burgers*, pp. 166–7. This matter was kept very secret – see PRO 30/6/32, no. 197, Carnarvon to Barkly, 8 March 1877.
5. CO 179/122, Natal 12875, Foreign Office to Colonial Office, 19 October 1876, minutes by Herbert and Carnarvon, 7 November 1876.
6. Goodfellow, *Great Britain and South African Confederation*, p. 116.
7. CO 107/2, GW 9102, Barkly to Carnarvon, 6 July 1876, minutes by Herbert and Carnarvon, 31 July 1876.
8. BPP, C1776, pp. 8–19, nos 13 and 16, Barkly to Carnarvon, 11 and 18 December 1876; CO 48/479, minute by Malcolm, 17 January 1877 on Cape 668, Barkly to Carnarvon, 18 December 1876, referring also to Cape 299, Barkly to Carnarvon, 11 December 1876.
9. GH 1219, p. 490, no. 205, Bulwer to Carnarvon, 3 November 1876.
10. BPP, C2144, p. 274, report on the province of the Transvaal by W.C. Sargeaunt, 15 August 1878; Uys, *Era of Shepstone*, pp. 215–19; De Kiewiet, *Imperial Factor in South Africa*, pp. 97–9 and 111; Appelgryn, *Burgers*, ch. 8.
11. SP 67, p. 1, Shepstone to Herbert, 23 October 1876.
12. *The Natal Witness*, 2 January 1877, 'Annual Retrospect'; *Natal Government Gazette Extraordinary*, Vol. XXIX, no. 1650, speech of Lieutenant-Governor opening Legislative Council, 7 June 1877.
13. *The Natal Witness*, 26 January 1877, editorial; *The Natal Mercury*, 2 January 1877, letter from special correspondent, Pretoria, 20 December 1877; ibid, 30 January 1877, 'Our North-Western Border'; CO 879/10, African no. 108, proceedings of a deputation of residents, merchants and others to Carnarvon, 26 October 1876, especially pp. 2 and 4.
14. TA, General Letter-book 2, Shepstone to Barkly, Pietermaritzburg, 3 December 1876.
15. PRO 30/6/12, p. 177, Carnarvon to Hardy, 20 September 1876; PRO 30/6/3, no. 36, Carnarvon to Victoria, 25 September 1876; BL Add Mss 60769, Carnarvon to Hardy, 17 September 1876; CO 48/479, minute by Herbert, 23 September 1876, on Cape 11509, Barkly to Carnarvon, 31 August 1876; PRO 30/6/3, no. 42, Carnarvon to Ponsonby, 6 October 1876; ibid, no. 44, Ponsonby to Carnarvon, 8 October 1876.
16. See ch. 3 p. 72.
17. SS 211, R1739/76, Rudolph to SS, 6 July 1876; SS 212, R2019/76, Rudolph to SS, 3 August 1876.
18. Laband, *Kingdom in Crisis*, pp. 59 and 70, n. 56; Cope, 'Political Power', pp. 23–5.
19. See ch. 3, pp. 66–8.
20. SS 210, R1608/76; SS 211, R1671/76 and R1739/76; SS 212, R2019/76 and R2072/76; all Rudolph to SS, 22 June, 1 July, 6 July, 3 August, 10 August 1876 respectively. See also the Utrecht correspondent's reports of 4, 13 and 20 July in *The Natal Mercury*, 13, 25 and 27 July 1876 respectively.
21. GH 1219, pp. 424 and 443, nos 139 and 156, Bulwer to Carnarvon, 13 July and 9 August 1876; SNA I/7/13, p. 9, message to Cetshwayo, 25 July 1876; SS 212, R2020/76, Rudolph to SS, 4 August 1876.
22. SNA I/7/13, p. 13, statement of messengers to Cetshwayo, 28 August 1876.

23. SS 212, R2072/76, Rudolph to SS, 10 August 1876; SS 213, R2130/76, Moll to SS, 16 August 1876; SS 213, R2187/76, Rudolph to SS, 24 August 1876.
24. SNA I/7/13, p. 11, message to Cetshwayo, 4 September 1876; ibid, p. 16, statement of messengers, 9 October 1876.
25. SNA I/7/7, p. 330, report on state of affairs in Zululand by ASNA, 11 October 1876; see also GH 1300, p. 63, Confid, Bulwer to Carnarvon, 13 October 1876, enclosing the former.
26. For more detail and sources, see Cope, 'Political Power', p. 22, and Cope, 'Characters of Blood?', pp. 13–14.
27. Cope, 'Characters of Blood?', p. 14.
28. SNA I/7/13, p. 15, message to Cetshwayo, 3 October 1876.
29. Webb and Wright, *Zulu King Speaks*, p. 72.
30. SS 214, R2267/76, Rudolph to SS, 31 Aug. 1876. On the chiefs and the marriage laws, see Cope, 'Political Power', pp. 22–3.
31. Cope, 'Political Power', pp. 11–18.
32. SNA I/7/11, p. 4, 'Addition to Report on Zulu Affairs of 20 November 1876', 24 November 1876; Mnyamana returned to Ulundi on 25 October – SS 219, R3073/76, Rudolph to SS, 31 October 1876, p. 44.
33. SNA I/7/13, p. 17, message from Cetshwayo, 2 November 1876. This message was spoken in Zulu to the messengers who, having borne it in their memory for about two weeks, delivered it in Zulu to the Acting Secretary for Native Affairs, who wrote it down in English. The substance may have been somewhat distorted and the language heightened in transmission, but it is probably substantially authentic: Cox, *Life of Colenso*, Vol. II, p. 518n; Etherington, 'Anglo-Zulu Relations', p. 51n.
34. GH 1300, pp. 66–7, Confid, Bulwer to Carnarvon, 2 November 1876; PRO 30/6/38, no. 89, Bulwer to Carnarvon, 3 November 1876.
35. See p. 117.
36. GH 1219, p. 487, no. 202, Bulwer to Carnarvon, 20 October 1876; GH 1300, p. 65, Confid, Bulwer to Carnarvon, 31 October 1876.
37. GH 1300, p. 66, Confid, Bulwer to Carnarvon, 2 November 1876.
38. SP 67, p. 8, Shepstone to Herbert, 12 November 1876.
39. GH 1300, p. 67, Confid, Bulwer to Carnarvon, 2 November 1876.
40. SS 219, R3073/76, Rudolph to SS, 31 October 1876.
41. TA, Engelbrecht Collection, Vol. 4, Section 16, p. 201, Rudolph to Burgers, 3 November 1876.
42. SP 67, p. 9, Shepstone to Barkly, 23 November 1876, quoting Rudolph's letter to him of 17 November.
43. Ibid, p. 13, Shepstone to Wolseley, 24 November 1876.
44. SP 71, Copy, Shepstone to Barkly, 13 December 1876.
45. SP 67, p. 21, Shepstone to Barkly, 23 December 1876.
46. Ibid, p. 17, Shepstone to Herbert, 2 December 1876; ibid, p. 21, Shepstone to Barkly, 23 December 1876.
47. TA, Engelbrecht Collection, Vol. 4, section 16, p. 201, Rudolph to Burgers, 3 November 1876; SP 71, Copy, Shepstone to Barkly, 13 December 1876.
48. Shepstone to Burgers, 20 December 1876, quoted Uys, *Era of Shepstone*, p. 242.
49. *The Natal Witness*, 9 January 1877, 'Sir Theophilus Shepstone'.
50. SS 227, R109/77, Rudolph to SS, 4 January 1877; SS 228, R377, Rudolph to SS, 24 January 1877; Webb and Wright, *Zulu King Speaks*, p. 22.
51. SP 67, pp. 33–4, Shepstone to Herbert, 26 January 1877.
52. SS 227, R228/77, Rudolph to SS, 11 January 1877.
53. *De Volksstem*, 27 January 1877, letter from Wakkerstroom correspondent, 18 January 1877; *The Natal Witness*, 6 February 1877, 'Utrecht', referring to letter dated 29 January;

ibid, 9 February 1877, 'Utrecht', referring to letter dated 25 January; *The Natal Mercury*, 13 February 1877, letters from Utrecht correspondent, 24 and 27 January 1877.

54. *The Natal Mercury*, 30 January and 13 February 1877, letters from Utrecht correspondent, 16 and 21 January 1877.

55. KC, Colenso Papers, File 27, KCM 50124, no. 10, Copy, Dunn to Shepstone, 28 December 1876.

56. SS 228, R377/77 and R449/77, and SS 229, R569/77, Rudolph to SS, 24 January, 1 February and 7 February 1877.

57. *The Natal Mercury*, 8 March 1877, letter of Utrecht correspondent, 20 February 1877.

58. SS 230, R862/77, Rudolph to SS, 26 February 1877; SS 231, R895/77, Hutchinson (Landdrost, Wakkerstroom) to SS, 3 March 1877; SS 231, R896/77, Rudolph to SS, 2 March 1877; *The Natal Mercury*, 20 March 1877, letter from Utrecht correspondent, 1 March 1877; *The Natal Witness*, 13 March 1877, letter from Wakkerstroom correspondent, 3 March 1877; *The Natal Colonist*, 16 March 1877, letter from Utrecht correspondent, 7 March 1877.

59. CO48/482, Cape 5576, Shepstone to Carnarvon, 3 April 1877, and enclosures.

60. SP 67, p. 129, Shepstone to Barkly, 28 March 1877.

61. Ibid, p. 79, Shepstone to Barkly, 23 February 1877; ibid, p. 81, Shepstone to Bulwer, 23 February 1877.

62. The most detailed account is in Uys, *Era of Shepstone*. As a corrective to Uys's hostile view of Burgers, the latter's biography by Appelgryn should be consulted.

63. See p. 122.

64. SS 230, R868/77, 'Vergadering ten Gouvernementskantore, Pretoria', 1 March 1877, printed in *Bijvoegsel tot de Staatscourant*, 24 March 1877. My translation.

65. Engelbrecht, *Burgers*, pp. 263–4.

66. See Cope, 'Shepstone, the Zulus', pp. 57–8, for my reasons for preferring the earlier version of Shepstone's words.

67. SP 17, Bulwer to Shepstone, 14 February 1877.

68. SP 67, pp. 66–7, Shepstone to Bulwer, 20 February 1877.

69. Ibid, pp. 78–9 and 102, Shepstone to Barkly, 23 February and 7 March 1877.

70. Ibid, pp. 117–8, Shepstone to Barkly, 20 March 1877.

71. BPP, C1776, pp. 107–10, Shepstone to Carnarvon, 6 March 1877; ibid., pp. 125–8, Shepstone to Carnarvon, 12 March 1877; ibid., pp. 157–9, proclamation by Shepstone, 12 April 1877, encl in no. 122, Shepstone to Carnarvon, 17 April 1877; SP 67, p. 225, Shepstone to Carnarvon, 23 July 1877.

72. See Giliomee, 'Processes'.

73. Bonner, 'Factions and Fissions'.

74. Newitt, *Portuguese Settlement*.

75. On the nature of white rule in the Transvaal at this time see Delius, *The Land Belongs to Us*, chs 1 (part 3), 6 and 8.

76. CO 879/10, African no. 110, pp. 58–9, Barkly to Carnarvon, 22 May 1876, encl Lobengula to Barkly, 10 April 1876, encl Lobengula to Burgers, 10 April 1876.

77. See p. 117.

78. Laband, *Kingdom in Crisis*, pp. 62, 64–5, 82, 154, 161, 175, 181, 223–4.

79. SS 232, R1196/77, Rudolph to SS, 29 March 1877; *De Volksstem*, 11 April 1877, report, Wakkerstroom, 31 March 1877; SNA I/4/1, no. 210, RM Umsinga to ASNA, 31 March 1877, encl statement of Makata, border guard, 31 March 1877; *The Natal Witness*, 11 May 1877, quoting letter, 2 April 1877 in *The Gold Fields Mercury*, 26 April 1877; *The Times of Natal*, 7 April 1877, letter from Biggarsberg correspondent, n.d.; *The Natal Mercury*, 17 April 1877, letter from Biggarsberg correspondent, 5 April 1877; *The Natal Colonist*, 13 April 1877, letter from Utrecht correspondent, 6 April 1877; *The Natal Mercury*, 24 April 1877, letter from Utrecht correspondent, 7 April 1877.

80. GH 1051, Robertson to Bulwer, 9 April 1877; SNA I/4/1/, no. 210, RM Umsinga to ASNA, 31 March 1877, encl statement of Mrilwa, 29 March 1877; SNA I/7/13, p. 26, report of messengers sent to Cetshwayo, 10 April 1877; SPG Vol. E32, p. 1989, no. 211, report of SM Samuelson, 31 March 1877; *The Natal Witness*, 11 May 1877, quoting letter, 2 April 1877, in *The Gold Fields Mercury*, 26 April 1877; *The Natal Mercury*, 10 April 1877, letter from Biggarsberg correspondent, 2 April 1877; SS 233, R1350/77, Rudolph to SS, 13 April 1877, reporting arrival of messengers from Cetshwayo, 7 April 1877; SNA I/3/29, no. 234, RM Umsinga to ASNA, 7 April 1877, encl statement of Maziana, 7 April 1877; Colenso, *Commentary*, pp. 755–6, 'Visit of the Bishop of Natal and Miss Colenso to Cetshwayo' (1 November 1880).

81. SP 18, Bulwer to Shepstone, 4 April 1877.

82. GH 789, Shepstone to Boast, 11 April 1877, encl in Shepstone to Carnarvon, 5 June 1877, encl in Shepstone to Bulwer, 6 June 1877.

83. Ibid, Boast to GS Transvaal, 15 May 1877, encl in Shepstone to Carnarvon, 5 June 1877, encl in Shepstone to Bulwer, 6 June 1877.

84. SNA I/1/29, no. 358, RM Newcastle to ASNA, 23 May 1877. The part of the message I have omitted simply explains who Mbilini was.

85. CO 179/124, Natal 8541, Bulwer to Carnarvon, 5 June 1877, and minute thereon by Carnarvon, 15 July 1877.

CHAPTER SIX

The Annexation of Zululand?

Reactions to the Annexation of the Transvaal, April to August 1877

Reactions to the annexation of the Transvaal varied. A petition against the annexation signed by 5 400 residents of the Cape expressed disappointment that Carnarvon had departed from the policy of conciliation with the Dutch that Froude had given them to understand he intended following.[1] Difficulty was experienced in getting up a petition in favour of annexation, particularly, as one would expect, among Afrikaners.[2] But as Frere said, in the western Cape 'the real welfare of the Transvaal very remotely affects commercial and agricultural interests'.[3] In the more English eastern Cape, where merchants were said to have been owed £1 000 000 by their Transvaal customers, the reaction to the annexation was much more favourable. The Port Elizabeth Chamber of Commerce went beyond mere debt collection and spoke in apocalyptic terms: but for the annexation a 'vast combination' of warlike tribes would have swooped on the Transvaal and elsewhere and 'thus forcibly thrust back civilisation in South Africa for many years, to the great loss of the agriculturalist, the capitalist, the merchant, and the distress of the Colonists generally'.[4]

Enthusiasm was greatest in Natal. The war in the Transvaal had disrupted the supply of labour needed for railway construction and had helped to cause a trade depression,[5] so the annexation of the Transvaal was 'heartily and gladly hailed'.[6] 'Durban was in a state of Saturnalia,' the Attorney-General told Shepstone, 'champagne in buckets . . .'[7] 'We may heartily congratulate our readers,' said The Natal Mercury, 'upon the improvement which that change seems to have effected in our prospects.'[8] The Natal Colonist expressed strong reservations about the fact that the ZAR was annexed without the consent of its citizens, but described it nevertheless as 'a consummation which, with probably the great bulk of the intelligent residents in South Africa, we have devoutly wished.'[9]

The reaction in Zululand to the annexation of the Transvaal was one of confusion and apprehension. Because they were not kept informed, and probably also because of the lack of resistance by the Boers, it was a long time before the Zulu grasped the nature of the political change that had taken place in the Transvaal. Shepstone, it will be remembered,[10] sent a message to Cetshwayo on 11 April concerning the annexation, but the annexation took place on the 12 April, so the message was not that the Transvaal *had* been put under the protection of the Queen but that it *would* be. Zulu messengers who saw Gert Rudolph (who stayed on as Landdrost of Utrecht) on 25 April did not know until

Rudolph told them that Shepstone was by then the ruler of the Transvaal.[11] They would have returned to Cetshwayo at about the same time as the rather indefinite message from Shepstone reached him, but even so the nature of the very surprising change in the Transvaal does not seem to have been grasped or believed. Cetshwayo sent two messengers to Pretoria to find out what Shepstone had done or was doing, and Shepstone said they told him that 'they were not aware of the extent and completeness of the measure I had taken', and that 'much of what they had heard from me was unknown' to Cetshwayo.[12] In his message of 11 April Shepstone had told Cetshwayo that he would send his eldest son to explain the 'true position of affairs and the altered circumstances of the country',[13] but Henrique Shepstone fell ill, so it was not until F.B. Fynney returned to Natal via Zululand and saw Cetshwayo on 12 June, two months after the annexation, and more than seven months after Shepstone's return to South Africa, that Cetshwayo was authoritatively informed of the British annexation of the Transvaal.

In the previously prevailing confusion all sorts of rumours were current among the Zulu, but the most widely believed was that part or the whole of Zululand was to be annexed by the British, or, as it was usually expressed, made to pay taxes. The building of a new *ikhanda* at the junction of the White and the Black Mfolozi rivers may have been the result of such a fear. The *ikhanda* was built following the Boer invasion scare of March 1877[14] and was given the name of 'Mayizekanye', meaning 'let the enemy come'. Magema Fuze, who visited Cetshwayo in July 1877, stated that the enemy in question were the Boers.[15] But the Boer invasion scare was soon discovered to be a false alarm, and it occurred at about the same time as reports – reports that were correct – of British troop movements to Newcastle in northern Natal, near the Zulu border, the troop movements being in support of Shepstone's imminent annexation of the Transvaal. The destination of the troops was kept secret, but *The Natal Witness* confidently asserted that they were intended not for the Transvaal but to occupy the disputed territory, or to take some action against the Zulu.[16] Cetshwayo may well have got to hear of these assertions. Bulwer commented in December 1876 that 'in Zululand they seem to know everything that passes with us', and there is evidence from a later date that Cetshwayo was kept informed of the contents of the Natal newspapers.[17] F.B. Fynney, who visited Cetshwayo in June 1877, was convinced that it was the fear of a British invasion that led to the building of Mayizekanye. He stated that it had been built at the junction of the two Mfolozis because it was believed that the thick bush of the area would render it unapproachable to an army (like a British army but unlike a Boer commando) encumbered with cannon and baggage waggons, and that the decision to build it had been made when Cetshwayo had heard of the movement of British troops to Newcastle and before he knew of their destination.[18]

The Zulu messengers mentioned above who saw Rudolph on 25 April inquired about Shepstone and the troop movements in Natal, and said they had heard that the English were 'going to make Zululand pay taxes'. Rudolph told them he had heard nothing of this. Shortly afterwards he received a letter from Charles Potter, a useful source of Zulu information since he ran a trading store where the Old Hunting Road crossed the Mphemvane river in the disputed territory, who said that there was 'now a settled conviction among the Zulus that Sir Theo. Shepstone intends to annex Zululand'. He said the head of the Qulusi *ikhanda*, an important Zulu military base in the area, had told him that Cetywayo had it on good authority from Natal, and that Shepstone had only gone to the Transvaal to 'blind their eyes'. Potter said that the *ikhanda* head and his attendants 'were very anxious to know the meaning of the massing of English troops at Newcastle'.[19]

On 12 May Cetshwayo asked the missionary Samuelson if he knew where Shepstone was and what he was doing, and said that he had 'heard that the English are going to compel the Zulus to pay taxes'. It was widely believed in Zululand that Fynney's purpose in going to Zululand in June was to announce to the King that Britain intended levying a tax on the Zulu. Fynney made no such announcement; nevertheless, Cetshwayo took the opportunity to point out to him that, although he regarded the British as friends and allies, it was important to understand that 'from the first the Zulu nation grew up alone, separate and distinct from all others, and has never been subject to any other nation'.[20] Even after Fynney's visit a belief persisted that Shepstone himself would soon be entering Zululand.[21] When Magema Fuze saw Cetshwayo in July the latter asked him if he had heard 'the story about Somtseu [Shepstone], that he is coming here to make us pay taxes?' Fuze replied that he had heard nothing to that effect; but Cetshwayo was clearly inclined to believe the story, and to believe that Shepstone was 'coming' not merely as an individual but with an armed force. As he had done with Fynney, Cetshwayo stressed to Fuze that

> this land and these people whom I rule are Senzangakona's, I have not *konza'd* for them to any one whatsoever; it is only myself in person that have *konza'd* to the English; I have not *konza'd* for these people of ours.

As late as August Robert Robertson said that 'for several months there has been a general expectation that Sir T. Shepstone would enter the country with English troops'.[22]

To the Zulu, Shepstone's mysterious movements must have seemed ominous. He had gone to England with the Zulu's statement of their case and all the other papers on the disputed territory, to lay the whole problem before the counsellors of the Queen. He had gone there primarily to attend Carnarvon's confederation conference, but as we have seen[23] it is likely that Cetshwayo and his advisers gained the impression that settling the territorial dispute was his primary or only purpose. He then returned, but said nothing to the Zulu. Instead he went to the Transvaal, and after a time reports began to be received that the Boers had come under the protection of the Queen. These reports were subsequently confirmed.

It must have looked to the Zulu very much as though the British had decided to take the side of the Boers and hence adopt an antagonistic stance towards the Zulu. Statements in the Natal press that the disputed territory or the whole of Zululand would or should be occupied by the British troops moving towards the frontier were calculated to add to this impression. Bulwer had made no reply to Cetshwayo's 'formidable message'; perhaps this was because only deeds and not mere words were considered adequate to avenge this insult.

The Annexation of Zululand Advocated, April to July 1877

The fear that persisted in Zululand even after the British troops had moved on from Newcastle to the Transvaal that the country was about to be annexed by Britain probably arose in large part from comment to this effect in Natal. As we have seen,[24] the head of the Qulusi said that Cetshwayo had it 'on good authority from Natal'. Cetshwayo's brother Hamu said Natal Africans had come to Zululand and reported that the English were about to attack the Zulu.[25] We have seen that the Zulu had some knowledge of the contents of Natal newspapers[26] and these newspapers both urged and expected the annexation of Zululand to follow the annexation of the Transvaal. The one was seen by many as the logical sequel of the other. *The Natal Mercury* noted that Shepstone's commission empowered him to annex any portion of extra-colonial South Africa and commented that 'the Transvaal makes a very respectable first instalment of this policy, but we are by no means sure that it will prove the last'. The *Mercury's* Utrecht correspondent urged the annexation of both the Transvaal and Zululand on the grounds that this would 'materially assist in the civilisation, christianisation and colonisation of South Africa'.[27] It was recognized that in taking over the Transvaal Britain had taken over its quarrel with the Zulu: the only permanently satisfactory solution to the disputed territory question would be to take over Zululand as well.[28] Shepstone claimed that only the annexation of the Transvaal had saved it from a Zulu invasion. These allegations of the aggressive intentions of the Zulu and the reports of military musterings and movements in Zululand[29] reinforced the desire to put the country under British rule. 'The pacification of Zululand,' stated *The Natal Witness*, 'would seem to be an even more important business than the annexation of the Transvaal.'[30]

The annexation of Zululand was justified on the grounds of humanity. It was said that Britain had not only an obligation to intervene on humanitarian grounds but a contractual right to do so. Reports began to be received from March onwards of attacks on mission stations and the murder of converts, and these were accompanied by further reports of more general slaughter in Zululand. 'There is abundant evidence,' stated *The Natal Mercury* 'to prove that kafir residents at mission stations are being constantly killed in cold blood.' It was said that Cetshwayo was killing his heathen subjects too at the rate of 50 a day, and that he had announced his intention of shedding more blood than Shaka and Dingane combined. 'It is high time,' ran a letter to *The Natal Witness*, that the British Government should step in and put an end to this wanton and reckless sacrifice of human life, remove the constant menace and danger to ourselves in Natal, but on higher grounds: our bounden duty to break the yoke of the tyrant and let the oppressed free.[31]

'Nor, indeed,' stated *The Natal Mercury,*

can England allow the King – who has been crowned by the hands of her own envoy, who has declared himself to be her child, and who has covenanted to respect human life within his territories – to set at naught his engagements with her by converting his country into a shambles and by singling out unoffending Christian converts as the particular victims of his fury.[32]

That there was an organized campaign of persecution directed against the missions appeared to be proved by the exodus of almost all the missionaries and their converts from Zululand during the second quarter of 1877. Appearances, however, proved to be deceptive. Some converts fled from Zululand because of rumours that a systematic campaign of murdering converts had been resolved upon by the Zulu authorities. But most of them left when their missionaries left; and their missionaries left, not because they thought they were in any danger from Cetshwayo, but because they shared the prevailing belief that Britain was about to intervene by force in Zululand.

The (quite untrue) story circulated among the missionaries that Bulwer had told one of their number that Zululand was to be annexed in a few months and that the matter was in the hands of Shepstone. Fynney (who later denied having done so) was understood to have warned some of the missionaries, after his visit to Cetshwayo, that the British government was about to take some decided step with regard to Zululand and that it would be advisable for them to leave. It was hope rather than fear that caused the missionaries to leave Zululand – hope that the old regime under which they had made so little progress was about to be replaced by one more sympathetic to missionary endeavour. This hope led them to do what they could to help to bring about a consummation they so devoutly wished: newspapers, private individuals, churchmen, public officials and missionary societies were plied with accounts of atrocities in Zululand and the consequent disaffection of a large part of the Zulu population towards their King.

These hopes were disappointed. Bulwer denied that any intervention in Zululand was intended by Britain, and refused even to make the representations to Cetshwayo which the missionaries requested. The missionaries argued that Shepstone's coronation of Cetshwayo in 1873, and the promises then made by the King, caused Zululand and Natal to become one country in Zulu eyes, and entitled Britain to intervene. Bulwer pointed out that Shepstone had been unable to obtain any guarantees for mission work in 1873 except that missionaries should not be expelled without the assent of the Natal government. He pointed out too that his remonstrances over the 'marriage of the *inGcugce*' in 1876[33] had not been well received, and that any representations concerning missions were equally unlikely to be successful.[34]

Bulwer also carefully investigated the allegations concerning the killing of converts. It turned out that the total number of converts killed was two. In neither case did it seem that the killings had been carried out on Cetshwayo's orders, and in one of the two cases the fact that the victim was a Christian appeared to have nothing to do with his being killed. There was also a third man killed at about the same time on a charge of witchcraft arising out of a family quarrel; although the missionaries included him in the roll of martyrs it emerged that he was a lapsed convert and that his death had nothing to do with his former connection with the missions. Bulwer later summed up the result of his investigations thus:

> I have heard nothing tending to confirm the opinion so hastily arrived at and so hastily expressed that the attacks actually made were part of a hostile design against the missionaries and mission stations in the Zulu country, or to induce me to alter the opinion which I originally formed upon the information before me that the attacks, however unjustifiable they might be in themselves, were directed against individual natives for personal reasons.[35]

Rebuffed by Bulwer, most of the missionaries somewhat sheepishly returned to Zululand.[36] The stream of atrocity stories dried up; and this, together with the news that Lord Carnarvon had stated in the House of Lords that the British government had no wish or intention to annex Zululand,[37] caused the Natal newspaper campaign for British intervention in Zululand to come to an end, for the time being.

The two killings of mission station residents in March 1877 were not unprecedented. In 1871 a party of men had dragged off an old woman from S.M. Samuelson's station and killed her as a witch. According to Samuelson the men had been sent by Cetshwayo, and he commented: 'Several other missionaries in Zululand have also lately been persecuted. It seams [*sic*] as the authorities are becoming more opposed to Christianity than ever.'[38] The authorities in Zululand had always been totally opposed to Christianity; but this killing did not lead to any concerted outcry by the missionaries or any allegations of systematic persecution. The essential ingredient lacking in this earlier case was any belief that Britain was on the point of intervening in Zululand. In 1877 a vicious circle was established for a time. The belief that Britain was intending to annex Zululand led the missionaries to speak and write and act in such a way as to give added impetus to the demand that Zululand should be annexed. Only Bulwer's calm and firm handling of the situation short-circuited the chain-reaction.

In 1875 a similar circuit had developed.[39] The fixed points in the circuit then had been stories of atrocities in Zululand, Wolseley's and Shepstone's designs on Zululand, and Robert Robertson's knowledge of these designs. In 1877 there is no doubt that Robertson was the principal purveyor of Zulu atrocity stories. He wrote to Bulwer, Shepstone, Frere and to the Anglican Metropolitan in South

Africa as well as to the editors of newspapers. His letters referred not only to the supposed campaign against missions but to the cruelties that Cetshwayo was allegedly practising upon his heathen subjects. In the memorial the missionaries sent to Bulwer, which Robertson drafted, he said that executions had increased since Cetshwayo's accession in 1873, and he wrote privately to Bulwer of 'almost daily executions' and of 'the hundreds of executions which every year take place in this country'. To the editor of *The Natal Colonist* he wrote that he was 'glad to see that you are taking up the wretched state of Zululand. It is like a tree with rotten roots, it needs only a blast to lay it low.' He went on to describe the 'misrule and terrorism' that prevailed in Zululand – and also the natural richness of the land. He urged its annexation and colonization by British subjects: 'a finer field can hardly be imagined for the varied operations of White men'. He concluded with this amiable sentiment:

> I hope you will make Zululand the 'Carthago dilenda [*sic*] est' of the 'Colonist', & I feel certain that if you do you will gain your end in time. You will not have lived in vain if you put an end to such barbarities & add a land so fair to the British Empire.

In a letter to his missionary society in England, which was printed in its journal, Robertson said that he prayed that the conquest of Zululand might be effected with little bloodshed, but he added that 'even if 3,000 or 4,000 are killed, it will be cheaply bought, for in so many years that number would be killed for witchcraft'. In another such letter (not printed) he said that he intended leaving Zululand, but added: 'I mean to volunteer to return with the first forces that are sent into the country if such are sent. I mean of course as chaplain.'[40]

The missionaries had so strong an interest in anything that would help to bring about British rule in Zululand that their testimony of persecution, despotism and killings in that country has to be treated with great caution. They were not as well informed as they claimed to be, relying on rumour and being very ready to jump to the most sinister conclusions. It is true that executions were common in the Zulu kingdom – in a country without prisons it could scarcely be otherwise – but the number was probably not nearly as great as that suggested by the lurid rhetoric of the missionaries, and they were by no means all the work of the King, who had no monopoly of capital punishment. There is evidence moreover that Cetshwayo took steps to protect his subjects from being condemned for witchcraft. I have elaborated on these themes elsewhere.[41] In his own day Cetshwayo was largely rehabilitated in the eyes of the British by the researches and advocacy of Bishop Colenso – but only after his defeat in 1879. In the years before the war the missionaries' campaign against him was not without its effect, and the impression they conveyed was strengthened by other circumstances.

The Image of Cetshwayo and the Zulu Kingdom

Bulwer was well aware of the interested motives of the missionaries. 'Some of them,' he wrote privately to Carnarvon, perhaps thought that the annexation of the Transvaal was leading inevitably to the annexation of Zululand, and this being a consummation devoutly to be wished by them ... the tendency of the influence they brought to bear upon the papers, & upon private persons & public opinion outside, and of the message they wished to bring upon me lay in that direction, in the direction of bringing on a crisis & hastening that consummation.

But although Bulwer knew that the missionaries were attempting to manipulate him he accepted in large measure their jaundiced view of Cetshwayo and drew appropriate political conclusions. 'He goes in fear of his life,' he wrote to Shepstone, 'being a tyrant and having reason to know that he is hated and dreaded by his own people.'[42] The cruelties of Shaka and Dingane were notorious. This was how Zulu Kings were expected to behave. To the extent that Cetshwayo had not hitherto conformed to this expectation, this was attributed to the moral influence of the Natal government. In his 'formidable message' of November 1876[43] which made a deep and lasting impression on Bulwer, Cetshwayo appeared to repudiate this moral influence, and the assumption was made that he would henceforth revert to the sanguinary methods of his predecessors. In this climate of expectation, the highly coloured stories of the missionaries and their converts gained more credit than perhaps they would otherwise have done.

Cetshwayo's frequently expressed desire to 'wash his spears' also did his image no good, although, as was later pointed out in the House of Lords, expressions such as 'fleshing maiden swords' were not unknown in the British army. A member of the House of Commons made some pertinent comments on Cetshwayo's savage candour:

> He said straight out what he meant. If he had been a European and Christian Emperor, he would have prefaced his intention of declaring war by issuing a Proclamation abounding in fine sentences and philanthropic phrases. He would have called God and man to witness that he had been driven into war against his inclination, for the purpose of freeing the bodies of his neighbours from physical thraldom, and their minds from degrading superstition. Not having learned the arts of modern Christian diplomacy, Cetywayo had the candour to declare that he meant to commence war for the simple purpose of showing his capacity as a chief for killing his enemy, and giving his braves an opportunity of washing his spears in the blood of hostile tribes.[44]

In fact, Cetshwayo did attempt something of this sort on occasion. His messengers told Rudolph that as a result of his not being allowed to punish the Swazi they had 'become disorganised' and were 'ready to have a civil war'. He told Shepstone that he wished to intervene in Swaziland because the Swazi 'are becoming very troublesome and are constantly fighting among themselves'.[45] But coming from a heathen savage such sentiments carried no conviction whatever.

It should also be pointed out that in the event Cetshwayo did not make war on the Swazi, in deference not only to the Natal and Transvaal governments but also to the prevailing sentiment among the Zulu people, which was against war in any form except in self-defence. Even the bombastic talk of the young regiments at the annual *umkhosi* was largely a matter of convention, as Robertson conceded and John Shepstone confirmed. When Bishop Colenso attended an *umkhosi* in Natal he received offers of war and threats of vengeance against his enemies, but he recognised this as simply the effervescence of youth.[46]

When the eminent Indian administrator Sir Bartle Frere succeeded Barkly as High Commissioner on 31 March 1877 he began almost immediately to receive numerous representations concerning the cruelties of Cetshwayo. He sent an example to Shepstone and asked him what he thought of it. Shepstone replied:

> I believe that a great deal of what is therein described is true: I think too that during the last twelve months that chief has been guilty of some terrible atrocities among his people, not spoken of in the paper you have sent me. I attribute the great change in his conduct to the effect of the Boer defeat by Sikukuni on his vanity. I went to England in July last year and up to that time there was no difficulty or sign of difficulty with Cetywayo.

At first sight it is not easy to see why a Pedi defeat of the Boers should enhance the Zulu King's vanity, nor why vanity should lead to atrocities. Presumably what Shepstone meant was that Cetshwayo had formerly ruled mildly only out of deference to the government of Natal, whose support he needed against the Boers, and that the defeat of the latter by Sekhukhune had shown him that he no longer needed this support. Shepstone sent Frere a letter from Robertson in confirmation of what he said about conditions in Zululand; it would, he told Frere, give him 'a very accurate idea of the state of the Zulu country just now'.

Frere was a militant Christian and he found in Robertson a kindred spirit. He was naturally susceptible to what he called the latter's 'very remarkable letters', which he received not only from Shepstone, but from the Bishop of Cape Town and directly from Robertson himself. He wrote to Carnarvon:

> He seems from all I hear to be a missionary of a very mediaeval type – great in stature & stout of heart and limb, with a wonderful influence over the Zulus, which he has always exercised for their good . . . he is evidently a person worth listening to, & I will learn all I can from him.

Cetshwayo's repudiation of British influence was not in Shepstone's view the only reason for the increase in his cruelties. Shepstone also advanced a psychological theory: that Cetshwayo's cruelties represented a displacement of the aggressive energies frustrated by the prohibition on foreign military campaigns. The annexation of the Transvaal, he told Carnarvon, had checkmated Cetshwayo. He had long wished to wash his spears: formerly he had wished to attack the Swazi, but since Sekhukhune's defeat of the Boers the latter had been promoted to the preference.

> The annexation of the Transvaal baulks both his purposes and condemns him to the ignominy of being a non-combatant Zulu King. He will continue to chafe under this,

but in my belief his chafing will end in destroying himself because it will take the form of domestic bloodshedding, and that will sooner or later produce revolution.

Shepstone's justification for annexing the ZAR without the consent of its government had been the imperative need to prevent its annihilation at the hands of the Zulu. He was therefore more or less obliged to maintain that, this necessary measure accomplished, the Zulu King was no longer a danger to his neighbours. He agreed with other observers that Zululand was in a restless condition, but continued:

> I cannot say that I feel very uneasy about it at present; I find that Sir Henry Bulwer does, and he may have grounds for so feeling of which I am ignorant. My opinion of Cetywayo's conduct is that he feels himself to be checkmated, and like a lassoed colt is kicking and plunging, but lassoed he is, and if we can only manage to keep clear of his heels until he finds kicking useless he will be quiet enough ... The chief danger is that by his reckless conduct he may bring about a revolution among his people, and then we must be ready to pick up the pieces, or they will be a trouble to us, and to Natal especially.[47]

As Shepstone indicated, others were not so sure that Cetshwayo was checkmated or that the danger of Zulu aggression was over. F.B. Fynney reported that Cetshwayo entertained exaggerated notions of the size and strength of his army, and that he contemplated the possibility of conflict with the British, not because he intended attacking them but because he fancied himself strong enough to resist any British interference. It was of course the Swazi whom Cetshwayo wished to attack. Fynney reported that Cetshwayo had asked him to ask Shepstone for permission to make 'one little raid only, one small swoop'. Fynney believed that the two messengers sent to Pretoria had been charged to make the same request (although from Shepstone's reports it does not appear that they did) and that if the request were refused Cetshwayo would risk an attack on the Swazi all the same.[48]

Bulwer was of the opinion that the disturbed condition of Zululand and of the King's mind could easily lead to war. He believed that the collapse of the Boer offensive against Sekhukhune had shown Cetshwayo that he no longer needed British protection and could henceforth act more independently. He received reports that the young regiments were clamouring to wash their spears and were increasingly dissatisfied at not being permitted to do so. Cetshwayo, he believed, had never had much friendly feeling towards the British, and was now vexed at their protecting his enemies after having restrained him for so long. 'But', he continued, in transmitting Fynney's report to Carnarvon,

> there undoubtedly remains a belief in and a certain fear of English power, though even these are qualified by the great blow to the prestige of the white man in South Africa that was struck last year in the Transvaal; and by an overweening confidence in the strength and prowess of the Zulu army; and probably the real state of the case at the present moment is this – that he has no wish to try conclusions with the English

unnecessarily, but that he is in such a frame of mind that he is quite prepared to fight, not merely to defend himself and his authority as an independent King but to fight upon the slightest provocation, regardless of all consequences.

To Sir Bartle Frere, the danger of Zulu aggression seemed inherent in the nature of the Zulu military system.

I cannot see how the present state of things there can last. If there is any truth in the pictures drawn by Mr. Fynney as well as others, of the Zulu force, its maintenance must be a burden far beyond the power of such a territory & people as the Zulus to support, without a constant succession of foreign wars, & 'eating-up' of the conquered after the orthodox Kaffir fashion. To maintain a standing army of 40 000 unmarried young men, would task the resources of a country as rich as populous & industrious as Belgium, & if Cetywayo can manage it, without a constant succession of conquests, he is fit to be War Minister to any great military power in Europe.

Frere's idea of the Zulu army was in fact a complete misconception. Even Shepstone, who received this letter while engaged in acrimonious negotiations with the Zulu, and who was consequently very disposed to agree with Frere that the maintenance of the Zulu army was 'a burden much too heavy for the Zulu people long to bear', nevertheless felt bound to point out that Cetshwayo did not have 40 000 *unmarried* soldiers, and that they were supplied with food by their families when called up.[49] The crucial point is that a 'standing army' was precisely what the Zulu army was not. There were no regular, professional, full-time soldiers in Zululand. The Zulu army was a citizen army, and its members spent most of their time engaged in productive labour at their homes. Even when called up, they were primarily engaged in working for the King, tilling the fields around the *amakhanda*, tending livestock, building, hunting and so forth, as well as acting as a police force. Far from being a burden on the state, the *amabutho* system, or 'military system' as it was misleadingly called, was what maintained the state. It resulted in a funnelling of wealth to the central government. It could be described as the Zulu system of taxation. In more developed states taxes are paid in money, the equivalent of commodities, which possess value because they embody labour. In the Zulu kingdom tax was paid directly in the form of labour. Foreign wars were not necessary to maintain the Zulu army. The fact that the Zulu had not waged war for a quarter of a century might have suggested this had Frere been at all susceptible to such a suggestion.

Frere's private secretary commented on one occasion that his 'whole heart & soul is in India. He is always thinking of it, talking of it. He compares everything with Indian things.' His conception of the Zulu army was certainly based on his Indian experience. He wrote:

We have always been quite as much harrassed in our Indian conquests, as here, by the inordinate numbers of the hereditary military classes who swallowed up all the resources of a native state. There, as in Kaffraria & Zululand, all the best muscle, as well as money, of the country was absorbed by idle warriors who found but scanty provision in the smaller and more compact Sepoy armies of their English conquerors. More of them turned their swords into plough shares than would be possible here – though, even among the most indolent Kaffirs there seem more ways of making them take to honest work, than their European critics always admit.[50]

This letter was written in July 1877. A year and a half before the British invasion of Zululand Frere was contemplating conquering the Zulu and making them take to 'honest work'. Nor was this some personal quirk. The conversion of 'idle warriors' into honest workers was part of the great project Frere had been sent to South Africa to carry out. But what, in practical terms, were the immediate intentions of the imperial government in the period after the annexation of the Transvaal?

The Imperial Government and the Zulu, May to September 1877

As noted above,[51] the fact that Shepstone's commission did not specify the Transvaal but empowered him to annex any territory bordering on a British colony led to the expectation that Zululand would be next on the list. In fact Zululand had for a time been tentatively placed first on the list. After Shepstone arrived in Britain in July 1876 and impressed on Carnarvon the danger that the ZAR's war with the Pedi might develop into a war with the Zulu, Carnarvon wrote to Bulwer: 'I cannot, with the absence of all real information, attempt to give you any instructions. My *impression* is that what is now occurring may lead to our taking Cetawayo and his Zulus under our protection.' Malcolm minuted a few days later: 'Perhaps Mr. Shepstone's policy of the establishment of a protectorate over Cetewayo's country and the gradual absorption of it as a "territory" of Natal akin to the Basuto Land of the Cape may be the solution.' Even after the Boers' failure against Sekhukhune and the promotion of the Transvaal to the top of the list, the possible annexation of Zululand as well was still envisaged. Carnarvon referred to a supposed desire in the Transvaal for British rule, and continued:

> On the other hand I have the information that Secocoeni, with whom the President is now at war, wishes to place his country under the Queen's protection, and that Cetywayo, on the part of the Zulus, is inclined to the same course.

In another despatch of the same date Carnarvon told Barkly that Shepstone was to be appointed Special Commissioner to 'the Transvaal Republic and to the Zulus and other native tribes in the neighbourhood of that Republic and of Natal, with large discretionary powers'. He continued, in words later omitted from the published version of the despatch: 'These powers will extend to the acceptance . . . of any territory whether of the Transvaal republic or of Native Tribes which may be offered to Her Majesty.'[52]

If it was Shepstone who advised Carnarvon that Cetshwayo was disposed to place his country under British protection, he was disabused of this notion when

.he returned to Natal and learnt of the Zulu King's defiant message to Bulwer. And once the Transvaal was annexed his superiors in Britain told him that they had decided against any further annexations in South Africa for the time being. Herbert warned Shepstone that 'H.M. Govt. are rather nervous as to the probability of their being pressed to take Zululand also immediately', and urged him to 'prevent any actual annexation of that country for a year or so'. There was still a large body of opinion in the British Parliament, and in the country generally, opposed to imperial expansion, or apprehensive of the complications and expense it might entail. Expansion had therefore to be undertaken cautiously and in such a manner as to avoid giving shocks to public opinion.[53]

There was, however, never any doubt that Zululand's destiny, sooner or later, was to come under British rule. The annexation of Zululand, wrote Carnarvon in June 1877, 'must & ought to come eventually: but not just now'. 'The time would doubtless come when it would become necessary,' he told Parliament in May. 'Of course it is by bringing Zululand under Shepstone & not by leaving it outside British rule, a prey to European & native savages, that war is to be averted,' wrote Herbert; political considerations precluded the immediate annexation of Zululand: 'it is however certain that it must before long become British'.[54]

The discussions on the subject in the Colonial Office were almost all concerned with the necessity of staving off the inevitable annexation of Zululand, and the means by which its annexation might be avoided for the time being. The possibility that the Zulu might resist being annexed went almost unmentioned. It was assumed that the annexation of Zululand would not involve war, or would require only a brief and slight war. The lack of resistance to the annexation of the Transvaal probably reinforced the Victorian idea that progress and the supersession of savagery by civilization, and of native states by the British empire, was an inevitable and natural process that needed to be regulated and even checked on occasion but which needed no artificial impetus. If Shepstone, representing the British empire, could so overawe the Boers, what could he not do with simple savages whose King acknowledged him as his 'father'? But there was another, more particular, reason why it was assumed that the annexation of Zululand could be easily effected. This was the belief that the Zulu people were greatly disaffected towards their cruel and tyrannical ruler. The missionaries conveyed the impression that the British annexation of Zululand would be hailed with joy by most of its inhabitants. Robertson told Bulwer (and through him Frere) that this was true of the common people, and that there was a rumour that some of the great men would desert the King in his hour of need. He described the Zulu kingdom as the sick man of South Africa and the Zulu power as doomed beyond redemption. Fynney stated that conflict with the British was likely to lead to the disintegration of the Zulu kingdom.

> While the Zulu nation to a man would have willingly turned out to fight either the Boers or Amaswazi, the case would be very different, I believe, in the event of a misunder-

standing arising between the British Government and the Zulu nation. I have reason to believe that in such an event the King could not rely upon either Uhamu or Mapita's sons (to say nothing of less powerful chiefs). These two alone would carry with them the whole of the northern part of Zululand. I further believe from what I heard, that a quarrel with the British Government would be the signal for a general split up amongst the Zulus, and the King would find himself deserted by the majority of those upon whom he would at present appear to rely.

Fynney at one point drew a distinction between the generations. He stated that some Zulu homestead heads told his African attendants that they were willing to pay taxes, but that the young men said they would fight rather than do so. Similarly, at about the same time, a Natal African border guard in the Umsinga district reported:

> In general conversation with the Zulus I learn that the old men wish for British rule so that they may live in peace, but the young men would like to fight, they say, before they would become servants and have to pay taxes.

But the prevailing view among white observers was that no fighting or virtually no fighting would be necessary. Shepstone, indeed, believed it possible, as we have seen[55] that the Zulu kingdom might disintegrate without Britain having to do anything except 'pick up the pieces'. The assumption that the kingdom was rent with strife and would collapse when touched was very deep-seated. Even Carnarvon, 6 000 miles away, thought he knew more about the political temper of the Zulu people than the Zulu King himself. 'Unfortunately,' he wrote, 'he does not seem to be under the restraint which a knowledge of the disaffection existing amongst a part of his people wd. impose.'[56]

The historian, with the benefit of hindsight, knows that this hubris was destined to be overtaken by a terrible nemesis at Isandlwana. But at the time that they were expressed these opinions were not as unreasonable as they might now appear. The history of the Zulu kingdom had been marked by internal conflict and division. Shaka had faced numerous rebellions before being assassinated by his brother Dingane. Dingane had been overthrown when a large proportion of his subjects followed his brother Mpande and went over to the trekkers. Mpande's reign was marked by a civil war in which his intended heir was defeated and killed, and he believed that he himself was saved from death thereafter only by the support of the British government. Fynney's statement that Cetshwayo could not rely on either 'Uhamu or Mapita's sons' was a remarkable pointer to the future. The King's brother Hamu did indeed defect to the British in 1879, and in the civil war of 1883 it was the forces led by Hamu and Maphita's son Zibhebhu that overthrew Cetshwayo. Even during the war of 1879 the solidarity of the Zulu against the invader was not as strong as Isandlwana and the other great battles might suggest: besides the defections of Hamu and Dunn, there were, as Laband has shown, many waverers among the *izikhulu*, and many against whom the King had to use the threat of force to prevent them from negotiating a separate peace with the British. When the Zulu were finally defeated and were told nonetheless that their independence and their land and cattle would not be taken from them, they showed no disposition to continue fighting for the King, who was rapidly captured and exiled.[57]

But before the war, despite tensions between the central government of the King and the local government of the *izikhulu*, and between the King and his counsellors on particular occasions, there was no serious separatist or disloyal movement against the King among the *izikhulu*, let alone among the young men of the regiments. As long as the kingdom, its resources, the power of the *izikhulu* and the people's freedom from taxes and wage-labour were under external threat, loyalty to the King was in the interests of the Zulu people as a whole.[58]

Shepstone and the Zulu, May to September 1877

Shepstone had inherited from the Boers their border dispute with the Zulu, and this, together with his long association with the Zulu, meant that he had the primary responsibility for dealing with them. It is to his thoughts and actions that we must now more particularly turn. Herbert had urged Shepstone to avoid any annexation of Zululand for a year or so, and had suggested a system of Residents 'if anything has to be done soon'. Shepstone replied:

> I think there will be little difficulty in staving off for a time the necessity for formally annexing that Country, but sooner or later the step will be inevitably forced upon you. My own view is that just now it would be better to let things here calm down a little before taking such a serious step with Zululand; but something must be done to quiet the South-eastern border of this Country in the matter of the disputed territory as well as to bring more restraining influence to bear upon the Zulus themselves & their King.

What that something should be Shepstone hoped to be in a better position to judge after his intended visit to the Zulu border. He believed that the appointment of a Resident would simply lead to the collapse of the Zulu state: the oppressed people would turn to him for protection and he would thus unwittingly become the catalyst for revolution. A revolution would result in a flood of refugees entering Natal, and Shepstone said he had always been opposed to the appointment of a Resident for that reason.

> Here however the matter is different – the times and circumstances are changed, and it will be impossible to tolerate the existence for any length of time, in a position such as that occupied by the Zulus with regard to what is now British Territory, [of] a source of perpetual disquiet and menace. If the men were allowed to go to Natal or elsewhere to work instead of being embodied in Regiments & kept idly at home the danger would be less, but so long as this continues Zululand is a dangerous, although I think manageable volcano.[59]

Previously Shepstone had supported the Zulu kingdom in its border dispute with the ZAR as a means of keeping the Boers from the sea. But now the Boers were under British rule, the Zululand border dispute was with a British possession, and the imperial government was no longer averse to expansion in South Africa, there was no longer any reason why the Zulu should delay the fulfilment of their destiny as workers in Natal or elsewhere.

Another reason for the ending of Zulu independence was the renewed reports of Cetshwayo's contacts with his non-British neighbours. In July Robert Bell, the Native Commissioner on the Swazi border, reported that Zulu messengers were in Swaziland. All the Swazi would admit was that Cetshwayo had urged them not to ally with the whites but to return to their allegiance to the Zulu King, and that they, the Swazi, had rejected this demand. Bell, however, was convinced that the Zulu had proposed an offensive alliance against the whites and that the Swazi would join whichever side they thought the stronger. Shepstone later heard that the Swazi King was in negotiation to marry Cetshwayo's sister, and commented that there seemed to be a tendency for the Zulu and Swazi to enter into friendly relations with each other. He also received a report that Cetshwayo had sent an embassy to Delagoa Bay to establish more intimate relations with the Portuguese authorities.[60]

Shepstone believed that Cetshwayo was intriguing with Sekhukhune as well. Although the British government had treated the ZAR's war with Sekhukhune as an unjustifiable attack upon an independent ruler, Shepstone required Sekhukhune to pay the fine of 2 000 cattle which he had agreed, under great pressure, to pay the Boers, and required him also to become a subject of the Transvaal. It is true that he offered him a choice; but the choice was between accepting British rule or leaving the Transvaal. The offer of subjection was thus an offer Sekhukhune could not refuse. But he tried to interpret his acceptance of the Queen's sovereignty to imply a diplomatic relationship with the Pretoria government rather than one of simple subjection. He also made difficulties over the payment of the cattle. This was interpreted by Shepstone as stemming from his disinclination to settle down under British rule. In fact the difficulty in supplying the cattle was genuine. Drought as well as the ravages of war had caused a food shortage in the Pedi country, and cattle were needed in order to purchase grain. The war had also resulted in a weakening of Sekhukhune's authority within his always somewhat fragile polity, and a cattle levy upon his subjects in these circumstances would have been politically disastrous. Shepstone, however, believed that he could easily pay the cattle demanded of him if he wanted to, and attributed his tardiness in complying with the demand to his being puffed up with his success against the Boers, to messages from Cetshwayo advising him not to submit to the British government, and to his belief that the Zulu were more powerful than the British.[61]

It seemed to Shepstone that Cetshwayo wished to 'get up a disturbance by means of instigating others to commit themselves while he awaits events'. His conclusion was that 'Cetywayo must have his wings clipped'.[62]

Bulwer also received reports of a similar nature. It was said that Cetshwayo had sent to Mqikela, the Mpondo paramount, to propose a concerted invasion of Natal. Bulwer's comments on these reports were considerably more enlightened and perceptive than Shepstone's, and show a greater capacity for appreciating how things looked from Cetshwayo's standpoint. He pointed out that the annexation of the Transvaal had taken the Zulu King by surprise,

and there can be little question that it has considerably disturbed him, for he has seen the English protection thrown over the people of that country – an act that he cannot understand – and, moreover, in consequence of mischievous reports spread about, he has been half led to anticipate that the English might have some designs upon his own country. In this troubled state of mind it is not to be wondered at if, determined as he is to resist to the utmost any attack made upon his sovereignty, he has taken steps to look out for auxiliaries, and the communication that he has now made to the Amapondo King is probably with a view of ascertaining how far he may rely upon the support and co-operation of the Amapondo in the event of any cause bringing him into collision with the English.

It is indeed likely that Cetshwayo, fearing the intentions of the British, would try to repair or establish good relations with his other neighbours. His communications were probably for this essentially defensive purpose. Mqikela heard the reports that Cetshwayo had sent a message to him, and assured the British authorities that it was not hostile to them:

The object of his sending to me was to encourage a friendly feeling [and] intercourse between the Pondos and the Zulu people, that, whereas formerly our fathers Tshaka and Faku were at variance with each other, we might be on more amicable terms.[63]

Before his meeting with the Zulu on 18 October 1877 (to be discussed in the following chapter), Shepstone, like many others, believed that he had a great personal influence over Cetshwayo. He probably thought that Cetshwayo's 'formidable message' of November 1876 was the result of his absence from Natal, and that Cetshwayo would never have dared address his father Somtsewu in such terms. One may perhaps infer that this is what he thought from his statement to Frere about his relationship with Cetshwayo, that 'he will bear a great deal from me, because by the Zulu law I stand in the position of Father to him and am entitled to lecture him'. He implied that this status in Zulu law would enable him to bring Zululand under British rule.

My relations with the Zulus are peculiar. In virtue of a law specially enacted by them in 1861 I hold supreme rank in their country and am entitled to the same salute as the King, according to that law I am the King's father! I do not think that there would be much difficulty in establishing British rule in Zululand when we are ready for it and our security will sooner or later demand it.

He evidently hoped that his visit to the Zulu border would enable him to do more than settle the border question. En route to Utrecht he wrote to Colonel

Durnford (who had asked for the post of Resident in Zululand) stating that he fully agreed with him that 'more thorough control of the Zulu Country is an absolute necessity, whether this be gained by means of annexation or otherwise', adding, however, that the home government was 'rather nervous about it and would be glad to see annexation avoided for a year or two'. He said that he would communicate with Cetshwayo once he reached Utrecht.

> I shall after that be in a position, at least I think so, of recommending or taking some definite course which shall have the object of attaining more control over the politics of the Zulu country than we now have.[64]

That Zululand would have to be annexed sooner or later had become the conventional wisdom among colonists, missionaries, local officials and the imperial government. Shepstone believed the special position he occupied in relation to the Zulu would enable him to take this necessary step without too much difficulty. His complacency was about to receive a rude shock.

Notes

1. CO 879/11, African no. 129, p. 77, no. 78, Frere to Carnarvon, 25 June 1877.
2. CO 537/124A, f. 125, Ebden to Hampden Willis, 29 May 1877.
3. CO 48/482, Cape/Tvl. 7790, Frere to Carnarvon, 5 June 1877.
4. Molteno, *Life of Molteno*, Vol. II, pp. 122 and 132; Schreuder, *Scramble*, p. 30; CO 879/11, African no.129, p. 87–8, no. 91, Chamber of Commerce, Port Elizabeth, to Colonial Office, 5 July 1877.
5. *Natal Government Gazette*, Vol. XXIX, no. 1657, 10 July 1877, Consulting Engineer to Resident Engineer, 18 October 1876; *The Natal Witness*, 21 January 1877, editorial; *Natal Government Gazette Extraordinary*, Vol. XXIX, no. 1650, 7 June 1877, speech of Lieutenant-Governor in opening Legislative Council, 7 June 1877.
6. *The Natal Mercury*, 24 April 1877, editorial.
7. SP 19, Gallwey to Shepstone, 3 May 1877.
8. *The Natal Mercury*, 24 April 1877, editorial. See also editorials in *The Natal Witness*, 20 April 1877 and *The Times of Natal*, 18 and 24 April 1877.
9. *The Natal Colonist*, 20 April 1877, editorial.
10. See ch. 5, p. 133.
11. TA, LU, Vol. 13, no. 90, Rudolph to GS, 25 April 1877.
12. TA, Administrator's Letter-book 6, no. 42, Shepstone to Carnarvon, 7 August 1877.
13. GH 789, Shepstone to Boast (Acting RM Newcastle) 11 April 1877, encl in Shepstone to Carnarvon, 5 June 1877, encl in Shepstone to Bulwer, 6 June 1877.
14. See ch. 5, p. 133.
15. Magema Magwaza [Fuze], 'Visit', p. 424.
16. *The Natal Witness*, 27 March 1877, editorial; ibid, 3 April 1877, 'Monthly Summary' and editorial.
17. SP 16, Bulwer to Shepstone, 21 December 1876; BPP, C2374, p. 52, statement of trooper Grandie, 16 April 1879.
18. BPP, C1961, p. 48, report on Zululand by F.B. Fynney, 4 July 1877.
19. TA, LU, Vol. 13, no. 90, Rudolph to GS, 25 April 1877; SS 236, R1769, Potter to Rudolph, 30 April 1877, encl in Rudolph to GS, 3 May 1877.

20. SPG Vol. E32, p. 1993, Samuelson, quarterly report, June 1877; BPP, C1961, pp. 49 and 45, report on Zululand by F.B. Fynney, 4 July 1877; see also SNA 1/3/29, no. 443, RM Umsinga to ASNA, 26 June 1877.
21. SNA 1/3/29, no. 451, RM Umsinga to ASNA, 30 June 1877.
22. Magema Magwaza [Fuze], ' Visit', pp. 430 and 426; GH 1052, Robertson to Bulwer, 7 August 1877.
23. See ch. 3, pp. 73–4.
24. See p. 141.
25. SS 242, R2956, Nunn to Shepstone, 7 July 1877.
26. See p. 140.
27. *The Natal Mercury*, 24 April 1877, editorial, and 'Our North Western Border'.
28. *The Natal Witness*, 13 April 1877, editorial; ibid, 1 May 1877, 'Monthly Summary'; *The Natal Mercury*, 22 May 1877, letter from Utrecht correspondent, 25 April 1877.
29. See ch. 5, pp. 132–3.
30. *The Natal Witness*, 27 April 1877, 'Short Notes – the Pacification of Zululand'; see also ibid, 8 May 1877, letter from 'SCW', 2 May 1877; *The Natal Mercury*, 24 April 1877, 'Zululand'; ibid, 29 May 1877, letter from Biggarsberg correspondent, 12 May 1877; *The Times of Natal*, 14 April 1877, 'The Fortnight'.
31. *The Natal Mercury*, 8 May 1877, editorial; *The Natal Witness*, 1 May 1877, 'Monthly Summary'; *The Natal Mercury*, 10 April 1877, 'Summary'; *The Natal Witness*, 15 June 1877, 'Zulu Atrocity', letter to editor, 6 June 1877.
32. *The Natal Mercury*, 8 May 1877, editorial.
33. See ch. 5, pp. 117–18.
34. GH 1397, petition of Zululand missionaries to Bulwer, 18 May 1877; GH 1325, no. 396, Bulwer's reply to the above, 24 July 1877.
35. GH 1220, no. 193, Bulwer to Carnarvon, 27 November 1877.
36. My account of this episode in Zululand mission history is based on documents too numerous to itemize, most of which are in the GH series and the Colenso Papers, vol. 3, in the Natal Archives; the SPG papers, vols D 46 and E 32; and the Selected Records of the Archbishop of Cape Town, Ab 3.4, in the University of the Witwatersrand Library. See also [Fuze] 'Visit', and BPP, C2252, pp. 11–24, encl in no. 4, Frere to Hicks Beach, 30 December 1878. For a more detailed account of this episode and more documentation, see Cope, 'Characters of Blood?', pp. 7–9. For secondary sources on Zululand missionaries in general, see ch. 3, fn. 55.
37. *The Natal Witness*, 26 June 1877, 'Lord Carnarvon'.
38. SPG Vol. E26, pp. 1375–6, report of Samuelson for quarter ending June 1871.
39. See ch. 3, pp. 54–5.
40. GH 1397, petition of Zululand missionaries to Bulwer, 18 May 1877; ibid, Copy, Robertson to Bulwer, 9 April 1877; ibid, Robertson to Bulwer, 26 June 1877; Natal Archives, Colenso Papers, Vol.3, Robertson to Sanderson, 9 April 1877; ibid, Robertson to Sanderson, 20 April 1877; *The Net*, 1 September 1877, p. 130, letter from Robertson, 19 June 1877; SPG, Vol. D46, p. 329, Robertson to Moore, 2 July 1877.
41. Cope, 'Characters of Blood?', pp. 4–13 and 15–17.
42. PRO 30/6/38, no. 108, Bulwer to Carnarvon, 14 September 1877; SP 23, Bulwer to Shepstone, 1 August 1877.
43. See ch. 5, pp. 118–19.
44. HL Deb, Vol. CCXLIV, col 1661, Lord Stanley of Alderley, 25 March 1879; HC Deb, Vol. CCXXXV, col. 1778, J. Cowan, 24 July 1877.
45. TA, LU, Vol. 13, no. 90, Rudolph to GS, 25 April 1877; SS 259, R2431, Dunn to Shepstone, 8 May 1877.
46. GH 1052, Robertson to Bulwer, 7 August 1877, and report on this letter by the Acting SNA, J.W. Shepstone, 28 August 1877; Colenso, *Ten Weeks*, p. 109.

47. SP 20, Frere to Shepstone, 31 May 1877; SP 67, p. 214, Shepstone to Frere, 20 June 1877; PRO 30/6/33, no. 86, Frere to Carnarvon, 19 July 1877; SP 67, p. 226, Shepstone to Carnarvon, 23 July 1877; ibid, p. 251, Shepstone to Frere, 1 August 1877.
48. BPP, C1961, pp. 44–50, report on Zululand by F.B. Fynney, 4 July 1877 (quotation p. 46); GH 1397, report on Zululand by Fynney to the Natal government, 13 July 1877.
49. GH 1300, pp. 94–5, Confid, Bulwer to Carnarvon, 23 July 1877; SP 25, Frere to Shepstone, 28 October 1877; SP 68, p. 291, Shepstone to Frere, 23 November 1877.
50. UWL, Littleton Papers, no. 84, Littleton to his mother, 5 January 1879 (I deal more fully with Frere's Indian background in ch. 8); SP 22, Frere to Shepstone, 17 July 1877.
51. See p. 142.
52. PRO 30/6/38, no. 78, Carnarvon to Bulwer, 5 August 1876; CO 48/478, minute by Malcolm, 11 August 1876, on Cape 9594, Confid, Barkly to Carnarvon, 14 July 1876; GH 274, two despatches, both Secret, Carnarvon to Barkly, 22 September 1876, encl in Secret, Carnarvon to Bulwer, 28 September 1876 – the published versions are in BPP, C1748, pp. 103–4, nos 73 and 74.
53. SP 20, Herbert to Shepstone, 7 June 1877; PRO 30/6/33, no. 45, Carnarvon to Frere, 7 June 1877.
54. CO 179/123, minute by Carnarvon, 5 June 1877, on Natal 6658, Confid, Bulwer to Carnarvon, 27 April 1877; HL Deb, Vol. CCXXXIV, col 981, Carnarvon, 15 May 1877; BL Add Mss 60793, Confid, Herbert to Carnarvon, 10 May [1877]; CO 48/483, minute by Herbert, 21 August 1877, on Cape 9982, Secret, Frere to Carnarvon, 21 July l877.
55. See p. 148.
56. GH 1052, Robertson to Bulwer, 7 August 1877 (copies of this and other letters of Robertson were sent to Frere and are in CO 959/1); BPP, C1961, p. 49, report on Zululand by F.B. Fynney, 4 July 1877; SNA I/4/1, no. 436, report by African border guard, 22 June 1877, encl in RM Umsinga to ASNA, 22 June 1877; CO 48/483, minute by Carnarvon, 5 September 1877, on Cape/Tvl 10665, Shepstone to Carnarvon, 24 July 1877, encl Fynney's report, 4 July 1877.
57. Laband, 'Cohesion'.
58. Cope, 'Political Power'.
59. SP 20, Herbert to Shepstone, 7 June 1877; SP 67, pp. 234–5, Shepstone to Herbert, 23 July 1877.
60. SS 242, R2957, R2958, R2960, R2961, Bell to GS, 8, 16, 22 and 24 July 1877; SP 68, p. 262, Shepstone to Frere, 12 September 1877; TA, Administrator's Letter-book 6, no. 35, Shepstone to Carnarvon, 31 July 1877.
61. Delius, *The Land Belongs to Us*, pp. 227–31; SP 68, p. 259, Shepstone to Frere, 15 August 1877; ibid, p. 262, Shepstone to Frere, 12 September 1877; ibid, p. 268, Shepstone to Herbert, 5 October 1877.
62. SP 68, p. 259, Shepstone to Frere, 15 August 1877; SP 67, p. 248, Shepstone to Bulwer, 25 July 1877.
63. SNA I/4/1, no. 743, RM Alfred to ASNA, 24 September 1877; SNA I/1/29, no. 765, Hancock to ASNA, 3 October 1877; GH 1220, pp. 219–20, no. 168, Bulwer to Carnarvon, 4 October 1877; SNA I/4/1, no. 936, Mqikela to Blyth (Chief Magistrate, East Griqualand), 15 November 1877, encl in Mrs Jenkins to RM Alfred, 22 November 1877, encl in RM Alfred to ASNA, 25 November 1877.
64. SP 67, p. 251, Shepstone to Frere, 1 August 1877; ibid, p. 215, Shepstone to Frere, 20 June 1877; SP 71, Shepstone to Durnford, 17 September 1877.

CHAPTER SEVEN

The Border Dispute
and the Threat of War

Shepstone's Negotiations with the Zulu, September to November 1877

On 16 August 1877 Shepstone set out on his tour of the eastern and south-eastern districts of the Transvaal. He travelled via Middelburg, Lydenburg, the gold fields, New Scotland and Wakkerstroom, reaching Utrecht on 21 September. This tour revealed to him the dimensions of the problem he had taken over in annexing the Transvaal: he found the eastern frontier in dispute along virtually its entire length. He seems to have supposed this to be a recent development, a product of the previous year's war, and he seems to have assumed that his task (as in the case of the Pedi)[1] was to enforce the claims which the Boers had put forward but had been unable to make good. He expressed the belief that the prestige of the white man had been permanently damaged by Sekhukhune's defeat of the Boers and stated that this complicated the task of government by tempting Africans to 'aggressive conduct and offensive language'.[2]

On the Transvaal-Zulu border, however, all was quiet, and had been for several months. 'Everything is so quiet that it becomes almost monotonous after the late periodical scares and alarms,' reported *The Natal Mercury's* Utrecht correspondent on 22 July 1877. 'Everything is dead still in this locality,' wrote *De Volksstem's* correspondent on 10 September.[3] It was the calm before the storm. Both Boer and Zulu were waiting for Shepstone to enforce their respective claims, and their claims were mutually incompatible.

While they waited, the effective boundary between the Transvaal and Zululand was the following line: the Ncome or Blood river, its tributary the Lynspruit (Dudusi), a more or less direct line from the latter's source to the junction of the Phongolo and the Ntombe rivers, and from the Ntombe northwards to approximately the vicinity of the Mkhondo or Assegai river. There were Zulu on the Transvaal side of this line, some of whom refused to pay tax to the Transvaal government, for fear, they said, of Cetshwayo. There were still a few whites living on the Zulu side of this line, but they remained only by Zulu permission. East of the Ntombe, wrote Colonel Durnford, who visited the area in June, 'the Zulus are masters and the Whites submit'. South of the Phongolo there were many deserted farmhouses along the 'Old Hunting Road', formerly the limit of white occupation, but it appears that only two whites still lived on the Zulu side of the line described above, south of the Phongolo. Charles Potter was still at his trading store, at the point where the Old Hunting Road crossed the Mphemvane river, and Cornelius Van Rooyen still occupied his farm west of the White Mfolozi. Potter had *khonza'd* to Cetshwayo, recognizing his sovereignty and paying him tribute, and it is very likely that Van Rooyen had done the same.[4]

Shepstone had told Cetshwayo's messengers in Pretoria that he would be going on a tour of the border and that Cetshwayo might then make some communications with him on the subject of the disputed territory. As soon as he reached Utrecht he caused Cetshwayo to be informed of his arrival and that he was awaiting a response to this invitation. The reply came on 4 October. Cetshwayo expressed delight that his 'father' was so near, and said that he would collect all the heads of the nation and send them to meet Shepstone. Shepstone commented:

> It appears that the Zulus have been in considerable anxiety as to my intention, they expected that I intended to annex them and their country and my confining my communication to the question of the disputed territory is a relief to them, at least to the headmen; the common people would not I think much disapprove, and so this anxiety and relief from it may enable [me] to at once settle amicably the territorial question.

Shepstone continued:

> Cetywayo alluded to annexation privately and in somewhat jocular strain to the messenger; he said, annexation means that we lose our chieftainship and pay taxes: well, as far as I am personally concerned I am perfectly willing to pay what my father may demand from me, he is my father and I am bound to obey him, and I am ready to do so at once; but the Zulu people are not my property as I am his, they belong to my forefathers and I don't know what they would say!! If I find myself in a position to make a desirable arrangement I shall not dare to lose the opportunity, for so good a one may not occur again, but I shall press nothing, and not put my hand out further than I can pull it back again comfortably.[5]

There can be no doubt that Shepstone seriously misinterpreted the tone of Cetshwayo's remarks. There was nothing jocular about them. Cetshwayo was in deadly earnest. He had stressed to Fynney that the Zulu nation had 'never been subject to any other nation', and had told Fuze that the Zulu people were Senzangakhona's and that he had not *khonza'd* to the English for them.[6] Cetshwayo was prepared to acknowledge that Shepstone was his patron and that he had assisted him to attain his rightful place as King of the Zulu without the necessity for fighting the rival pretenders. But he wished it to be clearly understood that this personal relationship with Shepstone implied nothing concerning the relationship between the Zulu people and the British government. He expressed himself in similar vein at about the same time in a conversation with Robertson, and Robertson's account makes it very clear that Cetshwayo saw the question as no joking matter:

Lately the King said to me, 'I love the English. I am not Umpande's son. I am the child of Queen Victoria. But I am also a King in my own country & must be treated as such. Somseu (Sir T.S.) must speak gently to me. I shall not hear dictation.' (And he added with great emphasis) 'I shall perish first.'[7]

Shepstone believed that the suspicion and distrust with which he was now regarded by the Zulu would facilitate an amicable settlement of the border dispute, but he could not have been more mistaken. Unlike Cetshwayo's Swaziland ambitions, this was a question on which the King, the *izikhulu*, and the nation at large were united and on which they felt very strongly. It is probable that the population of Zululand was increasing, and there is no doubt that in the later 1870s rainfall was undergoing a decline, which reached its nadir in the great drought of 1878.[8] The disputed territory was mostly upland country that was healthy for man and beast and which tended to receive more rain than lower land. In a time of drought it was becoming increasingly valuable, and secure possession of it was becoming increasingly important. The territorial dispute with the Transvaal had festered for 16 years. Boers had occupied Zulu territory, seized Zulu cattle, destroyed Zulu crops, burnt Zulu grazing, and assaulted and murdered Zulu people. The Zulu had submitted to all this without resistance; instead, they had begged Shepstone to intervene. Shepstone had urged them to show moderation and restraint, which they had done, but still the question had remained unsettled. Then, when the Boers had tried to tax the Zulu, beating them and seizing their cattle, Cetshwayo had risked an armed demonstration. This had proved surprisingly effective. The tax had been abandoned and many Boers had fled. It had also seemed to galvanize Shepstone into action, for he had asked the Zulu for a full statement of their case in writing, which they had given him, and he had gone to England with all the papers on the question to see the advisers of the Queen about it. In the meantime the failure of the Boers against Sekhukhune had showed that they were not so much to be feared as the events of Dingane's time had suggested. Shepstone had then returned, said nothing to the Zulu, entered the Transvaal, and the next thing the Zulu had heard was that he had taken the Boers under his protection. Incredible though this seemed, it turned out to be true. Then he said he would come and talk to them about the border question. Now he had come. But what would he say?

'The Zulus just now are in a high state of expectation,' reported Robertson on the eve of the conference with Shepstone. 'All sorts of rumours are afloat as to the intentions of the English Govt. regarding the country.'[9] The Zulu hoped, now Shepstone was in control of the Transvaal, that a grand inquest into the whole border question would be held, that they would be able to confront the Boers with their crimes, and that their wrongs would be righted and their land restored. What they feared was that Shepstone had taken the side of his fellow whites. Circumstances indicated this, and white men were even saying that he intended claiming the whole of Zululand and imposing taxes upon its people. This the Zulu were determined to resist to the uttermost.

As the time for the meeting approached, Shepstone's earlier optimism began to ebb. News of the conflict between the Cape and the Gcaleka Paramount Sarhili ('Kreli') reached him, and he feared it would have disturbing effects. He said he was glad that Frere was taking a strong line, since in the wake of the ZAR's failure against the Pedi any apparent weakness would encourage 'a struggle of colour against colour'; but he also said that if he had known of 'the imminence of matters between Sir Bartle Frere and Krili, I should have avoided this meeting for the present'.[10] Another disturbing piece of news was that the Zulu deputation coming to see him was very large. He sent to its leader, the King's Chief Counsellor, Mnyamana kaNgqengelele, to say that if there was to be any demonstration of force he would refuse to meet the deputation; but Mnyamana 'deprecated the idea of any demonstration and begged me to meet them'.[11]

The meeting took place on 18 October 1877. Shepstone did not wish large numbers of Zulu to traverse land occupied by Boers, so the meeting was held on a large flat-topped hill, subsequently known as Conference Hill, just west of the Ncome river, near its junction with the Lynspruit. Shepstone was accompanied by his son Henrique, whom he had appointed as the Transvaal's Secretary for Native Affairs, by Gert Rudolph, the Landdrost of Utrecht, by other officials and an escort of 45 soldiers. No farmers were permitted to attend as Shepstone feared that their presence might cause the discussions to become too heated. About 500 Zulu were present, of whom 300 were men of rank, who referred to themselves as 'the Zulu nation'.[12]

Shepstone had hoped that the Zulu, relieved to find that he had come only to settle the border question and not to annex their country, would prove complaisant and amenable. He was shocked at their attitude. They were, he reported to his superiors,

> exacting and unreasonable in their demands, and the tone they exhibited was very self-asserting, almost defiant and in every way unsatisfactory. At no moment during the whole interview was there apparent the smallest hope of any reasonable arrangement; the arrogant and overbearing tone adopted by the Prime Minister was of course concurred in by all his colleagues.

Shepstone told Herbert that the Zulu 'were respectful and civil to me personally'. He later told Carnarvon that 'their bearing was haughty . . . and it seemed difficult for them to treat me with the respect that they had usually paid me'.[13] Other accounts of the meeting suggest that, in fact, in these statements Shepstone considerably played down the disrespectful manner in which he was treated. Cetshwayo later stated that Shepstone 'became very angry' at being called 'Somtseu' to his face instead of being addressed as 'Inkosi'. Bulwer stated, apparently on the basis of private letters, that the Zulu did not treat Shepstone with their usual marks of respect, 'and by some one of them he was grossly insulted'.[14]

There is a consensus among historians that this Zulu hostility towards Shepstone on 18 October 1877 was the result of his attempt to claim for the Transvaal all the land the Boers had claimed in their days of independence. 'It is well known that Shepstone reversed his opinions on the Transvaal-Zulu border dispute as soon as he raised the British flag in Pretoria'. 'Desperately in need of Boer support for the annexation he tried to win their approval by travelling to the border and using his influence over the Zulu to settle the boundary dispute in a way which would be satisfactory to the Boers'. 'A demonstration of imperial power over the boundary question was therefore necessary to humble Cetshwayo, bring Sekhukhune to his senses and mollify the Boers. Shepstone set about this objective. On 18 October 1877, after a series of incidents in the border area, he met a Zulu delegation at Conference Hill'. 'Shepstone met a Zulu delegation to discuss the territory disputed with the republic – and in his new guise as administrator of the Transvaal backed the Boer claims to the hilt'.[15]

Despite this consensus, when Shepstone met the Zulu delegation on 18 October 1877 he did not claim for the British Transvaal what the Boers had claimed for the ZAR. He did not claim the line marked A-A on the map, let alone A-B, the line incorporating the extra slice claimed in 1875. He still assumed, as he had assumed when in Natal, that the transactions of 1861, by virtue of which the Boers claimed the line A-A, were fraudulent, and that the Zulu had ceded no land on that occasion. He adopted the Boer claim only after the 18 October meeting, and partly as a result of it. The acrimony at this meeting was a product of two things: the distrust the Zulu felt for Shepstone, and the way in which he attempted to go about settling the dispute.

Shepstone opened the proceedings by asking the Zulu delegation to state what they claimed as the boundary. The Zulu objected to this procedure. They said they had always reported everything concerning the border dispute to him and had nothing to add since he already knew their causes of complaint. They had expected to be brought face to face with the Boers and that the two parties would be questioned concerning their respective claims. Shepstone stated that he did not wish to go into the old disputes, which could only embitter feelings; he wished the disputes to be forgotten and a mutually satisfactory boundary to be decided upon, irrespective of old quarrels. It was this that first caused the Zulu to accuse Shepstone of having become a Boer. It was precisely the old quarrels that the Zulu wished to be investigated; they wished their rights to be established and their wrongs redressed; there could be no question of compromise between right and wrong. For 16 years they had deferred to Shepstone's counsels of restraint, but now that he was in a position to expose the truth and enforce strict justice, he wished instead to protect the Boers from a full investigation.

Shepstone insisted that the Zulu should name the boundary that they claimed, so Mnyamana eventually stated that the boundary the Zulu knew was the Mzinyathi (Buffalo) to the Drakensberg, and the Drakensberg as far north as the sources of the Vaal. This was rejected by Shepstone as unthinkable. He proposed instead the Blood (Ncome) river and the Lynspruit to its source. He did not state where the boundary should run beyond that, but presumably he meant it to go in a straight line in a northerly direction to the Phongolo. He also suggested leaving a belt of territory of unspecified width 'beyond' this line, presumably meaning on the Zulu side of it, unoccupied except by a British agent who would hear complaints from either side, the ultimate possession of this belt to be left for future consideration in perhaps five years time. He did not specify the Phongolo as the northern boundary, but he always took it for granted that this was the limit that the Zulu could claim in that direction. Part of the difficulty between Shepstone and the Zulu was that they were talking about different things. For Shepstone, the disputed territory was the land the Boers claimed by virtue of the alleged cession of 1861. This excluded the land west of the Ncome, or Ncome-Lynspruit, which had allegedly been ceded in 1854 by Mpande; it also excluded the land north of the Phongolo, which the Transvaal did not recognize as ever having been the Zulu's and which it claimed by virtue of a cession by the Swazi.

Shepstone thus considered that he was virtually conceding the Zulu case in the matter of the disputed territory. The commission appointed by Bulwer in 1878, which is usually described as having found in favour of the Zulu case, also accepted the 1854 cession and rejected the 1861 cession. Its terms of reference did not require it to investigate the trans-Phongolan question. The only difference between the 1878 commission and Shepstone on 18 October 1877 was that the commission interpreted the 1854 line as being the Ncome (Blood) river (although the map which accompanied its report showed the line as running along the Klein Bloed, a tributary of the Ncome flowing into it from the Zulu side),[16] while Shepstone interpreted it as the Ncome and the Lynspruit. As we shall see, Cetshwayo later modified the Zulu cis-Phongolan claim to the line of the Ncome river. Later still, he privately indicated to the Colenso family that he was prepared to confine his trans-Phongolan claim to a thin slice of territory north of the upper reaches of the river. By so doing he was abandoning almost all of the Zulu claim to land north of the Phongolo. This huge concession was made in the context of his attempt to bypass the Shepstone family, who stood between him and the British government in both Natal and the Transvaal, by appointing the Bishop's son Frank and his legal partner as his Diplomatic Agents.[17] I take this concession to be a confidential intimation to his lawyers of the absolute minimum he would settle for, if necessary, to avoid war.[18]

In short, the differences between the Transvaal and the Zulu claims were perhaps not unbridgeable. With goodwill and a determination to avoid war on both sides, a settlement might have been reached. The historian, with the benefit of hindsight, can see that the Zulu were in a very vulnerable position. On the eve of the partition of Africa any African kingdom's chances of survival were slim. The Zulu's only hope of survival as anything like independent people (such as a 'Protected' people retaining most of their land) was to act in a compliant and innocuous fashion, giving no possible excuse for invasion. Had the Zulu delegation in October 1877 been able to see into the future they would have accepted Shepstone's offer, with suitable professions of gratitude to their Father, and confined their negotiations to attempting to obtain the most favourable line northwards from the Lynspruit and the most temporary and narrowest neutral belt.

But although one can see that this would have been in their best interests one can also see that they could not have acted in this way. In their circumstances, in the historical context in which they found themselves, it was impossible for the Zulu to be so compliant. Filled with expectation after years of tension, their apprehensions heightened by the disturbing events of recent months, they saw their meeting with Shepstone as a day of reckoning. They wanted a full investigation, and they wanted their rights restored. They were in no mood to do a deal. Shepstone's insistence that they should name the boundary they claimed was certainly a mistake. They were bound to tell him, as they had told him in 1873,[19] that they regarded all Boer settlement below the Drakensberg as an encroachment, and having told him that, they were bound to insist upon all their rights, in the absence of any inquiry, and thus in the absence of any reason for relinquishing any of their rights.

The Zulu delegation therefore rejected Shepstone's proposed boundary as indignantly as he had rejected theirs. Shepstone attempted to prove that the Zulu had recognized the Boers' right to the land west of the Ncome river by pointing out that Boer farms east of the river had been abandoned while the Boers west of the river had not been molested. This aroused more Zulu indignation. They argued that they had not driven the Boers away because they had sought a peaceful solution to the dispute. Instead of resorting to force they had referred everything to Shepstone and trusted him to settle the question. They had obeyed his injunctions to exercise restraint, and now that he had joined the Boers he used their restraint as an argument for depriving them of land which they had never ceased to claim.

The Zulu delegation did eventually modify its claim to a line running along the Mzinyathi (Buffalo) river, the Ngcuba river (near the town of Utrecht) to its sources, a watershed parallel to the Drakensberg running northwards to the Mkhondo (Assegai) river and then that river eastwards. But Shepstone rejected this as just as impossible as their earlier claim. Since it was apparent that no agreement could be reached, Shepstone proposed referring the matter to Cetshwayo. The Zulu delegation opposed this proposal. They stated that they represented the Zulu nation, that Cetshwayo and Mpande were present in them, that they had full powers to settle the question, and that no one would gainsay what they decided. Shepstone said he could come to no agreement with them, and that even had he been able to do so he would not have considered it final until Cetshwayo had also agreed. Since Shepstone would not discuss the matter any further, the Zulu reluctantly agreed to this course of action, and with this the meeting broke up.[20]

The following day Shepstone sent his two envoys, Lazarus Xaba and Sabulawa, to Cetshwayo and departed himself for Pietermaritzburg to pay a hurried visit to his family and to see Bulwer. He returned to Utrecht on 5 November to find that Xaba and Sabulawa had returned a few days earlier. Cetshwayo did not repudiate the Zulu chiefs as Shepstone had hoped, but reacted to Shepstone's proposals in much the same way. He, too, wanted a full investigation of all the complaints against the Boers which he had made known to Shepstone over the years. He regretted that he had relied exclusively on Shepstone in the past: 'I should have spoken to all the governments who would all have heard my complaints and acted for me and I would not today have been thrown over by my Father.' He emphasized again that his personal relationship with Shepstone did not mean that Zululand was the latter's property: 'I am his, but the Zulu nation belongs to Senzangakona.' Shepstone's proposed boundary was completely unacceptable: 'Has there ever been anyone who has been closed in right across his own doorway?' He would continue to claim the land which rightfully belonged to the Zulu nation, but by words, not deeds. He had no wish for war. 'I would retaliate though, if attacked, as even a wife beaten by a husband protects herself by catching hold of the stick.'

Despite all this, he did modify, in the Transvaal's favour, the line claimed by the Zulu chiefs at the 18 October conference. The boundary he was prepared to accept was the Ncome (Blood) river to its sources, thence to Magidela's Nek, thence along a watershed east of the Drakensberg and parallel with it, and then (apparently) the watershed between the Mkhondo (Assegai) and Phongolo rivers. But this modified claim would still have required the removal of many Boers from their farms, and was thus quite unacceptable to Shepstone.

Cetshwayo told Shepstone's messengers to report first to the members of the Zulu delegation, who were still in the vicinity of the disputed territory, and then to proceed with certain members of it to report his words to Shepstone. When, however, Mnyamana and his colleagues heard of Cetshwayo's modification of the Zulu claim, they expressed anger at their betrayal by the King, declared that he must be in league with Shepstone, and refused to allow the men named by Cetshwayo to proceed to Utrecht. Instead they required them to return with them to confront the King.[21]

This public airing of disagreement between the Zulu King and his counsellors was a remarkable occurrence, but disagreement between them was not in itself anything unusual (as we have seen in connection with Cetshwayo's Swaziland ambitions,[22] and this particular disagreement was not long-lasting. On 23 November messengers arrived in Pietermaritzburg from the Zulu King to tell Bulwer what had passed. They included one of the men whom Mnyamana had refused to allow to go to Utrecht, and the message included Cetshwayo's modification of the line that the Zulu delegation had claimed. This suggests that the conflict between Cetshwayo and his counsellors had been resolved and that Cetshwayo's view had prevailed. This is more clearly shown by the message

Bishop Colenso received two weeks later from Cetshwayo, Mnyamana and Hamu, stating among other things that they had abandoned their claim to part of the disputed territory.[23]

Cetshwayo's reply to his message was not the only unwelcome news awaiting Shepstone on his return to Utrecht on 5 November. The calm that had prevailed on the border for several months had broken. Shepstone had suggested at the 18 October meeting that undisturbed occupancy was a proof of rightful ownership. The Zulu evidently took him at his word, for on the day after the meeting farmers still in the disputed territory were ordered to leave, and similar orders were made on subsequent days. It appears that the parties of Zulu who served these eviction notices were instructed to do so by Mnyamana. Shepstone sent messengers who succeeded in raising doubts in these Zulu's minds as to whether their instructions really represented the wishes of Cetshwayo, and they desisted from making any further eviction orders.[24]

Although these eviction orders appear to have been unauthorized by the King, there was and is no doubt that the next attempt by the Zulu to establish their occupation of, and hence their right to, the disputed territory was ordered by the Zulu King. On the evening of 16 November Charles Potter, the storekeeper, rode into Utrecht with the news that 2 000 armed Zulu had that morning marched up to the Phongolo river with orders from Cetshwayo to build an *ikhanda* or 'military kraal' within three miles of Luneburg. They had been ordered, according to Potter, to molest no one, but if fired on to return the fire. Mpande had built an *ikhanda* in this position, but it had been destroyed by the Boers. There had been talk from time to time of rebuilding it, but nothing had been done. Although he knew the project was not a new one, Shepstone was greatly alarmed by the news that an attempt was now being made to carry it out. An *ikhanda* in the position proposed would, he believed, command most of the districts of Utrecht and Wakkerstroom, block communications with Swaziland, and cause the evacuation of great numbers of farms hitherto unaffected by the border dispute. 'I feel therefore,' he wrote to Bulwer late in the evening that he heard the news, 'that the building of this kraal must be prevented at all hazards.' He asked him to make the troops at Newcastle available to him should he need them. He also despatched Captain Clarke and Gert Rudolph to find the Zulu force and attempt to induce its commanders to delay any action while he remonstrated with Cetshwayo.[25]

Clarke and Rudolph located the force on 18 November near the junction of the Ntombe and the Phongolo rivers. Its commanders stated

that their intentions were purely pacific, that Cetywayo had ordered them to build a kraal to accommodate his native subjects who were living on farms occupied by Boers in this district, that the land belonged to the Zulu nation who had a right to do what it liked with its own, [and] that their orders were not to molest the white inhabitants or to injure their property but to go home after their work was done.

Clarke and Rudolph pointed out that the land could not be flatly asserted to be Zulu territory: the question was in dispute, negotiations were pending, and in these circumstances the building of the *ikhanda* was an act of aggression. The Zulu admitted the force of this argument, but said that they dared not disobey Cetshwayo's orders. As a compromise, they stated that they would build only the framework of the *ikhanda*, which could easily be removed if necessary, and then return home at once.

On the following day the Zulu force retired, having constructed only a small cattle enclosure and stacked some poles on the ground. Nevertheless the passage of the Zulu force through the disputed territory caused about 20 more farmers to abandon their farms, and a number of deserted farmhouses were pillaged and damaged by the Zulu returning home.[26]

On 21 November an embassy of 16 Zulu men of rank came to Utrecht with a conciliatory message from the Zulu King. Cetshwayo now stated that he approved of the answers which Shepstone had made to the chiefs at the conference of 18 October, that their demands had been excessive, and that he wished his 'father' to say where the boundary ought to be, and that he would object if he did not agree with it. The members of the embassy had not been authorized to say anything about the recent *ikhanda*-building expedition, of which they had in fact heard only on the way up. Nevertheless, they pointed out that it was an old ambition, and said that it should not be interpreted as a hostile act.[27]

Shepstone had earlier decided to send his son Henrique and Gert Rudolph to Cetshwayo to attempt to establish a temporary boundary, pending a final settlement, as well as to complain of the action of the Zulu in the disputed territory. The *ikhanda*-building expedition was now added to the list of complaints. Shepstone wrote to Frere that the Zulu embassy of 16, which included several military commanders, saw very clearly that matters had become very serious and was anxious they should not get worse; this gave him 'every hope that the Zulus have by their injudicious conduct given me the whip hand in the coming negociations'. To the members of the embassy itself, however, he said he had 'but little hope of any very satisfactory issue'. To Bulwer he wrote that he was 'unable to judge' how likely Henrique Shepstone and Gert Rudolph were to succeed.[28]

Shepstone's Search for an Explanation, November 1877 to January 1878

Searching for an explanation for the unexpected hostility and refractoriness of the Zulu delegates at the 18 October meeting, Shepstone was much struck by the counsellors' public denunciation of Cetshwayo when his messengers returned from the Zulu King.[29] In this he thought he had discovered the clue he sought. The conventional view of Zulu politics was that there was a war party headed by the King and supported by the young regiments, and a peace party, headed by the grave old counsellors and supported by the majority of the older married men.

Now, however, it was the counsellors who were the extremists and the King who was relatively moderate. It appears that it was this inversion of expectations that led Shepstone to see a hidden meaning in the public conflict between Cetshwayo and his counsellors. This conflict, he told Frere,

> is a novel picture in Zulu affairs and appears to me to point to the possibility of a revolution in Zululand, and as the only chance of gain to the revolutionary party would be to drag us into hostilities with the Zulu King, the danger is that an attempt may be made to do this.

This was no mere passing speculation. He continued to express this view even after the conflict between the King and his counsellors had been resolved, and he made this view the basis of his policies and actions. Three weeks later he wrote again to Frere:

> I have a very strong suspicion that the headmen are pressing things to their extremes to bring about confusion and relieve them from the present state of things. I can account for their conduct only in this way.

A further five weeks later he wrote:

> My impression that the revolutionary spirit in Zululand is the main strength of this exacting conduct is daily growing stronger. It requires a disturbance for its own ends, and it requires too that this disturbance should be with us or they that favour it fear those ends would not be attained.[30]

The most polite comment one can make upon this hypothesis is that it was a very bold piece of inference and that the evidence in its favour was very scanty. As we shall see, it seemed to Bulwer an entirely unnecessary hypothesis; to him the circumstances of the border dispute provided a sufficient explanation for all the Zulu's words and actions, and Shepstone's wrong-headed view of the matter was one of the reasons that led him to intervene and cause the conduct of the negotiations to be removed from Shepstone's hands.

Why should Shepstone have espoused such an extravagant hypothesis? The reason seems to be that it provided him with an excuse for his failure. The 'Africander Talleyrand', as Frere called him, the master of African diplomacy, the Great White Father of the Zulu King, could not admit, even to himself, that he had misjudged the situation and mismanaged the Zulu. There had to be additional or extraneous factors to account for things having gone so wrong. He told Frere that in normal circumstances he would have had little fear of failure, but if 'the balance is disturbed by any revolutionary tendencies, an element of uncertainty is introduced into one's calculations'.[31]

Another extraneous factor was the war on the Cape eastern frontier, and the exaggerated reports of British reverses which Shepstone was sure were reaching Zululand. 'Such reports,' he told Frere, 'are doubtless calculated to keep up the excitement of the war party and to stimulate the feelings of all in the direction of a struggle with us.'[32]

Shepstone and others believed another extraneous influence was at work. Cetshwayo himself was cast in the role of outside agitator in relation to Sekhukhune and increasingly in relation to every case of 'native trouble' in South Africa. But there was a growing suspicion that the agitator himself was subject to external manipulation. F.B. Fynney, after a visit to Zululand, made the mysterious statement that 'the King in all he does is acting under advice, by whom given I am not prepared to say'. Shepstone wrote that the reason for the Zulu's conduct was 'a mystery to me unless I attribute it to representations from near Maritzburg, made in ignorance of my real intentions and with the object of thwarting them whatever they may be'.[33] There is no doubt as to whom they were referring. The arch-manipulator was the sinister Dr Colenso.

Shepstone was at first prepared to believe that Colenso was not deliberately malicious, and that the danger was only that Cetshwayo might 'put a very different construction upon the Bishop's words to what the Bishop intends'. But later he came to believe that Colenso was intentionally mischievous. Nor was he alone in this view. Herbert minuted on a despatch from Shepstone:

> It is impossible to guess what Bishop Colenso may do or meditate. All that one can predicate of him is that he will work mischief if he can, & will not be over particular as to his doings. It is conceivable that he may be egging on Cetewayo to claim an extended frontier with the view of taking up his residence with him and controlling the Zulu policy.

The frenzy of whites in the border districts knew no bounds. Colenso was threatened with assassination should he visit Utrecht; and the Utrecht correspondent of *The Transvaal Argus* wrote:

> The great difficulty in the way of a settlement seems to lie in the intervention of the powerful wirepuller behind the Zulu scenes, and the powerful and pernicious influence he exercises at Exeter Hall, the meddling priest who is actuated purely by a mania for notoriety, and who does not care a brass farthing for the true interests of the black races; who would sit Nero-like on an ant-heap and sing his own praises while the Zulus were desolating the country with fire and assegai. Robben island is the only fitting place for such dangerous maniacs.[34]

Colenso was in communication with Cetshwayo at this time – that much was true. Cetshwayo sent a message to him after the meeting between Shepstone and the Zulu delegation saying that he was in great trouble over the boundary question and asking his advice. Colenso urged him not to think of fighting the British, which could only end in the ruin of himself and his people, and suggested that he should submit the matter to arbitration. On 5 December messengers came from Cetshwayo, Hamu and Mnyamana, stating that the Zulu had abandoned their claim to part of the disputed territory and were strongly desirous of maintaining peaceful and friendly relations with the British, that they had sent messages to this effect to Shepstone and Bulwer but that they were afraid that their words might have been 'lost on the way'. They therefore wished Colenso to write a letter to Bulwer and to the Queen clearly stating their proposals and wishes. Distrust of the Shepstone family, it emerged, was the cause of the Zulu fear that their words were not getting through. Cetshwayo suspected that Theophilus Shepstone had never, as he had promised to do, conveyed his complaints about the Boers to the Queen.[35] Theophilus Shepstone's brother John was the Acting Secretary for Native Affairs in Natal, and all Zulu communications to Bulwer passed through his hands. Thus, in both the Transvaal and Natal, a member of the Shepstone family stood between the Zulu and the British government. It was to bypass the Shepstones that the Zulu authorities asked Colenso to commit their words to writing.[36]

Colenso declined to interfere in this way, but since the messengers were very urgent he suggested they might engage a lawyer to do it for them. He told Bulwer he did not suggest his son Frank, but it was to the latter and his legal partner, Walter Smith, that they went.[37] Smith and Colenso junior informed Bulwer that they had been appointed Diplomatic Agents to the Zulu Government, and that all dealings with Cetshwayo should henceforth be conducted through them. But Bulwer refused to accept this arrangement, so Cetshwayo was obliged to hope that a distinction could be drawn between Natal and Transvaal Shepstones. He told Bulwer that he was 'quite satisfied that his Excellency will see all justice done him, and that Mr. J. Shepstone he looks on as in the place of his Brother Sir Theophilus [with] whom he had no fault to find whilst he was in Natal'.[38] It was these events, magnified and distorted by fear, suspicion, and rumour, that created the belief in the evil machinations of the Bishop of Natal.

Shepstone's Adoption of the ZAR Claim, November 1877 to December 1878

Shepstone seemed to be in two minds as to the likely success or failure of the mission of Henrique Shepstone and Gert Rudolph to Cetshwayo.[39] His indecision probably arose from the nature of the message which his son and Rudolph were to convey. The Zulu had earlier rejected his proposal that the Ncome (Blood) river and the Lynspruit should be the boundary. Rudolph and H.C. Shepstone were now commissioned to claim for the Transvaal all the land allegedly ceded in 1861; but, as a temporary arrangement, they were to accept the 'Old Hunting Road' as a provisional boundary. It was thus only in November 1877, well *after* the acrimonious meeting of 18 October, that Shepstone came to support the Boer claim to the disputed territory.

Shepstone said that he had been converted to the Boer case by his discovery, after his arrival in Utrecht, of 'the most incontrovertable, overwhelming and clear evidence' in its favour, evidence which had never been communicated to the government in Natal and of which he had therefore previously been ignorant.[40] He sent this evidence to Carnarvon in two confidential despatches dated 7 December 1877 and 18 January 1878.[41] It is not at all convincing. Many of the documents are *ex parte* statements, made long after the event by Boers involved in the transactions of 1861 and 1864, which prove nothing except that the Boers claimed the disputed territory. Other documents – reports of commissions to Mpande and Cetshwayo and so on – prove nothing but the continued opposition of the the Zulu to the line claimed by the Boers. Only four of the documents Shepstone sent to Carnarvon date from 1861, the year in which the cession was allegedly made. The most important is the treaty of 28 and 29 March, which contains Cetshwayo's alleged deed of cession. This had, however, been communicated to the Natal government: Shepstone had appended a copy of it to a minute he had written as Secretary for Native Affairs in June 1876, and it was printed in the British Parliamentary Paper C1961 on page 23. Another of these 1861 documents consists of the minutes of the meeting held on 1 April, at which it was decided to return the fugitives in consideration for which it was later claimed that Cetshwayo had agreed to cede land. In this document there is no reference to any cession of land: the reason for returning them is stated to be that their retention endangered the safety of the state, and that Cetshwayo had promised not to injure them.[42] Another document, dated 16 March 1861, purports to be a record of a message from Cetshwayo in which he offered to cede land. But it also purports to describe his meeting with Shepstone, a meeting which took place only in May; the document is thus palpably a subsequent fabrication.[43] The last of these four documents is Mpande's so-called ratification of 5 August 1861. It was in fact a denial of the validity of any cession by Cetshwayo, and a fresh deed of cession. It was signed by three frontier farmers and unwitnessed by a single Zulu. I have given reasons above[44] for believing that it is extremely unlikely that Mpande ever made such a cession.

The three last documents were apparently not communicated to the Natal government; but it will be seen that as evidence they cannot be described as 'most incontrovertible, overwhelming and clear'. Shepstone in fact seems to have attached the greatest weight to the assertions made to him in 1877 in Utrecht. He described them as 'the most important testimony',[45] and he told Carnarvon, when sending the documents which he claimed proved the Transvaal case, that 'having received the evidence of the chief actors in the events called in question, including that of the President himself, I have thought it best not to multiply documents unnecessarily'.[46] Ex-President Pretorius's testimony[47] is of interest. It purports to give an account of his visit to Mpande and Cetshwayo immediately after the alleged cession of 1861. The discrepancy, or rather complete contradiction, between this account of his visit and the reports he made at the time[48] can only be ascribed with great difficulty to forgetfulness. The original reports are in the Transvaal archives now and must have been there in 1877. Perhaps Shepstone or his aides did not succeed in finding them. Even so, the inherent implausibility of the statement must surely have cast doubt on its truthfulness. For example,

Pretorius stated that 'Panda said we had acted in a friendly way one to another, you by giving me my sons, and I by giving you a strip of land.' Shepstone must surely have known that the last thing Mpande had wanted in 1861 was the surrender of Mthonga, whom he wished to be his heir, into the clutches of Cetshwayo, the rival claimant to the succession.

It is impossible to believe that Shepstone's volte-face on the border question was the result of any process of argument or intellectual conviction. The fact is simply that in Natal he had believed the Zulu, but in the Transvaal he believed the Boers. He was quite capable, in a different context, namely that of the Boer agitation against British rule in the Transvaal, of characterizing the Boers at large as 'exceptionally deceitful'. But in the context of the Transvaal-Zulu border dispute it was convenient or necessary for him to believe everything they said and to dismiss the Zulu case as 'characterised by lying and treachery to an extent that I could not have believed even savages capable of'.[49]

The real reason for Shepstone's conversion must be found in the political situation in which he was now placed. The growth of Boer opposition to his rule, together with the conduct of the Zulu, brought home to him the logic of his new situation and the inappropriateness in this context of the views on the border question he had absorbed as Secretary for Native Affairs in Natal.

It was during Shepstone's stay in Utrecht that the Boer opposition to British rule[50] began to manifest itself. A fortnight after he arrived in Utrecht he could write: 'Wherever I have been during this trip I have been very warmly received and I believe that confidence in the new state of things is fast growing up among the Boer population.' Shepstone had travelled to Utrecht through the frontier districts of the eastern Transvaal, and in areas such as this, where strong government had been most sorely missed, there was some Boer support for the new regime. A little over three weeks later, on 28 October, he commented that there were still a good many Boers who hoped that the deputation to England would succeed in getting the annexation reversed. By 23 November he was referring to a 'good deal of anti-British feeling' in the Heidelberg district (which was far removed from any frontier).[51] By the time he eventually left Utrecht, at the end of February 1878, the Boer population of the country was in a state of incipient revolt, which was temporarily defused only by the sending of a second deputation to England.

When Shepstone first arrived in Utrecht he received a number of loyal addresses approving of the annexation. The wording of the addresses, however, made it quite clear what those who signed them expected from Shepstone, and quite clear also that their loyalty was conditional upon those expectations being fulfilled. What they wanted and expected, in the words of one of the addresses, was that Shepstone should 'make the integrity of this State respected by the barbaric neighbouring nation, and its despotic ruler'. In his replies to these addresses Shepstone promised only 'the fullest consideration, and such action as justice and prudence may suggest'.[52] The rebuff he received from the Zulu at the

meeting of 18 October, and the subsequent disturbances in the disputed territory, were not such as to encourage such an even-handed approach; rather, they
were such as to incline him to adopt the more obvious course of upholding the
interests of the state of which he was the ruler. It was, he said, after the Boers
had brought to his notice 'the danger I appeared to be in of surrendering the just
rights of the Transvaal' that he changed his mind.[53] 'I need scarcely say,' he told
Carnarvon, 'that the White population in this country expect that Her Majesty's
Government will be better able to vindicate those rights than that which it has
superseded.'[54] The white population of the Transvaal had every reason to expect
this, for this was virtually what Shepstone had promised them when he had
annexed their country. His justification for the annexation had been the inability
of the republican regime to protect its citizens against the encroachments of the
black hordes that surrounded it. In a despatch written a month before the
annexation, and which bears all the marks of having been intended for publication, Shepstone referred specifically to Cetshwayo in these terms:

> Since the Sekukuni fiasco he has assumed the exercise of sovereignty over a portion of
> Transvaal territory. He has ordered this farmer to leave his farm, and granted to another
> the privileges of remaining on his. These orders have been obeyed, numbers of farms
> have been abandoned, and the houses and standing crops of the Boers have been taken
> possession of by the Zulus; so that the process that has been going on for years in the
> North of abandoning farms and houses and other property to the natives, is now
> commencing in the South.[55]

Having annexed the Transvaal ostensibly in order to rescue it from these conditions, there was something anomalous in his upholding even part of the Zulu
claims. To have continued to do so after the Zulu had caused more Boers to flee
their farms would have been very difficult. To have done so after growing Boer
discontent with British rule had manifested itself would have been suicidal. It is
easy to understand why he should have changed sides. But the change from one
view of the matter to another led him into tortuous arguments and assertions of
very doubtful honesty, and exposed him to the accusation (by an official of the
Colonial Office) of having 'turned his coat in the most shameless manner'.[56] The
very embarrassing situation he found himself in gave him a strong personal
interest in Lord Carnarvon's scheme to eliminate border disputes by bringing the
whole of South Africa under British rule, so abolishing borders altogether.

At the 18 October meeting, before his conversion, Shepstone had claimed for
the Transvaal the Ncome (Blood) river and Lynspruit line on the strength of the
1854 treaty with Mpande. After his conversion he professed to believe that the
line agreed on by this treaty had been the Old Hunting Road. The wording of the
treaty, though obscure, gives no support to this interpretation.[57] Shepstone,
however, claimed to remember that in 1873 Cetshwayo had said to him that 'he
supposed that as his father had given the road to the Boers, he should have to
consent to that'.[58] Shepstone's reports on his visit to Zululand in 1873 contain no

reference to any such remark, nor, indeed, to any such resigned attitude. On the contrary, he had reported then that 'the Zulu view is that the whole of the Transvaal occupation below the Drakensberg is an encroachment upon their territory', and he had emphasized the 'vehemence' and 'strong and angry feeling' of Cetshwayo and his counsellors on the question, feelings which could 'scarcely be described in language too strong'.[59] One can only surmise that the real reason for this change of professed opinion was that he felt that the 1861 cession would be much more difficult to sustain than the 1854 cession (and the conclusions of Bulwer's 1878 commission bore this out) and that he was therefore trying to get as much as possible on the strength of the 1854 cession.

The Breakdown of Shepstone's Negotiations and the Intervention of Bulwer, November to December 1877

We must return to the mission of Henrique Shepstone and Gert Rudolph. Shepstone instructed them to tell Cetshwayo that he had changed his mind and that he now claimed the line of 1861, but that he was prepared, without conceding any Transvaal rights, to accept the Old Hunting Road as a provisional boundary. Given these instructions, there was no chance of the mission being successful. It proved to be a disaster. Not only was Shepstone's new claim even more unacceptable than his old, but the Transvaal delegates complained bitterly of the way Shepstone had been treated at the 18 October meeting, treatment which Cetshwayo had already repudiated in his message of 21 November.[60] They also complained of the eviction notices served on the Boers in late October and early November, which had subsequently been withdrawn, and of the attempt to build an *ikhanda* in the Phongolo valley, which had subsequently been abandoned. The Zulu's attempt at conciliation, it seemed, produced no similar response in Shepstone, but rather led him to press home what he supposed to be his advantage. The results of H.C. Shepstone and Rudolph's mission were therefore entirely negative. The mission served only to harden the Zulu's attitude, and exacerbate the relations between Zululand and the Transvaal and between Cetshwayo and Shepstone.

Cetshwayo, with the support of his counsellors, rejected Shepstone's claim and repeated the claim he had made earlier. He stated that the whole problem had arisen because he had respected Shepstone's urgings in earlier years not to fight the Boers; if it had not been for this the Zulu would have enforced a settlement of the question long ago. He said that if Shepstone wished to cast him off there was a man of equal rank in Pietermaritzburg who would take him up and write to the Queen for him. This was almost certainly a reference to Bulwer, but Shepstone assumed it referred to Colenso. Cetshwayo told the Transvaal delegates to tell Shepstone to move the people living in the land he claimed or some accident would happen. He also stated that he intended to proceed with the building of the Phongolo *ikhanda* forthwith. He added, however, that he would not be the first to go to war.[61]

H.C. Shepstone and Rudolph returned to Utrecht on 1 December. Shepstone treated the message they brought as an ultimatum. He interpreted Cetshwayo's words as the announcement of his intention to occupy the territory he claimed by force. He consequently sent a counter-ultimatum to the Zulu King. He told him that he would not permit the erection of a 'military kraal' on the Phongolo, that he would henceforth regard the Old Hunting Road as the provisional boundary between the Transvaal and Zululand, and that if there were any further aggression north of this road the Zulu should not blame him for the consequences.[62]

At the time of the Zulu *ikhanda*-building expedition in November Shepstone had asked for permission to use the troops stationed at Newcastle should this prove necessary. He now asked the commanding officer in Newcastle to send as large a force as he could spare to Utrecht. He also had half the infantry and all the artillery in Pretoria moved by stages to Utrecht.[63] He considered the possibility of raising volunteers in the Orange Free State and calling out the Swazi.[64] He instructed the Landdrosts of Utrecht and Wakkerstroom to advise the burghers to place their families in secure positions and hold themselves in readiness for active service.[65] He appealed to Bulwer for co-operation: a demonstration that Natal and the Transvaal were acting in concert would, he believed, have a restraining effect on Cetshwayo. He suggested to Frere that a warship patrolling the Zululand coast 'might be of great service in deciding the Zulu King to adopt a more reasonable policy'.[66]

Shepstone hoped that his military preparations would reassure those farmers who still remained on their farms and put a stop to the evacuation of farms which was still proceeding. They had just the opposite effect. His advising the burghers to hold themselves in readiness for active service was interpreted as an intimation of an imminent outbreak of war; and what was described as a 'stampede' took place, as the border farmers removed not only their families but themselves from the scene of possible danger. For two days the roads to the Vaal were choked with 2 000 wagons and large herds of cattle, as the areas between the Ncome and the Mzinyathi rivers and between the Phongolo and the Mkhondo (Assegai) rivers, areas previously unaffected by frontier scares, were almost completely abandoned. Most Boers were determined not to give any assistance to Shepstone: he had annexed their country with the excuse that they were incapable of defending themselves, and now they believed it was up to him and his soldiers to defend the country.[67]

The anticipated Zulu invasion, like all anticipated Zulu invasions, never happened. In the territory claimed by Cetshwayo, Zulu helped themselves to abandoned property; west of the Ncome river, in territory not claimed by the Zulu, the desolation of the abandoned farms was not even thus disturbed. An officer in the Royal Engineers rode through the area south of the town of Utrecht in late December and reported:

In the two days we passed through a country showing abundant signs of settlement, but except the farms immediately near the town of Utrecht, the defence centres and Mr. Uys' farm, the country was deserted. The comfortable looking houses with doors and shutters fastened, the orchards and gardens with fruit rotting on the ground, the dogs, cats, geese and poultry which came round us when we dismounted, seeking for food, left a melancholy impression on our minds almost weird from the absence of ostensible cause. There was no appearance of fire; we saw no marks of violence anywhere.[68]

Shepstone in Utrecht was almost surrounded by a desolate countryside: a far wider area than ever before had been abandoned. And yet the Zulu did nothing. Cetshwayo's 'ultimatum' was a product of his temporary irritation and of Shepstone's failure of nerve. H.C. Shepstone and Rudolph had borne an unwelcome message and had conducted themselves in an undiplomatic fashion, and this had produced an irritable response from Cetshwayo. This response, perhaps exaggerated by Henrique Shepstone and Rudolph, was interpreted by Theophilus Shepstone as an ultimatum. But subsequent events showed that it was not intended as such. Subsequent Zulu statements were all of a pacific nature. The Zulu messengers to whom Shepstone delivered his counter-ultimatum on 3 December smiled at the thought of Cetshwayo going to war with Shepstone and said 'he was only talking to his "father" to gain his point'.[69] On 18 December a message came from Cetshwayo to say that he had heard it was believed he intended to attack the Transvaal but that he had no such intention. He said that he had heard as well that the Transvaal was preparing to attack him. He also stated that he was investigating reports that the force sent to build the *ikhanda* in November had damaged property, contrary to his orders. The messenger brought no reply to Shepstone's previous message, what I have called his counter-ultimatum, which, he said, Cetshwayo had 'not yet sufficiently consulted his great men about'.[70] The reply came six days later, and it was essentially that there was no reply he could make. He had named two boundaries both of which Shepstone had rejected. The Old Hunting Road on the other hand was right in Zululand. All he could suggest was that his father should point out a place sufficiently large for the Zulu people to move to. In referring to the 'man in Pietermaritzburg' and the letter to the Queen he said he was 'merely beseeching his father, remembering that he had brought him up and crowned him and hoping that therefore he would listen to him'. He also said he would pay compensation for all damage done by the *ikhanda*-builders once his inquiries were complete.[71]

Two days earlier (the suspense perhaps being unbearable) Shepstone had sent messengers to Cetshwayo to demand a reply to his counter-ultimatum: did he still intend to occupy by force the territory he claimed by building a military kraal on the Phongolo, and did he want a peaceful settlement or war? He also told him he intended to station troops on the west bank of the Blood (Ncome) river to reassure the few farmers still remaining in the lower Utrecht district. He was telling him this, he said, so the Zulu in the area would not take alarm and flee, as the Boers had done when Cetshwayo had sent a large force without any warning to build a military kraal.[72]

The men who took this message found Cetshwayo in the midst of the *umkhosi*, the annual military review. They stayed at Ulundi for three days. The King placed them near him to see the regiments dancing. The soldiers knew who they were and made contemptuous references to Shepstone, demanding to be led to war against the white men and declaring they would die for the disputed territory. 'You hear what they say', said Cetshwayo, 'that is the Zulu people speaking, and I dare not go against what they say about the land; they would turn against me were I to do so.' He also remarked, however, that many of those who clamoured loudest would be the first to desert him if anything went wrong. Cetshwayo said that he could not accept Shepstone's territorial claim and could not relinquish his own. But he would not fight. Even if Shepstone sent an army against him he would not resist; when the army came it would find him unarmed, for he could not fight his father. If he had wished to fight, he would have fought the Boers, who had given him great provocation, but he had not done so in deference to his father. He could have no objection to Shepstone's stationing troops on the Ncome (Blood) river since he did not claim that territory. By the same token, however, there was no necessity for it. He also questioned its wisdom. Were he to send a force to the opposite bank of the river to give *his* people confidence, would it be possible for the two forces to face each other without conflict arising? He had, however, no intention of sending such a force.

Before leaving, the messengers saw Mnyamana and the other *izikhulu*. They said they agreed with Cetshwayo concerning the boundary line, but disagreed with his statement that he would not fight under any circumstances. They said that they would not commence hostilities, but they would resist the occupation of the disputed territory, and were prepared to die fighting on this question. 'Take your official message, however,' they said; 'what we say is only conversation, but it is the truth.'[73]

It was clear that there was no further possibility of fruitful negotiations between Shepstone and Cetshwayo. This was the conclusion reached by Sir Henry Bulwer, the Lieutenant-Governor of Natal; and Shepstone's appeal to him for assistance[74] enabled him to intervene, an intervention which had the effect of removing the conduct of negotiations with the Zulu from Shepstone's hands.

Bulwer had viewed the developing crisis with mounting disquiet. His disquiet was caused not so much by the Zulu as by Shepstone. His conviction grew that Shepstone's handling of the situation was unwise and potentially disastrous. He did not share Shepstone's belief that the Zulu *izikhulu* were bent on war with Britain as a means of bringing about revolution in Zululand. Such a hypothesis he considered extravagant, unsupported by the evidence, and unnecessary in order to explain the Zulu's words and actions, all of which he believed to be explicable solely in terms of the long-festering border dispute.[75] Shepstone's reactions to the Zulu's attempt to build an *ikhanda* near Luneburg caused Bulwer further misgivings. The timing of this attempt, while negotiations were proceeding, was certainly provocative; but the aspiration to build it was an old one, and the site was in territory claimed by the Zulu, territory which might turn out to be rightfully theirs. For Shepstone to state that a Zulu *ikhanda* in such a position would be a 'perpetual menace' to the Transvaal, and that its construction 'must be prevented at all hazards',[76] seemed therefore to Bulwer an alarming over-reaction. 'At all hazards' meant at the risk of war, for which the Transvaal and Natal were utterly unprepared. Bulwer feared that Shepstone was relying on his belief that the Zulu were deeply divided and that their military machine would disintegrate when struck. Such a belief Bulwer believed to be profoundly mistaken.[77] In the event, the Zulu withdrew, the *ikhanda* was not built, and so the threat of war temporarily receded. But Bulwer's misgivings remained. He felt that Shepstone was coming unduly under the influence of the Boers, a feeling that can only have been strengthened by Shepstone's conversion to the Boers' case in the matter of the border dispute. Bulwer was sceptical of the validity of the new information Shepstone said that he had received concerning the Transvaal's claims.[78] And Shepstone's determination to press the full Transvaal claim made a peaceful outcome less likely than ever.

It was the failure of Henrique Shepstone's and Rudolph's mission to the Zulu King that finally convinced Bulwer there was no possibility of the question being settled by further negotiations between Shepstone and Cetshwayo. It seemed clear to Bulwer that the Zulu had lost all faith in Shepstone, and that Shepstone (and his family) were embittered by the insulting and humiliating treatment accorded him by the Zulu, especially at the 18 October meeting. H.C. Shepstone and Rudolph were received in Zululand, Bulwer told Carnarvon, 'very badly and with the scantiest courtesy', about which members of the Shepstone family complained bitterly in their private letters.

> The reception was a bad beginning, nor were Henrique Shepstone and Rudolph the men to improve the matter. They committed some great mistakes at the interview with the King, and some part of the discussion, so I have been told on good authority, was about the behaviour and bearing of the Zulus to Sir T. Shepstone at the October interview. Shepstone's son being one of the mission, and the principal member of it, there was too much family feeling enlisted in the matter, and this part of the discussion was unprofitable and not at all calculated to help the far larger question at issue which was one of peace or war between the English and the Zulus.[79]

With the receipt of Shepstone's despatches conveying the news of Cetshwayo's apparent ultimatum and Shepstone's counter-ultimatum, it was evident to Bulwer that a crisis had been reached. Relations between Shepstone and Cetshwayo had never been more hostile. Neither would give way. Cetshwayo had declared his intention of occupying the disputed territory and of building the Phongolo valley *ikhanda*; Shepstone had made it clear that any such action would be resisted by force. All possibility of a settlement of the dispute by direct negotiation between Shepstone and Cetshwayo was at an end.[80] At the same time Shepstone appealed to Bulwer for his assistance. 'Family feeling' was involved here too.

Bulwer heard that he was being blamed for 'inaction, remissness, omission' by members and connections of Shepstone's family. It was evidently felt that he was not giving Shepstone proper support. Shepstone's vaguely-worded appeal for co-operation in settling the dispute might have been intended to veil a similar reproach.[81] Bulwer did not know what Shepstone wanted him to do, but with the threat of war imminent he dared not risk delay. On 8 December, therefore, he sent a message to Cetshwayo proposing arbitration. He expressed his great concern at Cetshwayo's apparent intention to occupy the disputed territory by force, a proceeding incompatible with a peaceful settlement of the dispute, and urged him to desist. He pointed out that the Transvaal was now, like Natal, British territory, and that an injury to one was an injury to the other. The friendly relations which had always existed between the British and the Zulu should enable an amicable settlement to be arrived at. Specifically, Bulwer offered to write to the Queen's ministers or to the High Commissioner asking them to send a fitting person to examine the question with a fresh mind and make a decision on it.[82]

An anxious month passed before any reply to this message was received.

Shepstone Urges the Ending of the Zulu Kingdom, December 1877 to January 1878

Shepstone, meanwhile, had also reached the conclusion that the question could not be settled by negotiation; but the alternative he looked to was not arbitration, but war.[83] 'I am fully satisfied,' he told Frere, 'that no permanent peace can be hoped for until the Zulu power has been broken up.'[84] As we have seen,[85] Shepstone, Frere, Carnarvon and Herbert were all agreed that Zululand would sooner or later have to come under British rule. Events since the meeting of 18 October 1877 convinced Shepstone that the sooner it were done the better.

Shepstone's situation was deeply humiliating. He had annexed the Transvaal on the ostensible grounds that its white population was unable to defend itself against the black tribes that surrounded it, and he had represented the Zulu as constituting the greatest threat. He had the reputation of having great influence with the Zulu. And yet under British rule the Transvaal's Zulu frontier was in a worse condition than it had ever been under the republic. Since Shepstone had opened negotiations with the Zulu, more farms than ever before had been abandoned. Fear of the Zulu had extended to districts never before affected. The Pretoria newspaper, *De Volksstem*, made the point in scathing terms: Shepstone's 'Kafir diplomacy', it stated,

> now that it is disclosed shows what a dead failure it is and what a sham it has been. The long vaunted boast of being father of the Zulus – whose word was paramount with Ketchwayo – has now as suddenly as painfully and humiliatingly collapsed. And the personal dislike and contempt which Ketchwayo and his Zulus bear for the great 'Somtseu' has considerably aggravated and increased our difficulties on the borders.

The situation, Shepstone admitted, was 'most embarrassing' and 'gives great occasion to that part of the Boer population which is opposed to British rule to excite disaffection'.[86]

Shepstone's letters in this period contain many references to the rising tide of Boer opposition to the British regime in the Transvaal. The Boers had acquiesced with surprising apathy to the annexation of their country. There seems to have been then a widespread feeling that the republic had failed, and that its replacement by a more vigorous and effective regime was an inevitable consequence of that failure, which it would be futile to resist. It was when the new regime showed itself to be as ineffective as its predecessor – even more so on the Zulu border – that the Boers recovered their self-confidence and began to demand the restoration of their independence. The failure of the expected reforms to materialize lost Shepstone the support of his natural allies, the Tranvaal British and the 'progressive' elements among the Dutch. This failure was ascribed to Shepstone's preoccupation with the Zulu question. He had left Pretoria on 16 August 1877 and did not return until 4 March 1878. 'While His Excellency remains on the Zulu Border,' wrote the Pilgrims Rest correspondent of *The Natal Witness* on 29 November 1877, 'these Pretoria officials let things "slide" as they may, and have not inaugurated a single one of those many reforms which are so much required.' Two and a half months later Shepstone was still on the Zulu border. The same correspondent wrote on 14 February 1878:

> Although English people in this Colony regret to appear in opposition to their own Government, they are yet being driven to it against their will, because they see all the interests of the country suffering, and affairs being allowed to drift into hopeless confusion, on account, apparently, of the want of an able head to guide and control them. While Sir Theophilus remains on the border, attending exclusively to one matter, and all others are allowed to "slide" for the present, people can scarcely be blamed for grumbling.[87]

Directly and indirectly the subjugation of the Zulu was necessary in order to secure the acquiescence of the whites in the Transvaal.

Shepstone believed that this was even more true of the blacks. The republican government had exercised little or no control over a large proportion of the Africans within the nominal borders of the ZAR. Shepstone took it for granted that it was his duty to enforce the sovereignty that the Boers had claimed but which they had lacked the power to exercise. This he felt would be very difficult to do as long as the Zulu continued successfully to defy him. He told Carnarvon that the Transvaal

> is in a most defenceless state, no portion of its boundary is in a satisfactory condition and irritating processes will be necessary along hundreds of miles of it before things are properly settled, these processes will be dangerous in proportion to the belief of the natives in our want of power to coerce, and they will gauge this by the issue of our present differences with Cetywayo ... the disadvantage that the Zulu matter will place us

in, unless we get out of it with flying colours, is that it will be difficult to make any such collection of native taxes as should be made.

The defunct republican government had imposed a fine of 2 000 cattle upon Sekhukhune, and Shepstone had insisted upon this being paid. He attributed Sekhukhune's failure to do so not merely to the Zulu example, but to the direct 'encouragement which he gets from Cetywayo who is anxious to avoid Sikukuni's falling peacefully under the rule of the Transvaal Government'.[88]

Shepstone attributed much of the current fighting on the Cape eastern frontier to 'messages from Cetywayo'[89] and his propensity 'always to be encouraging disaffection and disturbance'.[90] In fact, Shepstone concluded, 'the Zulu power . . . is the root and real strength of all native difficulties in South Africa.'[91]

> Cetywayo is the secret hope of every petty independent chief hundreds of miles away from him who feels a desire that his colour should prevail, and it will not be until this hope is destroyed that they will make up their minds to submit to the rule of civilisation.[92]

The necessity for putting down Cetshwayo became the theme of Shepstone's letters; 'there is no doubt that, if it were once done, all Native troubles in South Africa would for the future be but insignificant affairs'.[93]

Carnarvon had a high opinion of Shepstone and was much influenced by his views. He absorbed from him, directly as well as indirectly via Frere, the belief that it was the apparent lack of success of the Cape against Sarhili, coming on top of the ZAR's failure against Sekhukhune, that had produced a 'very threatening change' in Cetshwayo's 'language and conduct towards the Transvaal Government', and that a 'deliberate attack upon Her Majesty's Territories may ensue'. Another Shepstonian theme which finds an echo in Carnarvon is that 'a defeat of the Zulu King would act more powerfully than any other means in disheartening the native races of South Africa'.[94]

It was in the private letters cited above that Shepstone expressed himself most directly, and, one must assume, most candidly. Shepstone's despatch of 5 January 1878, which was published later that year, was less direct, but is of significance nonetheless. In an extended mechanical metaphor, he represented the Zulu kingdom as an anachronism doomed to self-destruction, an engine that no longer had a function but which continued to accumulate pent-up power. More specifically, it was a military machine with no outlet:

> The Zulu constitution is essentially military, every man is a soldier, in whose eyes manual labour, except for military purposes or in furtherance of military schemes, is degrading, he has been taught from his very childhood that the sole object of his life is fighting and war, and this faith is as strong in the Zulu soldier now, and is as strongly inculcated, as it was 50 years ago, when it was necessary to the building up and existence of his nation. Had Cetywayo's thirty thousand warriors been in time changed to labourers working for wages, Zululand would have been a prosperous peaceful country instead of what it now is, a source of perpetual danger to itself and its neighbours.

European settlement of the surrounding territory had left this military machine with no outlet. But the pent-up forces within it continued to accumulate and so were expended at home in indiscriminate bloodshed. This, together with the happy condition of the Zulu-speaking people of Natal, produced among Cetshwayo's subjects a great longing for change. Hence the disturbances on the Transvaal frontier. In an argument he first put forward in private letters,[95] he asserted that these disturbances were designed to bring about war with the British, not for its own sake, but 'for the purpose of securing for themselves and their country the benefits of a revolution, which in my opinion would happen the moment any active measure to enforce the claim of this Government were taken'. But no active measure was possible without the presence of a more powerful military force.[96]

In this tortuous way Shepstone sought to persuade the Secretary of State, and in time the British public, that the disastrous situation on the Transvaal-Zululand border was not something for which he could be blamed, but was simply a manifestation of the contradictions within the Zulu kingdom; that the kingdom needed to be destroyed and converted into a labour reservoir; that such a change would be a blessing to the Zulu as well as to the rest of South Africa; and that this change could be accomplished largely by the Zulu themselves with a relatively small expenditure of British blood and treasure. That the overthrow of the Zulu kingdom would require relatively little fighting was a view expressed in a number of his private letters as well.

Reactions to Bulwer's Arbitration Proposal, January to March 1878

On the same day that Shepstone wrote this despatch, Bulwer received the Zulu King's answer to his message suggesting arbitration.[97] This message, coinciding as it did with the advice given by Colenso, was a source of profound relief to Cetshwayo and his advisors. 'You have brought me good words which have allowed me to sleep,' the King told the Natal messengers. 'They show that the Natal Government still wishes Cetywayo to drink water and live.' The Natal messengers said, 'we saw that what we were saying lifted a weight from his heart'. Their message had the same effect on the *izikhulu*. 'After our message was delivered, all of them appeared like men who had been carrying a very heavy burden, and who had only then been told they could put it down and rest.'[98] Messengers from the Transvaal who arrived a few days later[99] commented on the altered demeanour of the King, which they attributed to the message from Natal, although Cetshwayo said nothing of its contents. 'It was Cetywayo', they said, 'but it was Cetywayo born again.'[100]

In reply to Bulwer, Cetshwayo denied any wish for war and denied that he had threatened war. All that he had done was to tell his people occupying the disputed territory not to move from it before the dispute was settled. He had sent men to build an *ikhanda* with no aggressive intention, but to control his subjects already living in that region. Since these men had dispersed he had taken no further steps in the matter. It was Shepstone who had 'quite altered his voice with the Zulu Nation' and spoke of war. Shepstone 'wishes to cast Cetywayo off, he is no more a father but a firebrand'. The Zulu King accepted Bulwer's suggestion of arbitration, but added a suggestion of his own:

> Before sending for people across the sea, for the settlement of the boundary, Cetywayo would be glad if the Governor of Natal would send his representatives to see what the claims of Cetywayo are, and hear what he says, and to hear what the others say, and if these cannot come to an understanding on the matter, then a letter can be sent beyond the sea for other people to come and see what can be done.

Bulwer in turn was greatly relieved by Cetshwayo's message. He was prepared to accede to the latter's request for a preliminary investigation by Natal commissioners, with a final arbitration by the High Commissioner or his agent, if necessary, and he urged Shepstone to do the same. Indeed, he told him that he did not anticipate any objection from him.[101]

In a private letter Bulwer expressed his uneasiness at Shepstone's apparent abandonment of any hope of a negotiated peace and his apparent view that war was inevitable. Shepstone had stated that Bulwer's message to Cetshwayo would enable him (Shepstone) to choose his own time for action, and that he would have to take action unless Cetshwayo gave way. 'But', protested Bulwer,

> I did not send my message merely to gain you time but in order if possible to bring about a peaceable solution of the question, and to prevent that action which you say is necessary. I speak to you frankly as a friend. What action do you mean? and what do you mean by Cetywayo giving way?

Cetshwayo, Bulwer pointed out, had abandoned the *ikhanda*-building project and had ceased to make his claim by force. Did his 'giving way' mean abandoning the claim itself? And did 'action' mean war? War in such a case would be entirely unjustified and unnecessary. 'If the Zulus are in earnest to have it settled peaceably we certainly ought to be very much in earnest with the same object.'[102]

In a later letter he commented on Shepstone's despatches of 2 and 5 January 1878:[103]

> You make no reference to the possibility of this question being settled by peaceful means in any one way or another, but are giving reasons for the destruction of the Zulu power, and for the Zulu Nation ceasing to exist as an independent Nation. Your Despatches, I take it, are working up to that point; but if this be the case, we are looking to different objects – I to the termination of this dispute by a peaceful settlement, you to its termination by the overthrow of the Zulu Kingdom.[104]

Shepstone in reply denied that by 'action' he had meant war, or at any rate any immediate and independent aggressive action on his part. But, he stated, Cetshwayo by *his* actions had caused the abandonment by whites of most of two districts of the Transvaal, an area more than 10 times greater than the area hitherto regarded as the disputed territory. This was an intolerable situation and some action to rectify it would have to be taken by the British government or the High Commissioner, after consultation with the Governors of the Transvaal and Natal. What that action should be would depend on circumstances.[105]

Shepstone's statement that it was Cetshwayo's actions that had caused the abandonment of most of the districts of Utrecht and Wakkerstroom was only very partially true. Most of the abandonment took place when Shepstone wrongly interpreted as an ultimatum Cetshwayo's irritable remarks conveyed by his son and Rudolph, who were angry at their discourteous treatment, and ordered the burghers of Utrecht and Wakkerstroom to place their families in secure positions and hold themselves in readiness for active service.[106] The only action Cetshwayo had taken was to send a force to build the Phongolo valley *ikhanda* in November 1877, a project soon abandoned. He had done nothing after his 'ultimatum'. But by February 1878 the farms were still abandoned and the farmers and their families were existing miserably in laager, still expecting a war.

Shepstone denied that he and Bulwer had different objects. He too wished for a peaceful solution. But 'the condition in which the Zulu nation now is relatively to the countries by which it is surrounded' meant that any peaceful solution could only be temporary. He would be misleading the Secretary of State if his despatches had concealed his conviction

> that from the nature of things any solution to the question must, although peaceably effected, be but temporary, unless great organic change takes place in the Zulu Government. I think further that this change is not likely to take place without violence either from internal convulsion or from external action forced upon its neighbours, or both.

In concluding this letter Shepstone repeated his desire for peace in suitably ambiguous terms: he would, he wrote, 'hail with pleasure any arrangement by which a temporary solution even could be permanently brought about'.[107]

Shepstone's renewed belief in the possibility of a peaceful solution, even if only a temporary one, was based on his belief that Cetshwayo would back down. There had seemed to be no chance of this at the time of his 'ultimatum'. But Cetshwayo's acceptance of arbitration caused Shepstone's courage and self-confidence to revive. He came to believe once more that the Zulu King would accept his claims – or, rather, that he would have done so had Bulwer not interfered. Cetshwayo's reply to Bulwer's offer of arbitration, Shepstone wrote, showed

> that he never intended to fight, that his plan was to threaten, and bluster, & injure the Boers as far as he dare, but that he would ultimately have given way to what he, of all men in the world must and does know is a righteous demand.

Shepstone now claimed to have known this all along, and, a month after he first heard of it, expressed resentment at Bulwer's offer of arbitration, which he said had the effect of 'taking the negotiations in a summary way out of my hands' and 'cutting the ground from under my feet'.[108] Bulwer's message to the Zulu King had been made in response to a plea for help from Shepstone; but Shepstone now said that all he had wanted him to do was to apply some additional pressure, not offer arbitration. Shepstone now claimed to have known all along that there was no real danger of war. He claimed to have been in perfect control of the situation throughout, until Bulwer so unnecessarily pushed him aside:

> Every message I sent and every step I took was experimental, I thought at length that a little pressure from your side would suffice, would cause our claims to be listened to, and if listened to, I believed that they would be acquiesced in, and our difference ended; but the reins had not slipped out of my hands, nor had I any intention of letting them slip; I take it that the description given by your messengers of the relief and satisfaction afforded to Cetywayo and his Indunas by your message, shows that I was not far wrong in my estimate of the situation at that moment; naturally they would all say that your words were unlike my words; that yours were comforting while mine were disturbing; mine put pressure upon them, yours took it off, and relieved them from the necessity of further negotiating with me on a question upon which they must feel themselves in the wrong.

The inevitable result of Bulwer's interference was delay, and in the meantime the districts of Utrecht and Wakkerstroom would remain in their existing deplorable condition.[109]

Shepstone's claims and accusations illustrate his capacity for self-deception. They must have been infuriating to Bulwer. Shepstone had raised no objection to Bulwer's offer of arbitration when it was made; he objected only after Cetshwayo accepted it. It had been Cetshwayo's change from a threatening demeanour to one of compliance that had revived Shepstone's courage; but then he objected to the means by which this change had been brought about. His representation of himself as the master of the situation, shrewdly judging to a nicety just when a little additional pressure was needed, was utterly false. His incoherent plea to Bulwer for help had been the product of panic and despair. Even after he knew of Bulwer's message to the Zulu King, but before the King replied, he had still been writing in this vein:

> I do not think that we shall get through this Zulu affair safely till Cetywayo sees somehow that the two Governments are acting in concert. How this is to be accomplished I scarcely know, but it is quite clear that if I get into difficulties here, hostilities I mean, for God knows I have difficulties enough, your Colony will be involved instantly too and you ought to have some say in the first instance and may save the worst coming.[110]

Bulwer replied to Shepstone's complaints with some heat:

> You called upon me to act. You did not say how. If you had only told me plainly what it was you wished me to do, then my way would have been pointed out to me, and so far as

I could have done what you wished me to do I would have done it. But you did not say, you did not point out the way, you left it to me to find out.

Bulwer pointed out that Shepstone's despatches written after the return of his son and Rudolph from Cetshwayo showed quite clearly that he had believed a war to be imminent, that there was no time to be lost by prior consultation, and that it was necessary to seize any chance of averting the calamity of war without delay.

> You say now that if let alone the Zulus would have listened to your claims and acquiesced in them. I think you are most mistaken in this. All that we have heard tends to show that your claims would never have been listened to or been acquiesced in; and that the Zulus would have gone to war, no matter the final consequences, rather than yield to the Transvaal Government the claims of the latter.[111]

There can be little doubt that Bulwer understood the motives and attitudes of the Zulu much better than the supposed great authority on the subject, and that for this reason also, and not only because Shepstone was a party to the dispute, Bulwer was better qualified to deal with the matter. This seems to have been the conclusion of the Colonial Office. Humiliating though it was for Shepstone to be superseded by a mere neophyte, his supersession was confirmed by the Secretary of State for the Colonies.[112]

Since Bulwer had replaced the world authority on the question it was very important for him that his interference should prove successful, and this gave him a personal vested interest in the maintenance of peace. Cetshwayo was very anxious to avoid a war he knew that he would lose and so he eagerly grasped the way out that arbitration seemed to offer. But Bulwer found very little support for his peace initiative in the Transvaal or Natal.

Shepstone sent him a memorial signed by 79 frontier farmers, and said that other similar memorials were being signed. This memorial left no room for doubt concerning the attitudes of the frontiersmen of Utrecht and Wakkerstroom towards arbitration. They stated that they had heard with anxiety of the proposed arbitration, which they feared would 'decide in favour of a crowned robber, murderer and breaker of his word'. They stated that Cetshwayo (thus unflatteringly described) had voluntarily ceded the land in question and that therefore arbitration was 'an absurdity and an impossibility'. They stated that they would resist by all legal means a decision regarding their property, which they knew would be unlawful and unjust. They urged Shepstone to use force to defend their property, stated that war was unavoidable, and pledged themselves to 'assist in subduing the Zulu nation and making it harmless'. Shepstone described their 'strong' language and 'deep feeling of distrust' towards arbitration as

> scarcely to be wondered at when it is remembered that these men are compelled to occupy with their families fortified camps, while their farms in the neighbourhood are

being occupied by Zulus, while their crops are being reaped and their cultivated lands are being tilled by Zulus, and while the timber of their houses is being used as Zulu firewood.[113]

Bulwer was critical of the memorialists, and, by implication, of Shepstone, who had supported or excused them. Of course if they wanted war they would be opposed to anything like arbitration, which might avert it. Their conviction that an arbitration would go against them was remarkable and accorded ill with a statement of the leading men of the district, reported earlier by Shepstone, that they had no misgiving that arbitration would not show the justice of their claims. If the delay occasioned by arbitration caused impoverishment, the havoc of war would do the same to a greater degree. This would be true of Natal too, since the latter could not remain unaffected by a war between Zululand and the British Transvaal.[114]

But, according to *The Natal Mercury*, Bulwer's offer of arbitration was generally opposed in Natal too, the feeling being that the matter should have been left in the hands of Shepstone. 'No-one attaches any value to the enquiry, and the step is regretted on all sides.'[115] If newspapers are any guide to public opinion, the prevalent assumption among the colonists of Natal was that the award would be adverse to the Zulu, that Cetshwayo would refuse to accept it, and that arbitration would therefore merely delay the inevitable war and the consequent ending of Zulu independence, a step necessary for the peace and progress of South Africa.

Sir Bartle Frere's views were much the same, but he did not consider the delay a disadvantage, since it would 'increase our means of defending whatever we may find to be our unquestionable rights'. In approving Bulwer's arbitration proposal he wrote:

> I cannot say that I see much hope of any permanent peace being attainable by means of intervention at the present stage. I should rather expect, from what you have sent me on the subject, that the Zulu King like many other Military Despots, will be willing to accept an intervention which may give him what he desires without fighting for it; but that he will not accept with equal readiness any decision adverse to his own claims . . . Unless both Cetywayo and his army and people have been greatly misrepresented, I do not see what reasonable hope we can entertain of their laying aside schemes of Military Conquest, and taking to the ways of peace . . . and if Cetywayo were to get all that he demands, without a trial of strength, his subsequently remaining content with what he had got would be a phenomenon which the usual habits of Military despotism, civilized as well as uncivilized, hardly justifies our expecting. Even if immediate hostilities be averted our position must, I fear, long continue to be one of armed observation, ready to defend ourselves against further aggression; but this, in my opinion, only makes it more desirable that, before hostilities commence, there should be no reasonable room for doubt as to the justice of all our claims.[116]

W.R. Malcolm, an Assistant Under-Secretary at the Colonial Office, reviewing the correspondence between Shepstone and Frere on the arbitration question, commented:

Nobody seems to think that the arbitration or enquiry will be much more than a farce. It is clear that directly a decision is given we must be prepared to support it . . . We have however now gained time & have sent out to S. Africa a force sufficient to deal with the Zulus. The Authorities will therefore now probably hasten on the crisis.[117]

It was under these gloomy auspices that the Commission appointed by Bulwer began its work on 12 March 1878. It consisted of the Attorney-General, M.H. Gallwey; the Acting Secretary for Native Affairs, J.W. Shepstone (Sir Theophilus's brother); and the Colonial Engineer, Lieutenant-Colonel A.W. Durnford. The Transvaal delegation consisted of the Secretary for Native Affairs, Henrique Shepstone; the Landdrost of Utrecht, Gert Rudolph; and a prominent and old-established local farmer, Piet Uys. The Zulu delegation consisted of Mundula, an old *induna* of Mpande; Gebula, a messenger and envoy who had taken part in most of the negotiations with the Boers; Sihayo, the Chief of the Qungebe, who lived in the border region; and, as a personal representative of the King, his attendant Sintwangu. They met on the farm of James Rorke, near a drift through the Mzinyathi (Buffalo) river. It was not the sitting of this commission but the war it failed to avert that caused this obscure spot to become so well known.

Notes

1. See ch. 6, p. 154.
2. SP 68, p. 262, Shepstone to Frere, 12 September 1877; see also ibid, pp. 267–8, Shepstone to Herbert, 5 October 1877; SPG, WP, no. 23, Carlsen to Robertson, 5 October 1877.
3. *The Natal Mercury*, 7 August 1877; *De Volksstem*, 26 September 1877.
4. GH 78, no. 457, memo on present condition of border between Transvaal and Zululand by A.W. Durnford, 5 July 1877, encl in Shepstone to Carnarvon, 24 July 1877, encl in Carnarvon to Bulwer, 11 September 1877; BPP, C2242, pp. 61–2, Clarke to Shepstone, 14 November 1877.
5. SP 68, pp. 271–2, Shepstone to Herbert, 5 October 1877.
6. See ch. 6, p. 141.
7. SPG, WP, no. 193, Robertson to Macrorie, 23 October 1877.
8. Colenbrander, 'Zulu Political Economy', pp. 84–5; De Kiewiet, *Imperial Factor in South Africa*, pp. 205–6. See the rainfall figures for Durban from 1875 onwards and the magistrates' reports from the various districts of Natal in the Natal Blue Books. There are no such systematic reports for Zululand, but see the incidental remarks of SM Samuelson in SPG, Vol. E31, p. 1265, quarterly report, December 1876, and Vol. E32, p. 1992, quarterly report, June 1877; and *The Net*, 1 May 1877, p. 80, letter from Robertson, 20 February [1877]. Since the missionaries left Zululand in early 1878, this source of information is not available for that year.
9. SPG, WP, no. 193, Robertson to Macrorie, 23 October 1877. The conference in fact took place on 18 October, but no news of it had reached Robertson.
10. SP 68, pp. 276–7, Shepstone to Herbert, 11 October 1877.
11. SP 6, Shepstone's diary for 1877, entry for 16 October.
12. Ibid, entry for 18 October; SP 68, pp. 281–2, Shepstone to Herbert, 28 October 1877; BPP, C2242, p. 51, appendix III, no. 1, Shepstone to Carnarvon, 1 December 1877.
13. SP 68, p. 282, Shepstone to Herbert, 28 October 1877; BPP, C2242, p. 52, appendix III, no. 1, Shepstone to Carnarvon, 1 December 1877; SP 68, p. 282, Shepstone to

Herbert, 28 October 1877; BPP, C2242, p. 52, appendix III, no. 1, Shepstone to Carnarvon, 1 December 1877.

14. Guy, *Destruction of the Zulu Kingdom*, p. 47; GH 1351, p. 31, no. 9, Bulwer to Carnarvon, 24 December 1877.

15. Respectively: Etherington, 'Anglo-Zulu Relations', p. 39; Guy, *Destruction of the Zulu Kingdom*, p. 46; Laband, *Kingdom in Crisis*, p. 9; Marks, 'Southern Africa', p. 391.

16. BPP C2220, p. 382 and map opposite p. 390, report of Border Commission, 20 June 1878.

17. See pp. 170–1.

18. According to Harriette Colenso, the King's messengers described this line as follows: 'Cetywayo marks the boundary (1) along the Blood River (Income) from Rorke's drift to the mountain Magidela *where it rises*. (2) along the watershed of Magidela. (3) from Magidela to the mountain Ingcaka in the Mnyamayenja district. (4) from Ingcaka to the Pongolo River.' She added: 'I don't know at what point, but I think near the Ingcaka.' – KC, Colenso Papers, File 13, KCM 49152, Harriette Colenso to Frank Colenso [date uncertain – it looks like 11 October, but this cannot be correct. It may be 11 December 1877]. The same boundary is described more summarily in ibid, KCM 49151, Harriette Colenso to Frank Colenso, 11 December [1877].

19. See ch. 2, pp. 34–5.

20. The principal sources for the events of this meeting are TA, SN 6, minute by H.C. Shepstone, 16 January 1878 (also printed in CO 879/13, African no. 150, pp. 91–5) and the report of Lazarus Xaba and Sabulawa, 3 November 1877, the envoys sent by Shepstone to Cetshwayo after the 18 October meeting, whose report includes an account of what they told the Zulu King concerning the events of the meeting. Also useful are Shepstone's report of the meeting to Carnarvon, BPP C2242, pp. 51–3, appendix III, no. 1, Shepstone to Carnarvon, 1 December 1877; and Cetshwayo's report to Bulwer, SNA I/7/13, p. 41, message from Cetshwayo, 23 November 1877.

21. TA, SN 6, report of Lazarus Xaba and Sabulawa, 3 November 1877.

22. See ch. 3, p. 60, and ch. 5, p. 117.

23. SNA I/7/13, p. 41, message from Cetshwayo, 23 November 1877; GH 1398, papers on claim of Smith and Colenso to be Cetshwayo's agents, statements of Umfunzi and Nkissimane to Attorney-General, 5 February 1878.

24. SS 258, R4609, Potter to H.C. Shepstone, 15 November 1877; SS 258, draft, H.C. Shepstone to Potter, misdated 12 November 1877; BPP C2242, pp. 59–60, statement of Manyosi, Nongamulana, and Sabulawa, 13 November 1877.

25. GH 789, Confid, Shepstone to Bulwer, 11 pm, 16 November 1877.

26. BPP, C2242, pp. 62–3, Clarke and Rudolph to Shepstone, 19 November 1877; GH 789, Confid, Shepstone to Bulwer, 23 November 1877.

27. GH 789, Confid, Shepstone to Bulwer, 23 November 1877; BPP, C2242, p. 51, appendix III, no. 1, Shepstone to Carnarvon, 1 December 1877.

28. SP 68, p. 290, Shepstone to Frere, 23 November 1877; GH 789, Confid, Shepstone to Bulwer, 23 November 1877; SP 68, p. 295, Shepstone to Bulwer, 26 November 1877.

29. See p. 166.

30. SP 68, pp. 286, 296 and 317–18, Shepstone to Frere, 9 November 1877, 1 December 1877 and 5 January 1878.

31. Ibid, p. 287, Shepstone to Frere, 9 November 1877.

32. Ibid, p. 299, Shepstone to Frere, 7 December 1877.

33. BPP, C2242, p. 85, report of mission to Zulu King and nation, by Fynney, 22 April 1878; SP 68, p. 340, Shepstone to Bulwer, 31 January 1878.

34. SP 68, p. 296, Shepstone to Frere, 1 December 1877; CO 291/1, minute by Herbert, 11 February 1878, on Tvl 1524, Confid Shepstone to Carnarvon, 7 December 1877; KC, Colenso Papers, File 29, KCM 50279, fragment in Colenso's handwriting, n.d. but

early 1878; *The Natal Witness*, 3 January 1878, reprint of letter from Utrecht correspondent of *The Transvaal Argus*, 14 December 1877.

35. GH 1398, papers on claim of Smith and Colenso to be Cetshwayo's agents, statements of Umfunzi and Nkissimane to Attorney-General, 5 February 1878.
36. SNA I/4/1, no. 12, Dunn to Bulwer, 21 December 1877, conveying message from Cetshwayo.
37. GH 1052, Colenso to Bulwer, 2 September 1878.
38. GH 1052, Colenso to Bulwer, 2 September 1878; SNA I/4/1, no. 93, Dunn to Bulwer, 1 January 1878. On the 'Diplomatic Agents' episode, see also Colenso and Durnford, *History*, pp. 137–40.
39. See p. 168.
40. BPP, C2079, p. 54, no. 38, Shepstone to Carnarvon, 2 January 1878.
41. CO 879/12, African no. 147, p. 196, Confid Shepstone to Carnarvon, 7 December 1877; CO 879/13, African no. 150, p. 90, Confid Shepstone to Carnarvon, 18 January 1878.
42. See ch. 2, pp. 25–6.
43. See ch. 2, pp. 23–4.
44. See ch. 2, p. 26.
45. BPP, C2242, p. 56, appendix III, no. 1, Shepstone to Carnarvon, 1 December 1877.
46. CO 879/13, African no. 150, no. 58, p. 90, Confid, Shepstone to Carnarvon, 18 January 1878: BPP, C2242, p. 56, appendix III, no. 1, Shepstone to Carnarvon, 1 December 1877.
47. BPP, C2242, p. 99, statement of M.W. Pretorius, 22 December 1877.
48. See ch. 2, p. 26.
49. SP 68, p. 351, Shepstone to Herbert, 19 February 1878; ibid, p. 302, Shepstone to Bulwer, 10 December 1877.
50. On this generally see Van Zyl, *Protes-Beweging*.
51. SP 68, p. 275, Shepstone to Frere, 5 October 1877; ibid, p. 281, Shepstone to Herbert, 28 October 1877; ibid, p. 292, Shepstone to Frere, 23 November 1877.
52. BPP C1961, pp. 153–7, no. 79, Shepstone to Carnarvon, 4 October 1877, and enclosures.
53. BPP, C2079, p. 54, no. 38, Shepstone to Carnarvon, 2 January 1878.
54. BPP, C2242, p. 58, appendix III, no. 1, Shepstone to Carnarvon, 1 December 1877.
55. BPP, C1776, p. 127, Shepstone to Carnarvon, 12 March 1877.
56. Guy, *Destruction of the Zulu Kingdom*, p. 46, quoting Edward Fairfield in 1885.
57. BPP, C2220, p. 371, Border Commission report, 20 June 1878.
58. BPP, C2242, p. 57, appendix III, no. 1, Shepstone to Carnarvon, 1 December 1877.
59. SNA I/7/10, no. 62, minute on the relations of the Zulu with the government of the ZAR as described from a Zulu point of view, 20 February 1874.
60. See p. 168.
61. TA, SN 6, H.C. Shepstone and Rudolph to Shepstone, 4 December 1877.
62. BPP C2242, p. 77, appendix III, no. 2, Shepstone to Carnarvon, 4 December 1877.
63. TA, General Letter-Book 2, Shepstone to Major Tucker, 5 December 1877; to Commandant, Transvaal, 1 December 1877; to OC Heidelberg, 8 December 1877; to OC Standerton, 15 December 1877.
64. SP 68, p. 299, Shepstone to Frere, 7 December 1877.
65. Ibid, p. 311, Shepstone to Frere, 15 December 1877; TA General Letter-Book 2, H.C. Shepstone to Landdrost M.W. Stroom, 13 December 1877. This volume does not contain the instruction to the Landdrost of Utrecht, which was probably given verbally. A memorial of 79 burghers dated 2 February 1878, enclosed in GH 790, no. 9, Shepstone to Bulwer, 8 February 1878, shows that such advice was received from the Landdrost of Utrecht.

66. GH 789, Confid, Shepstone to Bulwer, 4 December 1877; SP 68, p. 314, Shepstone to Bulwer, 24 December 1877; TA, General Letter-Book 2, Shepstone to Frere, 22 December 1877.

67. GH 790, no. 9, Memorial dated 2 February 1878, signed by 79 Utrecht and Wakkerstroom burghers, encl in Shepstone to Bulwer, 8 February 1878; *De Volksstem*, 18 December 1877, 'The Zulu Difficulty'; ibid, 1 January 1878, letter from Wakkerstroom correspondent, 20 December 1877; ibid, 8 January 1878, quoting letter from Utrecht, 27 December 1877; *The Natal Mercury*, 22 January 1878, letter, 12 January 1878.

68. SS 258, R2649, Macdowil (?) to (?), 26 December 1878.

69. BPP, C2242, p. 78, appendix III, no. 2, Shepstone to Carnarvon, 4 December 1877.

70. CO 879/13, African no. 150, no. 1, Confid, Shepstone to Carnarvon, 20 December 1877; SP 6, Shepstone's diary for 1877, entry for 19 December.

71. TA, SN 6, statement of Piti, Faku, Ungexeni and Usizibana, 24 December 1877.

72. TA, General Letter-book 2, Shepstone to Frere, 22 December 1877; SP 6, Shepstone's diary for 1877, entry for 22 December.

73. BPP, C2079, p. 51, no. 38, Shepstone to Carnarvon, 2 January 1878; ibid, p. 56, statement of Nongamulana and Sabulawa, 31 December 1877.

74. See p. 176.

75. SP 25, Bulwer to Shepstone, 14 November 1877.

76. See p. 167.

77. SP 25, Bulwer to Shepstone, 14 and 21 November 1877; GH 1351, p. 18, no. 6, Bulwer to Frere, 26 November 1877.

78. SP 25, Bulwer to Shepstone, 5 December 1877.

79. GH 1351, pp. 31–2, no. 9, Private, Bulwer to Carnarvon, 24 December 1877. A description by Gert Rudolph of his and H.C. Shepstone's unfriendly reception by Cetshwayo, taken down by Sir Bartle Frere's military secretary, Henry Hallam Parr, n.d., is in BPP, C2367, pp. 17–18, reprinted in Parr, *Sketch*, pp. 133–7. Rudolph told Shepstone that Parr's notes were inaccurate in many points, and that Cetshwayo had not spoken in a disrespectful way of Henrique: SP 46, Confid, Rudolph to Shepstone, 15 December 1880. Lazarus Xaba later described to James Stuart the discourteous way in which H.C. Shepstone and Rudolph were received: KC, Stuart Papers, File 19, KCM 23467, pp. 121–2.

80. GH 1325, no. 446, Bulwer to Frere, 10 December 1877.

81. SP 27, Bulwer to Shepstone, 6 February 1878; SNA I/3/30, no. 530, minute by Bulwer, 31 May 1878.

82. SNA I/7/13, p. 49, message to Cetshwayo, 8 December 1877.

83. For Shepstone's views in this period, see his private letters to Bulwer, Carnarvon, Frere and Herbert in SP 68, p. 296 onwards.

84. Ibid, p. 319, Shepstone to Frere, 8 January 1878.

85. See ch. 6, pp. 150–1.

86. *De Volksstem*, 22 January 1878, editorial; BPP, C2079, pp. 52–3, no. 38, Shepstone to Carnarvon, 2 January 1878.

87. *The Natal Witness*, 14 December 1877; ibid, 2 March 1878.

88. SP 68, pp. 309–10 and p. 307, Shepstone to Carnarvon, 11 December 1877.

89. Ibid, p. 312, Shepstone to Frere, 18 December 1877.

90. Ibid, p. 307, Shepstone to Carnarvon, 11 December 1877.

91. Ibid, p. 300, Shepstone to Frere, 7 December 1877.

92. Ibid, p. 309, Shepstone to Carnarvon, 11 December 1877.

93. Ibid, p. 312, Shepstone to Frere, 18 December 1877.

94. Cape GH 4/6, Confid, Carnarvon to Frere, 23 January 1878.

95. See pp. 168–9.

96. BPP, C2079, pp. 54–6, no. 39, Shepstone to Carnarvon, 5 January 1878.
97. This exists in three forms: SNA I/7/13, p. 57, statement of Kilane and Umgovu (the Natal messengers who conveyed Bulwer's message to Cetshwayo) 5 January 1878; ibid, p. 59, statement of Tshikela, Mange and Bovolo (Zulu messengers) 5 January 1878; SNA I/4/1, Dunn to Bulwer, 21 December 1877 (a letter brought by the Zulu messengers).
98. SNA I/7/13, p. 68, statement of Kilane and Umgovu, 17 January 1878.
99. See pp. 177–8.
100. BPP, C2079, p. 52, no. 38, Shepstone to Carnarvon, 2 January 1878.
101. GH 1325, no. 468, Bulwer to Shepstone, 8 January 1878.
102. SP 26, Bulwer to Shepstone, 9 January 1878.
103. See pp. 182–3.
104. SP 27, Bulwer to Shepstone, 16 January 1878.
105. SP 68, p. 321, Shepstone to Bulwer, 14 January 1878.
106. See p. 176.
107. SP 68, p. 332, Shepstone to Bulwer, 22 January 1878.
108. Ibid, p. 321, Shepstone to Bulwer, 14 January 1878.
109. Ibid, pp. 340–1, Shepstone to Bulwer, 31 January 1878.
110. Ibid, p. 314, Shepstone to Bulwer, 24 December 1877.
111. SP 27, Bulwer to Shepstone, 6 February 1878.
112. BPP, C2000, p. 153, no. 98, Hicks Beach to Bulwer, 14 February 1878; and ibid, p. 152, no. 96, Hicks Beach to Frere and Shepstone, 14 February 1878, encl copies of no. 98.
113. GH 790, no. 9, Shepstone to Bulwer, 8 February 1878, encl memorial, 2 February 1878.
114. GH 1326, no. 40, Bulwer to Shepstone, 23 February 1878.
115. *The Natal Mercury*, 4 February 1878, 'The Month'; ibid, 11 March 1878, 'The Week'.
116. GH 599, no. 2, Frere to Bulwer, 26 January 1878.
117. CO 179/126, minute by Malcolm, 28 March 1878, on Natal 3602, Bulwer to Hicks Beach, 13 February 1878.

CHAPTER EIGHT

The Border Commission and Sir Bartle Frere

The Commission and the Border, March to July 1878

The Border Commission began its work at Rorke's Drift on 12 March 1878.[1] As instructed by Shepstone,[2] the Transvaal delegates claimed the line allegedly ceded in 1861 and beaconed in 1864 (A-A on the map), thus dropping the claim to additional territory made in Joubert's proclamation of 1875.[3] The Zulu delegates, on the other hand, were evidently instructed to claim the maximum possible, for they claimed the Mzinyathi (Buffalo) to its sources and then a line extending far into the eastern Transvaal, north of the Olifants river. They thus made a formal claim to the territory between the Mzinyathi (Buffalo) and Ncome (Blood) rivers, territory to which Cetshwayo had earlier abandoned his claim. The extravagant Zulu claim to territory north of the Phongolo fell outside the scope of the Commission, which had been instructed by Bulwer to consider only the territory alleged to have been ceded by the Zulu to the Boers. The Transvaal claim to territory north of the Phongolo was based on a Swazi cession of 1855 (which the Zulu claimed the Swazi had no right to make) and not on a Zulu cession.[4] This was therefore a separate question. Nevertheless, it needed to be solved, as the Commission pointed out. The reason why the Commission was not asked to do so was probably simply the fixed assumption on the part of whites that the Zulu could have no claim north of the Phongolo.

P.L. Uys, who was also one of the Transvaal delegates, was the first witness to give evidence. When the Zulu delegates were invited to cross-examine him they declined to do so, saying that everything he said was false, that they had come only to state their claim, and that they had received no authority from Cetshwayo to question Transvaal witnesses or to call any of their own.[5]

This unco-operative attitude arose from the Zulu's initial distrust of the Commission and their lack of faith in its impartiality.[6] The presence on it of John Shepstone probably had a lot to do with this. As the Commission's proceedings continued the Zulu lost their initial distrust. The Commissioners dealt with the Transvaal and Zulu delegates on a level of strict equality, which was a source of great dissatisfaction to Henrique Shepstone and his father,[7] but which seems to have reassured the Zulu. They certainly called witnesses, and though it is not clear whether they questioned the Transvaal witnesses, the members of the Commission subjected both sides to searching questioning. After the conclusion of the inquiry, Cetshwayo sent a message to Bulwer stating that he now saw the Natal government wished to do him justice and expressing perfect satisfaction with the way the enquiry had been conducted.[8]

Part of his satisfaction may have arisen from a belief that the Zulu had got the better of it; and, conversely, part of the Transvaal delegates' dissatisfaction with the inquiry may have arisen from a fear that they had not been successful. H.C. Shepstone's diary suggests that things did not go well for the Transvaal. Two days after Uys completed his evidence H.C. Shepstone described him as having 'amended' it. He described other witnesses as having 'made a mess of it', having 'made a regular mess of it', and as being 'forgetful' or 'very forgetful',[9] though he described others as having given their evidence well. The inadequacy of some of the Transvaal witnesses was apparent to others. William Ngidi, one of Colenso's converts, wrote to another, Magema Fuze, that

> the Dutch are beaten, they are unable to confirm the boundary, their paper has been lost – it has rotted away – it has had something spilt over it – it has been destroyed. Any how, the Dutch have lost their case, & are much blamed by the English for being unable to confirm the boundary.[10]

Reports along these lines then began to surface in the press. *The Natal Witness* stated on 13 April that rumours kept arriving that the Transvaal witnesses had failed to prove their case, and its Biggarsberg correspondent wrote on 22 April that it was 'rumoured pretty freely here that as far as the case has gone, it does not look favourable for the Transvaal'.[11] It is likely that a similar impression prevailed in Zululand. Cetshwayo's message to Bulwer expressing satisfaction with the inquiry reveals an expectation that its outcome would be favourable to the Zulu:

> Cetywayo and the Zulu people are awaiting with beating hearts what the Lieutenant Governor of Natal will decide about the land that the Boers have given them, the Zulus, so much trouble about – for the Zulus wish very much now to occupy the land they never parted with, as it is now the proper season for doing so.[12]

The Transvaal Boers also wished to occupy the land. Both sides in fact made attempts to reoccupy the land after the sitting of the Commission, with the result that May 1878 was characterized by renewed tension and alarms in the border area. Some of the Boers who had been living in laager were evidently encouraged by Shepstone to resume the occupation of their farms, but were driven off by groups of Zulu. The Zulu went further than this, however: they ordered farmers who had remained on their farms to quit, including farmers as far north as the Mkhondo (Assegai) river, and also in the area west of the Ncome river, territory to which Cetshwayo had earlier relinquished his claim. All this was done in the name of the Zulu King, and the impression evidently prevailed among the Zulu that Bulwer had granted them all the land they had claimed at the Rorke's Drift inquiry. Parties of Zulu also began building homesteads in the territory they claimed, including one at Luneburg, where the attempt six months earlier to build a 'military kraal' had caused such alarm. The 'kraal' that was built, however, proved to be an ordinary residential *umuzi*, not an *ikhanda* or 'military kraal', and the commander of the building party, the *induna* Faku, whose residence the *umuzi* was to be, contradicted the earlier Zulu orders to the Luneburgers to leave, and stated that Cetshwayo had ordered that Transvaal subjects were not to be molested or disturbed in the occupation of their land. It is possible, indeed, as Colenso argued, that the building of the Luneburg *umuzi* was Cetshwayo's response to the frontier disturbances, and that Faku was sent to Luneburg to control the local Zulu and prevent them from disturbing the peace.[13]

Shepstone's response to the frontier disturbances could almost be described as sulky. In reply to letters and petitions from his alarmed subjects he invariably replied that Zulu matters had been taken out of his hands and that they should direct their pleas and requests to Bulwer.[14] He evidently felt deeply humiliated by the removal of the negotiations with the Zulu from his hands. Bulwer did not agree that his offer of arbitration had made him responsible for the preservation of order on the Transvaal-Zululand border.[15] Nevertheless, he sent a message to Cetshwayo urging him not to anticipate the border award, as it was reported that some of his subjects were doing.[16] Cetshwayo denied having acted aggressively, and stated that all he had done was to ask Rudolph not to permit the Boers to reoccupy the farms, pending the outcome of the inquiry, for fear of disturbances.[17] Rudolph ascertained that the earlier orders to quit had been sent by local border chiefs.[18] In June Cetshwayo sent messages countermanding these orders, and it was reported that he had given strict orders against any further destruction of homesteads or molestation of white people. Although Zulu continued building homesteads in the disputed territory, these measures by the King produced a greater degree of calm among those whites who still remained on their farms.[19]

The Border Commission, Gallwey, Durnford and J.W. Shepstone, left Rorke's Drift on 14 April, and completed their report on 20 June. Sir Henry Bulwer then sent it to the High Commissioner, Sir Bartle Frere. The ninth and last war on the Cape eastern frontier had just ended, and Frere was henceforth able to give his undivided attention to the problems of Zululand and the Transvaal.

Sir Bartle Frere

I have had occasion to refer to Frere before this; from this point on he dominates the story, so it is necessary to make some more connected remarks about his background, his attitudes, and beliefs.

Sir Bartle Frere was then 63 years of age, and had behind him a long and illustrious career in the Indian Civil Service, which he had joined at the age of 19. He had distinguished himself as Commissioner of Sind by his coolness and courage during the Indian Mutiny. In 1859 he was appointed a member of the Supreme Council at Calcutta, the seat of the Indian government at that time, and in 1862 he was made Governor of the Bombay Presidency, where he remained until he left India in 1867. He left under something of a cloud, being criticized (most unfairly according to his biographers) for not having done enough to prevent the failure of the Bombay Bank. Nevertheless, he was appointed to the India Council in London, and in 1873 successfully undertook a mission to induce the Sultan of Zanzibar to end the slave trade, an action which won him esteem in philanthropic circles. In 1875 he was chosen to accompany the Prince of Wales on his visit to India. He had been knighted in 1865 and appointed to the Privy Council in 1873, and in 1876, on returning from India for the last time, he was made a baronet. His reputation as a great imperial administrator, statesman and humanitarian was at its height.

Commenting on his appointment to South Africa, *The Times* stated that the Aborigines Protection Society 'could safely claim him as almost one of themselves'. A Liberal member of Parliament described his appointment as fortunate because of his 'great sympathy for the native races'. Carnarvon commended him to Queen Victoria as a humanitarian and friend to native welfare. Frere's biographer came close to describing him as a saint:

> The description given me of him by those who knew him seemed too good, too faultless to be true. I asked for the reverse of the shield, for the shadows without which the lights seemed monotonous and unreal. I asked in vain . . . If it is too good to be true, I cannot help it. I cannot paint shadows which I do not see. If I am blind, at least I am blind in good company.

The author of the official *Life and Correspondence* might be suspected of undue partiality; but Philip Mason, a distinguished scholar as well as an eminent Indian Civil Servant, wrote in the same vein:

> Sir Bartle Frere is a man for whom one's admiration grows steadily . . . his wide sympathies, his chivalrous courtesy, his courage, his calm, his common sense, his obedience to duty – all are impressive . . . He judged every question by his own standards, which were absolute and admitted of no compromise. He did not consider whether his views would please his superiors or magnify his importance but whether they were right.[20]

When one turns to a historian of South Africa, one can scarcely believe that one is reading about the same man: 'Frere was the sort of villain cinema audiences love to hate . . . sanctimonious, pig-headed, officious, self-righteous . . .' Thus Norman Etherington; and he is not propounding a paradox or putting forward some radical reinterpretation of Frere's character. On the contrary, he is stating what he considers to be, within the context of South African historiography, the traditional and accepted view of Frere, a view which he says 'there is no reason to revise'. His argument is that the very obviousness of Frere's villainy has obscured the deeper causes of the Anglo-Zulu war: 'When a bully with a black hat and moustache is caught with a smoking gun in his hand, posses and juries don't ask very penetrating questions. Neither, it is embarrassing to admit, do historians.'[21]

One must agree that the villainy of Sir Bartle Frere is a most inadequate explanation for the Anglo-Zulu war, though many of his contemporaries found it sufficient. Lady Frere complained that his critics saw him as 'a very bad villain in a novel. They seem really to have believed two years in South Africa completely changed his character.'[22] It is Frere's villainy, real or supposed, his apparent reversal of character, that needs to be explained. What were the forces and circumstances in South Africa that led him to act in such a way as to change his reputation so drastically?

Frere was condemned in his own day as well as later for having launched an unjust, unnecessary, bloody and expensive war in defiance of his instructions. One might argue that Frere was simply unlucky in South Africa: that the methods of imperialism were much the same in India and South Africa, but that in India he got away with it whereas in South Africa he failed and was found out. Had it not been for the disaster at Isandlwana – had the war been the short and successful campaign he had expected it to be – he would almost certainly have escaped censure by the Colonial Office,[23] and would probably have escaped the censure and indeed the attention of the British public. Isandlwana focused the attention of the previously indifferent British Parliament, press and public on South Africa, and Frere's actions and writings were subjected to minute scrutiny. Cetshwayo turned out to be nothing like the ferocious monster depicted in Frere's despatches. When Natal lay at his mercy he did not counter-attack but instead sent repeated messages urging peace. A careful reading of Bulwer's despatches showed that a different view of Cetshwayo and the Zulu people was possible, and led to the conclusion that had things been left to Bulwer there would have been no war.

A further misfortune for Frere was that the Zulu had in Bishop Colenso an advocate and polemicist of genius – a polemicist, moreover, who owned a printing press. Colenso analysed the Blue Books, collated their contents with information from other sources, and relentlessly exposed the equivocations, misrepresentations and untruths with which Frere attempted to conceal the injustice of his attack upon the Zulu. These printed 'digests' he sent to the Aborigines Protection Society, to members of Parliament and to other interested parties, with the result that Frere was subjected to a well-informed onslaught such as few public men have had to endure. These attacks had a desolating effect on one grown used to unalloyed eulogy;[24] at one time he seriously feared that he would be put on trial.[25] Colenso's work continues to exert its influence, and helps to explain why in South African historiography Frere is represented so starkly as a villain. Reading Colenso's commentary on Frere's policy one experiences a growing sense of revulsion towards Frere, and it becomes all but impossible to avoid seeing him as nothing but a sanctimonious humbug and, in Colenso's words, 'rotten to the core'.[26]

A satisfactory comparison of Frere in India with Frere in South Africa would require an expert knowledge of both countries' histories and a serious biography (as opposed to hagiography) of Frere. But as far as I can tell, there was little in his relations with Asian rulers which would have enabled one to predict that he would act as he did towards the Zulu kingdom. There seems to have been a real inconsistency between the two. It is true that Frere was an advocate of what was known as a 'forward policy' in relation to Afghanistan. A memorandum he wrote on the subject in 1874 was published in *The Times* in October 1878, and this resulted in his being blamed for the disasters that ensued in both Afghanistan and Zululand.[27] But the policy he advocated in India was not one of conquest and annexation. He had opposed the policy of wholesale annexation pursued by Lord Dalhousie.[28] He wished to treat the Amir of Afghanistan as an independent ruler, to support his authority, to cultivate friendly relations with him, and thus to extend informal British influence over his country so that it would serve as a buffer against Russian expansion.[29] He wished in fact to see established with the Amir of Afghanistan the same kind of relations he had established as Commissioner of Sind with the Khan of Khelat. The Khan was the nominal overlord of many frontier tribes. It had been Frere's policy to recognize and strengthen this overlordship and to maintain peace on the frontier by co-operating with the Khan as an ally.[30] Not as an equal ally to be sure – Frere did not doubt the superiority of European to Asian civilization, and in the relations between the British and Indian rulers, the British, in Frere's view, had always to be the senior partner.[31] What he advocated in fact was the sort of relationship which had long existed between the government of Natal and the Zulu King, a relationship which he himself was to bring to a summary and violent end.

In view of the prominent part apparently played by missionaries in the formulation of Frere's policy toward the Zulu, and the demands he made concerning Christian missions in the ultimatum he sent to Cetshwayo, it is interesting and relevant to note that he strongly opposed the attempts made by some of the more zealous and militant Christians among the soldiers and civil servants in India to 'rely on the temporal power of Government to influence the natives in matters of belief'. He even opposed voluntary Bible classes in government schoolrooms for fear that this might constitute, in practice, an indirect form of pressure. 'With regard to missions,' he wrote, 'I hold that all that is required from Government is to leave them alone, and I look on any Government enterprise or support as in the last degree mischievous.'[32]

An element of continuity between Frere in India and Frere in South Africa was the strong conviction of his own rightness and the impatience of control which he always showed. This is of relevance to the way he responded to the situation in which he found himself in South Africa. It was his firm belief that the man on the spot should be free to act at his own discretion without the necessity for first referring back for instructions. The responsibility of officers to their superiors, he said, 'should always be retrospective in the shape of praise or blame for what is done, and should never involve the necessity for previous sanction'.[33] And he assumed the reaction would be praise rather than blame: 'I maintain that there is always in India some need for public servants acting without orders, on the assurance that, when their superiors hear their reasons, their acts will be approved and confirmed.' He would have reduced the Secretary of State for India to little more than a public relations officer for the Indian government.[34] When he put these principles into practice as Governor of Bombay he sometimes came into conflict with the Viceroy and the home government.[35] But his methods usually succeeded. When the Sultan of Zanzibar at first refused to end the slave trade, Frere had no authority to tell him that, in future, British ships would stop the transport of slaves to and from Zanzibar and that his customs service would be supervised by the British Consul; but the Sultan submitted and the Cabinet acquiesced.[36] Frere's conviction of his own rectitude and his readiness to assume responsibility were for most of his career justified and encouraged by success. Nemesis finally overtook him in South Africa. It was his overweening self-confidence that encouraged him to believe that the intractable difficulties of the task he had undertaken in South Africa could be overcome by a powerful exertion of will and that whatever he needed to do to achieve his great task must be right.

Carnarvon encouraged these tendencies. In offering him the Cape, he told him that 'a strong hand is required' and said: 'I propose to press, by all means in my power, my confederation policy in South Africa.' The post of Governor of the Cape was inferior in importance and status to that of Governor of Bombay to which Frere had been appointed 14 years earlier, but Carnarvon asked him to go to the Cape only 'nominally as Governor, but really as the statesman who seems to me most capable of carrying my scheme of confederation into effect, and whose long administrative experience and personal character give me the best chances of success'.[37] Frere replied:

> I should not have cared for the ordinary current duties of Governor of the Cape of Good Hope, but a special duty I should look upon in a different light, and there are few things which I should personally like better than to be associated in any way with such a great policy as yours in South Africa, entering as I do into the imperial importance of your masterly scheme, and being deeply interested personally from old Indian and African associations in such work.[38]

This interchange explains much about Frere's actions in South Africa. He could not just jog along, performing the ordinary current duties of Governor, dealing with troubles as they arose, and merely doing what he could to promote confederation as opportunities occurred. Having accepted the special duty entrusted to him by Carnarvon, he had to create the opportunities, force the pace and attempt to forge a confederation out of what proved to be most unyielding materials.[39]

He was all the more determined to succeed because of the strong personal interest in the success of the scheme given him, as he told Carnarvon, by his 'old Indian and African associations'. Much of the trade of East Africa was in the hands of Indian merchants, and so the Governor of Bombay necessarily had much to do with Africa. Following his visit to Zanzibar in 1873 Frere noted that Britain had 'succeeded without seeking it and almost without knowing it, to a dominant position and immense commercial interests in East Africa'. There was, he said, a 'tempting opening for an Empire in East Africa at the disposal of any great naval power'.[40] In a speech given in January 1874, Frere commented on the discrepancy between the vast resources of Africa and its relatively insignificant trade. It was the temperate belt extending from east Africa to the Cape Colony that he believed held the greatest potential for development by virtue of its climate, fertility, mineral riches and accessibility to the world's markets. He also referred to the labour of the African population as 'a mine of wealth to the employer', and to the desirability of 'welding together the loose elements of a great South African Empire'.[41] Thus Frere shared Carnarvon's views on the potential commercial importance of Africa, and long before his appointment as High Commissioner – before even Carnarvon's appointment as Secretary of State for the Colonies – he explicitly favoured the confederation or 'welding together' of the South African territories. He returned to this theme in 1875, again long before there was any question of his being appointed to carry out the task, expressing the hope that eastern and southern Africa might cease to be 'almost a blank in the commercial map of the world':

> It is clear that any Government which could ensure protection of life and property in such a position, and allow capitalists to attract the abundant labour of the continent by freedom and fair wages, might aspire to a great position among nations. Our South African colonies possess some of the elements of such a dominion.[42]

Like Carnarvon, Frere was concerned about foreign interference in Africa. 'Heretofore,' he said in 1874, 'we have had things pretty much our own way, and we have succeeded in keeping other powers at arm's length. But it is different now.'[43] As High Commissioner in 1878 he argued that the coastlines of southern Africa should be under British control:

> Supposing the whole coast east and west from the Cape of Good Hope to the Portuguese frontiers to be under the sovereignty of the British Crown, the chief step necessary to excluding all hostile European influence in South Africa is undoubtedly a Confederation of South African Colonies and States under the British Crown.[44]

This expansionism did not, as de Kiewiet implied that it did,[45] represent an original policy. Before Frere's appointment the Colonial Office had attempted to persuade a resistant Foreign Office of the desirability of such a step.[46] It was to Frere that Carnarvon wrote of colonising to the Zambezi and of a Monroe doctrine over much of Africa.[47] But it is true that Frere was not just expressing as a matter of duty the policy of his superiors: it was something in which he himself strongly believed.

The same was true of 'native policy'. The extension of British sovereignty to the Portuguese lines necessarily implied the subjection to British rule of the Zulu, as well as the still independent peoples beyond the Cape eastern frontier. But this was not simply an incidental by-product of a policy designed to exclude foreign powers. Bringing the indigenous population of South Africa under white control was an end in itself, for both Frere and the Colonial Office.[48] Despite the evidence of his opposition to expansion in India, Frere seems to have had no doubts about the desirability of extending British rule in South Africa. He seems to have drawn a fairly sharp distinction in this respect between Africans and Asians, regarding the latter as distinctly higher in the scale of civilization. 'The difference will be appreciated,' he wrote in 1875, 'if we contrast the worst of Arab *walis*, or local governors, with the best of such pure negro sovereigns as the rulers of Ashantee and Dahomey.'[49] Frere believed that Arab rulers had on the whole a civilizing influence in Africa, and that the Sultan of Zanzibar in particular (once the slave trade was abolished) deserved support.[50] There is no sign that Frere regarded the dominion of any indigenous African ruler as worthy of preservation. Indeed, he argued that the 'reign of barbarism' was doomed to disintegration as soon as it came into contact with civilization. For as soon as missionaries had demonstrated a higher life and traders had created new wants and shown how they could be gratified, the reign of barbarism, which rested only on force, 'must crumble away' of its own accord.[51] Most of the subjects of African rulers he seemed to regard simply as a potential labour supply for the colonizers of Africa, 'abundant labour' that would be a 'mine of wealth to the employer'.[52] His views on 'native policy' were thus entirely consonant with those of the Colonial Office. As High Commissioner he envisaged the African 'lower classes' becoming

> the free labouring population of states which protect them. They are in this respect a great benefit, and a very decided advantage to European Colonies, which do not seem likely to prosper on this continent if restricted to exclusively white labour.[53]

The Zulu, he said, were not irreclaimable savages:

> They belong to the same race which furnishes the good humoured volatile labourers and servants who abound in Natal, men capable of being moulded in the ways of civilisation, and when not actually trained to manslaughter not naturally blood-thirsty nor incurably barbarous.[54]

It seems clear that it was not simply opposition to manslaughter, or a political need to do away with the Zulu kingdom, that motivated such statements, but a positive desire for economic development and civilization. But there was no chance of the Zulu becoming good-humoured labourers as long as they had a King whose 'military system kept in compulsory idleness all the thews and sinews of industrial life', and as long as Zululand's 'utter insecurity of life and property, which strangles industry and commerce' was allowed to continue.[55]

There is no doubt that Frere was determined to get rid of the Zulu monarchy. What did he intend to put in its place? It has been argued that he did not intend the annexation of Zululand:

> Zululand would not be annexed, but would be subjected on the Indian model to a system of indirect rule by compliant chiefs under a British agent. Taught who was master, the demilitarised Zulu would be easy to manage and civilise. Thus Zululand would be slotted into its assigned place in the confederation rather like an Indian 'subject ally'.[56]

The evidence for this comes from statements Frere made in December 1878. He wrote privately to Hicks Beach, the Colonial Secretary:

> I do not think you need be the least anxious for the future government of the country. Once taught who is master, the Zulus will, I expect, not be difficult to manage under their own petty chiefs ... An English gentleman as Resident and supreme chief in place of Cetywayo will, I expect, make all the difference between war and peace as the *summum bonum* of Zulu aspirations.[57]

Similarly, in an official despatch of December 1878, he referred to the view 'that it is impossible to improve our relations with neighbours like the Zulus by any process short of ... annexing their territory to ours' and 'governing them as a subject race by our own officers, enforcing our own laws', and commented:

> This view seems to me a very seriously erroneous one. Experience in every part of the world, but especially in India, proves that it is quite possible for a native and comparatively uncivilised power to co-exist alongside a European power, and to be gradually raised by it to a higher stage of civilisation, without losing either its individual existence, or such natural customs as are not inconsistent with civilisation.

These statements, however, are somewhat misleading. They were made on the eve of the war, at a time when he was particularly concerned to reassure the Colonial Secretary, whose instructions he had exceeded, that his actions were not as drastic as they might seem and that all would be well. Having made the last-quoted statement, he immediately went on to qualify it. 'But,' he wrote,

> it is absolutely necessary that the Government which is civilised on European principles should have the upper hand. I know of no instance in history when a native Government, ruling on native and uncivilised, as opposed to European and civilised principles, has succeeded either in ruling European subjects or in preserving its own independence in the neighbourhood of a European power.

The reign of barbarism could not survive contact with civilization. Attempts had been made in the past, he said, to leave native territories as 'a sort of Black Alsatia', but the 'result has always been exactly the same. The natives do not become less barbarous, but they become much more dangerous', losing their respect and fear of the white man and acquiring evil habits and modern weapons.

Black Alsatias were not only 'dangerous to the peace and inimical to the civilisa- tion of the country', but 'a serious impediment to industrial progress', producing the 'evils inseparable from scarcity of native labour'. By the time Frere had warmed to his theme and concluded his despatch he had qualified his initial statement to the point of almost complete extinction.[58]

The impossiblity of uncivilized neighbours retaining their independence was a common theme of Frere's writings. His biographer quotes a letter to Hicks Beach which he states 'is only one amongst many others to the same effect'.

> You must be master, as representative of the sole sovereign power, up to the Portuguese frontier, on both the East and West Coasts. There is no escaping from the responsibility which has been already incurred, ever since the English flag was planted on the Castle here. All our real difficulties have arisen, and still arise, from attempting to evade or shift this responsibility. The attempt always ends in and can have no other result than that of substituting the gun-runner and the canteen-keeper for the English magistrate. There is often an interregnum of missionary influences, but guns and brandy carry the day, ultimately, unless there is a civilized magistrate of a settled Government to keep peace and enforce order. I have heard of no difficulty in managing and civilizing native tribes in South Africa which I cannot trace to some neglect or attempt to evade the clear responsibilities of sovereignty.[59]

This was written in August 1878, well before there was any need to defend himself against possible charges of exceeding orders and war-mongering.[60] Similarly, a minute of June 1878 on the government of the territories between the Cape and Natal may give a better clue to what Frere intended for Zululand than his explicit writings on the subject at a time when his chief concern was to defend himself. Among the existing territories he distinguished six 'different degrees of assimilation to the position of integral parts of the Cape Colony . . . every stage . . . a decided improvement on its predecessor and all on the normal condition of uncivilised Kafirdom'. He wanted to bring them all under the British flag, either as part of the Cape Colony, or as a province of the South African confederation, for which he proposed a system of government in which African chiefs and landholders would have some representation. But, he con- tinued:

> The principles of the administration and of the law administered must be everywhere those of modern civilisation, not of Kaffirdom, embodying the ruling ideas of the English, Dutch, and Roman law-givers, not of the Kafir Chief and his councillors.

These principles Frere held should apply to property as well as to persons. He was confident that a people with the capacity for improvement that the Mfengu had already shown would readily adopt these principles.[61]

In January 1879 Frere wrote to Chelmsford, from whom he had no need to disguise or extenuate his intentions, and made his plans for Zululand quite explicit. It is clear that the annexation of Zululand was exactly what he intended:

Acting as Glyn's & Wood's columns are now doing, you will virtually annex & settle the country as you proceed, & greatly simplify proceedings when Cetywayo is disposed of. I have no idea of recommending any revival of a paramount chief or King or of any separate Zulu nationality. An active & absolute Military Administrator, with a firm grasp of the country, by means of the pick of your native Regts. as Sepoys & Police, & supported by a backbone of H.M. Troops, will keep order among the chiefs who submit & obey, & will after putting down opposition govern directly, through Headmen, the subjects of those who resist – all as subjects of Queen Victoria. Whether any slice shall be annexed to Natal or Transvaal, will be a subject for after consideration . . .'[62]

Despite later reservations and equivocations, it had been common cause in the Colonial Office that Zululand should sooner or later come under British rule.[63] The authorities in Britain had always shrunk in practice from taking any decisive step, but Frere was not the sort of man to shrink from anything; and he came to believe the Zulu kingdom to be the grand obstacle to the achievement of that special duty entrusted to him by Carnarvon, a duty in which he believed wholeheartedly and which he was determined to carry out. The overthrow of the Zulu kingdom became an obsession with him, and his determination and self-righteousness enabled him to sweep all obstacles, moral as well as material, from his path.

The Zulu Kingdom an Obstacle to Confederation

With the benefit of hindsight we can see that Carnarvon's confederation scheme was doomed to failure. Indeed, many contemporaries could see this. But for Frere such a conclusion would have relegated him to the position of a mere Governor of the Cape and constituted a confession of personal failure; so this was a conclusion he could not accept.

The reason why confederation was doomed was the lack of support for it in South Africa. The republics had no wish to lose their independence, and the annexation of the Transvaal, which was intended to facilitate confederation, instead produced growing opposition to it. This opposition grew, moreover, not only among the Boers of the Transvaal but among their sympathisers throughout South Africa. The Cape, as the biggest, richest and most powerful state in South Africa, containing a white population five or six times that of all other states combined, would have constituted the major component of a confederated South Africa. But the Molteno administration had no desire to assume responsibility for the disaffected Boers and unsubdued Africans of the interior. Frere came to believe that the essential cause of both Boer and African disaffection was the Zulu kingdom, and that its overthrow would reconcile the Boers and dishearten the Africans. The need to reconcile the Boers became the most urgent pressure upon Frere at a later stage, and will be dealt with in its chronological place.[64] First we must deal with his belief in the existence of a black conspiracy to overthrow white domination.

Such a belief became current from the time of the Pedi repulse of the ZAR army,[65] which, according to Shepstone, had 'sent the thrilling intelligence through all the immense masses of natives between the Zambesi and the Cape Colony' that such an enterprise was practicable.[66] When war broke out on the Cape eastern frontier, Shepstone told Frere and Carnarvon that it was partly the result of messages from Cetshwayo. He assured them in fact that the Zulu power was the root of all the native trouble in South Africa and that no peace could be expected until it was extirpated.[67]

Frere's experiences in India during the Mutiny perhaps made him susceptible to conspiracy theories.[68] His susceptibility is shown by the seriousness with which he took a bizarre letter he received concerning a Dutch secret society allegedly founded in South Africa in 1815 or earlier and still going strong, making use of Masonic organization, and so forth.[69] He was very susceptible to Shepstone, the great authority on Africans. Less than four months after his arrival in South Africa he told Carnarvon that he had 'seen enough to feel sure that Shepstone is quite right as to the widespread influence of any Kaffir disturbance, & still more of any Kaffir success, on the Kaffir population everywhere', and that such causes would sooner or later produce 'a "scare" at least, on our Kaffir Frontier'. Such a 'scare', which developed into a war, duly occurred on the Cape eastern frontier in the very next month, and Frere's belief that one 'Kaffir disturbance' was likely to lead to another hardened into the conviction that a deliberate attempt at a concerted movement was afoot. In March 1878, while the ninth frontier war was still being fought, he expressed to Herbert his conviction 'that Shepstone and others of experience in the country were right as to the existence of a wish among the great chiefs to make this war a general and simultaneous rising of Kaffirdom against white civilization', and that although they were incapable of formal combination 'there was a widespread feeling among them, from Secocoeni to Sandilli', that the time had come to resist the changes threatening 'the idle, sensuous elysium of Kaffirdom'. By June 1878 he appears to have reached the conclusion that the seemingly unconnected outbreaks then occurring were in reality the products of a single cause. He wrote to the Secretary of State:

> as you will see from the accounts we send you from the Pondo & Zulu Borders, from the Transvaal Goldfields & from the Diamond Fields, it is quite clear that the war spirit is abroad, as Shepstone & most frontier men told us it was, a year ago; - the joint result of a long peace, the growth of a generation of Kaffirs who know not the power of the White races in war, the unrestrained possession of firearms, & the breakdown of the Transvaal Boers in their last Kaffir War . . . The letters I send you officially will show you how little the best informed men on the spot could foresee or account for these disjointed outbursts of rebellion. It was just the same after the Indian Mutiny.[70]

As he became more convinced that there was a deliberate conspiracy, so he became more convinced that it was led by Cetshwayo. During the war on the Cape eastern frontier he made a number of references to the presence of emissaries from Cetshwayo among the disaffected chiefs.[71] By September 1878 he reported that, while all was now peaceful on the Cape eastern frontier, it was clear that

> along the whole border of Natal, the Transvaal, and the Orange River border, wherever the Zulu influence is felt, the 'war fever', as it has been appropriately termed, has not been allayed, and that it must be mitigated and subdued before we can hope for a condition of permanent peace.

By November he had reached the conclusion, to which he adhered for the rest of his life, that the outbreaks on the Cape eastern frontier had been 'simply premature explosions of a combination in which Cetywayo was the moving spirit', and that 'in dealing with Kreli and Sandilli, we were trying to cure the symptoms, and that the real seat of the disease is here, in Zululand'.[72]

The overthrow of the Zulu kingdom would end Cetshwayo's intrigues and be a salutary lesson to Africans everywhere. The Cape would be reconciled to entering a confederation responsible for the administration and defence of a pacified country. The British would have fulfilled their promise to protect the Transvaal from the Zulu and other Africans, and the Boers would settle down to a restoration of self-government within a confederation under the British flag. After a few years as Governor-General of this splendid new dominion, a peerage and the applause of a grateful nation might bring an illustrious career to a fitting climax.

Obstacles to Overthrowing the Zulu Kingdom

There were many obstacles to the overthrow of the Zulu kingdom – not only the power and organization of the kingdom itself, but the timidity and lack of vision of Frere's superiors, colleagues and subordinates. He lacked the support he needed from the Colonial Office and from the governments of the Cape and Natal.

Carnarvon was committed in principle to the absorption of Zululand, but in practice always urged delay, for which he always had some good reason. In the aftermath of the annexation of the Transvaal in April 1877, it was the fear of parliamentary and public opposition to further annexations.[73] At the end of 1877 the crisis produced by the failure of Shepstone's negotiations with the Zulu coincided with the much greater crisis produced by the fall of Plevna and the advance of the Russians towards Constantinople. Britain could not have a war with Zululand as long as there was a danger of war with Russia. Carnarvon told Frere that he had written to Shepstone

> that however aggressive and ill-conditioned Cetywayo may be, he must not under present circumstances allow a collision. We cannot now have a South African war on our hands and if the worst comes to the worst you must all temporise and wait for a better opportunity of settling these controversies.[74]

The crisis in eastern Europe did not lead to war with Russia; but what it did lead to was equally disheartening to Frere: it led to the resignation of Lord Carnarvon. This was a 'great blow' to Frere: his private secretary half expected him to resign. Frere told Carnarvon that the news had 'utterly taken the heart out of me . . . it is peculiarly trying to us just now, when there seems at last a prospect of a break in the clouds'.[75]

This break in the clouds was his success in getting rid of the obstructive Molteno ministry and replacing it with a ministry under J.C. Sprigg composed entirely of eastern Cape men who were favourably disposed to confederation.[76] The immediate cause of Frere's conflict with Molteno had been the latter's refusal to agree that reinforcements from Britain were necessary for the war on the Cape eastern frontier. The real purpose for which Frere wanted additional troops, it seems almost certain, was the prospective war with the Zulu; but immediate and manifest necessity was more likely to secure them than references to possible future contingencies, which might be met by instructions to 'temporise'.[77]

Carnarvon had urged Frere to 'temporise', but he had also held out the prospect of a 'better opportunity' in the future. As the annexation of the Transvaal showed, Carnarvon could act boldly when necessary. Frere had reason to believe that Carnarvon would eventually support him in taking the decisive action his personally chosen agent deemed necessary to carry out a policy in which he took such a close and, indeed, proprietorial interest. But his successor, Sir Michael Hicks Beach, had no such personal interest, and the Colonial Office was growing weary of the mounting problems in South Africa and becoming increasingly inclined to avoid trouble rather than strive for confederation. Fairfield began to look back on the Sand River and Bloemfontein Conventions with nostalgic and disillusioned regret. Hicks Beach did not conceal from Frere his doubts as to the prospects for confederation, and in his first private letter to him he made it clear that he wanted a peaceful settlement with the Zulu.[78]

The disinclination of the Colonial Office for war, both before and after Carnarvon's resignation, created a great difficulty for Frere. He could not openly state that the destruction of the Zulu kingdom was necessary for the achievement of confederation and that he was therefore going to send an ultimatum which would inevitably lead to war, and that he needed further reinforcements for this purpose. Such candour was more than likely to produce in response a direct prohibition of the step which he saw as essential. He had therefore to represent his intended measures as essentially defensive, and portray the Zulu as the aggressors. A letter to Carnarvon written in December 1877, during the Transvaal-Zulu border crisis, illustrates the ambivalence that characterized his communications, official and private, with the home government. He stated that collision with the Zulu was inevitable, and that they would have to be made to realize they had met their match. This statement might seem to indicate aggressive intent, so he added that 'they will probably provoke a contest'. He said that reinforcements were needed, and continued:

Your object is not conquest, but simply supremacy up to Delagoa Bay. This will have to be asserted some day & the operation will not become easier by delay. The trial of strength will be forced on you; & neither justice nor humanity will be served by postponing the trial if we start with a good cause.[79]

This passage bristles with anomalies and contradictions. Why does he draw a distinction between 'supremacy' and 'conquest'? How was the one to be achieved except by means of the other? If supremacy was to be achieved by some means other than military conquest, why the reference to a trial of strength and the call for additional troops? Why was it necessary to argue against postponing the trial of strength if the trial was going to be forced upon the British anyhow?

The confusion in this letter reflects the confusion in Frere's mind. Had he made a conscious and deliberate decision to wage a war of aggression and to deceive the Secretary of State about his intention, he could have written more clearly. Straightforward lies need contain no ambiguities. But Frere was an English Christian gentleman absolutely convinced of his own rectitude and of the loftiness of his aims. Deliberate deception was an impossibility for such a man. He had to deceive himself before he could deceive others. He was convinced that the overthrow of Cetshwayo was necessary for the achievement of the policy entrusted to him. He therefore had to convince first himself and then his superiors that Cetshwayo's overthrow would come about through his own aggression. Since Cetshwayo resolutely refused to play the part allotted to him – a war with the British was the last thing he wanted – Frere became in consequence increasingly entangled in a web of ambiguity, self-deceit and misrepresentation.

There was an abundance of material available to construct an aggressive and dangerous image of the Zulu.[80] The cruelties and conquests of Shaka and the treachery of Dingane were legendary. Zululand was a military kingdom: as in Prussia, the army was the state. Frere believed the army to be a 'standing army' and that its maintenance required a succession of wars.[81] It was true that the British colony of Natal, with its small and vulnerable white population, had co-existed peacefully with its Zulu neighbours for nearly 40 years, ever since its foundation. But there were special reasons for this, reasons that no longer obtained. The Zulu had suffered a signal defeat at the hands of armed white men at the battle of Blood river in 1838. The reign of Mpande had been a period of internal conflict, but Cetshwayo had striven to restore the vigour and unity of the kingdom, had armed his warriors with guns, and made no secret of his wish to 'wash his spears'. The need to retain the support of Natal against the Transvaal Boers had acted for a time as a restraint, but this disappeared when the Boers revealed their weakness against Sekhukhune. Cetshwayo threw off the mask, defied Bulwer and announced his intention of shedding blood without restraint. The Transvaal was annexed to save it from the Zulu but even then Cetshwayo asked Shepstone (who of course refused) to be allowed to make 'one small swoop'. The subsequent Zulu defiance of Shepstone and the disturbances on the

frontier from October 1877 seemed designed to provoke war. Shepstone himself, the great authority on the subject, was convinced that this was so. But if
Cetshwayo was bent on war with the British, Natal was a much more tempting
target than the more distant and sparsely inhabited Transvaal frontier lands.[82]

In this way Frere convinced himself that Natal was in imminent danger of a
Zulu onslaught. The same facts could be interpreted very differently, as I have
tried to show in earlier chapters, but this was the interpretation Frere needed to
believe. It was also necessary and easy for him to believe that the missionaries
were right, that British action against Cetshwayo would be a blessing to the Zulu
people, and that it would therefore encounter little resistance, provided the
British were able to field a credible force and gain initial success.

The immediate occasion for war seemed likely to stem from the border
dispute with the Transvaal. Frere approved of the inquiry, not because he
thought it would bring permanent peace, but because the delay would enable the
British forces to be strengthened. Frere did not expect the inquiry to bring peace
because he did not believe Cetshwayo would accept an adverse decision or even
remain content for long with a favourable one.[83] He recognized that a decision
favourable to the Zulu would be politically disastrous. He wrote to Bulwer:

> As at present advised, I do not see how these Zulu claims can be admitted without the
> Transvaal giving up portions of territory which have for years been unquestioned as
> belonging to the Transvaal Republic. Apart from all other objections to such a course,
> any such surrender would be inconsistent with the pledges given by Sir T. Shepstone to
> the inhabitants of the Transvaal, that, in taking them over, the British Government
> would maintain the integrity of their State, and repel the unjust encroachments of native
> tribes.

But to conciliate the Boers at the expense of justice to the Zulu was not
something that Frere could ever admit to doing, so he had to deny that 'any
possible concessions to the Zulu demands will render our Frontier more secure
against further unjust aggression by the Zulu Chief and his allies'.[84]

Bulwer's reply to this despatch showed that he was inclined to take a very
different view of matters, and that he was likely to prove an obstacle to the policy
Frere considered it necessary to pursue. He denied that Shepstone's pledges to
the Boers to maintain the integrity of the Transvaal could be held applicable to
the disputed territory since this had never been an unquestioned part of the
Transvaal. He seemed to imply that the Zulu claim might well turn out to be
valid, and he stated that since the British had restrained the Zulu from asserting
their claim by force, and since they were now parties to the dispute, the Transvaal
having become British, no other course could be followed than to ascertain the
merits of the dispute and act upon them.

Bulwer cast considerable doubt on Frere's belief that there was a danger of
unprovoked Zulu aggression. Their actions were intelligible without resorting to
such an explanation. Far from being reassured by the British annexation of the

Transvaal, as Frere suggested they should have been, it seemed to them that the British had taken the side of their enemies; it was their determination to defend what they held to be their just rights that led them to behave in so assertive a manner. Bulwer had no high opinion of Cetshwayo himself, but he believed that he would be restrained by the more prudent part of the nation who were opposed to any action disapproved of by the British.

Bulwer also threw liberal quantities of cold water over Frere's belief in an inter-tribal conspiracy against whites. He conceded that the acquisition of fire-arms had given Africans a feeling of greater confidence in their ability to contend with the white man, and that exaggerated accounts of the Boers' failure against the Pedi had strengthened this feeling of confidence. He accepted, too, that chiefs were in communication with each other, and that the news of what was happening in one part of the country might have an unsettling effect on another. But, he said, 'there has been nothing to show that what has taken place in different parts of the country are portions of any general combination, move-ment, or understanding among the natives'. Supporting his argument in some detail, he stated that 'what has taken place – whether it has been actual distur-bance, or an indication of disturbing elements at work – can all, I believe, be traced to local causes and influences, independent of one another'. The possibil-ity existed that the various elements of disturbance might be brought together in one general movement, but this should be avoided by localising every trouble, 'dealing with it separately and distinctly as a separate and distinct matter – and by treating in the usual manner and with the usual confidence all those which are not concerned in it'.[85]

Bulwer had earlier been inclined to give some credence to the inter-tribal conspiracy thesis,[86] but there can be little doubt that his considered opinion against it was correct. The most plausible part of the thesis was that Cetshwayo and Sekhukhune were acting in concert, but it has been shown elsewhere[87] that when the evidence for this is clearly examined the impression that there was such an alliance melts away. Frere made frequent references to the 'evidence', 'much evidence', 'hundred little bits of evidence', 'unmistakable evidence', 'irresistible body of evidence', 'vast number of concurrent items of evidence',[88] for this conspiracy, but he never actually produced any. There was certainly evidence of communication between chiefs in different parts of the country, and distur-bances certainly occurred in different parts of the country. Frere seems simply to have assumed that the one was the cause of the other. He wrote on one occasion:

> What may have been the nature of the communications on this subject between the various native tribes it is impossible to say, for no written word ever passes between two chiefs unless they have been educated in the schools of Europeans, and it is only by results that the nature of such communications can in general be known.[89]

Magistrates and other officials had no difficulty in accounting for disturbances in their areas in terms of Bulwer's 'local causes'.[90] Frere wrote shortly before the beginning of the 1879 war with the Zulu that Cetshwayo's allies were waiting to see what would happen. 'If he gives in, or is beaten, they will declare against him. If he resists and gains any initial advantage, they will join the swarm against us.' Had such an alliance really existed, Isandlwana would surely have been the signal for the concerted uprising. 'It means the probable rising of tribes all round,' wrote Frere's private secretary shortly after the battle.[91] But nothing of the kind occurred, and this must count heavily against the conspiracy thesis.

The Boundary Commission's Report and Frere's Response, July 1878 to January 1879

In mid-July 1878 Frere received the report of the Rorke's Drift Boundary Commission. It confirmed his worst fears. It reported in favour of the Zulu.

The Commission took it as common cause that the territory between the Mzinyathi (Buffalo) and the Phongolo (which is all they were concerned with) had belonged to the Zulu before 1854. The Boers, by basing their claim on alleged cessions by the Zulu in 1854 and 1861 accepted the prior claim of the Zulu. The question therefore was whether these cessions were valid. The Commission concluded that the very defective evidence produced by the Transvaal did not prove their case, and that their claims were inherently improbable. Nevertheless, they awarded the area to the west of the Ncome (Blood) river to the Transvaal on the grounds of long occupation by Boers, and on the grounds that the Transvaal had exercised sovereignty over it for many years with the recognition and thus tacit sanction of the Zulu. The most striking instance of this had been in 1861, when Mthonga fled across the Ncome river: Cetshwayo had respected the sovereignty of the Boers over this territory by treating with them for the surrender of his brother. He had also in 1877 restricted his claim to the land east of the Ncome river.[92]

The Zulu had always protested against the Boer claim to the territory east of the Ncome river. The Commission went further than this, however, and stated that officers of the Transvaal government had never exercised jurisdiction in this area, and that the Boers had never occupied the territory in the sense of erecting homesteads there, but had only used the land for grazing. This, as Bulwer pointed out, was incorrect.[93] The Landdrost of Utrecht had exercised jurisdiction and homesteads had been erected down to the line of the Old Hunting Road. There were, however, Zulu living between the Ncome river and the Old Hunting Road over whom the Transvaal government had exercised no jurisdiction. Its attempt to tax them in 1876 had been successfully resisted,[94] and the experiment had not been repeated. What the Commissioners said of the territory between the Ncome river and the line allegedly ceded in 1861 was true only of the territory between the Old Hunting Road and the 1861 line. The Commissioners' error probably arose from the attempt of the Transvaal delegates at Rorke's Drift, following Shepstone's lead in his negotiations with the Zulu,[95] to represent the line ceded in 1854 as being the Old Hunting Road. Statements by Gert

Rudolph, the Landdrost of Utrecht, and one of the Transvaal delegates, regarding the land on the Zulu side of the '1854 line', meaning the Old Hunting Road, were probably interpreted by the Commissioners as referring to the land on the Zulu side of the 1854 line as they understood it, namely the Ncome river. As I have suggested above, Shepstone probably had doubts as to the Transvaal government's ability to prove the 1861 cession and feared it might have to fall back on the 1854 line and wanted as favourable an interpretation of it as possible. There was no justification for the interpretation he adopted. The Transvaal delegates at the Rorke's Drift inquiry had not expected to be called upon to prove the 1854 cession and, when they were, the only explanation they could offer for the Old Hunting Road not being mentioned in the 1854 document was that this must have arisen 'from some misconception on the part of the [1854] Commission'.[96]

The Commission accepted the Zulu argument that according to Zulu constitutional customs the land belonged to the nation, and that the Zulu King, as trustee for the nation, had no power to cede land without the clear assent and sanction of the Zulu people. Had there been any cession, the matter would have been submitted to the Council of Chiefs; but this was never done. The Commission therefore concluded

> that no cession of territory was ever made by the Zulu nation, and that even had such cession been made by either King Umpanda, or after him King Cetywayo, such would have been null and void unless confirmed by the voice of the Chiefs and people, according to the customs of the Zulus.[97]

Bulwer cleared up any possible ambiguity in this conclusion by asking

> whether he is to understand that in the opinion of the Commissioners there has been, or there may have been, a cession of land made by the Zulu King Panda, or the present King Cetywayo, but that there having been no confirmation of this by the nation at large, on that account the Commissioners have come to the conclusion that there has been no cession; or whether he is to understand that there has been no cession at all either by the kings past or present, or by the nation.

The Commissioners replied that they wished it to be understood 'that there has been no cession of land at all by the Zulu kings, past or present, or by the nation'.[98] The question of how land cessions should be ratified in Zulu custom was thus irrelevant, and it was unfortunate that the Commissioners raised it, as it gave Frere the opportunity to misrepresent them as having rejected an otherwise valid cession simply on the grounds that it had not been properly ratified.[99]

Frere immediately recognized the politically disastrous nature of the Commissioners' report. The Transvaal frontiersmen, he said, might well resist the arbitration.

> Even if they trek away they will carry discontent wherever they go, and furnish the Boer Agitators with a convincing proof of their charges of bad faith against our Govern-

ment. Security against Native aggression, and the integrity of the Transvaal boundary were among the prominent points guaranteed to the Inhabitants of the Transvaal when they were taken over, and it will be difficult to maintain that promises have been kept in the presence of Boers, Missionaries, and other settlers driven away with the loss of all their immovable property from lands which the late Transvaal Government maintained, and the present Transvaal Government believes they were justly entitled to occupy as on Transvaal territory.[100]

Despite this and other difficulties with the report which he pointed out (including the fact that the trans-Phongolan dispute had not been investigated), Frere initially assumed that Bulwer would communicate its contents to both parties.[101] Bulwer, however, urged that Frere, as High Commissioner, should arbitrate, without the report itself being communicated to either party.[102] Frere agreed to arbitrate, but told Bulwer to send Shepstone a copy of the report for his comments,[103] while Cetshwayo, the other party to the dispute, was given no such opportunity. Shepstone confirmed the disastrous political effects the report was likely to have.

I very much regret the tone in which the report is written and fear that, when it is published, it will produce a bad effect upon the minds of the Transvaal people; they will chafe terribly under both the scant courtesy with which they are spoken of, and the decision itself.[104]

Frere hoped that Shepstone would provide him with the ammunition he needed to overthrow the report, but Shepstone's official, detailed objections did not arrive until November, when they were too late to be of any use. In the meantime, Frere assailed the report in every way he could. He suggested that the Commission had rejected the documentary evidence in favour of the Transvaal claim simply because all the literate parties to the agreement were on one side, a procedure that would make any agreement between literate and illiterate parties impossible. But the Commission was able to show that the documents had many suspicious characteristics and included at least one outright fabrication.[105] Frere stated that although the documents had not been accepted by the Commission as evidence for the Transvaal claims, 'they appear to have been allowed considerable weight in various ways in evidence against them', stating this to be of 'doubtful equity'. The Commissioners stated that they had considered the documents 'as a written narrative on the part of the Dutch relative to these land transactions rather than as binding treaties'.[106] Considered thus as historical rather than as legal documents, they could be used much more safely as evidence against the Transvaal case than for it; so Frere's statement may have been true, but the Commission was not necessarily unjustified in using the documents in this way.

The Commission had taken as its starting point that before 1854 the disputed territory had belonged to the Zulu. It might seem that it would be impossible to question the original rights of the Zulu to the territory since the Transvaal claimed it by virtue of alleged Zulu cessions. Frere nevertheless did so. Both the

Boers and the Zulu, he said, were semi-migratory peoples without fixed and definite boundaries:

> I confess I fail to find in the recorded history of either people any better claim which either party could advance to the lands they stood on than that of possession, and power to hold and govern.

This seems to imply that since the Zulu claim to the territory rested only on conquest and occupation, the fact that the Boers had wrested the territory from them should be held to constitute a claim of equal or (because subsequent) greater validity. It might further be argued that since the Zulu had (in Frere's view at least) subsequently driven the Boers off most of the disputed territory it should be held to be rightfully theirs once again. But Frere would not concede that Zulu force conferred as much right as Boer force. In an astonishing passage, which evoked much comment when it was later published, and did much to damage his reputation, he wrote:

> Pure brutal force constituted the sole recognized local title to possession; the Boers had force of their own, and every right of conquest; but they had also what they seriously believed to be a higher title in the old commands they found in parts of their Bible to exterminate the Gentiles and take their land in possession. We may freely admit that they misinterpreted the text, and were utterly mistaken in its application, but they had at least a sincere belief in the divine authority for what they did, and therefore a far higher title than the Zulus could claim for all they acquired.[107]

Ultimately Frere recognized that he could not set aside the decision of the Commissioners. He was not convinced by their arguments, nor by their conclusion, which he later stated – in a public despatch – was the product of 'strong prejudice in favour of the Zulus and against the Transvaal claims', prejudice which 'would quite incapacitate the Commissioners from being impartial judges'.[108] But the British were now parties to the dispute, a British Governor had appointed British subjects to investigate its merits, and they had decided against the British claims. To set aside such a verdict would be impossible to reconcile with any reputation for honesty or justice. 'It seems to me,' Frere wrote to Shepstone, 'that however inconvenient the consequences may be we must abide by them, and make the best of it.'[109]

By making the best of it, it transpired, Frere meant misrepresenting the grounds of the Commissioners' verdict, and accepting it only in form while nullifying it in practice. Frere represented the Boers as having acted in good faith, the Zulu as having dishonestly evaded the necessary legal fulfilment of their promise, and the Commissioners as having decided against the Transvaal on these narrow technical grounds. In a memorandum which he forwarded to Bulwer for distribution and publicity he wrote:

> The Commission ultimately decided that Cetywayo's cession of a tract of land, relied on by the Transvaal claim, was promised when he was only Heir Apparent, and that the

cession had not been subsequently formally ratified by his father, Panda, nor by the Great Council of the Zulu nation.[110]

Since the Commission's report had not yet been published, there was no way the public could know that the Commission had decided that Cetshwayo had not made any cession.

Frere intended nullifying the award in practice by granting Cetshwayo only a nominal sovereignty over the disputed territory, while permitting the Boers to retain the 'individual rights of property which were obtained under the Transvaal Government', under a British guarantee, to be enforced by the British Resident he intended imposing on the Zulu. Fairfield compared this to 'giving the shells to the Zulus and the oyster to the Boers'. Frere justified it on the grounds that when a state ceded land to another it ceded only sovereignty, not rights of private property. The Transvaal, however, was not ceding land, but returning land it had wrongfully appropriated to its rightful owners; and as Colenso argued – a view confirmed on a 'strictly legal view of the matter' by the Chief Justice of the Cape – a state which had wrongfully appropriated land could convey no valid title to private property within it.[111] Frere feared that his substantial nullification of the award would not be enough to allay Boer discontent. All the Boers would see was that a portion of the Transvaal, the territorial integrity of which Britain had undertaken to protect, had been transferred to Zululand, and that a community of Boers had been placed under the rule of a heathen savage. The only satisfactory solution was to bring the disputed territory under British rule. Writing to Colenso after the start of the war he brought about to achieve this end, Frere stated that the question of private property in the disputed territory 'which would have been one of great practical importance had Cetywayo's conduct averted war, is now of little but quasi historical importance'. In a minute written three weeks after the start of the war, he stated:

> Whatever may be the future sovereignty of the disputed territory, whether it is to be governed separately or annexed to one of the neighbouring British Colonies, I cannot entertain a doubt that guarantees will be taken for its future management on a system which will make life and property fully as secure in the territory referred to as in any part of the Transvaal.[112]

With the territory annexed to the neighbouring British colony of the Transvaal, the nullification of the award would be complete.

Notes

1. Some information on the day-to-day proceedings of the Commission is to be found in Natal Archives, H.C. Shepstone Papers, Vol. 3, diary for 1878, and in GH 790, report made to Theophilus Shepstone by the Transvaal delegates, 20 April 1878, encl in no. 9, Shepstone to Bulwer, 18 May 1878.
2. TA, SN 6, minute by Shepstone for the guidance of the Transvaal delegates, 12 March 1878.
3. See ch. 3, p. 61.
4. See ch. 2, p. 21.
5. Natal Archives, H.C. Shepstone Papers, Vol. 3, diary for 1878, entry for 15 March; GH 1300, p. 118, Confid, Bulwer to Frere, 24 April 1878.
6. BPP, C2242, pp. 80–5, Bulwer to Frere, 24 April 1878, message from Bulwer to Cetshwayo, 29 March 1878, and report by Fynney, 22 April 1878.
7. GH 791, no. 34, Shepstone to Bulwer, 28 June 1878, and minute on this by Bulwer, n.d.; SP 69, p. 132, Shepstone to Frere, 12 October 1878; Durnford, *Soldier's Life and Work*, pp. 178–9.
8. SNA I/7/13, p. 114, message from Cetshwayo, 15 May 1878.
9. Natal Archives, H.C. Shepstone Papers, Vol. 3, diary for 1878, entries for 18 and 20 March and 1 April.
10. KC, Colenso Papers, File 29, KCM 50268, trans, 23 March 1878, encl in File 29, KCM 50269, Colenso to Chesson, 14 April 1878, in which the writer and recipient of KCM 50268 are identified. The translation from the Zulu is by Colenso.
11. *The Natal Witness*, 13 April 1878, 'Mail Summary'; ibid, 27 April 1878, letter from Biggarsberg correspondent, 22 April 1878; see also *The Natal Mercury*, 8 April 1878, 'The Week'.
12. SNA I/7/13, p. 114, message from Cetshwayo, 15 May 1878.
13. Colenso, *Commentary*, 1st section, p. 90. Information on the disturbances following the sitting of the Rorke's Drift Commission comes from a large number of sources: GH 790, no. 29, Shepstone to Bulwer, 18 May and enclosures; GH 791, nos 32 and 33, Shepstone to Bulwer, 3 and 8 June 1878, and enclosures; GH 1326, no. 93, Bulwer to Shepstone, 7 June 1878; SNA I/4/1, no. 606, H.C. Shepstone to J.W. Shepstone (ASNA), 16 May 1878, encl Rudolph to H.C. Shepstone, 10 May 1878, and Engelbrecht to Rudolph, 11 May 1878; SNA I/3/30, no. 90, R.M. Newcastle to J.W. Shepstone (ASNA), 18 May 1878, encl Rudolph to R.M. Newcastle, 16 May 1878; SS 283, R1761, Rudolph to GS, 25 May 1878; SS 284, R1877, Böhmer to Shepstone, Luneburg, 31 May 1878, encl in Rudolph to G., 3 June 1878; *The Natal Witness*, 21 May 1878, letter from Utrecht correspondent, 15 May 1878; ibid, 25 May 1878, letter from ibid, 16 May 1878.
14. EG, GH 353, Osborn (Transvaal GS) to Filter, 1 June 1878, encl in no. 32, Shepstone to Bulwer, 3 June 1878; GH 354, GS to Engelbrecht, 28 June 1878, encl in no. 34, Shepstone to Bulwer, 28 June 1878.
15. GH 791, minute by Bulwer, n.d., on no. 34, Shepstone to Bulwer, 28 June 1878.
16. SNA I/7/13, p. 116, message to Cetshwayo, 23 May 1878.
17. SNA I/4/1, no. 815, Dunn to Bulwer, 14 June 1878. He also sent a message to the same effect to Rudolph: SS 293, R2503, Rudolph to H.C. Shepstone, 12 July 1878, encl Dunn to Rudolph, 14 June 1878.
18. SS 282, R1674, Rudolph to GS, 19 May 1878.
19. *The Natal Witness*, 15 and 25 June, 2 and 20 July 1878, letters from Utrecht correspondent, 6, 9, 16, 25 and 30 June 1878; SS 291, R2365, Böhmer to Shepstone, 5 July 1878.
20. Goodfellow, *Great Britain and South African Confederation*, p. 124, quoting *The Times* of

24 January 1877; Currie, 'Thoughts', p. 405, lecture, 7 June 1877, comment by the Hon Evelyn Ashley; Carnarvon to Victoria, 23 November 1876, in Buckle, *Letters of Victoria*, Vol. II, p. 502n; Martineau, *Life of Frere*, Vol. II, p. 453; Woodruff (pseudonym of Mason), *Men Who Ruled India*, p. 42.

21. Etherington, 'Anglo-Zulu Relations', pp. 13–14.
22. Emery, 'South Africa's Best Friend', p. 30.
23. See Hicks Beach to Disraeli, 13 January 1879, in Monypenny and Buckle, *Life of Disraeli*, Vol. VI, p. 423.
24. Frere to Hicks Beach, 22 September 1879, in Martineau, *Life of Frere*, Vol. II, p. 327; see also ibid, pp. 448–9.
25. Frere to Clarke, 16 October 1880, in ibid., p. 434.
26. KC, Colenso Papers, File 29, KCM 50310, Colenso to Chesson, 12 July 1882. Collections of the 'digests' distributed by Colenso exist in the British Library, the Natal Archives and the Killie Campbell Africana Library. I have consulted the last-named, which has 'Bishop Colenso's Commentary on Frere's Policy' printed on the spine. Probably none of these collections is complete. See Jeff Guy's remarks in his *Destruction of the Zulu Kingdom*, pp. 253–4. Colenso published much 'commentary' in the introduction and notes to Vijn, *Cetshwayo's Dutchman*.
27. Martineau, *Life of Frere*, Vol. I, pp. 490–1.
28. Ibid, Vol. I, pp. 55–71 and 370–5.
29. Ibid, Vol. I, pp. 490–8, and Vol. II, pp. 140–9, 153–8.
30. Ibid, Vol. I, pp. 242–50; Woodruff, *Men who Ruled India*, pp. 34–5.
31. Martineau, *Life of Frere*, Vol. I, p. 70; Duthie, 'Further Insights', pp. 190–1.
32. Martineau, *Life of Frere*, Vol. I, pp. 255–65, quotations from pp. 260 and 262.
33. Ibid, Vol. I, p. 272.
34. Ibid, Vol. I, p. 347.
35. Ibid, Vol. I, ch. XI, *passim*.
36. Woodruff, *Men Who Ruled India*, pp. 41–2.
37. Carnarvon to Frere, 13 October 1876, in Martineau, *Life of Frere*, Vol. II, pp. 161–2.
38. Frere to Carnarvon, 18 October 1876, in ibid, p. 163.
39. John Benyon attaches great importance to the powers of the High Commission and to their enhancement during Frere's tenure of the office: Benyon, *Proconsul and Paramountcy*, pp. 148–9 and 162; Benyon, 'Overlords of Empire', pp. 175–6 and 193. In my opinion, Frere's formal legal powers explain little about his actions: he after all *exceeded* his authority and was censured for doing so.
40. Etherington, 'Frederic Elton', p. 257.
41. Emery, 'South Africa's Best Friend', p. 27.
42. Frere, 'Zanzibar', p. 288.
43. Hoskins, 'British Policy in Africa', p. 142.
44. CO 879/14, African no. 162, Confid, Frere to Hicks Beach, 5 September 1878, pp. 330–2.
45. De Kiewiet, *Imperial Factor in South Africa*, p. 128.
46. See ch. 4, p. 101.
47. See ch. 4, p. 106.
48. See ch. 4, pp. 82–4 and 90–3.
49. Frere, 'Zanzibar', p. 285.
50. Ibid, pp. 285 and 288; see Emery, 'Geography and Imperialism', p. 348, where Frere is quoted as comparing the 'civilizing colonization' of the Arabs and Persians with the 'Portuguese blight'.
51. Frere, 'Future of Zululand', p. 585.
52. See p. 201.

53. BPP, C2222, p. 213, no. 54, Frere to Hicks Beach, 14 December 1878. See also Frere to Hicks Beach, 26 April 1880, in Worsfold, *Sir Bartle Frere*, p. 320.

54. BPP, C2260, p. 27, no. 5, note by Frere, 3 February 1879, on his despatch of 16 November 1878.

55. Frere, 'Future of Zululand', p. 589; BPP, C2222, p. 214, no. 55, Frere to Hicks Beach, 16 December 1878.

56. Laband, *Kingdom in Crisis*, p. 194.

57. Frere to Hicks Beach, 23 December 1878, in Martineau, *Life of Frere*, Vol. II, pp. 263–4.

58. BPP, C2222, pp. 211–13, no. 54, Frere to Hicks Beach, 14 December 1878.

59. Frere to Hicks Beach, 10 August 1878, quoted in Martineau, *Life of Frere*, Vol. II, p. 259.

60. Unlike the statements of 14 and 23 December quoted above (see fns 57 and 58), and unlike his article 'On the Future of Zululand' published in November 1882, after he had come under such attacks.

61. BPP, C2144, pp. 165–8, Minute for Ministers, 4 June 1878.

62. NAM 6807-386-12, no. 9, Frere to Chelmsford, 21 January 1879. Most of this passage is quoted in French, *Lord Chelmsford*, p. 83, and, from the latter source, in Guy, 'British Invasion', p. 12.

63. See ch. 6, p. 151.

64. See pp. 213–6 and ch. 9, pp. 233–5.

65. See ch. 5, pp. 119–20.

66. BPP, C1776, p. 108, Shepstone to Carnarvon, 6 March 1877.

67. See ch. 7, p. 182.

68. GRO, PCC/1/8 and 12, Frere to Hicks Beach, 3 June and 16 July 1878.

69. GRO, PCC/2/37a and b, Frere to Hicks Beach, 24 November 1879, encl Copy – to Frere, 10 November 1879.

70. PRO 30/6/33, no. 86, Frere to Carnarvon, 19 July 1877; Frere to Herbert, 18 March 1878, quoted in Martineau, *Life of Frere*, Vol. II, pp. 223–4; GRO, PCC/1/8, Frere to Hicks Beach, 3 June 1878.

71. PRO 30/6/34, Frere to Carnarvon, 11 and 14 Nov. 1877; GH 686, Confid, Frere to Bulwer, 18 November 1877; Frere to Herbert, 18 March 1878, in Martineau, *Life of Frere*, Vol. II, pp. 224–5.

72. Frere to Hicks Beach, 10 November 1878, in Worsfold, *Sir Bartle Frere*, p. 111.

73. PRO 30/6/33, no. 45, Carnarvon to Frere, 7 June 1877.

74. PRO 30/6/34, p. 262, Carnarvon to Frere, 2 January 1878.

75. UWL, Littleton Papers, no. 53, Littleton to his mother, 20 February 1878; Frere to Carnarvon, 17 February 1878, quoted in Martineau, *Life of Frere*, Vol. II, p. 219.

76. BL Add Mss 60797, Frere to Carnarvon, 27 February 1878; Walker, *History of Southern Africa*, p. 371.

77. Blachford, 'South African Policy', pp. 277–8; Molteno, *Life of Molteno*, Vol. II, pp. 295–8, 334–6; Lewsen, 'First Crisis', pp. 241–52.

78. CO 48/486, minute by Fairfield, 8 October 1878, on Cape 12769, Frere to Hicks Beach, 5 September 1878; Hicks Beach to Frere, 25 July 1878, in Worsfold, *Sir Bartle Frere*, p. 79; Hicks Beach to Frere, 7 March 1878, in ibid, p. 69.

79. PRO 30/6/34, Frere to Carnarvon, 19 December 1877.

80. See Martin, 'British Images of the Zulu'.

81. See ch. 6, p. 149.

82. Frere himself, so far as I am aware, never explained why he thought it was Natal in particular that the Zulu were likely to invade; this explanation is contained in BPP, C2234, p. 14, memo by Thesiger, 28 September 1878, which was written after Frere's arrival in Natal and shows signs of his influence.

83. See ch. 7, p. 188.
84. GH 599, p. 80, Frere to Bulwer, 7 May 1878.
85. GH 1326, no. 96, Bulwer to Frere, 12 June 1878.
86. See ch. 5, pp. 119–20.
87. See ch. 3, pp. 70–1.
88. GH 599, p. 80, Frere to Bulwer, 7 May 1878; BPP, C2079, p. 2, no. 2, Frere to Hicks Beach, 9 January 1878; Frere to Herbert, 18 March 1878, in Martineau, *Life of Frere*, Vol. II, p. 224; BPP, C2222, p. 182, no. 45, Frere to Hicks Beach, 10 December 1878; BPP, C2252, p. 51, no. 18, Frere to Hicks Beach, 24 January 1879.
89. BPP, C2252, p. 51, no. 18, Frere to Hicks Beach, 24 January 1879.
90. Gordon, 'Frere and the Zulu War', pp. 7–17.
91. Frere to Herbert, 10 November 1878, in Worsfold, *Sir Bartle Frere*, p. 112; UWL, Littleton Papers, no. 91, Littleton to 'Ciss', 14 February 1879.
92. BPP, C2220, p. 381, Border Commission report, 20 June 1878.
93. GH 1326, no. 112, Bulwer to Frere, 17 July 1878.
94. See ch. 3, pp. 66–8.
95. See ch. 7, pp. 174–5.
96. GH 790, H. Shepstone, Rudolph and Uys to GS, 20 April 1878, encl in no. 29, Shepstone to Bulwer, 18 May 1878; TA, SN 6, minute by H. Shepstone, Rudolph and Uys to Commissioners, 12 April 1878.
97. BPP, C2220, p. 380, Border Commission report, 30 June 1878.
98. BPP, C2220, pp. 385 and 386, Bulwer to Commissioners, and reply, 6 July 1878.
99. EG, BPP, C2222, p. 130, no. 38, Frere to Hicks Beach, 2 December 1878; *The Natal Witness*, 14 January 1879, memo by Frere, n.d.; BPP, C2252, p. 47, no. 18, Frere to Hicks Beach, 24 January 1879; ibid, pp. 55 and 60–2, Frere to Colenso, 6 and 22 January 1879.
100. BPP, C2222, p. 25, Frere to Bulwer, 15 July 1878.
101. Ibid, p. 24; BPP, C2222, p. 28, minute by Frere, n.d.
102. BPP, C2222, p. 32, Bulwer to Frere, 12 August 1878.
103. SP 32, Frere to Shepstone, 27 August 1878.
104. SP 68, p. 104, Shepstone to Frere, 2 September 1878; see also SP 69, p. 130, Shepstone to Frere, 12 October 1878.
105. BPP, C2222, pp. 27 and 38–40, memo by Frere, n.d., and replies by Commissioners, 27 September 1878.
106. BPP, C2222, pp. 42 and 38–9, memo by Frere, n.d. and replies by Commissioners, 27 September 1878.
107. BPP, C2222, p. 45, minute by Frere, n.d.
108. BPP C2454, p. 130, no. 54, Frere to Hicks Beach, 30 June 1879.
109. SP 33, Frere to Shepstone, 7 October 1878.
110. *The Natal Witness*, 14 January 1879, memo by Frere, n.d. See above, note 99.
111. *The Natal Mercury*, 20 December 1879, memorandum on the appointment of a Resident in Zululand, by Frere, 27 November 1878; CO 48/489, minute by Fairfield, 10 March 1879, on Cape 3217, Frere to Hicks Beach, 26 January 1879; BPP, C2252, p. 55, Frere to Colenso, 6 January 1879; ibid, pp. 59–60, Colenso to Frere, 14 January 1879; BPP, C2367, p. 140, memo by De Villiers, 29 March 1879.
112. Frere to Hicks Beach, 5 January 1879, in Worsfold, *Sir Bartle Frere*, p. 139; BPP, C2252, p. 62, Frere to Colenso, 22 January 1879; BPP, C2316, p. 33, minute on the settlement of the disputed territory, by Frere, 31 January 1879.

CHAPTER NINE

Frere and the Road to War

Preparations for War, July to September 1878

The overthrow of the Zulu kingdom could not be effected without an invasion of Zululand. Bulwer opposed Frere's plan to send more troops to Natal ostensibly for its defence. He argued that the massing of troops in Natal would imperil a peaceful settlement, by arousing Zulu suspicions that the British were simply using the delay following the sitting of the Commission to make preparations for settling the question by force.[1] Since this was exactly what Frere intended, Bulwer was overruled, and the troops were sent. Only later did it become clear to Bulwer that the military preparations were not simply for the defence of Natal, as Frere maintained, but for an invasion of Zululand.[2] General Thesiger (who became Lord Chelmsford on the death of his father on 5 October 1878) moved to Natal and soon came into conflict with Bulwer, who opposed the troop dispositions the former wanted on the same grounds that he had opposed the troops being sent to Natal in the first place. Thesiger was anxious therefore that Frere should follow him to Natal to settle the dispute. 'Sir Henry has high notions of subordination', he said, '& will I feel sure be only too glad to recognise your Excellency as his chief in your capacity as High Commissioner.'[3] More ominous to Frere were the signs that Thesiger might acquiesce in Bulwer's opinions. Thesiger stated in an official despatch that Bulwer was opposed to anything being done which might be interpreted by Cetshwayo as indicating aggressive intentions, and that 'therefore at present all preparations against Cetywayo are temporarily deferred, indeed it is possible that the anticipated disturbance may yet be brought to a peaceful issue'. Bulwer later stated that Thesiger was less anxious for war than Frere.[4]

Frere did not consider that Thesiger had enough troops for war with the Zulu. It is clear that Frere was more anxious than Thesiger that the latter should have additional troops. This may perhaps be because Thesiger was thinking in terms of a defensive war, or even no war at all, whereas Frere wanted to present the Colonial Office with a *fait accompli* in the form of a swift and successful conquest of Zululand. Whether or not this is so, it is remarkable that it should be the civilian High Commissioner who suggested to the General commanding that his numbers were 'very inadequate' rather than the other way round.[5] Hicks Beach had earlier written privately to Frere, with specific reference to the growth of Boer disaffection in the Transvaal, that he took it for granted that if Frere and Thesiger considered more troops were necessary they would ask for them, making it clear, however, that he hoped they would not. Frere reported this to

Thesiger on 5 August, saying that 'on this point I need hardly say I shall be guided mainly by your opinion'. This, however, produced no response, so Frere telegraphed Thesiger on 31 August, on the newly opened line between Cape Town and Pietermaritzburg, saying 'as demand for troops at home less urgent and Diamond Fields are not yet quiet, would you like me to apply for another regiment or more staff officers?' By 10 September this had produced no response either, so Frere wrote to Hicks Beach on his own initiative asking for two more battalions. He suggested that they were needed for peace rather than for war: the Zulu 'war fever' had to be 'mitigated and subdued before we can hope for a condition of permanent peace', he said, and disaffection in the Transvaal should be dealt with by making concessions from strength. He explained Thesiger's reticence by Bulwer's opposition to further troops in Natal. But he said his own opinion was that it was 'quite possible that such reinforcements might avert or arrest a tedious and expensive war and greatly conduce to the peaceful settlement of the Transvaal'. In a private letter he expressed his 'belief that the Natal believers in Cetywayo's peaceful intentions are dreaming, and that those who, believing that our making preparations might lead to a collision, forbear to prepare, entirely mistake the way of inducing gentlemen like Cetywayo to keep the peace'. Two days later a telegram at last arrived from Thesiger stating that 'should hostilities break out with the Zulus' he would need specific reinforcements. Frere sent on the request to Hicks Beach and made preparations to move to Natal.[6]

Frontier Incidents, July to October 1878

Frere arrived in Durban on 23 September 1878. On the same day he telegraphed Hicks Beach to say that the urgency of supporting Thesiger's request was even greater than he had supposed. He followed this a week later with a despatch stating that 'it would be impossible to imagine a more precarious state of peace', that the preservation of peace depended on the sufferance of Cetshwayo, and that while the Zulu King professed a desire for peace, 'every act is indicative of an intention to bring about war'.[7] The acts Frere referred to seemed rather to suggest Zulu anxiety that the British intended to attack them. Bulwer had feared that a troop build-up in Natal would suggest the British intended to settle the border dispute by force, and this fear proved to be amply justified. The arrival of the troops led to much speculation in the newspapers and elsewhere that a war with the Zulu was imminent. Cetshwayo told Bulwer:

> I hear of troops arriving in Natal, that they are coming to attack the Zulus, and to seize me; in what have I done wrong that I should be seized like an 'Umtakata' [sorcerer or wrongdoer], the English are my fathers, I do not wish to quarrel with them, but to live as I always have done, at peace with them. Cetshwayo says that he sees that his Excellency is hiding from him the answer that has returned from across the sea, about the land boundary question with the Transvaal, and only making an excuse for taking time so as to surprise him.[8]

In early September a large Zulu force assembled near the lower Thukela and conducted what was ostensibly a hunt, but which was widely believed to be a counter-demonstration of force. There were also reports of regiments assembling at the royal residence, and of Zulu being ordered to keep a day and night watch on the border. To reassure the Natal population near the Zulu border, troops were sent to Greytown and Verulam. This in turn was likely to alarm the Zulu, so Bulwer sent a message to Cetshwayo explaining the reason for the move.[9] But the Zulu uneasiness was not allayed. Mounting mutual suspicion produced a situation in which any small incident might spark off war and thus vindicate, or be used to vindicate, Frere's assessment of the situation.

There had already been an event on the Natal-Zululand border which Frere was able to use against Cetshwayo. Towards the end of July two wives of Sihayo, Chief of the Qungebe, of the Nquthu district, were accused of adultery and fled with their paramours to what they supposed would be the sanctuary of Natal. Bands of armed Zulu led by two sons of Sihayo entered Natal, seized the women from the homesteads of Natal government employees, and took them back to Zululand, where they were executed. No British subjects were harmed. Bulwer sent a message to Cetshwayo requesting him to send the sons of Sihayo to be tried in Natal. Cetshwayo was not inclined to take so serious a view of this incursion, which he described as 'a rash act of boys, who in the zeal for their father's house, did not think of what they were doing'. He offered £50 in compensation, and stated that he would not have taken any notice of a similar case the other way round. He added that there had been cases of delinquents from Natal being followed into Zululand and removed from it by Natal policemen without the permission of the Zulu authorities, and that no notice had ever been taken of such acts.[10] This was quite true.[11] Another probable reason why Cetshwayo was not inclined to take the incident too seriously was that when a very similar incident occurred in November 1876 Cetshwayo had merely been informed of it by Bulwer, who had demanded neither the surrender of the offenders nor a fine – the information had not even been accompanied by a remonstrance. This had been on the advice of Shepstone, who had been anxious to avoid any possible complication with the Zulu on the eve of his mission to the Transvaal.[12]

Bulwer attached no political significance to the Sihayo incident, and would have been content with a larger fine. Frere, making the most of this stroke of luck, put a very different gloss on it. He wrote to Hicks Beach about the danger of a Zulu invasion, and said the occurrence 'looks very much like what school boys would call "trying it on".' He described Sihayo as 'extremely anti-English', and stated that he had of late received unusual marks of favour from Cetshwayo for this reason.[13] Sihayo was if anything pro-English,[14] but the action of his sons was to figure prominently in the ultimatum that Frere eventually sent to Cetshwayo.

Towards the end of September another border incident took place which Frere was able to use. A surveyor named Smith in the Colonial Engineer's department was sent to inspect a drift across the Thukela near Fort Buckingham and report on 'what would be necessary to be done to make the drift passable by wagons, etc'. He was accompanied by a friend named Deighton, who held no official position. A road to this drift had been made on Sir Garnet Wolseley's orders, and had always been looked upon with great suspicion by the Zulu, who were now keeping a day and night watch on their borders. When, therefore, Smith and Deighton walked into the almost dry river bed they were threatened by a group of armed Zulu who caught hold of them and made them sit down and explain what they were doing on what they described as Cetshwayo's land. After an hour or two of interrogation they were released, having had some small articles removed from their pockets. Smith did not consider the matter sufficiently important to report to the government, which heard of it only when Deighton, hearing that Smith had not reported it, took it upon himself to do so. Bulwer was more annoyed with the Colonial Engineer's department than with the Zulu, whose action, at a time when troops were pouring into Natal and it was being openly stated they were to invade Zululand, he described as 'not to be wondered at'.[15] But 'the rape of Mr. Smith's pipe and pocket-handkerchief' was one of the acts which a few months later Britain was 'avenging with carnage and ruin'.[16]

At about the same time, towards the end of September, it was reported that Faku, the *induna* of the *umuzi* established near Luneburg in May, had, in the King's name, ordered the Luneburg settlers to leave, stating that the land was required for grazing the King's cattle. Bulwer remonstrated with Cetshwayo, pointing out that the settlers were British subjects. Cetshwayo replied that he had not known they were British subjects, and he also stated that he knew nothing of Faku's order to them to leave. In a later message to Rudolph at Utrecht, Faku being one of the messengers, Cetshwayo admitted having ordered them to leave, claiming again that he had not known they were British subjects. He also retracted the order. It is difficult to believe that Cetshwayo really did not know that white people on the Transvaal border were under British protection, and difficult to believe that Faku would have ordered them to leave without authority. But it is equally difficult to understand why Cetshwayo should have issued such an order at such a delicate time. Rudolph expressed the fear that the departure of the Luneburg settlers and the other farmers of the area would enable the Zulu to gain access to rugged country containing many caves in the rear of Utrecht. It is possible that Cetshwayo, fearing that war was inevitable, sought to gain these defensible positions. What happened in the event was that a detachment of British troops was sent to Luneburg.[17]

In early October Mbelini, the Swazi pretender living under Cetshwayo's protection, raided two groups of Swazi, one a group of refugees on the Ntombe river near Luneburg, subjects of Cetshwayo, and the other a community in southern Swaziland. According to a newspaper report, between 40 and 50 of the Ntombe river people were killed, and four of the other group. These events caused great excitement in Swaziland, and much alarm among the whites in the border district. Rudolph stated that it was generally believed that Mbelini acted under secret orders from Cetshwayo; he thought the events were 'a feeler and of great significance', and that further raids on a much larger scale would ensue. There were, however, no further raids, and a fortnight later Rudolph reported that he had heard that Cetshwayo was very angry with Mbelini and had summoned him to his presence. John Dunn stated that Cetshwayo had known nothing of the raid beforehand, that he was so incensed that he gave orders for a party to go and kill Mbelini, who escaped after being warned by Mnyamana. Mbelini's massacres were presumably carried out in pursuit of his personal political aims. Cetshwayo told Bulwer that Mbelini had left Zululand with the avowed object of wresting the Swazi throne from his brother, and that if he returned he would have him killed.[18]

Frere summed up his view of the Sihayo, Smith and Deighton, and Mbelini incidents, and Cetshwayo's part in them, by saying that they 'were not accidents, but acts on system to keep up the terror he believed he had inspired, and to try how far he might go'.[19]

Opposition to Frere in Natal

Frere received the Border Commission's report in mid-July, and arrived in Natal on 23 September. But it was not until 11 December that the border award was made known to the Zulu. Frere explained the delay by saying that he could not make a final judgement until he had received Shepstone's comments on the report. He did not receive them until 7 November, but long before that he had made it clear that whatever Shepstone said he would be obliged to accept (in form) the Commissioners' decision.[20] What he really needed from Shepstone was advice concerning the ultimatum that he intended presenting to the Zulu together with the award, and an expression of support for the ultimatum policy.[21]

He was in particular need of Shepstone's support because of the lack of support and even outright opposition he encountered in Natal. Since he represented himself as having come to rescue Natal from a Zulu onslaught, it was highly embarrassing that the objects of his professed concern seemed not to realize that they needed rescuing. 'The people here seem slumbering on a volcano,' he wrote a week after his arrival.[22] His private letters to his old patrons, Carnarvon and Herbert, reveal the irritation he felt at the 'blindness, inconsistency and ignorance', the 'self-delusion and procrastination', the 'incapacity' and the 'blind and narrow provincialism' of the 'obstinate, ill-informed, short-sighted and reluctant' officials of the Natal government, or the 'official clique at Pietermaritzberg [*sic*]' as he called them.[23] He was shocked at their connivance in John Dunn's arming of the Zulu. Dunn was a salaried agent of the Natal government (for the purpose of facilitating the passage of Tsonga labourers through Zululand) and in his defence he said:

in arming the Zulus with guns it was under the impression that the Natal Government coincided with what I did, as I know from conversation with the Secretary for Native Affairs, that he (Sir T. Shepstone) sided with the Zulus and had no friendly feeling toward the Dutch of the Transvaal.

Dunn also stated that Gallwey, the Attorney-General (and later the chairman of the Border Commission), 'advised me to get my supplies from Delagoa Bay, and this is what first put the idea in my head'.[24] The arms trade between Natal and Delagoa Bay conducted by Dunn was perfectly legal, until it was eventually prohibited in 1877, the year that the Transvaal was annexed. There is evidence that in 1870 Shepstone expressed opposition to Dunn's arming of the Zulu,[25] and Frere wrote that Gallwey 'shows the untruth of much that Dunn says'. But Frere also wrote that the Natal government sailed very close to the wind and that 'there can be no doubt that Natal sympathy was strongly with the Zulus as against the Boers, and what is worse, is so still'.[26]

Frere did not describe Bulwer, who was after all an English gentleman and a fellow Governor, in the terms he used for Bulwer's officials, but it is evident that by the time he left Natal his irritation with him had become intense.[27] Bulwer was quite out of sympathy with Frere's policy, but he could not be ignored or contemptuously dismissed; he had to be 'brought round', and this took time. Frere explained to Hicks Beach that Bulwer had 'never had much to do with military affairs, and many things which are burnt into one after a few years dealing with Natives in India have to be explained to him'. Why a few years in India would have given Bulwer more insight into Natal's problems than the few years he had spent in Natal, Frere, who had spent a week in Natal at the time that he wrote this, did not explain. It was not until 8 December that Frere was able to report to Hicks Beach that Bulwer had been brought round, and that 'though the process was often tedious and somewhat laborious, the final result, when he agreed, was well worth the trouble'.[28]

Frere's difficulties came not only from Bulwer and his officials but from a large section of the colonists. More than two months after his arrival in Natal he was still complaining of

> how half-hearted is the support we get not only from gunrunners & pseudo-philanthropists, but from a mass of half-informed & prejudiced people, who to much contempt & ill-will towards the T.V. Boers, add a curious sort of sympathy for Cetywayo, such as one might feel for a wolf or hyena one had petted. Then there are many who, from habit, mistrust all we do, because it is done by government or by what they call "imperial" & not by Colonial people. The net result is that our own countrymen hereabouts are only half of them heartily with us, in all we do, & our difficulties are as much from our own people as from Cetywayo.

Bulwer later stated that 'the idea of a Zulu war had not yet occurred to anyone' in Natal before the troops that he had asked not to be sent arrived; it was only then that a Zulu war became a popular panacea for all difficulties and dangers. Bishop

Colenso, who had no reason for undue partiality towards the colonists, stated that 'they never desired the war in the first instance – they never urged it on, or even dreamt of it, till Sir B. Frere came up here and wheedled them into following his lead'. The editor of *The Natal Witness*, an opponent of Colenso, said the same thing. Frere was not wholly satisfied with the results of his wheedling. Less than two weeks before the invasion, after the ultimatum had been delivered and made public, he told Hicks Beach that while he thought he had 'a great majority of the straightforward common-sense of the colony entirely with us . . . there are enough of an opposite way of thinking to give much trouble hereafter, if we are not careful'. Shortly after the war began, Frere (evidently in a somewhat excited state of mind – perhaps the result of a premonition of disaster?) wrote to Chelmsford:

> As long as all goes smoothly & successfully . . . the opposition here will only murmur. But a slight check, or small inroad of Zulus, would bring them out open-mouthed, & a revolution – 'antimilitary & anti-imperialist' – with the Lt.-Gov. & Colonial service at its head, & all true colonists as followers, would be threatened, & if the present tone of home letters continues, the good people there will be only too glad of evidence to show how wise they were in sending us all to act on the defensive, whilst Bp. Colenso & the Natal Govt. tried conciliation & pure reason.[29]

This letter shows how aware Frere was of the risks he was taking in forcing on a war without home or local support. He wrote it on 22 January 1879, on the very day when, unknown to him, not a 'slight check' but a terrible disaster was taking place at Isandlwana, which was to leave all his plans in ruins and irreparably destroy his reputation.

Natal colonists were in an inherently precarious situation: even Colenso was prepared to admit that 'the Zulu Military System was in some sense a "standing menace" to the peace of Natal'.[30] This makes it all the more remarkable that the most senior British official in South Africa, normally resident far from the Zulu frontier, considered it necessary not to allay panic on the frontier but on the contrary to counteract complacency. The unconcern of the Natal colonists, however, can be explained. One must not exaggerate or sentimentalize their pacifism. There can be little doubt that white Natalians saw Zululand as their hinterland and eventual avenue of expansion. But they had no immediate and pressing need for the land and labour of Zululand. Their first priority was to complete the colonization of Natal. Within Natal there were vast tracts of land owned by absentee landlords and occupied only by Africans who were thus relieved of the necessity for wage-labour.[31] The prevailing assumption among the colonists was that this land should be occupied by white farmers and that these Africans should be working for them. They no doubt considered that the same processes of civilization and progress (or expropriation and proletarianization, as they are more likely to be called today) should one day extend to the barbarous domain beyond the Thukela; but the extinction of barbarism in Natal itself came first. Their immediate concern about Zululand was that they might be pre-empted by the Boers of the Transvaal. In default of a British annexation, the best way of keeping the Boers out of Zululand was to support the Zulu against them. Dunn argued that had he not armed the Zulu (which he did with the assistance of Natal merchants and the connivance of Natal officials), 'the Boers would long ago have provoked a war, and that nothing but knowing that the Zulus were armed with guns kept them in check'.[32] Many in Natal would have agreed with him. Thus for the time being the interests of white Natalians, both officials and colonists, led them to adopt those pro-Zulu and anti-Boer policies and attitudes that Frere found so shocking.

By the same token, the Zulu found them reassuring. There was no border dispute with Natal, and it normally seemed to pose no threat to the Zulu kingdom. Cetshwayo and his advisers knew very well that Natal was a mere outpost of an empire that wielded far more power than anything the Boers could muster. They had every reason to cultivate friendly relations with such powerful but unthreatening neighbours, and no possible motive for invading Natal. All this was well understood in Natal, and explains the unconcern of the colonists at what, on a superficial view, seemed their dangerously vulnerable situation. The Transvaal becoming British in 1877 might have been expected to have changed everything, but, although Shepstone, the Zulu's erstwhile friend, went over to the Boers and became their enemy, Bulwer and his advisers, including even Shepstone's brother, seemed disposed to continue the traditional Natal policy of supporting the Zulu against the Transvaal. This disposition was noted by Cetshwayo with appreciation and by Frere with the strongest disapproval.[33]

Frere and the Colonial Office

Frere's need to win support for his policy was one reason for his delay in presenting the border award, together with its indispensable accompaniment, an ultimatum which would nullify it, to the Zulu. Another was the weather. The summer rains were late, the veld was parched, and transport and hence military operations were virtually impossible. It was not until 20 November that Frere was able to report the glad news that the country was green again and that General Thesiger (now Lord Chelmsford) hoped to be able to move in any direction in about three weeks.[34] A further reason for delay was that Frere was hoping to hear that his representations concerning the critical situation in Natal had been heeded by the home government and that reinforcements were on their way. We must now examine the reaction of the Colonial Office to South African events. A complication to be borne in mind here is the time-lag: despatches and letters took three or four weeks between London and Cape Town and four or five weeks between Pietermaritzburg and London, while telegrams had to travel by ship between Cape Town and Madeira, which took about two weeks.

The impression formed at the Colonial Office by the reports received of the failure of Shepstone's negotiations with the Zulu in late 1877 was that war was inevitable.[35] Even the news that Cetshwayo had accepted arbitration did little or nothing to alter this. It was assumed that the decision would go against the Zulu and that they would refuse to accept it. Arbitration was considered useful only because the delay it entailed would enable the necessary military preparations to be made, including the sending to the Zulu frontier of the troops Frere had requested ostensibly for the war on the Cape eastern frontier.[36]

The first suggestion in the Colonial Office minutes of 1878 that a war with the Zulu might not be inevitable occurs in September, when the report of the Border Commission was received. Fairfield wrote:

> If the views of the Commission & of Sir Henry Bulwer are adopted there is no occasion to go to war with Cetywayo. It has been generally assumed that Cetywayo was in the wrong and would have to be repressed. Now he is pronounced to have been in the right, as indeed everyone always supposed he was until after the Transvaal had been annexed and Sir T. Shepstone took up a position adverse to his claims. But it appears to be a foregone conclusion in everybody's mind that there is to be a war.

Fairfield pointed out that war was in the career interests of the military; but there appears to have been no inkling in the Colonial Office at this stage that Frere himself was bent on war. Fairfield suggested that since Frere was 'so much surrounded by the military elements' it might be as well 'to give him some lead in favour of the inclination which he would naturally have towards peace'. Wingfield commented that Frere would 'scarcely require encouragement in a pacific direction'. Herbert wrote that 'a good deal is no doubt said, not very prudently, of the necessity of now breaking the power of Cetywayo', but pointed out that Frere apprehended that Cetshwayo himself would go to war, and for this reason he expressed fear that 'we are in for (if not already in) a war with the Zulus'. He continued, 'any how I think we must be very careful not to take large tracts of Zulu country without justification, & so do that which we charged the Transvaal Republic with having done', a sentiment with which Hicks Beach expressed agreement.[37]

If the Commissioners' report made war with the Zulu seem avoidable, news received a little later made the avoidance of such a war most desirable. The Congress of Berlin in July checked Russian expansion in eastern Europe; but in the same month the reception of a Russian mission in Afghanistan raised the spectre of Russian expansion at the expense of British interests in Asia. The Viceroy of India demanded that the Amir of Afghanistan receive a British mission. Towards the end of September the news came that the Amir had refused to do so. War with Afghanistan seemed likely. Were Britain to be simultaneously engaged in wars in Asia and Africa, it was feared that Russia would consider it safe to ignore the undertakings she had made in Berlin, under British pressure, in respect of eastern Europe.[38]

It was in these circumstances that Frere's first request for further reinforcements was received on 5 October.[39] South Africa already had far more than its normal complement of British troops, but Hicks Beach immediately referred Frere's request to the Cabinet, which had met to consider the crisis in India. It declined to send further troops to South Africa. Thesiger (Chelmsford) had not at this stage asked for reinforcements, and Hicks Beach knew that the Border Commissioners had reported in favour of the Zulu claim, and that Bulwer did not believe in the imminence of war, so he cabled Frere, who was still in the Cape:

> Her Majesty's Government will await the result of your personal interview with Sir Henry Bulwer and General Thesiger before coming to a decision on the subject. I am led to think from the information before me, that there should still be a good chance of avoiding war with the Zulus.[40]

A few days later Hicks Beach received Frere's telegram of 14 September stating that Thesiger had asked for reinforcements, and then his telegram of 23 September from Durban stating that the need for reinforcements was greater even than he had supposed.[41] Hicks Beach pointed out to Disraeli that the general had now asked for reinforcements and that Bulwer was unlikely to change his and Frere's minds, and suggested the request should be complied with. But Disraeli and the Cabinet did not agree, so Hicks Beach sent a despatch to Frere designed, as he told Disraeli, to throw 'as much cold water as possible upon his evident expectation of a Zulu war'. The despatch, dated 17 October, stated that the government was

> not prepared to comply with the request for a reinforcement of troops. All the information that has hitherto reached them, with respect to the position of affairs in Zululand, appears to them to justify a confident hope that by the exercise of prudence, and by meeting the Zulus in a spirit of forbearance and reasonable compromise, it will be possible to avert the very serious evil of a war with Cetywayo.[42]

On 1 November the Colonial Office received Frere's alarming despatch of 30 September from Natal.[43] It was with 'the greatest possible reluctance', said Hicks Beach, that he again urged Disraeli that the matter should be considered by the Cabinet. He said he was by no means convinced that a Zulu war was necessary or that the troops in South Africa were insufficient, but pointed out that if war broke out with the Zulu, and the Boers took the opportunity to rise, Frere might be in great difficulty and the government would be blamed for not supporting him. But the Cabinet was more concerned about eastern Europe and India, so Hicks Beach had to tell Frere again that his request had been refused and urge him to redouble his exertions to avoid war.[44] On 18 November a telegram came from Frere stating that 'the news from Zululand is as threatening as possible, short of actual hostilities'. On 20 November, in response to much stronger urging by Hicks Beach, the Cabinet very reluctantly agreed to send reinforcements. In informing Frere of this, Hicks Beach told him he could 'by no means arrive at the conclusion that war with the Zulus should be unavoidable', and that in supplying these reinforcements it is the desire of Her Majesty's Government not to furnish means for a campaign of invasion and conquest, but to afford such protection as may be necessary at this juncture to the lives and property of the Colonists.[45]

But this despatch arrived only after the ultimatum had been delivered, and the troops themselves arrived on the eve of the invasion of Zululand, for which they were of course used.

Frere's apologists make much of the 'reversal of policy', which they allege the initial refusal to send reinforcements represented.[46] They say that Hicks Beach's statements that it should be possible to avoid war with the Zulu were insincere and inconsistent with his earlier statements, that the real reason for not sending reinforcements was the European and Indian situation, and that by not sending them the Cabinet left Frere in the lurch. But it is clear that the report of the Border Commission made it possible to see the actions of the Zulu in a new light. If the Zulu were indeed the aggrieved party, what had seemed indicative of aggressive intentions could well be seen as only a determination not to forfeit their just rights; and if their just rights were upheld, there was no reason to suppose that they would deviate from the policy of peace and friendship towards the British which they had followed ever since the latter had become their neighbours. Bulwer made it clear that this was his view of the matter. And the Cabinet increasingly suspected that it was Frere rather than Cetshwayo who harboured aggressive intentions.[47]

This raises the other accusation against Hicks Beach – that he failed to control Frere. This is of course true, but it was not necessarily his fault. 'I cannot really control him without a telegraph,' he wrote (adding in parenthesis 'I don't know that I could with one').[48] The delay in communication meant Frere had to be left a wide discretion. And Frere was not only headstrong, but Hicks Beach's senior in years and administrative experience, which probably also inhibited any impulse to issue peremptory commands. Moreover, it only gradually became clear to Hicks Beach that Frere needed controlling.

Frere's first mention of an ultimatum was in his despatch from Natal dated 30 September 1878 in which he wrote that if the sons of Sihayo were not handed over as demanded 'it will be necessary to send to the Zulu King an ultimatum which must put an end to pacific relations with our neighbours'.[49] This reached London on 1 November. Had Hicks Beach immediately telegraphed Frere not to send any ultimatum without it first being cleared by the British government, such a telegram would have reached Pietermaritzburg (despite its being conveyed by ship between Madeira and Cape Town) before John Shepstone left on 4 December for the Lower Thukela Drift to deliver the ultimatum to the Zulu delegation. It might even have reached Pietermaritzburg by 16 November, when messengers were despatched to the Zulu King requesting him to send the delegation.[50] Whether Frere would have obeyed even such an explicit instruction at so late a stage is another question. But no such instruction was sent. Hicks Beach and his advisers seem not to have noticed Frere's brief reference to an ultimatum, presumably because it was so surrounded and smothered by such very different statements – the despatch was otherwise almost entirely concerned with the alleged warlike intentions of the Zulu. Surprisingly, Frere seems to have forgotten about it, too. He never used it in his defence against the charge of failing to inform the Colonial Office of his intentions. Frere's apologists have not used it either. The statement seems to have lain unnoticed in the Blue Books from the day it was printed to the present.[51]

This lapse into clarity by Frere was an aberration. After 30 September, as before, his professions were all pacific while every warlike intention was attributed to Cetshwayo. He represented the reinforcements he asked for as being needed to repel or discourage a Zulu attack. In his letters and despatches to Hicks Beach he described the ultimatum in such terms as a demand for 'further securities for peace' or 'a statement of the guarantees which we consider necessary in order to ensure peace'.[52] It was not until well into December, when Hicks Beach saw a letter from Frere to Shepstone dated 7 November, a copy of which Frere had sent to Herbert, asking for Shepstone's 'opinions regarding the kind of ultimatum that ought to be sent to Cetywayo' that Hicks Beach clearly grasped that Frere intended to send an ultimatum that might result in war.[53] This was in fact only one of many repetitions of a request that Frere had first made to Shepstone a month earlier.[54] But Frere was never so straightforward in his letters to Hicks Beach.

As late as 10 November he was still only hinting at his intentions, and diluting his hints with statements of an opposite tendency. Statements concerning the necessity of 'employing an adequate force' to take 'immediate action' were mixed up with statements that 'the time for taking action no longer rests with us' and that 'it rests, not with you, nor with us here, but with a conceited savage to say whether he will have peace or war'.[55] To divine Frere's true intentions from the confused and multifarious deluge of paper he sent Hicks Beach was an almost impossible task. It was not until 2 January 1879 that the first draft of the ultimatum specifying the terms to be imposed on Cetshwayo reached London, and the final draft, in the form it was actually delivered to the Zulu, arrived only on 25 January, a fortnight after the war had begun and three days after the battle of Isandlwana.[56]

Brilliant parody is usually more effective than careful analysis, and much of the impression of feebleness on the part of Hicks Beach is derived from the summary of his despatches with which Sir William Harcourt entertained the House of Commons:

> My dear Sir Bartle Frere: I cannot think you are right. Indeed, I think you are very wrong; but then, after all, I feel you know a great deal better than I do. I hope you won't do what you are going to do; but if you do I hope it will turn out well.[57]

But this is really a summary – a fairly accurate summary in fact – of Hicks Beach's despatch to Frere of 23 January 1879,[58] rather than of his despatches in general. By this time Hicks Beach knew what Frere intended and had given up hope of controlling him. He was hedging his bets: while not approving of Frere having acted without prior approval, he was prepared to condone it, if it proved successful. Hicks Beach may well be criticized for allowing success or failure to influence his judgement on a matter of principle: Frere's apologists are almost certainly correct in saying that Frere would not have been censured had it not been for Isandlwana.[59] But it is much less fair to criticise Hicks Beach for failing to prevent Frere from invading Zululand, since Frere did not tell him (until it was too late to stop him) that he had any such intention, except so obscurely in his despatch of 30 September that not only Hicks Beach but everyone else failed to notice it.

Still less may one argue (though Frere himself did) that Frere did not know that the British government wished him to avoid war with the Zulu. In the first private letter he received from Hicks Beach, in April 1878, the latter stated that the troops to be transferred from the Cape to Natal 'should not make us relax our best efforts to obtain a peaceful solution'.[60] The telegram of 5 October stating that Hicks Beach believed there to be 'a good chance of avoiding war with the Zulus'[61] reached Frere by 3 November at the latest.[62] The despatch of 17 October, which expressed the 'confident hope'[63] that it would be possible 'to avert the very serious evil of a war with Cetywayo', reached Frere on 10 November.[64] It was not until 16 November that a message was sent to Cetshwayo requesting him to send representatives to the Lower Thukela Drift to receive the border award and what Frere described as 'further communications'.[65] A telegraphed summary of Hicks Beach's letter of 7 November[66] in which he urged him to redouble his exertions to avoid war was sent from Cape Town. The text of the summary does not survive, but it can scarcely have failed to include the statement that Hicks Beach underlined in the original: '*we cannot now have a Zulu war in addition to other greater and too possible troubles*'.[67] This telegram reached him on 30 November. It was on 4 December that John Shepstone left Pietermaritzburg to deliver the award and the ultimatum, and the die might be said to have been cast.[68]

Frere and the Danger of Revolt in the Transvaal

Frere knew that the home government did not wish him to send an ultimatum to the Zulu King, but he sent it nevertheless. He was convinced that 'everything in South Africa hangs on this question – Transvaal contentment and Transvaal finance, and all chance of Confederation depend on its being settled, to say nothing of the peace of this border'.[69] He calculated (quite rightly) that the government would acquiesce in a successful *fait accompli*. He gambled and he lost – and proved to be an extraordinarily bad loser, spending the rest of his life insisting upon the absolute rectitude of all his actions.

'Transvaal contentment' – the danger of a Boer revolt – was the major reason why Frere was so inexplicit about his plans until it was too late for Hicks Beach to veto them. It was the major reason why he brought about a war with the Zulu against the wishes of the government. Mounting discontent in the Transvaal had been temporarily allayed by the decision in April 1878 to send a further deputation to Britain to request the restoration of independence. But Hicks Beach warned Frere in July that Kruger and Joubert were quite intractable, that reforms, promises of telegraphs and railways and so forth were unlikely to satisfy them, and that when they returned 'with their little request refused, I fear there will be an outbreak'. According to Frere's private secretary, writing in October, the same belief was common in Pietermaritzburg.[70] Hicks Beach seems to have favoured the restoration of self-government within the framework of a British protectorate, with British control over foreign relations and native policy, along the lines of the later Pretoria Convention, a scheme which might have worked had it been conceded from strength and not in the aftermath of British military defeat. But Frere was opposed to any arrangement outside the framework of confederation, about the chances of which Hicks Beach was by now frankly sceptical. Frere was not interested in piecemeal settlements of local problems but in the implementation of his grand design. He did not accept that the Boers were irreconcilable. He did, however, believe that they would not be reconciled unless the Zulu problem were solved. He wrote privately to his former chief, Carnarvon:

> In the Transvaal, I need hardly tell you it is quite useless my saying a word to the Boers, unless we can settle the Zulu & other native questions. I have most encouraging accounts of their willingness to accept the past as irrevocable, if I can give them assurance as to the future. But how can I satisfy them as to the future, if, after annexing them because they provoked a Zulu difficulty, we leave that difficulty unsettled?[71]

Kruger and Joubert passed through Natal on their way back to the Transvaal, arriving in Pietermaritzburg on 28 November. They were due to report back on their mission on 10 January 1879. As things became more urgent, so Frere's language became more explicit. 'The Boers', he wrote to Hicks Beach on 8 December, 'will watch what we do here; &, if we prove the better men, will accept it as some sort of argument for the annexation of Transvaal, which otherwise they will resist as far as they dare'. To Shepstone he pointed out that 10 January was

> the same date on which the time given to Cetywayo will expire, &, unless he has completely given in, Ld. Chelmsford will take the matter in hand, & his preparations are so complete that I have every hope of his speedy success. I hope the discontented Boers will understand this & see what the Zulus can do, before they decide on their own future proceedings.

It was not simply the removal of the danger of Zulu aggression that he hoped would mollify the Boers but the nullification of what he called the 'most inconvenient – most disastrous' border award. In response to Hicks Beach's despatch telling him the reinforcements being sent were not to be used for a 'campaign of invasion and conquest',[72] an instruction he disregarded, Frere said that war with the Zulu might possibly have been deferred, but 'an insurrection or rebellion in the Transvaal would have been almost inevitable', adding only as an afterthought (between the lines of the letter) 'and would certainly have been followed by a Zulu invasion of Natal'. He went on:

> It would take months to convey to the Boers the devices by which I hoped the Commissioners' disregard of private rights might possibly be mitigated and corrected. Meantime it is probable the Boer discontent would have exploded in some form or other.

In April 1879, having been privately informed that he would be publicly censured, Frere wrote (from the Transvaal) that the evidence of Boer discontent had convinced him that the delay caused by a referral would involve 'dangers far greater than those of a Zulu war'. Hicks Beach might prefer Colenso's opinion to his on the danger of a Zulu invasion of Natal, he wrote:

> But there could be no doubt as to the state of Boer feeling, of which at the time you had little evidence before you. I felt, however, quite certain that, even if I could postpone for a few weeks or even months the inevitable Zulu War, it would be impossible to avoid a Boer rebellion. You will, I think, agree with me when you read my recent despatches about the Transvaal and reflect how much the danger we have so narrowly escaped here would have been aggravated had the malcontent Boers been able to point to Piet Uys and his gallant band, driven from their homes to make them over to the Zulus.[73]

The Ultimatum, the Zulu Response and the Invasion, November 1878 to January 1879

Frere needed to overthrow the Zulu kingdom to persuade a reluctant Transvaal and an almost equally reluctant Cape into confederation. He forced a war on the Zulu for imperial reasons, but he had to represent it as being forced on him for local, defensive reasons. It was therefore embarrassing for him to be obliged to admit that there was 'a considerable party in Natal and the Cape Colony who have taken, and advocated in the public press, views regarding Zulu affairs strongly opposed to the use of coercion'.[74] A further embarrassment was that while he was describing the aggressive blood-lust of the Zulu in ever more lurid terms in an attempt to scare the home government into sending out reinforcements, the Zulu themselves were doing nothing to justify this description. There were no frontier incidents after Mbelini's raids on the Swazi in early October.[75] On the same day that Frere telegraphed Hicks Beach to say that reinforcements were 'urgently needed to prevent war of races' and that the Zulu were 'insolent' and 'burning to clear out white men', a message was received from the Zulu King stating that he wished to 'sit down and rest and be peaceful'. His subsequent messages were equally pacific, as was a message received on 13 November from the *izikhulu*. The King's brother, Hamu, even while secretly informing the British of his intention to defect to them in the event of war, stated that Cetshwayo had no aggressive intentions. The Zulu people at large also showed no sign of a wish for war. The Border Agent on the Lower Thukela wrote:

> I am repeatedly assured both by our own natives just out from the Zulu country and by Zulus who visit their friends in Natal that the desire of the Nation is lasting peace with the English and that any other policy on the part of the Zulu King would not receive general support.[76]

But Frere needed the Zulu to be aggressive. 'Are we then forcibly to coerce the Zulus in order to secure the allegiance of the Transvaal?' he asked in one of his despatches advocating in effect just that. His explicit answer to his question however was: 'Certainly not, if any one can show us reasonable grounds for expecting that the Zulus will be content to remain in peace within their own borders.' But there could be, he insisted, no such expectation of one who sought 'to revert to Chaka's system of centralised military organisation, for the avowed purpose of conquest and aggression of the bloodiest and most barbarous kind'.[77]

Since Frere so needed the Zulu to be aggressive, he was unable to keep out of his numerous and voluminous letters and despatches all traces of his irritation at Cetshwayo's pacific demeanour. He attributed the Zulu King's failure to take advantage of many 'favourable opportunities' in the previous 18 months to 'half-heartedness'[78] or 'want of resolution'.

> Just at present Cetywayo seems a very ordinary kind of butcher; with some ability of a low cunning kind, but little personal courage, and no tinge of genius like Chaka. Had he Kreli's ability or popularity you would long since have had trouble in Natal.[79]

All Frere's problems would be solved if only Cetshwayo would strike the first blow.

> If some of Cetywayo's young regiments would try their strength against one of H.M.'s, I should have no fear of the result & the way would be clear. But if, as is very possible, he tries to gain time, & to wait for a more favourable opportunity, when we are not so well prepared – what should be our course to bring him to a clear issue?[80]

Frere's great fear was that Cetshwayo would accept the ultimatum. He was, he told Shepstone, 'at a loss to know what security I can get, or demand from Cetywayo, should he profess an intention to do as we require, & offer to repeat his broken Coronation promises'. There was, he said, 'a great disposition among many persons in Natal to be satisfied with such promises of amendment'; but this, he considered, would be 'a fatal error'. To obviate as far as possible the danger of its being accepted, Frere wished the ultimatum to be as comprehensive as he could make it. But he experienced difficulty in finding sufficient things of which to complain. He began to suspect that the Natal government was concealing Zulu outrages from him. He had been unable, he told Shepstone, to whom he appealed for help, to get from anyone in authority in Natal 'any clear or complete account [of] what we have to complain of '. He had given Bulwer a note of what had occurred to him on the subject, which most of the Natal officials had seen, but he had had no response. He knew of course of the Sihayo, Mbelini, and Smith and Deighton incidents, 'but for anything I know to the contrary there may be scores of similar misdeeds, during the last 12 months'.[81] But Shepstone was unable to produce any further Zulu actions to complain of, so the Smith and Deighton incident, which Frere had earlier been inclined to agree with Bulwer in regarding as of little significance, had to be promoted to the status of an 'outrageous insult'.[82]

Shepstone's official advice on the ultimatum arrived only after it had been drawn up. This was the result not only of his habitual dilatoriness but of his uncertainty as to whether Frere wanted an ultimatum that would be accepted or one which would lead to war. This was a delicate inquiry, made in private letters, and the answer to it was of a circumlocutory nature, but its essential meaning was clear enough, and Shepstone was relieved to learn that Frere intended the overthrow of Cetshwayo.[83] Shepstone in turn expressed the reassuring opinion that a demand for the surrender of the people involved in the border incursions and for the payment of a heavy fine would not be complied with, and that the Zulu kingdom would disintegrate at the first move made against it.[84]

Shepstone's official memorandum on Britain's relations with the Zulu, when it eventually arrived, was chiefly remarkable for its historical inaccuracy and its inconsistency with his earlier statements. His assertion, for example, that Britain had a 'sovereign right' over Zululand, derived curiously enough from the Voortrekkers' defeat of Dingane and installation of Mpande, was scarcely consistent with his statement in 1875 that no treaty or formal protectorate existed between Britain and the Zulu kingdom.[85] Even Frere commented on how greatly Shepstone's statements on the border dispute differed from the views he had expressed as Secretary for Native Affairs in Natal. Frere could afford to call attention to this inconsistency since he had decided to accept (in form) the Border Commission's decision. But Shepstone's observations on the necessity for intervention by force in Zululand were useful to him, and corresponded to his own views on the subject. Shepstone made it clear that a complete reformation of Zululand's government and social system could not be effected without the use of force, and that such a reformation was essential for the peace, progress and civilization of South Africa. He wrote:

> At this moment the Zulu power is a perpetual menace to the peace of South Africa; and the influence which it has already exercised and is now exercising is hostile and aggressive; and what other result can be looked for from a savage people, whose men are all trained from their youth to look upon working for wages and the ordinary labour necessary to advance the progress of a peaceful country to be degrading; and to consider the taking of human life as the most fitting occupation of a man![86]

By the end of November the ultimatum had been drawn up. It required the surrender of Sihayo's brother and sons, together with a fine of 500 cattle, within 20 days of the delivery of the ultimatum. A fine of 100 cattle was demanded in recompense for the Smith and Deighton affair, also to be paid in 20 days. The people responsible for Mbelini's raids were to be given up for trial in the Transvaal courts; no time limit was laid down in this case. The changes required within Zululand were then specified. The existing military system was to be abolished. Men were to be free to marry when they pleased. The obligation upon every able-bodied man to defend his country was to remain, but men were not to be called out or assembled in regiments without the consent of the British. The laws agreed to by Cetshwayo at his coronation were henceforth to be strictly observed: people accused of crimes were to be given a fair and open trial, there was to be a right of appeal to the King, and no executions were to be carried out without the King's consent. There was to be a British Resident in or on the borders of Zululand to see that the coronation laws and the military regulations were observed. All missionaries formerly in Zululand and their converts were to be permitted to return, and no obstacle was to be put in the way of Zulu wishing to listen to the missionaries. Any dispute concerning Europeans was to be heard by the King in the presence of the British Resident, and no Europeans were to be expelled from the country without the approval of the Resident. An affirmative answer to these proposals was required within 30 days.[87]

The ultimatum was signed by Sir Henry Bulwer. This seems strange when one considers how out of sympathy he was with Frere's policy towards the Zulu. Colenso's comments, in a letter of May 1880, on the circumstances of Bulwer's signing the ultimatum are of interest:

> I have heard *on very good authority* that Sir B.F.'s despatch requesting Sir H.B. to sign the ultimatum remained for some days unanswered – that, at last, as the two Governors were hardly on speaking terms, our Col[onial] Sec[retary] (Col. Mitchell) *urged* Sir H.B. to sign it for the sake of peace (!) – & that Sir H.B., when he sat down to sign it, hesitated for a while, then signed & dashed it from him, saying 'That's, I fear, the worst thing I ever did in my life.'

This account appears to be confirmed by Sir Garnet Wolseley's account of a conversation with Bulwer in June 1879:

> Bulwer was evidently very sore at having been induced by Frere to sign the ultimatum, and from what he said on the subject led me to believe that much pressure was brought to bear upon him to make him do so.

Although Colenso's statement appears to be supported by Wolseley's, it is entirely contradicted by a letter written by Bulwer to his brother a few days after he signed the ultimatum. He wrote that the demands made upon Cetshwayo were 'absolutely necessary and just, and therefore in requiring them we are doing no more than we have a right to do and no more than we ought to do'. He doubted that the demands would be accepted, and expected hostilities to ensue.

> However, there is no help for it. It is impossible to allow the king to keep up a standing army of thirty or forty thousand warriors – a perpetual menace – and without necessity, for there are no enemies to fear. By taking over the Transvaal we have become practically the only neighbours of the Zulus, and they have no need to fear us.

About Frere he wrote: 'I get on very well with him. We have not always agreed upon all points, but I am able to agree with what he has now asked and consider he has asked no more than necessary.'[88]

Bulwer resisted Frere's relentless pressure, but retreated virtually all the way and eventually capitulated on every important point, not only in substance but in spirit.[89] His principal concern was that justice should be done in the matter of the disputed territory, in which he had intervened and so acquired a sort of personal interest, and this he secured, though only in form. He opposed the massing of troops in Natal but was overruled. As he feared, their presence created a crisis. The Zulu fear of a British attack caused them to mobilize their own army, which led to British troops being sent to the border, which in turn increased Zulu fear and suspicion. The extra British troops could not remain indefinitely in Natal, and in the circumstances created by their presence they could not very well be withdrawn without some corresponding reduction in Zulu military power. Bulwer doubted Britain's alleged historical right to intervene in Zululand, but in the circumstances that had developed he considered some intervention unavoidable on grounds of self-preservation.[90]

The point was made in the crudest terms by Norman Macleod, the British Swazi Border Commissioner:

> My opinion is that unless we thrash the Zulus or dictate such ignominious terms to them as to make it plain they cannot fight us (and this will never happen) we shall lose what little prestige we ever had. All eyes, native eyes, are on the Zulus & ourselves now. They all believe, even our own Natal Kafirs, but certainly the Swazies and any independent tribe that the Zulus are the most powerful, and I believe the only chance of settling S. Africa once for all, is to lick the Zulus now right or wrong, justly or unjustly. I did not realize till I got among the Swazies what a poor opinion it was possible for a nigger to have of us, but when we show ourselves stronger than the Zulus our position would be acknowledged throughout S.A.[91]

The crisis created by the British military build-up in Natal could not be resolved by unilateral disarmament on the part of the British. Such a humiliating climb-down would too greatly damage the prestige on which they relied to hold down their subject populations. But bilateral disarmament meant the disbanding of the Zulu army, which meant the collapse of the Zulu monarchy, and this was something Cetshwayo could never agree to. By this stage, therefore, war was inevitable.

Bulwer clung for some time to the hope that the necessary changes in Zululand might be made without the sending of an ultimatum, but he failed to convince Frere of this. He argued that the Smith and Deighton and Sihayo incidents were not sufficient grounds for resorting to extremities: a nominal fine would be sufficient for the former, he considered, and an enhanced fine in place of the surrender of the culprits for the latter. But Frere would not agree to these suggestions. The most Bulwer secured was an extension of the time limit from the 15 days originally proposed by Frere to 30 and 20 days for the two categories of demand. Bulwer believed Cetshwayo himself to be a cruel tyrant. He was anxious that the Zulu people should understand that the British complaints were not against them but against their King, and that the changes envisaged would be to their benefit. To save this out of the wreck of his original hopes he was eventually reduced to the pitiful and absurd expedient of rewriting the ultimatum in more conciliatory language.[92] Frere's original draft had at least hinted that if the demands were not complied with there would be a resort to war. As rewritten by Bulwer, the ultimatum (or 'message' as it was officially known) said nothing about what would happen in the event of a failure to comply. It concluded that the King and his advisers should give their answer within 30 days

> in order that Her Majesty's High Commissioner may then know if the King and the Great Council agree to the words which are here given, and will give effect to these conditions, which are necessary both for the peace and safety of the Queen's subjects and allies, and also for the safety and the welfare of the Zulu people, to which the Queen's Government wishes well.[93]

There was thus a big discrepancy between the real and apparent meaning of the 'message'. The initial reaction among Natal's colonists, by then fully expecting a war, was that it was a 'milk and water' document. It was not until its 5 000 words had been more carefully studied and considered that its real implications became clear. *The Natal Colonist*, a Colensoite paper, at first warmly supported the 'message', but then developed doubts.[94] It is very probable that its real implications never became clear to the Zulu, and that Bulwer's inappropriately emollient language served only to produce that lack of urgency which characterized the Zulu reception of the ultimatum.

The British army showed how much real concern it had for 'the welfare of the Zulu people' by plundering and destroying their property as soon as it crossed the border.[95] This, together with the opprobrium that came to be attached to the war in general, seems to have aroused Bulwer's regret and anger that he should have allowed himself to become the instrument of Frere's aggression. Frere's later accusation that the military operations had been delayed by Bulwer's want of co-operation – described by Bulwer as a 'monstrous and iniquitous untruth' – turned him more decisively against Frere.[96] Bulwer was, indeed, as Wolseley said, 'induced' under 'much pressure' to sign the ultimatum, but the pressure and the inducement were psychological. It was not a case of external pressure and unwilling compliance, though Bulwer may later have come to believe that it had been.

Frere won an even more unexpected, albeit even more temporary, convert to his ultimatum policy. This was none other than Bishop Colenso. Colenso expressed to Frere his

> cordial assent to the main points of the message, viz., those requiring the disbanding of the military force and an entire change in the marriage system, as being, though measures of coercion, yet such as a great Christian power had the right and the duty of enforcing upon a neighbouring savage nation like the Zulus, brought into close relations with itself, whose King had been installed at their own request by the representative of the Natal Government, and to whom a signal proof of generosity and good faith had been given in the award, as was set forth emphatically in the forefront of the message itself.[97]

It was when Colenso discovered that the border award was in reality quite fraudulent – that the Zulu were to get only a nominal sovereignty while the Boers kept the land – that he was forced to face the fact that he had been duped by Frere into dwelling briefly in a 'fool's paradise'.[98] But Colenso's initial ignorance of the real nature of the award does not explain everything. It was still, as John Bramston in the Colonial Office observed, 'unexpected to find that the Bishop approves of those points of the ultimatum which really made war inevitable'. Fairfield commented that his approval was 'extremely important to Sir Bartle Frere or anyone wishing to take up his defence', a judgement borne out in the parliamentary debates.[99] That he should have so approved, even temporarily, is inexplicable if one sees him as a 'twentieth century liberal who somehow wandered into the wrong century'.[100] Colenso was a man of his time, his nationality, his class and his profession. As Jeff Guy's study of Colenso shows, as a critic of imperialism he had decided, if inevitable, limitations.[101] He could never entirely rid himself of the belief that British expansion was essentially a force for good, and that the injustices he encountered and fought were aberrations, the accidental products of the weakness or wickedness of individuals, and not intrinsic to the process.[102] All the signs pointed to the war with the Zulu which he dreaded; but he suppressed his doubts and clung desperately as long as he possibly could to the belief or hope that Frere, as an English Christian gentleman, would prove to be on the side of right and truth and justice, and that Cetshwayo would prove sufficiently enlightened to embrace the elements of civilization he was being required to accept.[103]

The award and the ultimatum were delivered on 11 December 1878 on the right bank of the Thukela, under what is now known as the Ultimatum Tree. The Zulu delegation was headed by Vumandaba kaNteti, a personal attendant of the late King Mpande, and the British delegation by John Shepstone, the Acting Secretary for Native Affairs in Natal. The award was read first. It defined the line decided upon by the High Commissioner as the Ncome (Blood) river to its main source in the Magidela mountains and thence in a direct line to a round hill between the two main sources of the Phongolo river. Much of the text of the award was taken up with the question of whites and Zulu living on the 'wrong' side of the line. It gave the impression of even-handedness, but this was highly misleading. What the award did not state was that all the land between the line it defined as the border and the line claimed by the Transvaal had been divided into farms, and that all these claims, whether marked out on the ground or only on paper, would be accepted as valid; whereas any Zulu on the Transvaal side of the newly-defined line could only be living on white-owned land, since Transvaal law did not allow Africans to own land, and therefore they would not have any right to the land they lived on or any claim to compensation if they moved. The Zulu delegates raised no objection to the award on this sort of ground, which shows that they had no idea of its real nature. They did object to the statement that Cetshwayo was not to attempt to exercise any sovereignty north of the Phongolo, but John Shepstone pointed out that the document also stated that any trans-Phongolan claim Cetshwayo considered himself to have should be submitted to the British government. The Zulu appeared to be satisfied with that.

There was a break for lunch, and in the afternoon the ultimatum was read. The award had been passively received, but the ultimatum produced manifest consternation. The Zulu delegates denied that the coronation laws had been broken, and stated that they could not understand why the disbandment of the army was required since it was an ancient and necessary institution. John Sheptone stated that in the presently existing circumstances the Zulu army could only attack British subjects, and that the Zulu knew that the British government presented no threat to them. One of the Zulu delegates pointed to the British troops present and asked what they were. Shepstone replied that they were for defence and that it was the actions of Cetshwayo that had brought them there. The Zulu objected that 30 days was far too short, and that on such important issues no time limit should be set. They also asked that a British representative should be present when the ultimatum was delivered to the King so that it might be certified as correct. Shepstone interpreted this as signifying a reluctance to bear sole responsibility for the conveying of such bad tidings, but it may also have stemmed from a lack of confidence in their ability to remember accurately so long and complex a communication. Shepstone replied that he had no authority to agree to such a request or to vary any of the terms of the ultimatum.[104]

The written documents were given to John Dunn, who sent messengers to the King, but who did not go to the King himself. Dunn's messengers reached the King before the official delegates, who were manifestly reluctant to convey such unpalatable news. It is possible that Cetshwayo and his advisers never received any very clear or accurate account of the ultimatum. The impression seems to have prevailed in Zululand that the surrender of Sihayo's sons was the chief demand of the British and that if this were complied with the other demands would not be insisted upon. The *izikhulu* were generally strongly in favour of their being surrendered, but Cetshwayo himself was reluctant to do so, and the younger regiments were strongly opposed. It may be doubted whether it was politically possible for Cetshwayo to have complied even with this demand. It was certainly impossible for him to comply with the demand for the disband-ment of the army and the abrogation of the marriage laws. This would have amounted to the abolition of the *amabutho* system, which would have meant the abolition of the monarchy and the disintegration of the state. The demand for cattle was the easiest to comply with, and there is much evidence that cattle were rounded up for this purpose. But even here insufficient importance appears to have been attached to the time limit. Cetshwayo seems not to have been convinced that the British, with whom the Zulu had been on friendly terms for so many years, really intended the conquest of Zululand. The ultimatum, as we have seen, announced no such intention, nor did it provide any explanation of the significance of the time period mentioned. Cetshwayo gave instructions that if the British troops entered Zululand they were not to be resisted, unless they took hostile action first, or constructed entrenchments and fortifications. He appears to have hoped to discuss the whole matter with them when they reached Ulundi.[105]

The first public response of the Zulu King to the ultimatum came in the form of a letter from John Dunn. Dunn reported that the messengers he had sent to the King had returned with a message requesting him to write that he agreed to give up Sihayo's sons and pay the fines of cattle, and that he would submit the other demands to his advisers. Cetshwayo begged that, should the 20 days expire before the arrival of the cattle and the wanted men, Frere would take no action, as the recent heavy rains had made communications difficult. Bulwer urged Frere to wait the full 30 days before taking any action, but Frere refused; the most he would concede was that the troops should halt at convenient posts across the Zulu border and there await the expiry of the term of 30 days. Frere was fairly confident that the terms of the ultimatum were such that it would be 'quite impossible for Cetywayo to submit', but he took no chances. Shortly afterwards an encouraging letter arrived from Dunn. Dated 24 December, it stated that although cattle were still being collected, Cetshwayo evidently did not attach sufficient importance to the time limit, 'and it will be impossible now for them to be up in time'. Dunn was therefore making arrangements to cross over into Natal. On 26 December a message was received by the Border Agent at the Lower Thukela. It stated that Cetshwayo agreed to pay the number of cattle demanded but asked for more time: 'Why does the Government name days, and count them out to him? He cannot get all the cattle together within the days mentioned, as the land is great and he has to seek them.'[106] Neither the cattle nor Sihayo's sons had been handed over by 31 December when the 20-day limit expired. On Frere's instructions,[107] the invasion began before the expiry of the full 30 days. It was on 6 January 1879 that Wood's number 4 column crossed the Ncome (Blood) river, by then the acknowledged Zulu border.[108] On 11 January

1879, the Border Agent at the Lower Thukela received a message from Cetshwayo that he had 'not yet refused to listen to the voice of government' and that 'the Zulu Nation' was gathered with him to consider the British demands. He asked for more time to send their reply.[109] But the 30-day limit had expired the previous day and the invasion was already in progress.

In accordance with Cetshwayo's instructions no resistance was offered by the Zulu. The British troops began looting cattle as soon as they entered Zululand, but the only opposition they encountered at first was verbal.[110] On 16 January Lord Chelmsford, who accompanied Glyn's number 3 column, wrote: 'I cannot help thinking that the Zulu has not much stomach for fighting. He ought to have attacked one of our columns before this if he really means business.'[111] A few days later he wrote to Pearson, the commander of number 1 column, that there was 'no sign of any armed force'. He told Pearson that Bulwer was 'in a great state of mind' about a large force of Zulu said to be in the Nkandla forest, and asked him to send troops to explore the forest, 'from which', he wrote, 'the Zulus will most probably scamper as those have done from before this column'. His letter was dated 'Insandlana Hill, 21 January 1879'.[112]

Notes

1. BPP, C2220, pp. 395–6, Bulwer to Frere, 18 July 1878.
2. BPP, C2584, p. 204, no. 94, Bulwer to Hicks Beach, 10 March 1880, quoting Commodore Sullivan and General Thesiger.
3. NAM 6807-386-29, no. 37, Thesiger to Frere, 11 August 1878; ibid, no. 38, Thesiger to Frere, 13 August [1878].
4. BPP, C2234, p. 1, no. 1, Thesiger to Surveyor-General of Ordnance, 12 August 1878; Preston, *Wolseley's Journal, 1879–80*, p. 48, entry for 30 June 1879.
5. NAM 6807-386-6-13, Frere to Thesiger, 10 September 1878.
6. Hicks Beach to Frere, 11 July 1878, quoted Worsfold, *Sir Bartle Frere*, pp. 75–6; NAM 6807-386-6-13, Frere to Thesiger, 5 August 1878; NAM 6807-386-32, p. 15, Confid telegram, Frere to Bulwer, 31 August 1878, asking him to convey the contents to Thesiger (the demand for troops at home was presumably less urgent because of the signing of the Treaty of Berlin on 13 July 1878); BPP, C2220, pp. 232–3, no. 74A, Frere to Hicks Beach, 10 September 1878; Frere to Hicks Beach, 10 September 1878, in Worsfold, *Sir Bartle Frere*, p. 89; NAM 6807-386-33, p. 15, Confid telegram, Thesiger to Frere, 12 September 1878; BPP, C2220, p. 254, no. 83A, Frere to Hicks Beach, 14 September 1878.
7. BPP, C2220, p. 255, no. 83B, telegraphic, Frere to Hicks Beach, 23 September 1878; ibid, p. 280, no. 105, Frere to Hicks Beach, 30 September 1878.
8. SNA I/7/13, p. 130, message from Cetshwayo, 16 September 1878; ibid, p. 134, Dunn to ASNA, 20 September 1878.
9. GH 1326, no. 136, Bulwer to Frere, 12 September 1878; SNA I/4/2, no. 40, BA Lower Tugela to ASNA, 14 September 1878; ibid, no. 43, RM Umsinga to ASNA, 18 September 1878; SNA I/7/13, p. 127, message to Cetshwayo, 12 September 1878.
10. SNA I/7/13, pp. 124–5, messages to Cetshwayo, 1 and 16 August 1878; ibid, p. 126, Dunn to ASNA, 24 August 1878; ibid, p. 140, Dunn to ASNA, 12 October 1878.
11. See, eg, SNA I/1/29, no. 955, RM Newcastle to ASNA, 30 November 1877.

12. SNA I/7/13, p. 19, message to Cetshwayo, 26 December 1876; SNA I/3/26, minute by Shepstone, 10 December 1876, on no. 994, RM Umvoti to ASNA, 4 December 1876.

13. BPP, C2222, p. 173, memo by Bulwer, 18 November 1878; Frere to Hicks Beach, 20 August 1878, in Worsfold, *Sir Bartle Frere*, p. 87; BPP, C2220, p. 278, no. 105, Frere to Hicks Beach, 30 September 1878.

14. Cope, 'Political Power', p. 30.

15. GH 1052, minute by Colonial Secretary, 9 October 1878, on Deighton to Bulwer, 27 September 1878, and on conversation with Smith; SNA I/4/2, no. 48, Confid, RM Umsinga to ASNA, 23 September 1878; GH 1399, Deighton to RM Umvoti, 25 September 1878, and Acting RM Umvoti to ASNA, 27 September 1878; GH 1052, minute by Bulwer, 10 October 1878, on Deighton to Bulwer, 27 September 1878. In the rearrangement of the GH records, letters and the minutes on them have been separated, and I have not been able to find Deighton's letter to Bulwer. Neither have I been able to find Smith's letter to the Colonial Secretary of 8 October 1878, formerly in what was GH 356.

16. John Morley's sardonic phrases in his 'Plain Story', p. 344.

17. SS 306, R3466, Rudolph to GS, 27 September 1878; SNA I/7/13, p. 139, message to Cetshwayo, 8 October 1878; ibid, p. 142, message from Cetshwayo, 29 October 1878; TA, SN 1, no. 310, Rudolph to H.C. Shepstone, 25 November 1878; TA, SN 1, no. 259, Rudolph to H.C. Shepstone, 22 October 1878.

18. *The Natal Witness*, 22 October 1878, letter from Utrecht correspondent, 15 October 1878; TA, SN 1, nos 242 and 247, Rudolph to H.C. Shepstone, 12 and 27 October 1878; Vijn, *Cetshwayo's Dutchman*, p. 106, Colenso's note, quoting *The Cape Argus* Special Correspondent's interview with Dunn; SNA I/7/13, p. 143, message from Cetshwayo, 29 October 1878.

19. GRO, PCC/2/4, Frere to Hicks Beach, 19 January 1879. This passage is misprinted in Worsfold, *Sir Bartle Frere*, p. 156.

20. BPP, C2367, p. 112, memo by Frere, 29 October 1878; SP 34, Frere to Shepstone, 7 November 1878; SP 33, Frere to Shepstone, 7 and 17 October 1878.

21. SP 33, 34 and 35, Frere's letters to Shepstone between 7 October and 30 November 1878 inclusive.

22. Frere to Hicks Beach, 30 September 1878, in Worsfold, *Sir Bartle Frere*, p. 91.

23. BL Add Mss 60797, Frere to Carnarvon, 16 November 1878; ibid, Frere to Carnarvon, 7 May 1879; Frere to Herbert, 10 November 1878, in Worsfold, *Sir Bartle Frere*, p. 113; BL Add Mss 60797, Frere to Carnarvon, 29 September 1880.

24. GH 1052, Dunn to Bulwer, 21 October 1878.

25. SNA I/1/20, no. 63, Dunn to Shepstone, 31 October and 17 November 1870.

26. Frere to Herbert, 12 January 1879, in Martineau, *Life of Frere*, Vol. II, pp. 238–9. For more detail on the acquisition of firearms by the Zulu, see Cope, 'Shepstone and Cetshwayo', ch. 4, and Guy, 'Note on Firearms', pp. 557–70.

27. NAM 6807-386-12, no. 17, Frere to Chelmsford, 20 February 1879; NAM 6807-386-6-13, Frere to Chelmsford, 18 March 1879; see also UWL, Littleton Papers, no. 91, Littleton to 'my dear Ciss', 14 February 1879.

28. Frere to Hicks Beach, 30 September 1878, in Worsfold, *Sir Bartle Frere*, p. 92; Frere to Hicks Beach, 8 December 1878, in Martineau, *Life of Frere*, Vol. II, p. 250.

29. SP 35, Frere to Shepstone, 3 December 1878; BPP, C2584, pp. 204–5, no. 94, Bulwer to Hicks Beach, 10 March 1880; KC, Colenso Papers, File 27, KCM 50001, Colenso to Chesson, 23 November 1879; Statham, *Blacks, Boers and British*, pp. 168–73; Frere to Hicks Beach, 30 December 1878, in Martineau, *Life of Frere*, Vol. II, p. 267; NAM 6807-386-12, no. 11, Frere to Chelmsford, 22 January 1879.

30. KC, Colenso Papers, File 27, KCM 50001, Colenso to Chesson, 23 November 1879.

31. See ch. 2, p. 12.
32. GH 1052, Dunn to Bulwer, 21 October 1878.
33. SPG, WP no. 201, Robertson to Jackson, 18 December 1877; SNA I/7/13, p. 114, message from Cetshwayo, 15 May 1878.
34. SP 34, Frere to Shepstone, 20 November 1878.
35. CO 291/1, minutes on Tvl 815 and 1524, Confid Shepstone to Carnarvon, 1 and 7 December 1877.
36. See ch. 7, pp. 188–9, and ch. 8, p. 208.
37. CO 179/127, minutes by Fairfield, 12 September, Wingfield, 13 September, Herbert, 15 September, and Hicks Beach, 17 September 1878, on Natal 11374, Bulwer to Hicks Beach, 24 July 1878.
38. Hicks Beach, *Life of Hicks Beach*, Vol. I, pp. 96–7.
39. See p. 222.
40. CO 48/486, Cape 12773, Frere to Hicks Beach, 10 September 1878, and draft telegram to Frere, 5 October 1878. This telegram is alluded to but not printed in BPP, C2242, p. 79; it is printed in HC Deb, Vol. CCXLIV, col 1860, Hicks Beach, 27 March 1879, and in Hicks Beach, *Life of Hicks Beach*, Vol. I, p. 98.
41. See p. 222.
42. Hicks Beach to Disraeli, 15 and 17 October 1878, in Hicks Beach, *Life of Hicks Beach*, Vol. I, pp. 99–100; BPP, C2220, p. 273, no. 92A, Hicks Beach to Frere, 17 October 1878.
43. See p. 222.
44. Hicks Beach to Disraeli, 3 November, and to Frere, 7 November 1878, in Hicks Beach, *Life of Hicks Beach*, Vol. I, pp. 103–4.
45. Hicks Beach, *Life of Hicks Beach*, Vol. I, p. 108; BPP, C2220, p. 320, no. 119, Hicks Beach to Frere, 21 November 1878.
46. Martineau, *Life of Frere*, Vol. II, pp. 261–2; Worsfold, *Sir Bartle Frere*, ch. IX, 'The Reversal of Policy', and pp. 123–30.
47. Hicks Beach to Victoria, 11 November 1878, and Disraeli to Victoria, 12 November 1878, in Buckle, *Letters of Victoria*, Vol. II, pp. 645–6.
48. Hicks Beach to Disraeli, 3 November 1878, in Hicks Beach, *Life of Hicks Beach*, Vol. I, p. 103.
49. BPP, C2220, p. 280, no. 105, Frere to Hicks Beach, 30 September 1878.
50. See p. 233.
51. Colin Webb, for example, in his useful 'Lines of Power' makes no mention of this reference to an ultimatum, and states (p. 34) that Frere's 'first intimation of his intention to make "demands" on the Zulu was in a private letter to Hicks Beach, written on October 14, 1878'.
52. Frere to Hicks Beach, 14 October 1878, in Worsfold, *Sir Bartle Frere*, pp. 158–9; BPP, C2222, p. 17, no. 11, Frere to Hicks Beach, 11 November 1878.
53. Hicks Beach to Frere, 11 December 1878, in Hicks Beach, *Life of Hicks Beach*, Vol. I, pp. 115–16; SP 34, Frere to Shepstone, 7 November 1878.
54. SP 33, Frere to Shepstone, 7 October 1878; SP 34, Frere to Shepstone, 26 and 29 October and 2 November 1878.
55. Frere to Hicks Beach, 10 November 1878, in Worsfold, *Sir Bartle Frere*, p. 110.
56. BPP, C2222, p. 23n, no. 19, Frere to Hicks Beach, 16 November 1878; ibid, p. 201, no. 53, Frere to Hicks Beach, 13 December 1878, encl border award and ultimatum.
57. HC Deb, Vol. CCXLV, col 85, Harcourt, 31 March 1879.
58. BPP, C2222, pp. 197–8, no. 51, Hicks Beach to Frere, 23 January 1879.
59. This is shown by Hicks Beach to Disraeli, 13 January 1879, in Monypenny and Buckle, *Life of Disraeli*, Vol. VI, p. 423.
60. Hicks Beach to Frere, 7 March 1878, in Worsfold, *Sir Bartle Frere*, p. 69.

61. See p. 230.
62. Hicks Beach stated he sent it 'to catch at Madeira the mail that left England on 3rd of October' (Hicks Beach, *Life of Hicks Beach*, Vol. I, p. 99); a letter from Hicks Beach to Frere dated 2 October reached the latter on 3 November (Worsfold, *Sir Bartle Frere*, p. 102); if the telegram was telegraphed from Cape Town to Pietermaritzburg, as it probably was, it would have reached Frere about a week earlier.
63. See p. 230.
64. Worsfold, *Sir Bartle Frere*, p. 106.
65. SNA I/7/13, p. 149, message to Cetshwayo, 16 November 1878; BPP, C2222, p. 107, no. 28, Frere to Hicks Beach, 25 November 1878.
66. See p. 230.
67. Martineau, *Life of Frere*, Vol. II, p. 318; Worsfold, *Sir Bartle Frere*, pp. 131 and 132.
68. SP 35, Frere to Shepstone, 4 December 1878.
69. Frere to Herbert, 10 November 1878, in Worsfold, *Sir Bartle Frere*, p. 112.
70. Hicks Beach to Frere, 11 July 1878, in Worsfold, *Sir Bartle Frere*, p. 75; UWL, Littleton Papers, no. 75, Littleton to his mother, 6 October 1878 (sheet 4).
71. Hicks Beach to Frere, 18 and 25 July 1878, in Worsfold, *Sir Bartle Frere*, pp. 76–7 and 79; Frere to Hicks Beach, 10 August, 15 September and 10 November 1878, in ibid pp. 83, 89 and 111; BL Add Mss 60797, Frere to Carnarvon, 16 November 1878.
72. See pp. 230–1.
73. GRO, PCC/1/31, Frere to Hicks Beach, 8 December 1878; SP 35, Frere to Shepstone, 19 December 1878 (long quote); SP 33, Frere to Shepstone, 17 October 1878: Frere to Hicks Beach, 5 January 1879, in Worsfold, *Sir Bartle Frere*, p. 139 – the original is in GRO, PCC/2/1; Frere to Hicks Beach, 25 April 1879, in Martineau, *Life of Frere*, Vol. II, p. 323. See also in the same vein, BPP, C2454, p. 140, no. 54, Frere to Hicks Beach, 30 June 1879.
74. BPP, C2222, p. 225, no. 58, Frere to Hicks Beach, 27 December 1878.
75. See pp. 224–5.
76. BPP C2222, p. 8, telegraphic, Frere to Hicks Beach, 5 November 1878; SNA I/7/13, p. 148, message from Cetshwayo, 5 November 1878: ibid, p. 157, Dunn to Bulwer, 10 November 1878; SNA I/4/2, message from Cetshwayo, 28 November 1878, encl in no. 91, BA, Lower Tugela, to ASNA, 28 November 1878; SNA I/4/2, message from Zulu chiefs, 13 November 1878, encl in no. 79, BA, Lower Tugela, to ASNA, 13 November 1878; TA, SN 1, message from Hamu, 6 November 1878, encl in no. 281, Rudolph to H.C. Shepstone, 7 November 1878; SNA I/4/2, no. 56, BA, Lower Tugela to ASNA, 7 October 1878.
77. BPP, C2222, pp. 6–7, no. 6, Frere to Hicks Beach, 5 November 1878.
78. BPP, C2252, p. 51, no. 18, Frere to Hicks Beach, 24 January 1879. This was written after the battle of Isandlwana but before Frere had heard of it.
79. Frere to Herbert, 10 November 1878, in Worsfold, *Sir Bartle Frere*, pp. 110–12.
80. SP 34, Frere to Shepstone, 20 November 1878.
81. Ibid, Frere to Shepstone, 15 November 1878.
82. Compare BPP, C2220, p. 305, no. 111, Frere to Hicks Beach, 6 October 1878, with BPP, C2222, p. 189, minute by Frere, 12 December 1878.
83. SP 69, pp. 173 and 183–4, Shepstone to Frere, 16 and 30 November 1878; SP 34, Frere to Shepstone, 20 November 1878.
84. SP 69, pp. 176 and 184–5, Shepstone to Frere, 23 and 30 November 1878.
85. See ch. 3, p. 63.
86. BPP, C2222, pp. 130–4 (long quote p. 133), memo on political position occupied by the British Government towards the Zulu King, by Shepstone, 18 November 1878; see also ibid, pp. 177–9, Shepstone to Frere, 30 November 1878; ibid, p. 62, memo by Frere, n.d.

87. Ibid, pp. 203–9, message no. II.
88. KC, Colenso Papers, File 27, KCM 50050, Colenso to Chesson, 23 May 1880; Preston, *Wolseley's Journal, 1879–80*, p. 48; Clarke, *Invasion of Zululand*, pp. 213–14.
89. The process may be followed in: BPP, C2367, pp. 113–8, memo by Bulwer, 25 October 1878, on no. 105, Frere to Hicks Beach, 30 September 1878, encl in no. 39A, Frere to Hicks Beach, 8 November 1878; BPP, C2222, pp. 169–76, memo by Bulwer, 18 November 1878, and note by Frere, 6 December 1878, encl in no. 42, Frere to Hicks Beach, 7 December 1878; BPP, C2222, pp. 186–90, minute by Bulwer, 29 November 1878, and comments by Frere, 12 December 1878, encl in no. 46, Frere to Hicks Beach, 12 December 1878.
90. BPP, C2584, pp. 203–6, no. 94, Bulwer to Hicks Beach, 10 March 1880.
91. NAM 6807-386-23, no. 9, Macleod to Crealock, 15 November 1878.
92. UWL, Littleton papers, no. 84, Littleton to his mother, 5 January 1879.
93. BPP, C2222, p. 209, message no. II.
94. *The Natal Mercury*, 17 December 1878, editorial; *The Natal Witness*, 17 December 1878, editorial; ibid, 21 December 1878, 'Mail Summary'; ibid, 7 January 1879, 'Short Notes'; *The Natal Colonist*, 14, 19 and 21 December 1878, editorials.
95. Preston, *Wolseley's Journal, 1879–80*, p. 48.
96. Clarke, *Invasion of Zululand*, p. 224.
97. BPP, C2252, p. 52, Colenso to Frere, 27 December 1878.
98. Guy, *The Heretic*, p. 267.
99. CO 48/489, minutes by Bramston and Fairfield, 10 March 1879, on Cape 3217, Frere to Hicks Beach, 26 January 1879; HL Deb, Vol. CCXLIV, col 1632–3, Cranbrook, 25 March 1879; HC Deb, Vol. CCXLIV, col 1931, Hicks Beach, 27 March 1879; ibid., col 1997, Hanbury, 28 March 1879; HC Deb, Vol. CCXLV, col 48, Sandon, 31 March 1879.
100. Norman Etherington's critical phrase, quoted in Guy, *Heretic*, p. x.
101. See especially ibid, pp. 353–5; but the whole of this illuminating book should be read by anyone interested in the history of British imperialism in South Africa in the nineteenth century.
102. See Hicks Beach's pertinent remarks on Colenso's inconsistent shrinking from the only means by which the ends he supported could be attained: HC Deb, Vol. CCXLIV, col 1931, Hicks Beach, 27 March 1879.
103. Guy, *Heretic*, pp. 262–7.
104. The award and the ultimatum are in BPP, C2222, pp. 201–9, messages I and II, encl in no. 53, Frere to Hicks Beach, 13 December 1878. My description of the delivery of the award and ultimatum is based on: ibid, pp. 209–11, Brownlee to Frere, 12 December 1878, and Littleton to Frere, 11 December 1878; ibid, pp. 216–17, Brownlee to Littleton, 16 December 1878; UWL, Littleton Papers, no. 83, Littleton to his mother, 14 December 1878; SNA, I/7/12, p. 36, report by J.W. Shepstone, 19 December 1878.
105. On the reactions of the Zulu to the ultimatum, see the reports of Border Agents in CSO 1925, Vijn, *Cetshwayo's Dutchman*, pp. 16–17 and 91–4, and Laband, *Rope of Sand*, pp. 200–4.
106. BPP, C2222, p. 227, Dunn to ASNA, 18 December 1878; ibid, pp. 227–31, memos by Bulwer, 26 December 1878, and by Frere, 24 and 28 December 1878; Frere to Hicks Beach, 23 December 1878, in Martineau, *Life of Frere*, Vol. II, p. 263; BPP, C2242, p. 10, Dunn to ASNA, 24 December 1878; SNA I/7/13, p. 165, message from Cetshwayo, 26 December 1878.
107. BPP, C2234, p. 39, no. 26, Chelmsford to War Office, 22 December 1878.
108. BPP, C2242, p. 24, no. 9, Frere to Hicks Beach, 13 January 1879. It appears Frere attempted to countermand his instruction, too late to prevent Wood's advance – NAM 6807-386-27, p. 8, Chelmsford to Frere, 1 January 1879. Pearson's no. 1 column was

prevented by rain from crossing before 12 January – Public Record Office, War Office records, WO 32/7707, Chelmsford to War Office, 14 January 1879.

109. CSO 1925, telegraphic, BA, Lower Tugela, to ASNA, 11 January 1879.
110. NAM 6810-38, no. 4, Chelmsford to Pearson, 12 January 1879; Public Record Office, War Office records, WO 32/7707, Chelmsford to War Office, 14 January 1879; French, *Lord Chelmsford*, p. 71; Vijn, *Cetshwayo's Dutchman*, p. 96.
111. NAM 6810-38, no. 7, Chelmsford to Pearson, 16 January 1879.
112. Ibid, no. 9, Chelmsford to Pearson, 21 January 1879.

CHAPTER TEN

Epilogue and Conclusion

Epilogue: The War and its Effects

The British camp at Isandlwana was not fortified. The wagons were needed for bringing up supplies and so were not used to make a laager; the ground was stony and so entrenchments were not dug; 'furthermore it seems that the camp, intended merely as a temporary base, was never considered to be in danger of attack'.[1] The Zulu attack on 22 January 1879 overwhelmed and destroyed the camp, and 1 250 men on the British side – 52 officers, 727 white troops and 471 black – lost their lives. Zulu deaths were probably not fewer than 1 000, but the Zulu remained in possession of the field and so won a spectacular if costly victory.[2]

It was not until early in the morning of 24 January that the first survivors of the disaster reached Pietermaritzburg and the news became generally known.[3] It had a shattering impact on the colony. Colenso reported that the 'excitement & consternation' was intense 'as it is well known that C[etshwayo] has expressed his determination to send in a force & sweep the Colony'. 'A panic is spreading broadcast over the Colony which it is difficult to allay,' reported Chelmsford. It was believed that the government was concealing even worse news from the public. 'The people here are in a terrible fright of being attacked,' wrote Frere's private secretary; 'the panic is a horrible thing to see.' The Newcastle district, with the exception of the town itself and an outlying fort, was reported to have been deserted. A laager incorporating the substantial public buildings was constructed in central Pietermaritzburg. A similar laager was constructed in Durban, together with a stockade across the Point, the narrow spit of land between the bay and the sea.[4]

The impact of the disaster on Britain was bigger than one might have expected. The *Annual Register* commented:

> The news that reached England on February 11, of the terrible disaster at Isandhlwana, was a shock for which the nation was totally unprepared. It was as complete and almost as horrifying a surprise as the Indian Mutiny, and nothing had occurred since then to stir public feeling about imperial affairs so profoundly. It was not indeed felt that there was any danger of a province being lost to the Crown, but there were the same fears for the safety of English colonists, an unarmed population exposed to the fury of overwhelming numbers of savage enemies.

Carnarvon heard that Disraeli was so impressed with the belief that there would be further disasters in South Africa that he dreaded going home for fear of the telegrams he might find there. Disraeli was at at the height of his power and success, having gained an extraordinary hold over aristocracy and people alike. But it was a fragile success: it still remained to be seen whether Russia would fulfil the obligations entered into at Disraeli's diplomatic triumph in Berlin; and the economic depression at home had become very severe. Isandlwana was an exhibition of British military incompetence, it diverted troops from Europe, and served notice that the war would be protracted and expensive. Carnarvon, now out of office, was told that 'the defeat in S. Africa has extraordinarily shaken the prestige and credit of the Govt.'. Disraeli told the Queen that 'this terrible news from S. Africa . . . will change everything: reduce our continental influence & embarrass our finances'. The Lord Chancellor described Isandlwana as 'the heaviest blow we have sustained since we came into office'. It prevented Britain from intervening in Egypt and raised the possibility that France would do so unilaterally. The Foreign Secretary, Lord Salisbury, explained that France would not intervene if Britain were in a position to do so too: 'But all our force is locked up – Oh! that Bartle Frere! I should like to construct for him a gibbet twice the height of Haman's.'[5]

Isandlwana had a greater effect on the course of South African history. It halted the phase of British territorial expansion that had began with the annexation of Basutoland in 1868. Isandlwana focused the attention of the previously indifferent British public and Parliament upon the war in Zululand. Not only the conduct of the war but its causes came under scrutiny. Journalists and members of Parliament were able to compare the views of Frere and Bulwer in the Blue Books, and some were assisted by the researches of Bishop Colenso. At first there was a tendency to accept the jaundiced picture of Cetshwayo painted by Frere, but the contrast between the latter's violent language and the former's act of sparing Natal when it lay at his mercy produced a reaction. Cetshwayo came to be described in Parliament as 'a gallant Monarch defending his country and his people against one of the most wanton and wicked invasions that ever could be made upon an independent people', and this and other similarly unpatriotic statements do not seem to have produced the outraged reaction one might have expected.[6] 'The fact is,' said Hicks Beach, 'that, unpopular as South African wars have always been in England, there never was one more unpopular than the Zulu war.' The war was seen as not only bloody and expensive but as unjust and unnecessary as well, and the demand arose that it should be ended. The wisdom of the old policy of the Conventions was increasingly praised. In the circumstances an annexation of Zululand was politically impossible. Frere was instructed in March not to make any Zulu settlement without the prior approval of the government, and a few days later Disraeli virtually assured Parliament that there would be no annexation. Hicks Beach told Frere (in connection with the Transkeian territories) that he could 'hardly imagine the reluctance to agree to anything that could by any possibility be twisted into a charge of extension of territory in South Africa'.[7]

Zululand could not be annexed. But the Cabinet did not know what to do instead. There was a widespread feeling that Britain's military honour and reputation had to be retrieved, and that the Zulu army, which even Colenso was prepared to acknowledge was a potential threat to Natal,[8] could not be allowed to remain in being. But how to dissolve the Zulu army without annexing Zululand seemed an insoluble problem. The solution eventually arrived at was to send out the imperial superman, Sir Garnet Wolseley, and leave it all to him.[9] His instructions were verbal and of the most general nature; they were summed up by Hicks Beach as: 'Bring peace about as soon as you can: but let it be made on such terms as you believe will last.'[10]

After Isandlwana the British invasion of Zululand was suspended for more than four months. The centre column was destroyed, the right-hand column under Pearson was besieged in Eshowe, and the left- hand column under Wood was in an entrenched position at Khambula, from which it was able to do no more than make forays against the Zulu. One of these, on the Hlobane mountain, proved disastrous, with 200 killed on the British side, including nearly 100 regulars. A little earlier a convoy bringing supplies to the camp had been surprised, and 80 had been killed, including 60 regulars. These were minor disasters compared to Isandlwana, but were not the sort of thing that was expected in 'small wars' or what Bismarck called 'England's sporting wars'. The Zulu also suffered serious losses. According to Zulu informants there was 'more crying than rejoicing' after Isandlwana. The attack on the camp at Rorke's Drift later the same day added 600 Zulu deaths to the nearly 1 000 Zulu lives lost at Isandlwana, and, also on the same fateful day, more than 300 Zulu died resisting Colonel Pearson's advance. Encouraged by their success at Hlobane, the Zulu made the mistake of attacking the entrenched camp at Khambula, from which they were beaten off with severe losses, possibly nearly as many as 2 000 losing their lives.[11]

The Zulu were thus ready to endure great losses, but they made no attempt to invade Natal, with the exception of the attack on the Rorke's Drift camp, just across the Mzinyathi. Natal's freedom from invasion was attributed by some to the reverse the Zulu suffered at Rorke's Drift, but this is scarcely credible. It would have been an easy matter for the Zulu forces to have avoided the British army posts and to have made devastating raids upon Natal.[12] The most plausible explanation and the best supported by the evidence, is that Cetshwayo had given orders that the war was to be fought on a strictly defensive basis. The attack on the Rorke's Drift camp was contrary to his orders.[13] Cetshwayo throughout the war sent numerous messengers with pleas for peace, all of whom were either turned away for a variety of reasons or excuses, or else imprisoned on suspicion of being spies.[14] Chelmsford did not want negotiations but an opportunity to restore his military reputation.

Yet he delayed the second attempt at an invasion for months. At the beginning of April he relieved Colonel Pearson and brought his force back from Eshowe to

Natal. Almost two months were then spent in elaborate preparations for the renewed invasion, during which time the war, in the sense of actual fighting, came to a virtual standstill. The major conflict that took place in this period was between Chelmsford and the Natal government, which he blamed for his transport difficulties. Eventually on 1 June 1879 Chelmsford and his army began their second invasion of Zululand. A month later they were in the vicinity of Ulundi, the royal capital. Cetshwayo still made attempts at negotiation and peaceful settlement, but both Chelmsford and the younger Zulu warriors wanted to fight. The ensuing battle of Ulundi took place on 4 July and was a complete victory for the British.

This was the final battle of the war. Whether it was the cause of the war's coming to an end is much more doubtful. It is true that the Zulu had cherished the belief that they could defeat the British if only the latter would come out from their fortifications and fight them in the open, and that the battle of Ulundi, which was fought in an open plain, disabused them of this notion. But to conclude that it was this battle that caused the Zulu to decide that 'they had had enough of war, and wanted peace and the withdrawal of the British so that they could go home and resume the normal course of their lives',[15] is surely to beg a very large question and ignore a very large factor. The Zulu had never wanted war with the British and had never wanted the normal course of their lives disrupted. They fought to keep their land and cattle and to remain free of taxes and forced labour. When the British invaded their country the Zulu naturally assumed that they intended to reduce them to the status of the *amakhafula* of Natal,[16] as indeed they did. Robert Robertson had earlier advised that in the event of an invasion, defections to the British 'would be largely increased if whoever is in command were able to proclaim that no one would be taxed or obliged to work. These two things are the great horror of the Zulus.'[17] Chelmsford proclaimed no such thing. But when Wolseley arrived immediately after the battle of Ulundi he announced that the Zulu would not be brought under British rule and that they would be allowed to keep their land and cattle. It was then that all resistance came to an end. Wolseley required the Zulu to surrender their arms and the royal cattle in their possession; but the young men who were heard to say that 'they never would have fought for Cetshwayo if they had known that this was all the British would have exacted from them',[18] entirely misunderstood the situation. Had they not fought, the British would have exacted a great deal more.

The Zulu chiefs and people were not prepared to carry on a desperate struggle simply for the sake of the monarch or the monarchy. Cetshwayo was progressively isolated as the *izikhulu* made their submissions to Wolseley. He became a fugitive in his own kingdom and was eventually captured on 28 August and deported to Cape Town.[19] In the place of the monarchy, Wolseley appointed 13 chiefs as independent rulers. He required them to agree that they would 'not permit the existence of the Zulu military system', that they would 'make it a rule that all men shall be allowed to marry when they choose', and that they would 'allow and encourage all men . . . to work in Natal or the Transvaal, or elsewhere, for themselves or for hire'.[20] As a means of providing Zululand with good government Wolseley's settlement was a disastrous failure, but it solved the immediate problem of breaking up the Zulu army without annexing Zululand.

Wolseley came out to South Africa not only as Commander-in-Chief, but as Governor of Natal and the Transvaal and as High Commissioner for South East Africa. Frere, though he retained the title of High Commissioner, was virtually relegated to being Governor of the Cape. As the man responsible for what was widely regarded in Britain as an unjust and unnecessary war, Frere came in for devastating attack not only from Liberals but from a great many Conservatives as well. 'The Duke of Wellington calls Sir Bartle Frere "a sniveller",' reported Theophilus Shepstone, who had gone to England in May, and who, as he had done in the Langalibalele affair, miraculously escaped responsibility for the conflict in Natal; 'he says that he talks religion to make his politics go right, and you have no idea what a strong feeling there is in this direction regarding Sir Bartle among some at least of the aristocracy of England'.[21]

The British government censured Frere for not referring the terms of the ultimatum to them before sending it, but it did not recall him. A motion in the House of Commons demanding his recall was defeated, but with a significantly reduced majority. Most of the Cabinet were in favour of his recall, but the Queen, who was a personal friend of Sir Bartle and Lady Frere and conducted a private correspondence with them, was strongly opposed to such a step.[22] Disraeli, whose private opinion was that Frere ought to be impeached, had to use all his magical arts to bring the Cabinet to accept the Faery's wishes.[23] An argument for retaining him was that he had acquired influence with the Cape colonists and so was the man most likely to achieve confederation. The British government still wanted a South African confederation, but not for the expansive reasons of Carnarvon's day. They now wanted it for much the same reason as the Liberals had earlier done, as a means of escaping expense and responsibility.[24]

It would have been better for Frere had he resigned when he was censured. Instead he hung on, hoping to justify himself by achieving confederation: this was to be for him what the battle of Ulundi was for Chelmsford. But the result of this decision was that he died a slow and agonizing political death in public. Wolseley's appointment denied him any control over Natal, Zululand and the Transvaal, which he argued unavailingly was necessary if confederation were to be achieved. He was denied even information, since Wolseley was jealous of any possibility of interference. Wolseley's appointment was temporary, but when he departed, instead of the High Commission being reunited, General Colley was appointed in Wolseley's place, and Frere's relegation to the Cape continued. The Liberal government that came into power in 1880 reduced his salary on account of his diminished duties. Shortly afterwards the Cape Premier failed to persuade his Parliament even to hold a confederation conference. The British government accordingly decided there was no possibility of confederation, and Frere was finally recalled.[25]

Frere felt the humiliation of his treatment very deeply. Had it all come at once he would almost certainly have resigned. Coming in stages, it led him to cling to the dwindling hope that he might yet snatch success from the jaws of failure. He refused throughout to admit that he had done anything wrong. He denied that he had exceeded or acted counter to his instructions.[26] He insisted that the war had been 'forced on us by Cetywayo – begun by him and not by us'. In long and intemperate despatches he defended himself not only against the censure of the British government but against all attacks from whatever quarter. Hicks Beach begged him not to supply his enemies with further ammunition, but to no avail. He believed that his despatches would one day be the means by which he would be exonerated. 'I shall not leave a name to be permanently dishonoured' he told Hicks Beach.[27] He was still defending himself on his death-bed. His last words were: 'Oh, if they would only read "The Further Correspondence"; *they must understand.*'[28]

Frere's calculation that the overthrow of the Zulu kingdom would conciliate the Transvaal Boers proved to be utterly mistaken. The Boers showed very little disposition to support the British against the Zulu; indeed their sympathies seemed to be with their fellow-victims of British imperialism. It was with much difficulty and only after much persuasion that Evelyn Wood, who had commanded a column throughout the war, secured the services of the small number of frontier farmers who fought under Piet Uys. After Isandlwana (where his son George was killed) Shepstone attempted to raise a force of mounted men in the Transvaal. 'But judge of my surprise,' he told another of his sons, 'when I found not only a disinclination to face the Zulus but an open sympathy with their success, and exultation at our defeat!'[29] There are reports of the Zulu attempting to enlist Boer support, as well as of Boers offering their services to the Zulu. It seems virtually certain that there were communications between the Zulu King and the Boer leaders, and that there was an agreement that the Boers would remain neutral. On a number of occasions cattle captured from the Zulu and sold at auction were seized by parties of Boers and returned to the Zulu.[30] By May 1879 many Transvaal frontier farmers had reoccupied their farms, and it was said that this was done by agreement with the Zulu.[31] Wolseley's setting aside of the Border Commission's finding and his award of most of the disputed territory to the Transvaal[32] had no effect on Boer loyalty, and Britain's Zulu War was followed 18 months later by a Boer War.

Another miscalculation concerning the effects of the war was that made by the missionaries. They had hoped that the overthrow of Cetshwayo would be the dawn of a brighter future for mission work. Instead they found themselves worse off. 'Grants of land by former Kings to Missionaries cannot be recognized by the British Government', stated a notice in the Natal Government Gazette. When missionaries attempted to resume the occupation of their stations they found that they were theirs no longer. They were now the property of the 13 chiefs, who were not obliged to allow the missionaries back. Some, notably John Dunn, whose territory contained more than half the stations in Zululand, decided to exclude them. Righteous indignation on the part of the missionaries and their supporters was as unavailing as their appeals to the legitimacy of the grants by the King whom they had tried so hard to overthrow. Eventually Dunn relented and allowed some of the missionaries back. Even so, there were fewer stations in operation in the 1880s than there had been before the war.[33]

But the real losers were of course the Zulu people. Their heroic defence of their country and their restraint in sparing Natal won them only a reprieve. The reaction in Britain made it politically impossible to annex their country, and so they retained their land – but only temporarily. They lost the political unity and stability which some of them perhaps had not previously valued as highly as they later came to when they saw the effects of its absence. Even in its own terms Wolseley's settlement was a botched job. Chiefs found a large proportion of their people in other chiefs' territories. Some of the most powerful and influential chiefs were not granted territories at all. Conflicts inevitably broke out, many of them between those prepared to collaborate with new ways and those loyal to the old. A strong movement developed among the latter for the restoration of Cetshwayo. This struck a responsive chord in the new Liberal government in Britain, which felt guilty and embarrassed about the continued exile of the Zulu King. Since Wolseley's settlement had clearly broken down, the British government decided to restore Cetshwayo. But Natal's colonists and officials were strongly opposed to his return. They feared a revival of Zulu military power, and, as Shepstone wrote to Frere, Cetshwayo was 'the representative of the sentiment and of all those that cherish it in South Africa which is opposed to civilization, Christianity and progress and cannot help occupying that position'.[34] Natal's officials also felt a sense of obligation to the anti-monarchist party which had collaborated with the colonial regime. They therefore saw to it that when Cetshwayo was restored in 1883, he was restored to only a portion of his former kingdom. This was a cause of great dissatisfaction to him and his followers, and gave his Zulu enemies a power base from which to operate. A civil war ensued, and Cetshwayo became a fugitive once again. He died, in somewhat mysterious circumstances, in 1884. His son and heir, Dinizulu, resorted to the desperate expedient of calling in the Transvaal Boers against his Zulu enemies. The latter were defeated, but the Boers seized most of Zululand as their reward. The British then stepped in to prevent the Boers gaining independent access to the sea, and they reduced the size of the territory the Boers had taken, annexing the rest of the country themselves. In 1897 this remnant was added to Natal, which had received 'responsible' (that is, settler) government in 1893. In 1905, 40 percent of this remnant was sold to white farmers. In this way the Zulu kingdom was reduced to the fragmented, eroded, impoverished, labour reservoir that came to be known as 'Kwazulu', north of the Thukela.[35]

Conclusion: The Origins of the War

The most immediate causes of the Anglo-Zulu war of 1879 were Sir Bartle Frere's determination that there should be a war and his ability to bring it about. The opposition of the British and Natal governments, which Frere had to defy or overcome to bring about the war he wanted, and the lukewarmness of the local colonists, shows that the will of this individual was an important cause of the war.

But it cannot be a complete explanation. Even the most headstrong and powerful individuals operate in a context, and it must be asked why Frere was so determined on war. Again, there is a simple explanation: to achieve confederation. Frere was no run-of-the-mill High Commissioner on a routine posting; he was, as we have seen in chapter eight, a 'statesman' entrusted with a special task, a task which chimed perfectly with his imperial vision, and which he was determined to carry out. Frere soon came to see the Zulu kingdom as the principal obstacle in his way. The Cape Colony was the biggest and richest state in South Africa and would bear the greatest share of the burden of defence; it would therefore not confederate until the Zulu danger was removed. Preventing the Transvaal from rebelling was a more urgent matter. It had been annexed to facilitate confederation, and Frere believed the Boers would become reconciled to the British flag if the undertaking to protect its borders against the Zulu and other Africans was fulfilled. But this required the findings of the Border Commission to be nullified, and this could only be done by overthrowing the independent Zulu kingdom.

Frere himself would have indignantly rejected the motives attributed to him in the previous paragraph. He could not have admitted even to himself that he wished to wage war upon an independent people, inevitably killing many of them, in order to achieve a political ambition. He had to believe that the war was necessary for self-defence, or for the good of the Zulu people, or that it was inevitable in any case; or preferably all three.

The Zulu kingdom was founded by the great warrior Shaka and had a history of conquests and raids upon its neighbours. The very nature of the state, with what was described as its large 'standing army', seemed to Frere to be predicated upon war. Natal's long freedom from invasion, Frere and his supporters believed, was simply the result of the Zulu ruler's need to have Natal's support against the Transvaal, or his policy of 'playing off' the one against the other as it was often described. When the Boers demonstrated their weakness against Sekhukhune the situation changed and Natal's exemption from the danger of invasion ended. Cetshwayo's aggressive intentions appeared to be demonstrated by numerous circumstances. There was his explicit desire to 'wash his spears', and his defiant message to the Lieutenant-Governor of Natal in November 1876 which served notice that he would no longer heed the latter's pacific counsels. His impis became a menace to the Transvaal, reaching such a pinnacle of peril in April 1877 that it became necessary to bring it under British protection. Then came the belligerent behaviour of his representatives towards Shepstone when the latter attempted to settle the border dispute with them in October 1877, the subsequent Zulu seizure of much of the territory in dispute, and the driving away of the frontier farmers. The murderous raids of Mbelini and Sihayo's sons Frere described as 'trying it on', trial runs for the inevitable onslaught to follow.

These events could be interpreted very differently, as I have tried to show. Bishop Colenso interpreted them very differently, and when the events of the Anglo-Zulu war showed beyond doubt that Cetshwayo had no aggressive intentions towards Natal, Colenso's skilfully disseminated interpretation came to prevail in Britain. But before the event it was possible for Frere to justify the invasion of Zululand as a pre-emptive strike against an otherwise inevitable attack. In this sense, the events alluded to in the previous paragraph can be included among the causes of the Anglo-Zulu war.

A pre-emptive strike against an otherwise inevitable attack was justified as essentially defensive. Frere, Shepstone and others believed that Cetshwayo was the leader of an inter-tribal conspiracy to drive out the white man. In this sense too the invasion of Zululand could be represented as essentially defensive, and such a representation facilitated the invasion.

It is most unlikely that Cetshwayo was the leader of any such inter-tribal conspiracy. It is, however, true that he possessed great prestige among Africans throughout South Africa as the ruler of the most powerful independent African state. The British believed that their prestige was essential to the maintenance of their position as the paramount power in southern Africa. From the time of Shepstone's confrontation with the Zulu on the frontier in October 1877 the destruction of Zulu prestige came to be widely seen as essential to the maintenance of British prestige and power. This was certainly Shepstone's view, and even Bulwer acknowledged that the British army assembled in Natal could not simply be withdrawn without the submission of Cetshwayo.

Cetshwayo was widely believed to be a cruel tyrant practising atrocities upon his people. We have seen the role of missionaries in propagating this belief and the reasons why they did so. Their propaganda found willing believers since it conformed to white expectations concerning savages in general and Zulu Kings in particular. It also seemed plausible to many, of course, because it justified the intervention that was desired for other reasons. The invasion of Zululand, it was said, was not directed against the Zulu people but against the Zulu King; it was essentially an act of benevolence towards the Zulu people, being intended among other things to free them from tyranny. It was this sort of argument that enabled Bulwer to sign the ultimatum. By the time he realized its hollowness it was too late.

The supposed cruelties of Cetshwayo facilitated the invasion in another way. It was widely assumed that most of the Zulu people would welcome the overthrow of their tyrannical ruler, and that resistance to the invading army of liberation would be slight. Shepstone, supposedly the great authority on the subject, held that the Zulu kingdom would disintegrate when touched. Chelmsford did little to prepare the camp at Isandlwana against attack but made extensive preparations for the reception of the 'considerable exodus of Zulus from their country', which he believed would follow an invasion since 'every reliable account received from that country shows conclusively that Cetewayo is most unpopular' and 'that an internal revolution is not only possible but probable'.[36] Frere believed the short, inexpensive and successful war he confidently expected would cause his acting without instructions to be overlooked. Such a war and the reasons for it would have attracted little interest or attention in Britain. Had Frere known that the war would be a disaster and would destroy his reputation he would surely have acted differently. His belief, supported as it was by the best authorities, that the Zulu people hated their King and that only a limited and short war would be necessary to overthrow him, encouraged him to force on the war.

The Zulu King, it was held, not only subjected his people to cruelties but kept them in barbarism. He was described by Shepstone as the enemy of civilization, Christianity and progress. Shepstone was entrusted with the restoration of Cetshwayo in 1883, and his report on the occasion was a scarcely veiled attack on the British government for having restored him. He emphasized the improvement in the condition of the Zulu people since the ending of Cetshwayo's rule – the freedom from military service, the freedom to marry, the freedom from fear, the adoption of European clothing and 'the facilities for their young men earning money by labour in the Colony', which they spoke of 'as a new and great privilege, and such it undoubtedly was'. Shepstone expressed anxiety lest 'we should blight all these new-born aspirations in the minds of, in many respects, a noble people, and thrust them back into the barbarism from which they were just beginning to emerge'.[37] The idea that the overthrow of Cetshwayo was the means of rescuing the Zulu people from barbarism surely helped to justify and thus facilitate the invasion of Zululand.

But justification and facilitation are not the same thing as motivation. It seems unlikely that the desire to benefit the Zulu people was an important part, or any part at all, of the motivating force behind the invasion. All the evidence suggests that Frere was determined to get rid of the Zulu kingdom as an obstacle to confederation. This raises the question of the purposes of the policy of confederation. I have concluded in chapter four that its purposes were to extend the territory under the British flag (in the form of a self-governing dominion) in order to exclude foreign powers, to achieve a greater degree of control over the black population and to promote economic development. The first and second of these implied bringing Zululand under British rule, and this was made explicit in a number of statements by members of the Colonial Office.[38] The confederation policy required the annexation of Zululand, not simply to remove a political obstacle to its achievement, but because it was an essential part of the policy itself.

What of the promotion of economic development? To return to the question posed in the introduction: was the Zulu kingdom invaded to facilitate the advance of capitalist production in South Africa? In an indirect sense, the answer is certainly yes. The economic development envisaged as following confederation was certainly of a capitalist nature, not peasant and artisan production, and the Zulu kingdom was an obstacle to the achievement of confederation. It might be argued, however, that in a more direct sense, too, the Zulu kingdom was invaded to facilitate capitalist production. It seems clear from the discussions of the 'uniform native policy' Carnarvon wanted, that the working class of the new state was to be drawn from its black population, and it seems equally clear that Shepstone and Frere envisaged such a future for the Zulu people.[39] The passage which is usually quoted in this context is by Shepstone:

> Had Cetywayo's thirty thousand warriors been in time changed to labourers working for wages, Zululand would have been a prosperous peaceful country instead of what it now is, a source of perpetual danger to itself and its neighbours.[40]

Modern preoccupations tend to cause certain words in this passage to attract more attention than others: 'labourers', 'wages' and 'prosperous', rather than 'warriors', 'peaceful' and 'danger'. But Shepstone wrote it during the crisis on the Transvaal-Zulu border caused by the breakdown of his negotiations with the Zulu, and there can be no doubt that it was the danger of war that preoccupied him at that time. Security was, as it had always been, his chief concern, and it might be argued that what appears to be a desire for proletarianization and the advance of capitalist production is really nothing more than his attempt to depict, for rhetorical reasons, and for the benefit of Lord Carnarvon, to whom he was writing, the sort of normal peaceful society (such as that of England) which the artificial military tyranny of the Zulu King made impossible in South East Africa.

One should not, however, attempt to draw too sharp a distinction between security and capitalist production, since the one was dependent on the other. A contemporary supporter of the policy that led to the Anglo-Zulu war made the point clearly. The Zulu kingdom, he wrote, was a 'standing menace to progress and prosperity':

> What good was there in opening up farms, in building houses, or in buying herds, with a not remote prospect of Cetywayo sweeping across the country like a destroying angel, burning, slaying, and pillaging wherever he went? How was capital to be invested, enterprise to be encouraged, with such a cause of terror constantly in the background?[41]

Security, peace, capitalist economic growth, Christianity and the social changes these things entailed, all constituted what might be called a programme and ideology of civilization and progress. One may distinguish between these things and discuss them separately for the purpose of analysis, but they were not separate in the minds of the British in South Africa and in Britain itself in the 1870s. I think we may legitimately conclude that Zululand was invaded to facilitate the advance of civilization in the sense in which the term was used in the nineteenth century, a sense in which capitalist production constituted an integral part of the concept.

In his essay on the absence of a telegraph and the genesis of the Anglo-Zulu war, Colin Webb concluded that 'the fate of the Zulu nation and the lives of thousands of human beings were, in 1878–9, twined into the cable coils that were the power-lines of late Victorian empire'.[42] Had there been a telegraph between Britain and South Africa in 1878 Frere might have been restrained (though Hicks Beach doubted even that); but would it have made any difference to the 'fate of the Zulu nation'? This seems much more doubtful. Doubts arise, apart from anything else, because Frere's critics were just as much imbued as he was with the ideology of progress and civilization. One of the charges they urged most strongly against him was that the war which he forced on, with all the loss of life and suffering that it entailed, was unnecessary to achieve the ends both he and they desired. Lord Blachford held that the Zulu kingdom was decomposing and that had it not been for the unifying effects of Frere's ultimatum it would have dissolved and become British in the natural course of events.[43] John Morley wrote:

> Civilisation would have extended in Zululand in the normal way. The people would have come down to Natal for the railways, and would have been silently influenced by what they saw there. Cetywayo and his chiefs might have been induced to send children down to Natal to school, as we know them to have been disposed to do. A few hundred pounds expended in such ways as those would have done more to extend our influence peacefully than millions of war-money and long trains of Gatlings. Patience, caution, moderation – but before all else patience – these are the keywords of a true policy if, in professing to civilise South Africa, you are not to rebarbarize England.

In the course of explaining the origins of the war Morley alluded to the annexation of the Transvaal, which he stated was as unjustifiable as would be a German annexation of Switzerland. 'Where is the difference? The Transvaal government was a government of Europeans, and not a kingdom of barbarians.'[44] A similar distinction was drawn by Colenso. He expressed 'cordial assent' to Frere's demand that the Zulu army and marriage system should be disbanded

> as being, though measures of coercion, yet such as a great Christian power had the right and the duty of enforcing upon a neighbouring savage nation like the Zulus, brought into close relations with itself, whose King had been installed at their own request by the representative of the Natal Government, and to whom a signal proof of generosity and good faith had been given in the [border] award.[45]

Only later did Colenso discover the fraudulence of the border award. Had it been what it seemed, he believed 'the desired reforms might have been gradually brought about in Zululand by judicious & peaceful measures on our part, instead of by this frightful war'.[46] He wrote that he had supposed

> that Sir B. Frere, after making a judicious exhibition on our frontier or, if need be in Zululand itself, of the power of England, would have sought, by wise and peaceful measures of negotiation, to bring about gradually the desired improvements in the Military and Marriage Systems of Zululand, in accordance with the principle laid down by himself on another occasion (2079, p. 7) that 'such changes, like all great revolutions, require time and patience to effect peacefully'; and there is every reason for believing that this work, worthy of the English Name, might have been done successfully.[47]

These statements take it for granted that the extension of British control and culture to the Zulu kingdom was desirable, justifiable and inevitable: in Blachford's and Morley's words, 'natural' and 'normal'. They also assume that the desired changes could be achieved without war, by cultural osmosis, patience, negotiation, or at most a show of force. Such statements and their underlying assumptions were the product of an imperial age, when Europe as a whole and Britain in particular was at the height of its military, economic and cultural power and self-confidence.

In a post-imperial age, with the benefit of hindsight, these statements and assumptions seem implausible in the extreme. It is difficult to see them as anything more than the products of over-weening self-confidence and wishful thinking. The Zulu did not go down to Natal 'for the railways' or for any other form of wage labour – they were not permitted to do so by their King. Cetshwayo and his chiefs were entirely opposed to the Christian education (the only form available) of the Zulu people. Cetshwayo could surely never have agreed to the dismantling of the marriage system or the army. These were the two institutions upon which, more than anything else, his power depended. Without the marriage laws, he said, he would be 'a shadow instead a king'.[48] Without the army he would be nothing at all.

Since even Frere's opponents desired changes incompatible with the existence of the Zulu kingdom, and considered that Britain had a right to demand them, it is difficult to see how one can avoid the conclusion that war was inevitable sooner or later. The war that actually took place might have been averted had something occurred to alter its direct political causes – had the telegraph line been completed earlier, or had Frere somehow disappeared from the scene. But the alternative seems to be a later war rather than no war at all. The Zulu had a history of success, of military glory, and of domination. They were not like the Mfengu, failures in traditional terms, who willingly embraced new techniques and ways of life. The Zulu were proud of their history and traditions and of their independence, and would not have been incorporated into a white-ruled state and a capitalist economy and civilization without a struggle.

It took a highly intelligent woman, uninhibited by any fear that her opinions might be taken seriously or have any effect – she described them as 'scarcely worth pen and paper' – to think the unthinkable and ask whether the Zulu needed to be 'civilized' at all. Mrs Colenso wrote:

> John Bull has been taught, it seems, that he is the Israel of this century, that every other of the many families of man on the globe ought to conform to his ideas, obey his laws, pay tribute to Queen Victoria etc. etc. But is it quite certain that the civilisation of Western Europe is good for Eastern Africa?[49]

Once the Zulu kingdom was safely a thing of the past and the practical effects on the Zulu of transforming them from warriors to wage labourers became apparent, there was a growing tendency among whites to wax nostalgic and romantic about the old Zulu order. This is most striking in the novels of Rider Haggard who, though an ardent British imperialist, contrasted the 'bloodstained grandeur' of the old independent Zulu kingdom with the meanness and vulgarity of civilized life.[50] The son of S.M. Samuelson, the Zululand missionary, wrote in 1929 in similar terms, and in very different terms from those of his father's reports of the 1870s:

> The country had, in those days, its natural and romantic beauty, which has since been destroyed by what is termed as 'Civilization'. The human inhabitants of the land, in those days, were the kindly, cheerful, hospitable and friendly Zulus before they were contaminated, and their self-respect and pride destroyed by the seamy side of European and Asiatic civilisation, and before these had taught them selfishness. They were, indeed, more contented and happier than they are now, in spite of the fact that they were sent to their last account without notice or trial. For death was quick in those days, and not made a prolonged torture. Nowadays, all that matters are sugar cane, cotton fields, the Almighty Dollar, commercial wrangling and strikes, all saturated with unlimited selfishness and non-consideration of others.[51]

At the time of the Anglo-Zulu war the conventional contrast was the other way round. In Natal, where the Zulu-speaking people had long been in contact with both missionaries and colonists, they were described, for example, in 1881 as having made 'remarkable progress' in their way of life and in their 'growing disposition to labour for others, and to cultivate the soil for market produce'. But, the same author stated, it was 'otherwise in Zululand': the 'degradation of the people there is complete', as they 'cling tenaciously to their barbarous customs and laws' and 'do not labour, and as a consequence are often in a state of semi-starvation'. 'Let us hope', he concluded, 'that the ploughshare of war that recently passed through the land . . . will yet prove to have been the harbinger of blessings manifold to that degraded people.'[52]

'The ploughshare of war' is a startling phrase, particularly from a writer on Christian missions, contrasting as it does so starkly with the familiar Biblical antithesis. Few expressed themselves so brutally, or perhaps one should say so thoughtlessly. But in a mental climate, and in the conditions that produced it, in which the sword could be equated with the ploughshare, war was all too possible.

Even opponents of the policy that led to the Anglo-Zulu war were inhibited from opposing the forces that led to the policy. The war of 1879 may have been Frere's war, but in the late nineteenth century there were many more impersonal and longer-term forces tending towards war between the British empire and the Zulu kingdom.

Notes

1. Laband and Thompson, *Field Guide*, p. 41.
2. Laband, *Kingdom in Crisis*, pp. 87, 90–1.
3. Martineau, *Life of Frere*, Vol. II, pp. 272–3.
4. KC, Colenso Papers, File 27, KCM 50091, Colenso to Chesson, 26 January 1879; Public Record Office, War Office records, WO 32/7706, copy of telegram from Frere, received 11 February 1879; UWL, Littleton Papers, no.88, Littleton to his mother, 26 January 1879; Natal Blue Book, 1879, p. JJ11; Thompson, 'Zulus are Coming!', and 'Defence of Durban'.
5. *Annual Register for the Year 1879*, p. 13; BL Add Mss 60913, Carnarvon's diary for January–June 1879, entries for 12 April and 18 February; Cabinet Reports, Cab 41, 12/6, Disraeli to Victoria, 11 February 1879; Swartz, *Politics of British Foreign Policy*, pp. 106 and 130.
6. HC Deb, Vol. CCXLIX, col. 973, Anderson, 14 August 1879. See also ibid, cols 150–3, Lawson, 4 August 1879. Sir Wilfrid Lawson stated that everyone agreed the war was wicked and unjust.
7. Hicks Beach to Frere, 28 August 1879, in Worsfold, *Sir Bartle Frere*, p. 297; BPP, C2260, p. 110, no. 16, Hicks Beach to Frere, 20 March 1879; HL Deb, Vol. CCXLIV, cols 1689–1690, Disraeli, 25 March 1879; GRO, PCC/23, Copy, Hicks Beach to Frere, 30 November 1879.
8. See ch. 9, p. 227.
9. Cabinet Reports, Cab 41, 12/15, 16 and 18, Disraeli to Victoria, 11, 19 and 23 May 1879.
10. GRO, PCC/8/1, Hicks Beach to Wolseley, n.d. but 27 May 1879. See also Hove Central Library, Wolseley Papers, SA 1, p. 32, Wolseley to Hicks Beach, 5 September 1879; and HC Deb, Vol. CCXLIX, cols 158–63, Hartington and Hicks Beach, 4 August 1879.
11. CO 959/1, extracts from letter from officer of naval brigade, 27 March 1879, quoting Zulu informants; all estimates of deaths from Laband, *Kingdom in Crisis*, pp. 90–1, 108, 120, 137, 152 and 164–5.
12. Colenso, *Commentary*, p. 466n, quoting military minute signed W. Bellairs, 8 February 1879.
13. KC, Colenso Papers, KCM 50081, Colenso to Chesson, 28 January [1879] citing four black wagon drivers who escaped from Isandlwana; BPP, C2454, p. 88, statement of Sibalo, 1 June 1879; ibid, p. 100, statement of Sihlahla, 3 June 1879; Vijn *Cetshwayo's Dutchman*, p. 31; Natal Archives, J.W. Shepstone Papers, Vol. 10, p. 30, 'Reminiscences of the Past', citing evidence of Zulu who took part in the attack on Rorke's Drift camp, which John Shepstone stated he 'fully believed'.
14. Laband, 'Humbugging the General?', pp. 45–67.
15. Laband, *Kingdom in Crisis*, p. 236.
16. Guy, *Destruction of the Zulu Kingdom*, p. 1; Vijn, *Cetshwayo's Dutchman*, p. 15; GH 1397, Robertson to Bulwer, 16 November 1877; see the statements by Sibalo and Sihlahla cited in fn 13; and see ch. 6, pp. 141 and 152, and ch. 7, p. 160. '*Amakhafula*' was a

derogatory term, probably derived from 'kaffir', used by the Zulu to refer to the Africans of Natal.

17. CO 879/13, African no. 150, p. 29, Robertson to Bulwer, 1 December 1877, encl in no. 23, Bulwer to Carnarvon, 14 January 1878.
18. Laband, *Kingdom in Crisis*, p. 237.
19. Guy, *Destruction of the Zulu Kingdom*, ch. 4; Laband, 'Cohesion'.
20. Theal, *History of South Africa*, Vol. X, pp. 347–8.
21. KC, Shepstone Papers, File 6, KCM 31408/3, Shepstone to [Henrique Shepstone] n.d.
22. Cabinet Reports, Cab 41, 12/10 and 19, Disraeli to Victoria, 8 April and 27 May 1879.
23. Zetland, *Letters of Disraeli*, Vol. II, p. 225; Hicks Beach, *Life of Hicks Beach*, Vol. I, p. 130.
24. Goodfellow, *Great Britain and South African Confederation*, pp. 173–86.
25. Hove Central Library, Wolseley Papers, WA 200, no. 2, Frere to Wolseley, 20 July 1879; Benyon, 'Passing of a Proconsul'.
26. BPP, C2740, p. 40, no. 26, Frere to Kimberley, 30 August 1880.
27. Frere to Hicks Beach, 22 September 1879, in Worsfold, *Sir Bartle Frere*, p. 300.
28. Worsfold, *Sir Bartle Frere*, p. 336.
29. Wood, *Midshipman to Field Marshal*, Vol. II, pp. 14, 22 and 23; SP 71, Shepstone to Offy Shepstone, 6 February 1879.
30. SP 69, pp. 222–3, Shepstone to Frere, 30 January 1879; SP 37, Osborn to Shepstone, 31 January 1879; SP 38, Osborn to Shepstone, 17 February 1879; TA, Letter-book 3, Administrator to High Commissioner, Confid Shepstone to Frere, 2 February 1879; ibid, Private, Shepstone to Wood, 5 February 1879.
31. CO 959/1, Macleod to Littleton, 26 May 1879.
32. BPP, C2482, p. 258, no. 87, Wolseley to Hicks Beach, 3 September 1879.
33. *Natal Government Gazette*, Vol. XXXI, no. 1799, 23 December 1879; Ballard, 'Reproach to Civilisation'; and see the correspondence in UWL, Selected Records of the Archbishop of Cape Town, Aa5.
34. SP 69, p. 68, Shepstone to Frere, 4 June 1880.
35. Wolseley's settlement and the civil war that followed is expertly analysed in Guy, *Destruction of the Zulu Kingdom*.
36. NAM 6807-386-13, no. 1, memo by Thesiger (Chelmsford) 30 October 1878; also in GH 1399 (no. 4051).
37. BPP, C3616, pp. 57–9, Shepstone to Bulwer, 27 February 1883.
38. See ch. 6, pp. 150–1.
39. See ch. 4, pp. 82–4 and 90–3; ch. 7, p. 182; and ch. 8, p. 202.
40. BPP, C2079, p. 55, no. 39, Shepstone to Carnarvon, 5 January 1878; this is quoted in its context in ch. 7, pp. 182–3.
41. Allardyce, 'Zulu War', p. 377.
42. Webb, 'Lines of Power', p. 36.
43. Blachford, 'Causes of the Zulu War'; HL Deb, Vol. CCXLIV, col 1634, Blachford, 25 March 1879.
44. Morley, 'Plain Story', pp. 352 and 330.
45. BPP, C2252, p. 52, Colenso to Frere, 27 December 1878.
46. KC, Colenso Papers, File 16, KCM 49320, Colenso to Ferguson, 13 April 1879.
47. Vijn, *Cetshwayo's Dutchman*, p. xiii, Colenso's editorial comment.
48. Webb and Wright, *Zulu King Speaks*, p. 72.
49. Mrs Colenso to Mrs Lyell, 25 April 1879, in Rees, *Colenso Letters*, p. 343.
50. Martin, 'British Images of the Zulu', pp. 334–6; Etherington, *Rider Haggard*, p. 106.
51. Samuelson, *Long, Long Ago*, p. 9.
52. Young, *Modern Missions*, p. 220–1.

Bibliography

For more detail on sections I and II, see my Ph.D thesis listed below.

I. UNPUBLISHED PRIMARY SOURCES

A. Official Records

(1) Natal Archives, Pietermaritzburg
(i)   Government House: G.H. 57–87, 274–5, 281–3, 596–602, 684, 686, 702, 747, 760, 788–92, 829, 854–6, 1049–54, 1139, 1163–4, 1218–21, 1300, 1325–6, 1351, 1388–9, 1396–1400, 1403, 1406–8, 1410–13, 1419–4, 1540–3, 1552, 1554–5
(ii) Secretary for Native Affairs: S.N.A. I/1/20–32, I/3/23–30, I/4/1–2, I/6/1–3, I/6/6, I/6/11, I/7/3–6, I/7/7–13
(iii) Colonial Secretary's Office: C.S.O. 1925, 2552–3

(2) Transvaal Archives, Pretoria
(i)   Administrator's Records: Letter-books 2, 3 and 6
(ii) Secretary for Native Affairs: S.N. 1, 1A, 5 and 6
(iii) State Secretary/Government Secretary: Incoming Letters: S.S. 19, 37–40, 62, 204–322
(iv) Landdrost of Utrecht: L.U. 13 and 25

(3) Cape Archives, Cape Town
Government House: G.H. 4/1–12, 7/1, 9/56–88, 10/5–6, 11/8–18, 19/11, 20/4

(4) Killie Campbell Africana Library, Durban
K.C., Uncatalogued Ms. 26515

(5) Public Record Office, London
(i)   Colonial Office
      Original Correspondence:
      Cape: C.O. 48/468–489; Griqualand West: C.O. 107/1–6; Natal: C.O. 179/111–132; Transvaal: C.O. 291/1; Supplementary: C.O. 537/124A
      Colonial Office Confidential Print, C.O. 879, African:
      Vol. 7, nos. 65 and 66; Vol. 8, nos. 80 and 81; Vol. 9, nos. 83a, 84, 86, 93, 94, 98, 99; Vol. 10, nos. 102, 103, 104, 105, 107, 108, 109, 110, 112; Vol. 879/11, nos. 121, 123, 125, 129; Vol. 12, nos. 142, 143, 144, 147; Vol. 13, nos. 150, 151, 154; Vol. 14, nos. 161, 162, 164, 165, 166, 167, 168, 169; Vol. 15, nos. 170, 171, 172, 173, 174, 184; Vol. 16, nos. 200, 203, 204; Vol. 17, nos. 208, 209, 212, 217
(ii) Foreign Office
      F.O. 63/1039, 541/20, 541/23A
(iii) War Office
      W.O. 32/7698–7708, 7717, 7740, 7745, 7747–9, 7752–3, 7762–3, 7773

(iv) Cabinet
Cab. 41, 3–14

B. Private Papers

(1) Natal Archives, Pietermaritzburg
(i) Theophilus Shepstone Papers: Vols. 3, 14–48, 67–9, and miscellaneous papers formerly in Vols. 22, 23 and 25 before rearrangement
(ii) H.C. Shepstone Papers: Vols. 1–3, 6–12
(iii) J.W. Shepstone Papers: Vols. 5–10
(iv) Colenso Papers: Vols. 1–3

(2) Transvaal Archives, Pretoria
(i) Engelbrecht Collection (Burgers Papers): Vol. 4
(ii) Lanyon Papers: Vol. 1

(3) Killie Campbell Africana Library, Durban
(i) Colenso Papers: Files 5, 7, 9, 11, 13, 16, 22, 25–9
(ii) Shepstone Papers: Files 1 and 6
(iii) Stuart Papers: Files 9, 19 and 58
(iv) Southey Paper: Files 2 and 7
(v) Lugg Papers: File 2
(vi) Dunn Papers
(vii) Fynn Papers
(viii) G.C. Cato Papers
(ix) Uncatalogued Mss

(4) University of the Witwatersrand Library, Johannesburg
(i) A. 721, Littleton Papers
(ii) A. 639, Diary of S.O. Samuelson
(iii) A. 55, Reminiscences of R.T.N. James

(5) South African Library, Cape Town
MSB 197, Bartle Frere Papers

(6) Public Record Office, London
(i) P.R.O. 30/6, Carnarvon Papers: Vols. 1–3, 5, 7–8, 10–12, 23, 32–4, 38, 43, 45, 47, 48–9, 52, 84
(ii) W.O. 132/1 & 2, Buller Papers
(iii) C.O. 959/1, Private Correspondence of Sir Bartle Frere

(7) British Library
(i) Carnarvon Mss: 60757, 60763–5, 60769, 60776, 60791–4, 60796–8, 60799A, 60805A, 60811, 60854, 60906–60917
(ii) Molteno Mss: 39299

(8) National Army Museum, London
(i) Chelmsford Papers: Papers *re* Anglo-Zulu War, 1878–1879: 6807-386: 6, 7–10, 12–14, 16, 21, 23, 27, 29, 32–3
(ii) Chelmsford Papers: Correspondence with Pearson: 6810–38

(9)   Gloucestershire Records Office, Gloucester
St Aldwyn (Hicks Beach) Papers: PCC 1–5, 8, 11, 13, 22–4, 35, 43, 75, 92

(10) Hove Central Library
Wolseley Papers: WA, NAT 1, SA 1–2

(11) Norfolk Record Office, Norwich
Bulwer Papers

C. Institutional Records

(1)   **United Society for the Propagation of the Gospel, London:** D. 38, 42, 44, 46, 48, 50; E. 25–35; Wigram Papers

(2)   **University of the Witwatersrand Library, Johannesburg:** Selected Records of the Archbishop of Cape Town, Aa5, Ab3, Ba3

(3)   **Standard Bank Archives, Johannesburg:** G.M.O. 3/1/5–7, J.A.H. 6/2/1

II. PUBLISHED SERIAL PRIMARY SOURCES

A. Official

(1)   **British Parliamentary Papers:**
412, C.1121, C.1137, C.1187, C.1244, C.1361, C.1399, C.1401-1, C.1631, C.1681, C.1732, C.1748, C.1776, C.1814, C.1883, C.1961, C.1980, C.2000, C.2079, C.2100, C.2128, C.2144, C.2220, C.2222, C.2234, C.2242, C.2252, C.2260, C.2269, C.2308, C.2316, C.2318, C.2367, C.2374, C.2454, C.2482, C.2505, C.2584, C.2676, C.2695, C.2740, C.3616

(2)   **British Hansard:** Parliamentary Debates, Vols. CCXIX–CCLIV

(3)   **Natal Blue Books:** 1874–1880

(4)   **Natal Government Gazette:** Vols. XXIV–XXXI

B. Unofficial

The Natal Witness, 1872–1879
The Natal Mercury, 1872–1878
The Natal Colonist, Selected Periods, 1873–1878
The Times of Natal, Selected Periods, 1873–1878
De Volksstem, 1877–1878
The Net Cast in Many Waters, 1873–1878
The Annual Register, 1872–1880

III. BOOKS, ARTICLES, THESES AND PAPERS

For ease of reference, this list includes everything that I have found useful that can be referred to by means of a person's name and a title, without distinguishing between books and articles, published and unpublished works, or primary and secondary sources.

Allardyce, M. 'The Zulu War', *Blackwood's Edinburgh Magazine*, Vol. 125 (March 1879).
Appelgryn, M.S. *Thomas Francois Burgers; Staatspresident 1872–1877* (Pretoria & Cape Town, 1979).
Atcherley, R.J. *A Trip to Boerland* (London, 1879).
Atmore, A., & Marks, S. 'The Imperial Factor in South Africa in the Nineteenth Century: Towards a Reassessment', *The Journal of Imperial and Commonwealth History*, 3 (1974).
Aylward, A. *The Transvaal of Today* (London, 1878).
Ballard, C.C. ' "A Reproach to Civilisation": John Dunn and the Missionaries 1879–1884', *South African Historical Journal*, 11 (November 1979).
Ballard, C.C. 'The Political Transformation of a Transfrontiersman: the Career of John Dunn in Zululand, 1857–1879', *Journal of Imperial and Commonwealth History*, VII, 3 (May 1979).
Ballard, C.C. 'John Dunn and Cetshwayo: the Material Foundations of Political Power in the Zulu Kingdom, 1857–1878', *Journal of African History*, 21 (1980).
Ballard, C.C. 'The Historical Image of King Cetshwayo of Zululand: a Centennial Comment', *Natalia*, 13 (Dec. 1983).
Ballard, C.C. *John Dunn: the White Chief of Zululand* (Johannesburg, 1985).
Beales, D. *From Castlereagh to Gladstone, 1815–1885* (London, 1969).
Benians, E.A., Butler, J., & Carrington, C.E. (eds.) *The Cambridge History of the British Empire, Vol III: the Empire-Commonwealth, 1870–1919* (Cambridge, 1959).
Benyon, J.A. 'Isandhlwana and the Passing of a Proconsul', *Natalia*, 8 (Dec. 1978).
Benyon, J.A. *Proconsul and Paramountcy in South Africa: the High Commission, British Supremacy and the Sub-Continent, 1806–1910* (Pietermaritzburg, 1980).
Benyon, J.A. 'Overlords of Empire? British "Proconsular Imperialism" in Comparative Perspective', *The Journal of Imperial and Commonwealth History*, XIX, 2 (1991).
Binns, C.T. *The Last Zulu King: the Life and Death of Cetshwayo* (London, 1963).
Blachford, Lord. 'The Causes of the Zulu War', *The Nineteenth Century*, V (March 1879).
Blachford, Lord. 'South African Policy', *The Nineteenth Century*, VI (Aug. 1879).
Blakely, B.L. *The Colonial Office 1868–1892* (Durham, 1972).
Bodelson, C.A. *Studies in Mid-Victorian Imperialism* (Copenhagen, 1924, reprinted London, 1960).
Bonner, P. 'Factions and Fissions: Transvaal/Swazi Politics in the Mid-Nineteenth Century', *Journal of African History*, XIX, 2 (1978).
Bonner, P. *Kings, Commoners and Concessionaires: the Evolution and Dissolution of the Nineteenth-Century Swazi State* (Johannesburg, 1983).
Boswell, J. *The Life of Samuel Johnson, 2 Vols.* (London, 1952).
Bourne, K. *The Foreign Policy of Victorian England 1830–1902* (Oxford, 1970).
Brookes, E.H., & Webb, C. de B. *A History of Natal* (Pietermaritzburg, 1965).
Buckle, G.E. (ed.). *Letters of Queen Victoria*, 2nd ser., (3 Vols. London, 1926–8).
Bundy, C. *The Rise and Fall of the South African Peasantry* (London, 1979).
Burman, S. *Chiefdom Politics and Alien Law: Basutoland under Cape Rule, 1871–1884* (Oxford, 1981)
Butler, W.F. *Sir William Butler: an Autobiography* (London, 1911).
Cain, P.J., & Hopkins, A.G. *British Imperialism: Innovation and Expansion 1688–1914* (London, 1993).
Cairnes, J.E. 'Our Defences: a National or a Standing Army', *The Fortnightly Review*, new ser., 9 (1871).
Carnarvon, Lord. 'Army Administration and Government Policy', *The Quarterly Review*, 131 (1871).
Carnarvon, Lord. 'Imperial Administration', *The Fortnightly Review*, new ser., 24 (1878).
Carnarvon, 4th Earl of, (ed. R. Herbert). *Speeches on the Affairs of West Africa and South Africa* (London, 1903).

Chamberlain, M.E. *'Pax Britannica'? British Foreign Policy 1789–1914* (London, 1988).

Child, D. *Charles Smythe, Pioneer, Premier and Administrator* (Cape Town, 1973).

Child, D. (ed.). *Portrait of a Pioneer: the Letters of Sidney Turner from South Africa 1864–1901* (Johannesburg, 1980).

Clammer, D. *The Zulu War* (Newton Abbot, 1973).

Clarke, S. (ed.). *Invasion of Zululand 1879: Anglo-Zulu War Experiences of Arthur Harness; John Jervis, 4th Viscount St. Vincent; and Sir Henry Bulwer* (Johannesburg, 1979).

Colenbrander, P.J. 'Warriors, Women, Land and Livestock: Cetshwayo's Kingdom under Stress?', unpublished seminar paper, 1977.

Colenbrander, P.J. 'The Zulu Political Economy on the Eve of the War', in A. Duminy & C. Ballard (eds) *The Anglo-Zulu War: New Perspectives* (Pietermaritzburg, 1981).

Colenso, F.E., & Durnford, E. *History of the Zulu War and its Origin* (2nd ed., London, 1881).

Colenso, J.W. *Ten Weeks in Natal: a Journal of a First Tour of Visitation among the Colonists and Zulu Kafirs of Natal* (Cambridge, 1855).

Colenso, J.W. *Bishop Colenso's Commentary on Frere's Policy* (Bishopstowe, n.d., in Killie Campbell Africana Library).

Cope, A.T. 'The Zulu War in Zulu Perspective', *Theoria*, 56 (May, 1981).

Cope, N.L.G. 'The Defection of Hamu', unpublished B.A. Hons dissertation, University of Natal, 1980.

Cope, R.L. 'Shepstone and Cetshwayo, 1873–1879', unpublished M.A. dissertation, University of Natal, 1967.

Cope, R.L. 'Shepstone, the Zulus, and the Annexation of the Transvaal', *South African Historical Journal*, 4 (Nov. 1972).

Cope, R.L. 'Christian Missions and Independent African Chiefdoms in South Africa in the 19th Century', *Theoria*, 52 (May 1979).

Cope, R.L. 'Political Power within the Zulu Kingdom and the "Coronation Laws" of 1873', *Journal of Natal and Zulu History*, VIII (1985).

Cope, R.L. 'Strategic and Socio-economic Explanations for Carnarvon's South African Confederation Policy: the Historiography and the Evidence', *History in Africa*, 13 (1986).

Cope, R.L. 'Local Imperatives and Imperial Policy: the Sources of Lord Carnarvon's South African Confederation Policy', *International Journal of African Historical Studies*, 20, 4 (1987).

Cope, R.L. 'C.W. De Kiewiet, the Imperial factor, and South African "Native Policy" ', *Journal of Southern African Studies*, 15, 3 (April 1989).

Cope, R.L. 'Written in Characters of Blood? The Reign of King Cetshwayo Ka Mpande 1873–1879', *Journal of African History*, 36, 1 (1995).

Cope, R.L. 'The Origins of the Anglo-Zulu War of 1879', unpublished Ph.D thesis, University of the Witwatersrand, 1995.

Coupland, R. *Zulu Battle Piece: Isandhlwana* (London, 1948).

Cox, G.W. *The Life of John William Colenso, D.D., Bishop of Natal*, 2 Vols. (London, 1888).

Cunynghame, A.T. *My Command in South Africa, 1874–1878* (London, 1879).

Currie, D. 'Thoughts Upon the Present and Future of South Africa, and Central and Eastern Africa', *Proceedings of the Royal Colonial Institute*, 8 (1877).

De Kiewiet, C.W. *British Colonial Policy and the South African Republics* (London, 1929).

De Kiewiet, C.W. *The Imperial Factor in South Africa: a Study in Politics and Economics* (Cambridge 1937, reprinted London, 1965).

Delius, P.N. *The Land Belongs to Us: the Pedi Polity, the Boers and the British in the Nineteenth-century Transvaal* (Johannesburg, 1983).

Dlamini, P. (comp. H. Filter, ed. & trans. S. Bourquin). *Paulina Dlamini, Servant of Two Kings* (Durban & Pietermaritzburg, 1986).

Dominy, G. ' "Frere's War"?: a Reconstruction of the Geopolitics of the Anglo-Zulu War of 1879', *Natal Museum Journal of Humanities*, 5 (Oct. 1993).

Drooglever, R.W.F. 'A Figure of Controversy: Colonel Anthony Durnford in Natal and Zululand, 1873–1879' (unpublished D. Litt et Phil. thesis, University of South Africa, 1982).

Duminy, A., & Ballard, C. (eds). *The Anglo-Zulu War: New Perspectives* (Pietermaritzburg, 1981).

Duminy, A., & Ballard, C. (eds). *Natal and Zululand from Earliest Times to 1910: a New History* (Pietermaritzburg, 1989).

Dunn, J. (ed. D.C.F. Moodie). *John Dunn, Cetywayo and the Three Generals* (Pietermaritzburg, 1886).

Durnford, E. *A Soldier's Life and Work in South Africa 1872 to 1879* (London, 1882).

Duthie, J.L. 'Some Further Insights into the Working of Mid-Victorian Imperialism: Lord Salisbury, the "Forward" Group and Anglo-Afghan Relations 1874–1878', *Journal of Imperial and Commonwealth History*, 8, 3 (May 1980).

Eldridge, C.C. *England's Mission: the Imperial Idea in the Age of Gladstone and Disraeli 1868–1880* (London, 1973).

Eldridge, C.C. (ed.). *British Imperialism in the Nineteenth Century 1815–1914* (London, 1984).

Emery, F.V. ' "South Africa's Best Friend": Sir Bartle Frere at the Cape, 1877–80', *Theoria*, 63 (Oct. 1984).

Emery, F.V. 'Geography and Imperialism: the Role of Sir Bartle Frere (1815–84)', *The Geographical Journal*, 150, 3 (Nov. 1984).

Engelbrecht, S.F. *Thomas Francois Burgers: a Biography* (Pretoria, 1946).

Etherington, N.A. 'The Origins of "Indirect Rule" in 19th Century Natal', *Theoria*, 47 (Oct. 1976).

Etherington, N.A. *Preachers, Peasants and Politics in Southern Africa, 1835–1880* (London, 1978).

Etherington, N.A. 'Labour Supply and the Genesis of South African Confederation in the 1870s', *Journal of African History*, 20 (1979).

Etherington, N.A. 'Frederic Elton and the South African Factor in the Making of Britain's East African Empire', *Journal of Imperial and Commonwealth History*, IX (1981).

Etherington, N.A. 'Anglo-Zulu Relations, 1856–78', in A. Duminy & C. Ballard (eds) *The Anglo-Zulu War: New Perspectives* (Pietermaritzburg, 1981).

Etherington, N.A. *Rider Haggard* (Boston, 1984).

Etherington, N.A. 'Natal's Black Rape Scare of the 1870s', *Journal of Southern African Studies*, 15, 1 (Oct. 1988).

Etherington, N.A. 'The "Shepstone System" in the Colony of Natal and Beyond the Borders', in A. Duminy & C. Ballard (eds) *Natal and Zululand from Earliest Times to 1910: a New History* (Pietermaritzburg, 1989).

French, G. *Lord Chelmsford and the Zulu War* (London, 1939).

Frere, H.B.E. 'Zanzibar a Commercial Power', *Macmillans Magazine*, 32 (July 1875).

Frere, H.B.E. 'The Native Races of South Africa', *The Transactions of the South African Philosophical Society*, I (1877–80) p.xii.

Frere, H.B.E. *The Union of the Various Portions of British South Africa* (London, 1881).

Frere, H.B.E. *Afghanistan and South Africa: a Letter to the Right Hon. W.E. Gladstone . . . regarding Portions of his Midlothian Speeches* (London, 1881).

Frere, H.B.E. 'On the Future of Zululand and South Africa', *The Fortnightly Review*, 32 (Nov. 1882).

Froude, J.A. *Short Studies on Great Subjects*, Vols. II & III (London, 1874 & 1877).

Froude, J.A. *Two Lectures on South Africa* (London, 1900).

Furneaux, R. *The Zulu War: Isandlwana and Rorke's Drift* (London, 1963).

Fuze, M. M. (trans. H.C. Lugg, ed. A.T. Cope) *The Black People and Whence They Came: a Zulu View* (Pietermaritzburg & Durban, 1979).

Fynney, F.B. *The Zulu Army and the Zulu Headmen* (Pietermaritzburg, 1879).

Gallagher, J., & Robinson, R. 'The Imperialism of Free Trade', *Economic History Review*, 2nd ser., VI (1953).

Gellner, E. *Nations and Nationalism*, (Oxford, 1983).

Gibson, J.Y. *The Story of the Zulus* (London, 1911, repr. New York, 1970).

Giliomee, H. 'Processes in the Development of the South African Frontier', in H. Lamar & L.M. Thompson (eds) *The Frontier in History* (New Haven, 1981).

Goodfellow, C.F. *Great Britain and South African Confederation, 1870–1881* (Cape Town, 1966).

Gordon, C.T. 'Frere and the Zulu War of 1879', unpublished B.A. Hons dissertation, University of the Witwatersrand, n.d. [1953].

Gordon, R.E. *Shepstone: the Role of the Family in the History of South Africa, 1820–1900* (Cape Town, 1968).

Guest, W.R. *Langalibalele: the Crisis in Natal, 1873–1875* (Durban, 1976).

Gump, J.O. *The Dust Rose Like Smoke; the Subjugation of the Zulu and the Sioux* (Lincoln & London, 1994).

Guy, J. 'A Note on Firearms in the Zulu Kingdom with Special Reference to the Anglo-Zulu War, 1879', *Journal of African History*, XII, 4 (1971).

Guy, J. *The Destruction of the Zulu Kingdom: the Civil War in Zululand, 1879–1884* (London, 1979).

Guy, J. 'The British Invasion of Zululand: Some Thoughts for the Centenary Year', *Reality: a Journal of Liberal and Radical Opinion*, II, 1 (Jan. 1979).

Guy, J. 'Cetshwayo kaMpande, c.1832–84', in C. Saunders (ed.) *Black Leaders in Southern African History* (London, 1979).

Guy, J. 'Ecological Factors in the Rise of Shaka and the Zulu Kingdom', in S. Marks & A. Atmore (eds) *Economy and Society in Pre-industrial South Africa* (London, 1980).

Guy, J. *The Heretic: a Study of the Life of John William Colenso, 1814–1883* (Pietermaritzburg & Johannesburg, 1983).

Haggard, H.R. *Cetywayo and his White Neighbours* (London, 1882).

Haggard, H.R. *The Days of My Life: an Autobiography* (London, 1926).

Hall, M. *Settlement Patterns in the Iron Age in Zululand: an Ecological Interpretation* (Oxford, 1981).

Hammond-Tooke, W.D. (ed.). *The Bantu-Speaking Peoples of Southern Africa* (London, 1980).

Hardinge, A. (ed. Lady Carnarvon). *The Life of Henry Howard Molyneux Herbert, Fourth Earl of Carnarvon 1831–1890*, 3 Vols. (Oxford, 1925).

Harries, P. 'Plantations, Passes and Proletarians: Labour and the Colonial State in Nineteenth Century Natal', *Journal of Southern African Studies*, 13, 3 (1987).

Harrison, F. 'The Effacement of England', *The Fortnightly Review*, new ser., 9 (1871).

Headlam, C. 'The Failure of Confederation, 1871–1881', in E.A. Walker (ed.) *The Cambridge History of the British Empire*, Vol. VIII (London, 1936).

Hernaes, P. 'The Zulu Kingdom, Norwegian Missionaries, and British Imperialism 1845-1879' in J. Simensen (ed.) *Norwegian Missions in African History*, Vol. 1, *South Africa 1845–1906* (Oslo, 1986).

Hicks Beach, V. *Life of Sir Michael Hicks Beach (Earl St. Aldwyn)*, 2 Vols. (London, 1932).

Hoskins, H.L. 'British Policy in Africa, 1873–1877', *Geographical Review*, XXXII (1942).

Hynes, W.G. *The Economics of Empire: Britain, Africa and the New Imperialism 1870–1895* (London, 1979).

Jeppe, F. *Transvaal Book Almanac and Directory for 1877* (Pietermaritzburg, 1877).

Kennedy, P.A. 'The Fatal Diplomacy: Sir Theophilus Shepstone and the Zulu Kings, 1839–1879', unpublished Ph.D thesis, University of California, Los Angeles, 1976 (University Microfilms International, Ann Arbor, 1978).

Kennedy, P. *The Rise of Anglo-German Antagonism 1860–1914* (London, 1980).

Kennedy, P. 'Continuity and Discontinuity in British Imperialism 1815–1914' in C.C. Eldridge (ed.) *British Imperialism in the Nineteenth Century 1815–1914* (London, 1984).

Kimberley, Lord (ed. E. Drus). 'Journal of Events during the Gladstone Ministry 1868–1874', *Camden Miscellany*, 3rd ser., XC (1958) 4.

Knatchbull-Hugessen, E. 'South Africa and her Diamond Fields', *The Edinburgh Review*, 134 (1871).

Knight, I. *Brave Men's Blood: the Epic of the Zulu War, 1879* (London, 1990).

Laband, J. 'The Cohesion of the Zulu Polity under the Impact of the Anglo-Zulu War: a Reassessment', *Journal of Natal and Zulu History*, VIII (1985).

Laband, J. 'Humbugging the General? King Cetshwayo's Peace Overtures during the Anglo-Zulu War', in J. Laband & P. Thompson, *Kingdom and Colony at War: Sixteen Studies on the Anglo-Zulu War of 1879* (Pietermaritzburg & Cape Town, 1990).

Laband, J. *Kingdom in Crisis: the Zulu Response to the British invasion of 1879* (Pietermaritzburg, 1992).

Laband, J. *Rope of Sand: the Rise and Fall of the Zulu Kingdom in the Nineteenth Century* (Johannesburg, 1995).

Laband, J.P.C., & Thompson, P.S. *A Field Guide to the War in Zululand 1879* (Pietermaritzburg, 1979).

Laband, J., & Thompson, P. *Kingdom and Colony at War: Sixteen Studies on the Anglo-Zulu War of 1879* (Pietermaritzburg & Cape Town, 1990).

Laband, J., & Wright, J. *King Cetshwayo kaMpande (c.1832–1884)* (Pietermaritzburg & Ulundi, 1980).

Lamar, H., & Thompson, L.M. (eds) *The Frontier in History: North America and Southern Africa Compared* (New Haven and London, 1981).

Le Cordeur, B.A. 'The Relations between the Cape and Natal, 1846–1879', *Archives Year Book for South African History*, 1965, Vol. I (Cape Town, 1965).

Lewsen, P.L. 'The First Crisis of Responsible Government in the Cape Colony', *Archives Year Book for South African History*, 1942, Vol. II (Cape Town, 1942).

Lewsen, P. (ed.). *Selections from the Correspondence of J.X. Merriman 1870–1890* (Cape Town, 1960).

Lewsen, P.L. *John X. Merriman: Paradoxical South African Statesman* (Johannesburg, 1982).

Leyds, W.J. *The First Annexation of the Transvaal* (London, 1906).

Lloyd, A. *The Zulu War, 1879* (London, 1973).

Lovell, R.I. *The Struggle for South Africa 1875–1899: a Study in Economic Imperialism* (New York, 1934).

Lucas, T.J. *The Zulus and the British Frontiers* (London, 1879).

Ludlow, J.M. 'The Reconstitution of England', *The Contemporary Review*, 16 (1871).

McGill, D.C. 'A History of the Transvaal (1853–1864) with a New Interpretation of the Transvaal-Zulu Relations which Culminated in the Zulu War of 1879' (unpublished Ph.D. thesis, University of Cape Town, 1943).

McIntyre, W.D. *The Imperial Factor in the Tropics 1865–1875* (London, 1967).

Mackenzie, A. (ed.). *Mission Life among the Zulu-Kafirs: Memorials of Henrietta Robertson, Wife of the Rev. R. Robertson* (Cambridge, 1866).

Macmillan, W.M. *The Cape Colour Question: a Historical Survey* (London, 1927).

Macmillan, W.M. *Bantu, Boer and Briton: the Making of the South African Native Problem* (London, 1929).

Macmillan, M. *Sir Henry Barkly* (Cape Town, 1970).

Mael, R. 'The Problem of Political Integration in the Zulu Empire' unpublished Ph.D. thesis, University of California, Los Angeles, 1974 (University Microfilms International, Ann Arbor, 1978).

Magema Magwaza [Fuze]. 'A Visit to King Ketshwayo', *Macmillan's Magazine*, XXXVII (1878).

Marinden, G.E. (ed.). *Letters of Lord Blachford, Under-Secretary of State for the Colonies 1860–1871* (London, 1896).

Marks, S. 'Southern Africa, 1867–1886', in R. Oliver & G.N. Sanderson (eds.) *The Cambridge History of Africa, Volume 6, from 1870 to 1905* (Cambridge 1985).

Marks S., & Atmore, A. (eds). *Economy and Society in Pre-industrial South Africa* (London, 1980).

Martin, S.J.R. 'British Images of the Zulu, c.1820–1879', unpublished Ph.D. thesis, Cambridge, 1982.

Martineau, J. *The Life and Correspondence of Sir Bartle Frere*, 2 Vols. (London, 1895).

Maurice, F., & Arthur, G. *The Life of Lord Wolseley* (London, 1924).

Molteno, P.A. *The Life and Times of Sir John Charles Molteno*, 2 Vols. (London, 1900).

Monteith, M.A. 'Cetshwayo and Sekhukhune, 1875–1879', unpublished M.A. dissertation, University of the Witwatersrand, 1978.

Monypenny, W.F., & Buckle, G.E. *The Life of Benjamin Disraeli, Earl of Beaconsfield*, 6 Vols. (London, 1920).

Moodie, D.C.F. *The History of the Battles and Adventures of the British, the Boers, and the Zulus*, 2 Vols. (Cape Town, 1888).

Moodie, G.P. 'The Population, Prospects, and Future Government of the Transvaal', *Journal of the Royal United Service Institution*, XXII (1879).

Morley, J. 'The Plain Story of the Zulu War', *The Fortnightly Review*, XXV, new ser. (1 March 1879).

Morris, D.R. *The Washing of the Spears* (London, 1968).

Munro, J.F. *Africa and the International Economy 1800–1960* (London, 1976).

Newitt, M.D.D. *Portuguese Settlement on the Zambesi: Exploration, Land Tenure and Colonial Rule in East Africa* (London, 1973).

Nourse, G.B. 'The Zulu Invasion Scare of 1861' (unpublished M.A. dissertation, University of Natal, 1949).

Oliver, R., & Sanderson, G.N. (ed.). *The Cambridge History of Africa, Volume 6, from 1870 to 1905* (Cambridge, 1985).

Parr, H.H. *A Sketch of the Kafir and Zulu Wars: Guadana to Isandhlwana* (London, 1880).

Peires, J.B. 'Paradigm Deleted: the Materialist Interpretation of the Mfecane', *Journal of Southern African Studies*, 19, 2 (June 1993).

Preston, A. (ed.). *The South African Diaries of Sir Garnet Wolseley, 1875* (Cape Town, 1971).

Preston, A. (ed.). *Sir Garnet Wolseley's South African Journal, 1879–80* (Cape Town, 1973).

Rees, W. (ed.). *Colenso Letters from Natal* (Pietermaritzburg, 1958).

Robinson, J. *An Essay on Marxian Economics* (London, 1976).

Robinson R.E., & Gallagher, J., with Denny, A. *Africa and the Victorians: the Official Mind of Imperialism* (London, 1969).

Samuelson, R.C.A. *Long, Long Ago* (Durban, 1929).

Sanderson, G.N. 'The European Partition of Africa: Coincidence or Conjuncture?', *Journal of Imperial and Commonwealth History*, III, 1 (Oct. 1974).

Sansom, B. 'Traditional Economic Systems', in W.D. Hammond-Tooke (ed.) *The Bantu-Speaking Peoples of Southern Africa* (London, 1980).

Sansom, B. 'Traditional Rulers and their Realms', in W.D. Hammond-Tooke (ed.) *The Bantu-Speaking Peoples of Southern Africa* (London, 1980).

Saunders, C. *C.W. de Kiewiet, Historian of South Africa* (Cape Town, 1986).
Schreuder, D.M. *The Scramble for Southern Africa, 1877–1895: the Politics of Partition Reappraised* (Cambridge, 1980).
Schreuder, D.M. 'The Cultural Factor in Victorian Imperialism – a Case Study in the "Civilizing Mission" ', *The Journal of Imperial and Commonwealth History*, IV, 3 (May, 1976).
Simensen, J. (ed.). *Norwegian Missions in African History*, Vol. 1, *South Africa 1845–1906* (Oslo, 1986).
Slater, H. 'Land, Labour and Capital in Natal; the Natal Land and Colonisation Company, 1860–1948', *Journal of African History*, XVI, 2 (1975).
Slater, H. 'The Changing Pattern of Economic Relationships in Rural Natal, 1838–1914', in S. Marks & A. Atmore (eds.) *Economy and Society in Pre-industrial South Africa* (London, 1980).
Stander, H. 'Die Verhouding Tussen die Boere en Zoeloe tot die Dood van Mpande in 1872', *Archives Year Book for South African History*, 1964, Vol. 2 (Cape Town, 1964).
Stanford, E. (pub.). *Stanford's Large Scale Map of Zulu Land* (London, 1879).
Statham, F.R. *Blacks, Boers and British: a Three-Cornered Problem* (London, 1881).
Swartz, M. *The Politics of British Foreign Policy in the Era of Disraeli and Gladstone* (Oxford, 1985).
Theal, G.M. *History of South Africa*, Vol. X (London, 1919).
Thompson, L.M. 'The Subjection of the African Chiefdoms, 1870–1898' & 'Great Britain and the Afrikaner Republics, 1870–1899', in M. Wilson & L.M. Thompson (eds) *The Oxford History of South Africa*, Vol. II (Oxford, 1971).
Thompson, P. 'The Zulus are Coming! The Defence of Pietermaritzburg, 1879', in J. Laband & P. Thompson, *Kingdom and Colony at War: Sixteen Studies on the Anglo-Zulu War of 1879* (Pietermaritzburg & Cape Town, 1990).
Thompson, P. 'The Defence of Durban, 1879', in J. Laband & P. Thompson, *Kingdom and Colony at War: Sixteen Studies on the Anglo-Zulu War of 1879* (Pietermaritzburg & Cape Town, 1990).
Thompson, W.A. 'Wolseley and South Africa: a Study of Sir Garnet Wolseley's Role in South African Affairs, 1875–1877', unpublished Ph.D thesis, Vanderbilt University, 1973 (University Microfilms International, Ann Arbor, 1976).
Trapido, S. ' "The Friends of the Natives": Merchants, Peasants and the Political and Ideological Structure of Liberalism in the Cape', in S. Marks & A. Atmore (eds) *Economy and Society in Pre-industrial South Africa* (London, 1980).
Uys, C.J. *In the Era of Shepstone: being a Study of British Expansion in South Africa (1842–1877)* (Lovedale, 1933).
Van Rooyen, T.S. 'Die Verhouding tussen die Boere, Engelse en Naturelle in die Geskiedenis van die Oos-Transvaal tot 1882' *Archives Year Book*, 1951, Vol. I (Cape Town, 1951).
Van Zyl, M.C. *Die Protes-Beweging van die Transvaalse Afrikaners 1877–1880* (Pretoria & Cape Town, 1979).
Vijn, C. (ed. J.W. Colenso). *Cetshwayo's Dutchman: Being the Private Journal of a White Trader in Zululand during the British Invasion* (London, 1880).
Walker, E.A. *A History of Southern Africa* (London, 1964).
Walker, E.A. (ed.). *The Cambridge History of the British Empire*, Vol. VIII (London, 1936).
Warren, C. *On the Veldt in the Seventies* (London, 1902).
Webb, C. de B. 'Lines of Power: the High Commissioner, the Telegraph and the War of 1879', Natalia, 8 (Dec. 1978).
Webb, C. de B. 'The Origins of the War: Problems of Interpretation', in A. Duminy & C. Ballard (eds.) *The Anglo-Zulu War: New Perspectives* (Pietermaritzburg, 1981).
Webb, C. de B., & Wright, J.B. (eds). *The James Stuart Archive of Recorded Oral Evidence*

Relating to the History of the Zulu and Neighbouring Peoples, Vols. 1–4 (Durban & Pietermaritzburg, 1976, 1979, 1982, 1986).

Webb, C. de B., & Wright, J. (eds). *A Zulu King Speaks; Statements Made by Cetshwayo kaMpande on the History and Customs of his People* (Pietermaritzburg & Durban, 1978).

Welsh, D. *The Roots of Segregation: Native Policy in Colonial Natal, 1845–1910* (Cape Town, 1971).

Wilson, M., & Thompson, L.M. (eds). *The Oxford History of South Africa*, Vol. II (Oxford, 1971).

Wood, E. *From Midshipman to Field Marshal*, 2 Vols. (London, 1906).

Woodruff, P. (pseud.). *The Men Who Ruled India: the Guardians* (London, 1954).

Worsfold, W.B. *Sir Bartle Frere: a Footnote to the History of the British Empire* (London, 1923).

Wright, J., & Hamilton, C. 'Traditions and Transformations: the Phongolo-Mzimkhulu region in the late eighteenth and early nineteenth centuries', in A. Duminy & B. Guest (eds) *Natal and Zululand from Earliest Times to 1910: a New History* (Pietermaritzburg, 1989).

Wright, J., & Manson, A. *The Hlubi Chiefdom in Zululand-Natal: a History* (Ladysmith, 1983).

Young, R. *Modern Missions: their Trials and Triumphs* (London, 1881).

Zetland, Marquis of (ed.). *The Letters of Disraeli to Lady Bradford and Lady Chesterfield*, 2 Vols. (London, 1929).

Index